'ME WRITE MYSELF'

For Leon Harper, who is woke, witty, and wise beyond his years.

'ME WRITE MYSELF'

The Free Aboriginal Inhabitants of Van Diemen's Land at Wybalenna, 1832–47

LEONIE STEVENS

© Copyright 2017 Leonie Stevens
All rights reserved. Apart from any uses permitted by Australia's Copyright Act 1968, no part of this book may be reproduced by any process without prior written permission from the copyright owners. Inquiries should be directed to the publisher.

Monash University Publishing
Matheson Library and Information Services Building
40 Exhibition Walk
Monash University
Clayton, Victoria 3800, Australia
www.publishing.monash.edu

Monash University Publishing brings to the world publications which advance the best traditions of humane and enlightened thought.

Monash University Publishing titles pass through a rigorous process of independent peer review.

http://www.publishing.monash.edu/books/mwm-9781925495638.html

Series: Australian History
Series Editor: Sean Scalmer

Design: Les Thomas

Cover image: John Skinner Prout, *Residence of the Aborigines, Flinders Island*. 1846, paper lithograph, 25.3 x 37.7 cm. Courtesy National Gallery of Australia, Canberra.

National Library of Australia Cataloguing-in-Publication entry:

Creator:	Stevens, Leonie, 1962- author.
Title:	'Me write myself': the free Aboriginal inhabitants of Van Diemen's Land at Wybalenna, 1832-47 / Leonie Stevens.
ISBN:	9781925495638 (paperback)
Subjects:	Aboriginal Australians--Tasmania--Wybalenna Correspondence.
	Aboriginal Australians--Tasmania--Wybalenna--Social conditions.
	Aboriginal Australians--Tasmania--Removal.
	Aboriginal Australians--Tasmania--Flinders Island--History.
	Aboriginal Australians--Tasmania--Flinders Island--Social conditions
	Flinders Island (Tas.)--Social conditions.
	Wybalenna (Tas.)--History.
	Wybalenna (Tas.)--Social conditions.

Printed in Australia by Griffin Press an Accredited ISO AS/NZS 14001:2004 Environmental Management System printer.

The paper this book is printed on is certified against the Forest Stewardship Council ® Standards. Griffin Press holds FSC chain of custody certification SGS-COC-005088. FSC promotes environmentally responsible, socially beneficial and economically viable management of the world's forests.

CONTENTS

About the Author vi

Acknowledgements vii

Introduction ix

Chapter 1
40,000 Years to Exile 1

Chapter 2
Exiled to Great Island 27

Chapter 3
The Promise of Wybalenna 71

Chapter 4
The Battle for VDL Souls 150

Chapter 5
Empire, Agency and a Humble Petition 218

Chapter 6
Defeating Wybalenna 260

Bibliography 332

Index 343

ABOUT THE AUTHOR

Dr Leonie Stevens researches and lectures in History. She has worked extensively as an editor, is the author of six novels, a variety of short fiction, and is addicted to B-grade disaster films.

ACKNOWLEDGEMENTS

I acknowledge that this book was written on Wurundjeri land, where I was born and bred, and I pay my respect to Elders of the Kulin nation past and present. I also pay my respects to the authors of those writings from exile which inspired this study; to the Pallawah peoples past and present; and to Aunty Patsy Cameron for her generous support in the early stages of the project.

This book would not have seen the light of day if not for Richard Broome, who steadied me through numerous storms. Working with him has been one of the great honours of my life. I am also indebted to Lynette Russell, Uncle Les Alderton, Katie Holmes, Henry Reynolds, Tony Ballantyne, Kat Ellinghaus, and the late, great Patrick Wolfe for their generosity. I especially honour the late Rhonda Jankovic, and thank my buddies Alan Petersen and Geoff Allshorn for their solidarity and the Code 7Rs. And of course, my wonderful family – Leon, Theodore and Alexandra Harper – ensured I was grounded, supported, fed, amused, housed and loved.

Finally, this project owes a huge debt to the Journey of Nishiyuu. Stanley George Jr and the other members of the Original Seven, plus the hundreds of young warriors who joined them, inspired me from the other side of this pale blue dot in ways that mere words cannot convey. To the Seven, the Walkers and the extended family – especially my cheer squad Elsie, Rhonda, Robert, Crystal, Nancy, Jennie, Mary, Barbara, Gloria, Sandra, and our beloved Bob, who celebrated every chapter completed and every deadline met – *meegwetch*!

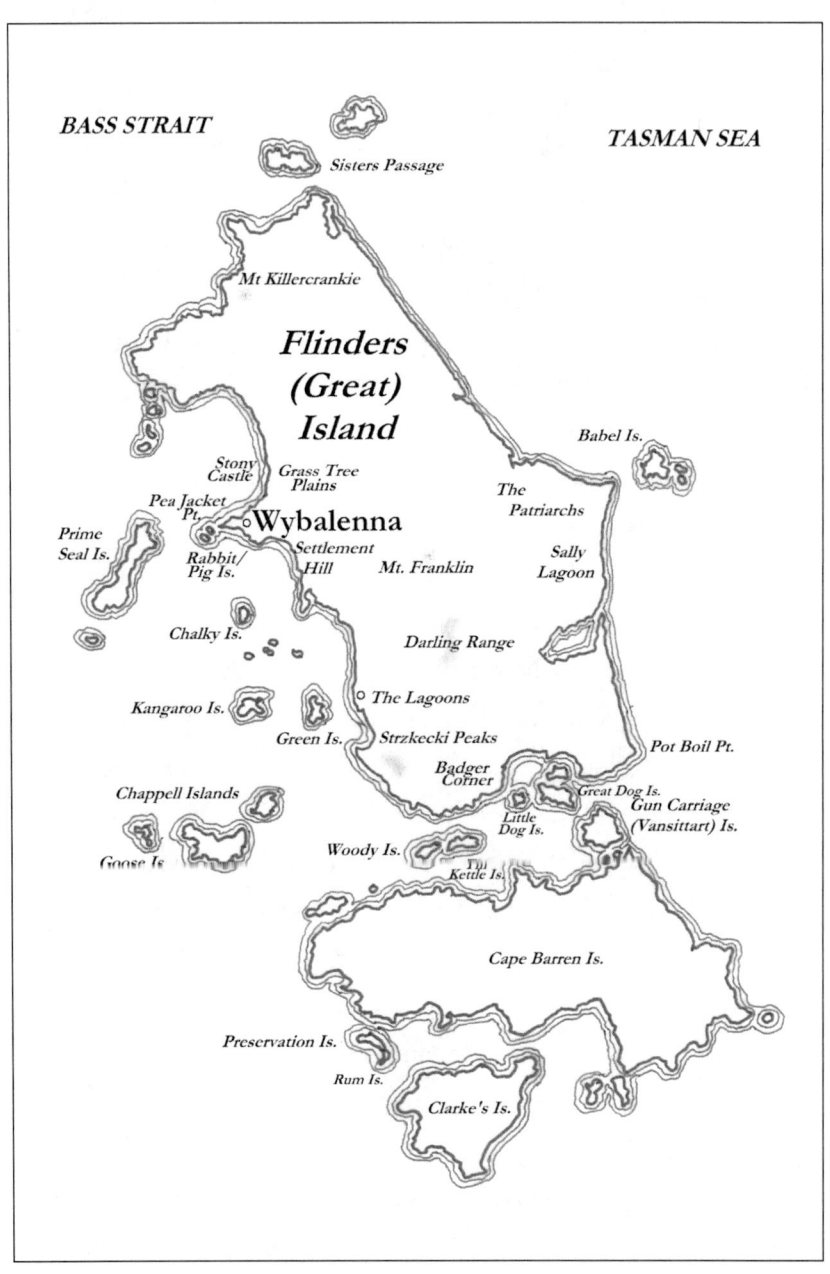

Flinders Island and the Furneaux Group, featuring places mentioned in the text.
© L. Stevens 2017

INTRODUCTION

> What the Aborigines thought about their captivity or of their future is almost entirely unknown. They recorded nothing themselves, and little of what they said is written down.
>
> N. J. B. Plomley, Weep in Silence¹

The exile of the First Nations peoples of Van Diemen's Land to Flinders Island in the 1830s and 1840s is one of the most infamous chapters in Australian, and world, history. A number of unique characteristics – not the least of which is the subsequent myth of racial extinction – have maintained its significance. In the long and often problematic historiography surrounding the First Nations peoples of Van Diemen's Land, one voice has largely been ignored: that of the people themselves. When two Big River nation elders wrote to the Governor in 1846, protesting the conditions of their exile, they signed their letter, proudly, 'Me Write Myself King Alexander, Me Write Myself King Alphonso'. This study takes them at their word.

The *Flinders Island Chronicle*, sermons, letters and petitions penned by the exiles at the settlement known as Wybalenna offer a compelling counter-narrative to the often erroneous Eurocentric representation of a depressed, dispossessed people's final days. Seen through their own writing, the community at Wybalenna was vibrant, complex and evolving. The exiles did not see themselves as prisoners, but as a free people. Their lives were difficult and at times traumatic, but

---

1   N. J. B. Plomley, *Weep in Silence: A History of the Flinders Island Settlement, with the Flinders Island Journal of George Augustus Robinson*, Hobart, Blubber Head Press, 1987, 99.

they were also full. They steadfastly maintained traditional language and culture, at the same time incorporating aspects of European culture and spirituality of their choosing. There were multiple spheres of power, authority, and resistance.

This is a narrative history, but also by necessity a critical one. And like the traveller to modern-day Tasmania, before we can even arrive on the island's shores, our baggage must be checked. There are now firm quarantine restrictions.

Baggage Check

If we imagine Van Diemen's Land historical studies as a room, it is immensely crowded. The walls are well insulated, double-lined with the tomes, articles and paper archives of two hundred years of reportage and scrutiny. The reduced floor space heaves with men, women and children: Indigenous and transplanted, convict and emancipist, the famous, notorious and nameless. There are warriors, survivors, colonial conduits and humanitarians; seamen, sealers, soldiers and slaves. We find the gentry, the aspirants and the no-hopers; and, circling furtively, the God-botherers. Some are treated kindly by history, some ill, some not at all.

The air is a pea-souper of ideas. Themes of Christianity, war, empire, race, moral responsibility, entitlement, civilisation and progress jostle for space, tempered by profound guilt, anger and regret. Proclamations of victory often ride on a cloud of self-doubt. It is a noisy, argumentative, anxious place. In this room there are ships, sheep and firearms. And historians – *many* historians.

Such is the vibrant, evolving, contested world in which this work is situated. This cornucopia of events, people and ideas will be examined in due course, but there are several key ideas which demand to be acknowledged from the outset. They are so profound to the popular imagination – and the historiographical tradition – as to give our room a false floor. At times, they obscure the foundations. These seemingly core understandings unconsciously prejudice attitudes and assumptions. They distort readings of the present and expectations for the future. They are the issues carried by any study of First Nations history that originates from the academy.

In our case, they stand out like a mountain of unchecked baggage. Some are massive trunks, suited to emigration; others are carry-on baggage, smaller but more insidious. Most are easily negotiable, but several are monsters of the mind.[2] These prevailing narratives about Van Diemen's Land (VDL) people in the colonial context, or issues related to the position of the scholar, form an undercurrent to VDL history, and it behoves us to look inside, however briefly.

Baggage Check 1: Language and Colonisation

Renaming of people, place and landforms is often the first act of taking possession. Many of the people in this study had numerous names, whether in-Country, married, initiated, in another's Country, or exiled at Wybalenna. Each of these names had significance: nomenclature was place-based, and complemented by social identity.[3] Ambiguous records and variable spelling meant errors in name and identity were common. At the receiving end of the archive, there are many inherited errors, as I. P. S. Anderson notes, mediated by the

---

2   Craig Stockings recently used a similar metaphorical line with his edited volume *Zombie Myth of Australian Military History*, UNSW Press, Sydney, 2010, 3 – the 'zombie myth' being one which seemingly will not die, a 'monster of the mind'.
3   Shayne Breen, *Contested Places: Tasmania's Northern Districts from Ancient Times to 1900*, Hobart, Centre for Tasmanian Historical Studies, 2001, 17.

colonial ear.⁴ Many otherwise sound histories of Van Diemen's Land contain serious errors when identifying individuals.⁵

To avoid confusion and ensure accuracy, this book has rebuilt these biographies from a bedrock of sources written by the exiles themselves. Individuals are therefore identified by the names by which they were known at Wybalenna, and which they used to sign their work. These are often European names. Those who did not write, and were not directly referred to in VDL texts, are identified by the names under which they 'speak' through Europeans in recorded testimonies. Original names are also attributed, where sources are credible.⁶

Use of these mostly European names in this study in no way implies that these bestowed names were more desirable, more utilised, or in any way preferred to original names by the community. Indeed, the conferring of European names is an obvious performance of colonisation, and has been widely recognised and criticised as such. Many decolonising histories deliberately employ Indigenous or non-European names and terminology, considering European names an example of attempted cultural genocide. However, there is ample evidence that such renaming was embraced.⁷ This ready adoption was almost certainly a strategic act: as Richard Broome points out, such

---

4   I. P. S. Anderson, 'A People Who Have No History', in A. Johnston and M. Rolls (eds.), *Reading Robinson: Companion Essays to Friendly Mission*, Hobart, Quintus Publishing, 2008, 59.

5   These will be corrected on a case-by-case basis throughout this study, where discrepancies of the record become apparent.

6   Chiefly, N. J. B. Plomley's transcriptions of G. A. Robinson's journals, which are a reliable translation. See *Friendly Mission: The Tasmanian Journals and Papers of George Augustus Robinson, 1829–1834*, second edition, Launceston and Hobart, Queen Victoria Museum and Art Gallery and Quintus Publishing, 2008, and *Weep in Silence*.

7   George Augustus Robinson's journals – both in VDL and later at Port Phillip – discuss the eagerness for bestowal of European names.

INTRODUCTION

a bestowal of names 'established an attachment and avoided the use of traditional names that were hedged with protocols and strictures'.[8]

Use of European names by First Nations peoples was also a pragmatic tactic. A global hallmark of Indigenous resourcefulness and adaptability has been the adoption of European clothing, language and business practice. Many First Nations people were colonial agents in their own right. Economic and ultimately political responses to colonisation can be seen in the active involvement internationally by First Nations communities with colonial entities such as the Hudson Bay, East India and Dutch East Indies companies, and within Australian sealing and whaling enterprises. Naming and writing systems were a key element of this participation in colonial economies, best exemplified by the creation of the Cherokee syllabary in 1828 by Sequoyah (George Gest), and its rapid embrace by the Cherokee leadership and population.[9] Language acquisition and the use of European names, then, can also be seen as an act of resistance, and ensuring cultural survival.

For the purposes of this study, the use of European names is at times essential, and there is no alternative. Walter George Arthur and Thomas Brune, the two most prolific VDL writers, had no other known names. Further, other writers cited in this study had a multitude of names, which begs the question of which name and spelling (or often, misspelling) to use. Ultimately, employment of the usually European names actively used in the VDL texts is the only way this researcher can claim categorically that, unless otherwise noted,

---

8 Richard Broome, *Aboriginal Victorians: A History since 1800*, Crows Nest, Allen & Unwin, 2005, 57.
9 See Ellen Cushman, 'The Cherokee Writing Syllabary; A Writing System in its Own Right', *Written Communication*, 28:3, 2011, 255-281; John B. Davis, 'The Life and Work of Sequoyah', *Chronicles of Oklahoma*, 8:2, June 1930, 149-180.

all information regarding individuals has been derived directly from primary VDL sources, seen with the researcher's own eyes.

The issue of collective naming is also a problematic one, and while this study does not intend to become distracted by etymology, this must be addressed. The First Nations people of Van Diemen's Land were not one homogenised people, but a range of diverse nations. The most commonly used terms in the historiographical tradition – *Aboriginal* and *Aborigine* – are European and therefore colonising terms, placing First Nations people as an Other to the coloniser. The tensions around this term are indicated by the work of Lyndall Ryan, with her 1982 study entitled *Aboriginal Tasmanians*, but the 2012 version retitled *Tasmanian Aborigines*. The title *Tasmanians* has been used to good effect by Henry Reynolds and others, but does denote a later colonial period than that covered by this study. Alternatively, *Pakana*, *Pallawah* and *Trowunna* are terms now in scholarly and popular usage. However, these terms were not commonly used in the VDL texts, and, as these are the authority in this study, I have used the terminology used therein.

The authors of the VDL texts always remained vocal patriots of their own Country. Their letters were often signed, or specifically mentioned, their Country of origin.[10] Collectively, they self-identified as Van Diemen's Land (VDL) blacks, VDL Aborigines, VDLs, blackfellows, Countrypeople and, most famously, The Free Aboriginal Inhabitants of Van Diemen's Land.[11] This study uses the collective of VDL, and then VDL exiles. On a broader scale, the

---

10 Walter George Arthur signed as Chieftain of the Ben Lomond Tribe; David Bruney signed as Chief of the Bruny Island Tribe; King Alexander and King Alphonso similarly claimed Big River.
11 This latter term was used in the Petition to Queen Victoria, January 1846.

INTRODUCTION

term 'First Nations' is used, as it places the exile of VDL people in a global, postcolonial context.[12]

Spelling and punctuation follows the original texts as far as possible. What might to modern eyes appear to be typographical or spelling errors, are actually markers of the evolution over time of both writer and language.[13] Editing the texts to conform to our idea of good grammar would be just another act of colonisation.

Baggage Check 2: The Many Guises of Scientific Racism

The second mountain of baggage clogging the floor of the metaphorical room of VDL historiography is Scientific Racism. White superiority was used as an excuse for dispossession and enslavement of First Nations people across a range of empires and times. It resounds in the Rousseauian ideal of the Noble Savage, and in the defence of colonialism in the early 19th century, even as populations were decimated. It was codified in evolutionary thinking, and finely honed in the rise of Social Darwinism, doomed race doctrine and eugenics. No discussion of the history of Van Diemen's Land, and its peoples, can avoid this baggage inspection.

Most settlers reflected the philosophy of empire: they had inalienable rights, and in fact a moral responsibility, to seize control of First Nations lands. They were bringing civilisation, and they made no apology. To the contrary, the colonists aggressively justified their actions through what Albert Memmi called the Nero (or usurper) complex, whereby the coloniser extols his own merits,

---

12 It must be remembered that the VDL exile was occurring contemporaneously with dispossessions and forced relocations across North America and what would become Canada.

13 As will be discussed, these texts have, where reproduced, usually been heavily corrected.

while simultaneously deriding the usurped.[14] In 1836, the Malthus-inspired naturalist Charles Darwin visited Hobart. Darwin opined on how Van Diemen's Land enjoyed the advantage of 'being free of a native population', and the 'cruel step' of forced exile did not prevent him from marvelling at the 'increase of a civilized over a savage people'.[15] Two years later, Sydney barrister Richard Windeyer also displayed the paradoxical lament. While asserting that First Nations had no relationship or right to land, he nevertheless questioned the usurper's deep-seated guilt – 'this whispering in the bottom of our hearts'.[16]

This lament was especially prevalent with British antipodean colonisation. Located temporally with the peak of the abolitionist movement and the rise of humanitarianism, there was a profound disconnect between morality – Windeyer's 'whispering' – and the necessities of colonisation, symbolised in Darwin's celebration. Even sympathetic administrators, humanitarians and missionaries, who sought to ameliorate conditions for First Nations people, ultimately had vested interests in ensuring the success of the colonial venture. Figures central to the VDL story such as Sir George Arthur and George Augustus Robinson gained power, prestige and profit, and even the Quakers George Washington Walker and James Backhouse, who Penelope Edmunds notes were not so much colonial agents as 'institutional

---

14 Albert Memmi, *The Colonizer and the Colonized*, London, Earthscan, 2003, 96-97; Richard Broome applies Memmi's notion of the usurper complex to early British claims of Eora land. Broome, *Aboriginal Australians*, 27-28.

15 Charles Darwin, *Voyage of the Beagle: Charles Darwin's Journal of Researches*, [1839], Abridged, London, Penguin, 1989, 329.

16 Richard Windeye, public lecture 'On the Rights of the Aborigines of Australia', discussed in Henry Reynolds, *This Whispering in Our Hearts*, St Leonards, Allen & Unwin, 1998, 21.

INTRODUCTION

opponents',[17] benefited socially and financially by the alienation of First Nations people from their land.

To assure legitimacy and assuage colonial guilt, colonised people needed to be framed as inferior and already doomed. Thus, they were, as the saying goes, the architects of their own demise. Their fall in the face of progress needed to be seen as inevitable, and their only possible hope was to abandon savagery, accept Christianity and civilisation, and assimilate. Racial extinction and cultural annihilation thus became synonymous with humanitarian duty.

Of course blame was shifted wherever possible. Conscience-stricken commentators and colonial officials held lower-class Europeans responsible for frontier violence, framing VDL First Nations peoples as sometimes vicious savages, but ultimately the wronged party.[18] The *Report of the Parliamentary Select Committee on Aboriginal Tribes* of 1837 held this line.[19] The characterisation of bloodthirsty convicts and scurrilous so-called gentlemen leading violent roving parties away from the humanitarian gaze certainly has a factual basis. However, the ethnic cleansing on New South Wales, Van Diemen's Land, and other, later frontiers, was sanctioned by the very nature of colonial invasion. And it was shortly to be justified by science.

---

17 See Penelope Edmunds, 'Travelling "Under Concern": Quakers James Backhouse and George Washington Walker Tour the Antipodean Colonies, 1832–41', *The Journal of Imperial and Commonwealth History*, 40:5, December 2012, 769–788.

18 James Bischoff, *Sketch of the History of Van Diemens Land*, [1832], Australiana Facsimile Editions No. 102, Adelaide, Libraries Board of South Australia, 1967; John West, *History of Tasmania*, Vol. II [1852], Australian Facsimile Editions No. 35, Adelaide, Libraries Board of Australia, 1966; see also the correspondence of Sir George Arthur.

19 *Report of the Parliamentary Select Committee on Aboriginal Tribes, (British settlements). Reprinted, with Comments by the 'Aborigines Protection Society'*, London, Ball, Chambers, Row, Hatchard & Son, 1837, 14.

Van Diemen's Land's history is inescapably linked to the codification of ideas about biological determinism and doomed races. From as early as 1832, racial unfitness became the defining characteristic of most discussions about VDL people. Ideas about race transformed, as Kay Anderson notes, 'from the conceptualisation of race as tribe-nation-kin to race as innate-immutable-biological'.[20] Concepts about the fixed nature of race were seized by the apologists for the excesses of colonialism, being a perfect fit for the narrative unfolding in Van Diemen's Land.

Literature about VDL First Nations routinely contained such markers as 'lost', 'doomed' and 'vanished'. This characteristic began with colonisation, and endured through the 20th century. The rise of Social Darwinism and eugenics blamed VDL people for their own demise, for being a race which 'remained in the stone age'.[21] A famous example of this is the problematic discourse around VDL people's alleged inability to make fire.[22] VDL First Nations became emblematic to historians, anthropologists and archaeologists as what Patrick Brantlinger evocatively depicted as the self-exterminating savage, the 'ghostly twin' of the Noble Savage.[23] As Wendy Aitken wryly observes, 'Really. Some people just can't be helped!'[24]

Scientific Racism's greatest success can be seen in the dissemination of the myth of VDL extinction. It was a fictive discourse, as

---

20 Kay Anderson, *Race and the Crisis of Humanism*, Routledge, London and New York, 2007, 191.
21 Russell McGregor, *Imagined Destinies: Aboriginal Australians and the Doomed Race Theory 1880–1939*, Melbourne University Press, Carlton, 1997, 59.
22 Discussed in an excellent overview by Rebe Taylor, 'Reliable Mr Robinson and the Controversial Dr Jones', in Johnston and Rolls (eds.), *Reading Robinson*, 118-123.
23 Patrick Brantlinger, *Dark Vanishings: Discourse on the Extinction of Primitive Races*, Ithaca and London, Cornell University Press, 2003, 3.
24 Wendy Aitken, 'Community Voices', in Johnston and Rolls (eds.), *Reading Robinson*, 95.

INTRODUCTION

Greg Lehman observes, 'rooted in the imaginary, rapidly taking on the mantle of historical fact'.[25] Framed as one of the great tragedies of modern world history, this myth is inextricably linked with the story of Trugernanner.[26] At her death in 1876, she was not – as we now know – 'the last Tasmanian'.[27] However, she *was* the last known VDL veteran of the war of dispossession. James Bonwick had laid the groundwork for her ascension to icon status six years before her death, with the publication of *The Last of the Tasmanians*.[28] Already famous for her central role in negotiations between the Crown and VDL people, in her advanced years Trugernanner was a celebrity in Hobart. With her death in 1876, the white population was offered a neat finale to their violent genesis: as historian Rebe Taylor observes, it was 'an appealing kind of shame … guilt without complication'.[29] VDL First Nations people were, as many well knew, alive and well on the Bass Strait islands, across the now-Tasmanian mainland, and even in Hobart.[30] Yet this did not get in the way of a good story.

For a time, VDL extinction played into Australia's growing national story, which predicted the disappearance of all First Nations

---

25 Greg Lehman, 'Telling Us True', in Robert Manne (ed.). *Whitewash: On Keith Windschuttle's Fabrication of Aboriginal History*, Black Inc. Agenda, Melbourne, 2003, 180.

26 Trugernanner/Truganiena/Truganini/Lydgudgeye/Lygdudge/Lalla Rookh, born around 1812, Port Esperence, South East nation. The subject of much attention, conjecture and faulty scholarship. These names from Plomley, *Weep in Silence*, 806 and 860. For poor scholarship, see Vivienne Rae-Ellis, *Truganini: Queen or Traitor*, Hobart, OBM Publishing, 1976; for a more reliable view, see Lyndall Ryan, *Tasmanian Aborigines: A History since 1803*, Crows Nest, Allen & Unwin, 2012.

27 The term 'The Last Tasmanian' has a historical life of its own, and echoes the romanticism of *The Last of the Mohicans*, etc.

28 James Bonwick, *The Last of the Tasmanians*, [1870], Facsimile Edition No. 87, Adelaide, Libraries Board of South Australia, 1969.

29 Rebe Taylor, *Unearthed: The Aboriginal Tasmanians of Kangaroo Island*, Kent Town, Wakefield Press, 2008, 139.

30 Fanny Cochrane-Smith was then receiving a government pension.

people. Writing in 1930, W. K. Hancock lamented a 'pathetically helpless' race, and its usurper which 'From time to time ... remembers the primitive people whom it has dispossessed, and sheds over their predestined passing an economical tear'.[31] This prediction of extinction – and deliberate silence on continuity – has been well documented by a range of eminent historians.[32] Nowhere, however, did it reach the levels of certainty – and fame – as in Tasmania.

VDL extinction has *always* been a myth. Like many mainland First Nations, VDL people were pushed to the brink, but their survival has been continuously noted in official and scholarly records.[33] As the linguist Terry Crowley so succinctly put it, the Tasmanian experience of violent colonisation was actually not so unusual: 'The only major difference is that nobody has tried to tell the Aboriginal people of Victoria, for example, that they no longer exist'.[34]

By the 1970s, this myth *should* have been well and truly slain by the emergence of the Tasmanian Aboriginal Centre, a powerful new voice. The residues – those scattered, ill-informed remnants alluding to racial unfitness in the face of a superior colonial power – should have been further countered by the efforts of the many archaeologists, linguists, anthropologists, sociologists, educationalists and historians who have painstakingly pointed out the disconnect between the

---

31 W. K. Hancock, *Australia*, [1930, London], Brisbane, Jacaranda, 1964, 21.

32 See particularly Henry Reynolds, *Why Weren't We told? A Personal Search for the Truth about Our History*, Camberwell, Penguin Australia, 1999.

33 Most notably by the continued presence of VDL descendants on Bass Strait islands, often known as 'Islanders'; documented in anthropologist and eugenicist Norman Tindale and Joseph Birdsell's 1939 visit and resulting study, and especially in more recent times by Bill Mollison and Coral Everitt's sometimes poorly regarded 'Stud Book' – *The Tasmanian Aborigines and Their Descendants: Chronology, Genealogies and Social Data*, Hobart, University of Tasmania, 1978.

34 Terry Crowley, 'Tasmanian Aboriginal Language: Old and New Identities', in M. Walsh and C. Yallop (eds.), *Language and Culture in Aboriginal Australia*, Canberra, Aboriginal Studies Press, 1993, 25.

INTRODUCTION

self-serving colonial narrative of extinction, and the actual historical and cultural record.

However, the extinction myth has proved an enduring one, grounded in systemic racism, snake-oil eugenics and, as N. J. B. Plomley wrote, the *glamour* of the doomed race.[35] No matter how often it is debunked, the myth emerges elsewhere. Gradually, its influence is diminishing, but having formed such a key role in VDL history and the international imagination, it may never be fully eradicated. While it does not necessarily demand debunking – this has already been theoretically accomplished, dozens of times over – its residue remains powerful, influencing almost all characterisations of the VDL people who were exiled at Wybalenna.

The doomed race representation extends to this day. The very title of N. J. B. Plomley's 1986 landmark history of the settlement, *Weep in Silence*, is anchored in this view, filtered as it were by the retroactive extinction myth. Plomley's view of Wybalenna places the indifference of Europeans front and centre: VDL people were passive objects, helpless children, lacking all agency. Elsewhere, Plomley highlighted the loss of hope, lamenting 'the realisation by the natives themselves that there was no hope for them'.[36] Flinders Island is dismissed as 'the graveyard of most of them'.[37]

This characterisation of a death camp has been enduring. Clive Turnbull, in his influential *Black War*, stated that at Wybalenna, the exiles' 'chief business was dying'.[38] Raphael Lemkin characterised the

---

35   N. J. B. Plomley (as Brian Plomley), *The Tasmanian Aborigines*, Launceston, Plomley Foundation, 1993.
36   N. J. B. Plomley, 'Robinson's Adventures in Bass Strait', in *Bass Strait: Australia's Last Frontier*, Sydney, Australian Broadcasting Commission, 1969, 41.
37   Plomley, *The Tasmanian Aborigines*, 93.
38   Clive Turnbull, *Black War: The Extermination of the Tasmanian Aborigines*, [1948], reprint, Melbourne, Cheshire-Lansdowne, 1965, 224.

last years of Wybalenna as 'a story of death'.³⁹ Lloyd Robson likewise depicted Wybalenna as where 'the disintegration of the culture of Van Diemen's Land Aborigines was achieved', and elsewhere as 'a sort of concentration camp where most of them perished'.⁴⁰ C. D. Rowley characterised Wybalenna as 'in fact a prison', and the exiles as 'bored and bewildered victims'.⁴¹ Art historian Robert Hughes mused, 'Little by little, they wasted away and their ghosts drifted out over the water'.⁴² Bruce Elder, in his influential *Blood on the Wattle*, claimed, 'If ever a group died of broken hearts it was the Aboriginal people who spent their last days on Flinders Island'.⁴³ British scholar David Davies wrote that VDL people 'sank into an apathy from which they never emerged'; Patricia Ratcliff, in her local history of Wybalenna, wrote of 'body after body languishing into death'; and Jean Edgecombe, in a Bass Strait islands history, wrote 'Hopeless and helpless, they sat inside their huts with nothing to do but drink and no future but early death'.⁴⁴ These are but a sample of the traditional death-narratives of Wybalenna.

Scientific Racism is not a major focus of this study; nor is the process of colonisation, the well-chronicled patriotic wars, or the famed conciliation of the 'Friendly' Mission, when George Augustus

---

39 Raphael Lemkin, 'Tasmania', *Patterns of Prejudice*, 39:2, 2005, 190.
40 Lloyd Robson with Michael Roe, *A History of Tasmania*, Vol. 1, Melbourne, Oxford University Press, 1983, 253; Lloyd Robson, *A Short History of Tasmania*, second edition, 1997, Oxford and New York, Oxford University Press, 1997, 13.
41 C. D. Rowley, *The Destruction of Aboriginal Society*, Harmondsworth, UK, Penguin, 1978, 50.
42 Robert Hughes, *The Fatal Shore*, Collins Harvill, London, 1987, 423.
43 Bruce Elder, *Blood on the Wattle*, third edition, Sydney, New Holland Publishers, 2003, 47.
44 David Davies, *The Last of the Tasmanians*, Sydney, Shakespeare Head Press, 1973, 200; Patricia Fitzgerald Ratcliff, *The Story of Wybalenna*, Launceston, The Glendessary Press, 1975, 30; Jean Edgecombe, *Flinders Island and Eastern Bass Strait*, Thornleigh, Edgekirk, 1986, 16.

INTRODUCTION

Robinson, at the behest of Sir George Arthur, toured the island with guides to broker peace. These facets of VDL history have already been discussed ably and at length by a range of eminent and emerging scholars.[45] This study is concerned with gaining a sense of the *lives people led* during the exile at Wybalenna, in their own words. To get a fresh sense of the VDL exiles' stories, however, we must acknowledge the baggage the very name of Wybalenna brings. We will certainly come across this baggage again – and again – on our journey.

Baggage Check 3: Credibility

> I am a man and a free man too.
>
> Walter George Arthur[46]

> Walter George Arthur was not a free man.
>
> Sally Dammery[47]

If Scientific Racism is the largest collection of metaphorical baggage in the room, there is another which is the most influential and insidious. The systematic and often unconscious discrediting of VDL perspective risks tripping us up from the moment we walk in the door, quietly undermining understanding of VDL writing and life for the exiles at Wybalenna. It is fed by generations of Scientific Racism, extinction myths, and doomed race doctrines. It is the reason that

---

45 For an overview, see the work of Henry Reynolds, Lyndall Ryan, Greg Lehman, Richard Broome, Marilyn Lake, Bain Attwood, Patsy Cameron, Nicholas Clements and Graeme Calder.
46 Walter George Arthur, Statement (Sent to Governor), 16 July 1846, AOT CSO 11/1/27 Correspondence Civil Branch C658, 114.
47 Sally Dammery, 'Walter George Arthur: A Free Tasmanian?', *Monash Publications in History*, 35, 2001, 49.

biographies of the VDL exiles remain riddled with inaccuracies and disinterest. It is the scaffold supporting colonising history. It is the unwitting cheerleader, perpetuating the old rumours of extinction and racial unfitness. It is the fundamental imbalance in a colonised historiography.

In her biography of Walter George Arthur, the young literate exile who spearheaded political activism at Wybalenna, Sally Dammery questioned whether Arthur was, as he repeatedly claimed throughout his adult life, a free man. This claim to be free was not idle or rhetorical: VDL exiles placed exceptional importance on being regarded as free people.[48] It is a central, recurring theme of their communications. However, Dammery – taking into account the colonial environment Arthur was forced to negotiate – concluded he could not possibly have been 'a free man'.

There are many grounds on which to contest this assessment. Most obviously, there is the issue of perspective. In the 1830s and 1840s, in a far-flung penal colony, *very* few people – be they convicts, workers, British or First Nations, soldiers, colonial officials – enjoyed the luxury of 'freedom' as it might be defined today. On a distant penal colony of a far-away empire, freedom is a relative concept. Underpinning any discussion of the definitions of freedom, subversion or sociological interpretations, however, is our third insidious mound of baggage.

Walter Arthur's own assertions are simply not credited. His voice and the claims of his Countrypeople over the decades are not taken seriously. Dammery's biography is ultimately that of a British colonial

---

[48] James Backhouse noted the importance of being seen as free, and not the equivalent of convicts, as early as 1832, in *A Narrative of a Visit to the Australian Colonies*, [1843], New York, Johnson Reprint Corporation, 1967, 169-170.

INTRODUCTION

subject, rather than an active agent. Likewise, most previous histories of Wybalenna, even when they focus on the VDL exiles, are effectively colonial histories, which are contaminated by the extinction myth. The First Nations protagonists are seen through the historical reality, noted by Greg Dening, of those 'who did not understand what they were seeing'.[49]

There is no need, at this stage, to reinvent the postcolonial wheel. A generation of academics have highlighted the problematic nature of Eurocentric bias when studying settler colonies. Yet there is still a natural and profound privileging of European sources – *any* European sources. They are always seen as the most credible, by virtue of being written by white colonists and experts. Yet simply stating the obvious has done little to remedy the imbalance.

Given the high level of interest in VDL and Tasmanian history, and the sizeable body of literature on its bloody colonial past, it might be expected that the newspapers, letters and other papers left by VDL people would have generated great interest, at least in recent decades. Yet, as will be seen shortly, they remain astonishingly underutilised. This is illustrated by the fact that this study is the first to study the VDL texts as a group. VDL people have been represented from the outset as a doomed race: it is thus hardly surprising that their writings were of little interest. The story, it has been assumed, was already known.

The privileging of European over VDL accounts is illustrated graphically by N. J. B. Plomley in his formidable *Weep in Silence*. To date the only significant history of the Wybalenna exile, it places a

---

[49] Greg Dening, *Islands and Beaches: Discourses on a Silent Land, Marquesas 1774–1880*, Honolulu, The University Press of Hawaii, 1980, 41.

small selection of VDL texts at the *very end* of the massive tome.⁵⁰ They receive two paragraphs of generally disparaging comment, being the final appendix, and then are followed directly by the bibliography. On a spatial level, they could not be more obscure. This hierarchy of racialised representation extends further in Plomley's prodigious tome – what I. P. S. Anderson calls 'patient Empiricism'.⁵¹ In the formatting of biographical material, even the lowliest convicts on Flinders are depicted in traditional biographies, written as paragraphs. Yet VDL First Nations people, even those who played a very significant role over many years, such as Walter and Mary ann Arthur, Doctor Wooreddy, Trugernanner and Mannalargenna, are relegated to lists. They are dehumanised: they do not even warrant sentences. In Plomley's work, individual people are an afterthought.

Scholars of Van Diemen's Land history are not alone in paying scant attention to texts generated by First Nations people. Academic rigour rarely, it seems, extends to consulting First Nation sources. While historians are expected to be familiar with the European writings and discourse around a colonial history, there is traditionally no such reciprocal imperative to consult Indigenous writings or perspectives. Dipesh Chakrabarty noted this unapologetic tendency toward 'asymmetric ignorance' with regard to the writing of Indian colonial history, observing that:

> ... insofar as the academic discourse of history – that is, 'history' as a discourse produced at the institutional site of the University – is concerned, 'Europe' remains the sovereign, theoretical subject of all histories ...⁵²

---

50 Pages 1008-1015.
51 I. P. S. Anderson, 'A People who Have No History?', in Johnston and Rolls (eds.), *Reading Robinson*, 76.
52 Dipesh Chakrabarty, 'Postcoloniality and the Artifice of History: Who Speaks for "Indian" Pasts?', *Representations*, 37, Winter 1992, 1.

INTRODUCTION

Hawai'ian historian Noenoe Silva likewise noted ignorance of a once well-known body of documentary evidence in her study of the Hawai'ian opposition to American colonisation.[53] In Silva's example, however, the fact that those long-ignored documents were in Hawai'ian language provides some explanation. The VDL texts allow no such excuse, being written in English and publicised since 1836.[54]

There is, then, a traditional bias in the way historical sources are valued, which has impacted on the way texts written by VDL exiles have been perceived. Quite recent studies have carried on this practice of casting doubt, even scorn, on VDL texts.[55] This extends to European sources being given precedence (or heightened credibility) by nature of being European sources, and VDL texts have routinely been seen as less credible. To get the most from the VDL texts – to get us closer to a conception of what life might have been like at Wybalenna during the exile – we must do more than just acknowledge this very problematic value system.

A revised hierarchy of credibility is a central tenet of the methodology of this study. This draws on Ann Laura Stoler's use of the term in her analysis of the way rumour and fact intersect on the colonial frontier.[56] VDL texts can be seen as occupying a similar discursive space to Stoler's frontier rumours or unofficial news, as their authenticity has routinely been questioned. The *Flinders Island Chronicle* has

---

53   Noenoe K. Silva, *Aloha Betrayed: Native Hawaiian Resistance to American Colonialism*, Duke University Press, Durham and London, 2004.

54   The *Chronicle* was discussed in the Hobart press in September 1836; James Bonwick discussed other writings in 1870.

55   Johnson and McFarlane dismiss the *Flinders Island Chronicle* as 'essentially meaningless'. In Murray Johnson and Ian McFarlane, *Van Diemen's Land: An Aboriginal History*, Sydney, New South Publishing, 2015, 244.

56   Ann Laura Stoler, '"In Cold Blood": Hierarchies of Credibility and the Politics of Colonial Narratives,' *Representations*, 37, Winter 2002; Ann Laura Stoler, *Along the Archive Grain: Epistemic Anxieties and Colonial Common Sense*, Princeton University Press, Princeton and Oxford, 2009.

almost universally been interpreted as not *really* the work of its authors, even in sympathetic readings. The petition to Queen Victoria similarly endures an ongoing cloud of doubt over its credibility and authorship. The writers are routinely perceived as puppets of interfering Europeans.

The concept of a hierarchy of credibility was also used with great effect by sociologist Howard Becker in his seminal essay 'Whose Side Are We On?'. Where Stoler uses the term to discuss rumour or unofficial news, Becker's interpretation is about power and representation:

> In any system of ranked groups, participants take it as given that members of the highest group have the right to define the way things really are.[57]

In Becker's model, those in authority who are positioned atop the *hierarchy of credibility* have the right to define reality over those without power. Adapting Becker's concept for this project, the traditional hierarchy of historical credibility posits European (superordinate) sources at the top, and VDL sources (subordinate) as least trustworthy.

The traditional hierarchy of credibility as discussed by Becker can be seen in action in a range of historiographical contexts. It is front and centre when Dammery declares Walter Arthur not a free man, ignoring his repeated, heartfelt, pragmatic self-representation. Arthur's reality and knowledge is simply not credited. It is physically illustrated by the way the most knowledgeable writer on Flinders Island, Plomley, presented VDL texts as obscurely as possible. And it is blatantly obvious by the fact that this study – a major examination of VDL texts – is the first of its kind, despite the long-held knowledge of the existence of many of these documents.

---

57   Howard Becker, 'Whose Side Are We On?' *Social Problems*, 14 (Winter 1967), 241.

INTRODUCTION

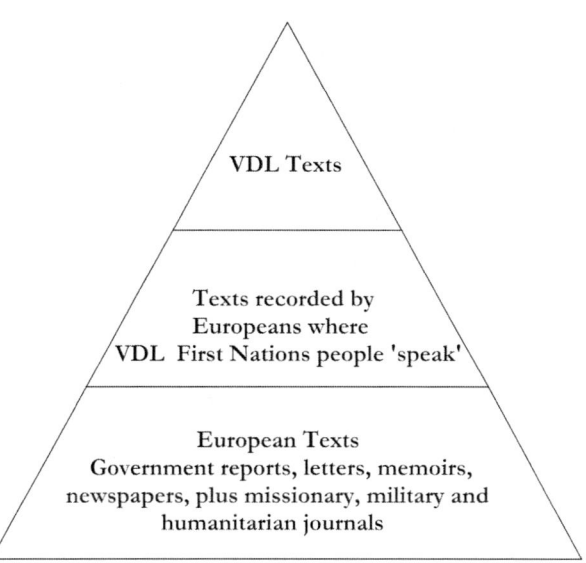

Revised Heirarchy of Credibility. © L. Stevens 2017

This study's methodology in applying this awareness of hierarchies of credibility to the VDL texts can best be described as an inversion. It consciously places VDL texts at the top of a conceptual hierarchy (here visualised as a pyramid: see figure above), followed by European texts quoting VDL First Nations, and ending with European texts, or versions. In this model, VDL texts and the information they contain are consciously prioritised.

This inversion is both a symbolic and a conceptual act. In previous hierarchical frameworks, texts written by First Nations peoples would be positioned at the bottom of the pyramid and viewed as curiosities or representing 'colour'. They are thus all but silenced, and mostly confirm the pre-formulated position of the enquirer – commonly, that European domination was ubiquitous, and VDL resistance was occasional. The response in this framework to Walter Arthur's claim to be a free man is, like Dammery's, *how could he be, given his situation?*

Yet when placed at the apex of the hierarchical structure, the VDL word takes on an urgency and new level of insight, revealing a more nuanced, personal, human story. If Walter Arthur says, repeatedly, that he is a free man, the inversion model demands that we enter history through his world: his story, worldview, community and options. When he writes those words, he *is* a free man, and fighting to stay that way.

The inversion model is straightforward – a mindfulness in how texts are approached – but its execution is more complex. To simply 'add VDL texts and stir' would still be a European recipe, marinated in problematic historiography, with VDL perspectives as seasoning. To successfully acquit this goal – to be aware of the baggage associated with asymmetrical representation and credibility, which has largely silenced VDL voices in the past – it is essential to go back to the sources: VDL sources, that is. This study deliberately consults, in the first instance, written VDL sources, then VDL sources or voices recorded by Europeans. When these are exhausted – and only then – this study consults European accounts of the day.

By this method, a new picture can begin to emerge. And while perhaps the writer and reader can never fully un-learn two hundred years of colonial history-making, saddled with its enduring baggage, this inversion of credibility offers a potential starting point.

Baggage Check 4: The White Historian

> We look into the past and inevitably write something about ourselves.[58]
>
> E. P. Thompson

---

58   E. P. Thompson, 'The Politics of Theory', in R. Samuel (ed.), *Peoples History and Socialist Theory*, London, Routledge and Kegan Paul, 1981, 407.

INTRODUCTION

The fourth and final baggage to be examined is the uncomfortable fit of white outsider writing about First Nations people. This is especially salient in the case of Van Diemen's Land and Tasmanian studies, as historians, anthropologists and archaeologists have played a leading role in the continuing colonisation of VDL people by the nature of their conclusions. It was white commentators and experts who made such fervent use of the extinction myth and ideas of racial unfitness.[59] In the 20th century, white writers fetishised frontier violence under the guise of critiquing it.[60] Even archive-rich studies perpetuated the European narrative of VDL history by over-reliance on colonial sources and perspectives.[61] Other more mendacious works used archival sources to create false narratives.[62]

Of all the baggage so far checked, this one may prove the most intractable. It is, after all, the space this work occupies. The spectre of Scientific Racism can be identified where it might be influencing conclusions, its ghosts negotiable, or at least navigable. We also have a clear strategy in how to read the VDL texts, by challenging the

---

59   James Bonwick's *Last of the Tasmanians* (1870) and *The Lost Tasmanian Race* (1884), and James Calder's *Some Account of the Wars, Extirpation, Habits etc. of the Native Tribes of Tasmania* (1875).
60   Turnbull's *Black War* and Elder's *Blood on the Wattle* are examples of well-meaning studies which, by fixating on frontier violence, nevertheless cement ideas about racial unfitness.
61   N. J. B. Plomley's monumental *Friendly Mission* and *Weep in Silence* succeed in presenting Robinson's journals, which are rich in observation and anecdote: however, Plomley's interpretations remain fixed in a doomed race perspective. James Boyce's *Van Diemen's Land*, Black Inc., Melbourne, 2009, likewise makes exhaustive use of colonial archives but makes little to no attempt to analyse their representation of First Nations narratives.
62   Clear examples are Vivienne Rae-Ellis's *Trucanini: Queen or Traitor* (1976) and *Black Robinson, Protector of Aborigines* (1988) and Keith Windschuttle's *Fabrication of Aboriginal History: Volume One: Van Diemen's Land, 1803–1847*, Sydney, Macleay Press, reprinted with corrections, 2003, all of which, by selective use of data, make spurious claims.

hierarchy of credibility. However, what of the white mainland historian in the 21st century?

The question of who is entitled to write Indigenous history is of vital importance, and for the purposes of this study there is no clear answer. First Nations scholars and communities may convincingly argue that white historians have no place at all writing First Nations histories. Histories have been a major instrument of colonisation, and First Nations people in a range of settler colonies have been dispossessed time and time again by this means. Mistrust is actually common sense.

However, the Wybalenna story is foundational to Australian and global colonial history. As such, there is no separating what are often individually termed 'Australian' and 'Indigenous' histories. They are bound, as Broome evocatively portrayed, in a 'colonial dance that needs to be understood in a conjoined way'.[63] The author of this study, a white 21st century mainland writer studying VDL history, must therefore be mindful of her position on the metaphorical dance card. Their study will be just one node in the continuum which is the long and complex discourse on VDL history. At its most useful, this study will be a facilitator of future scholarship.

Caution with analysis and representation must be employed at every turn, and reflexivity is essential. This study recalls Dening's observation that 'In re-presenting the past, in reconstructing the different, there is no avoiding our present or ourselves'.[64] This study is conscious of the way in which the VDL people exiled to Flinders Island have previously been seen as mere exotic specimens of the

---

63 Richard Broome, 'Entangled Histories: The Politics and Ethics of Writing Indigenous Histories', *Melbourne Historical Journal*, 33, 2005, 5.
64 Greg Dening, *Islands and Beaches*, 2.

INTRODUCTION

19th century ethnographer, or else victims bandied from pillar to post by technologically superior forces. Neither, though, should they be seen as nationalist revolutionaries to suit a 21st century assessment. This tension around representation was expressed succinctly by Donald Denoon and his co-authors in the depiction of the fraught postcolonial balancing act of celebrating Indigenous agency and power, while not glossing over the excesses of colonial violence and dispossession.[65]

This study attempts to tread that delicate line. It circles the baggage, working to highlight the very real power exercised by VDL people on Flinders Island, while not minimising the unthinkable devastation of invasion and exile. Exercising mindfulness of language, myths, representation and credibility, this study has the potential to greatly enhance the discourse on VDL history, by promoting a VDL voice.

Summary

We now return to our metaphorical room of VDL history. Having identified the baggage, we can see, beyond it, a comparatively small portion of that rambling colonial archive. It sits in a corner, under-lit and under-examined. This small section of data is easily accessible, and many of the commentators in the room at the very least know it is there. Yet this small section of the archive remains virtually unexamined. Commentators have often posed nearby like well-meaning dandies, and told one another what is in it, perhaps quoted one or two examples, and this has sufficed. A very few have peered

---

[65] Donald Denoon, with Stewart Firth, Jocelyn Linnakin, Malalma Meleisea and Karen Nero, *The Cambridge History of the Pacific Islanders*, Cambridge University Press, Cambridge, 2004, 20-31.

inside – sometimes to gain new perspective, but more often than not to confirm an existing idea. To date, this archive-in-the-shadows has not been given the attention it deserves, let alone looked at in its entirety.

This archive is of course the writings of VDL people themselves – in the words of Wendy Aitken, 'unhoped for treasure – *firsthand* accounts of Aboriginal country, perspective and events'.[66] In the jumbled, contested, noisy room of VDL history, the baggage had been obscuring the view:

> and I seen the Native women and what they was doing I cant tell
> and I saw a man carrying a ring tail possum
> and I also saw the Native men at work in the Garden
> and I think they are gathering the thistles that was Growing in the garden there was about 10 or 11 there was
> and I also saw some of the women awalking around the stock yeard and I also saw a running raise between two boys this morning
> I seen them run as fast as they whould
> and there names was Teddy and john franklin
> and franklin and Teddy began to fight
> And I also saw Charles Clark kill a redbreast.[67]

Introducing the VDL Texts

This is a narrative history, which presents ideas, analysis and critiques chronologically. Given that its focus is documents and perspectives which were previously all but silenced, it is fitting that its overall structure is dictated by the nature of the texts themselves. Four types or genres of texts are employed, created by VDL First Nations people between 1836 and 1847. Three of these groups of

---

66 Wendy Aitken, 'Community Voices', in Johnston and Rolls, *Reading Robinson*, 96.
67 Walter George Arthur, *Flinders Island Chronicle*, 24 October 1837.

INTRODUCTION

texts are handwritten, and one is comprised of recorded interviews and testimonies. Their respective genres neatly encapsulate the three main phases of VDL exile at Wybalenna: *The Chronicle*, covering social organisation (1836–37); the Sermons, covering the attempted hegemonic control of the Christianising mission (1838–42); and the Communications, covering the period of political agitation (1843–47).

The Flinders Island Chronicle, 1836–37

The first group of documents written by VDL First Nations people was *The Flinders Island Chronicle*.[68] This handwritten journal was produced between September 1836 and December 1837 by two teenagers, Walter George Arthur and Thomas Brune. Along with a group of younger boys, they had received a brief education at the Kings Orphan School in Newtown, just outside Hobart.[69] Both display remarkable writing talent given their minimal training, and a fine copperplate hand.

The content of the *Chronicle*, initially at least, was supervised closely by the then-superintendent (or Commandant) of the Flinders Island settlement, George Augustus Robinson. His editorial hand is obvious from the very first edition, leaving no doubt that the *Chronicle* was intended as a propaganda tool. There was no subtlety, no hidden agenda: the *Chronicle*'s stated purpose was to Christianise and civilise. A second purpose – as will be seen from a sequence of events following its first appearance in 1836 – was to assure the colonial administration

---

68 Contained in the papers of George Augustus Robinson, located in G. A. Robinson Letterbook 1838-39, ML A7045 (Vol. 24), SLNSW, photographed from QVMAG Microfilm Reel CY548; ML A7075 (Vol. 52) SLNSW; and the Plomley Collection, QVMAG, plus additional copies and drafts in colonial and personal archives.

69 Walter Arthur approximately three years, Thomas Brune four.

and humanitarians that the civilising project was paying dividends. The *Chronicle* itself clearly announced:

> The object of this journal is to promote christianity civilization and Learning amongst the Aboriginal Inhabitants at Flinders Island. The chronicle professes to be a brief but accurate register of events of the colony.[70]

The *Chronicle* has generally been taken at face value. In historical and literary analyses, it has often been framed – or dismissed – as an obvious and clumsy attempt at re-education. On a superficial level, it is. The very first edition calls on VDL people to forget their own land, language, cultural practices and belief systems, and embrace Christianity. Thomas Brune tells his Countrymen, 'we cannot look back on the events connected with our history, this we leave with the Divin[e]'[71] VDL people were encouraged to look ahead, to a civilised future. Although obviously orchestrated by the Commandant to impress Sir George Arthur, this acquiescence with the new order reached dizzying heights with the *Chronicle*. This is not to say, of course, that the re-education was successful.

Astonishingly, the *Flinders Island Chronicle* has only ever been partially published. In all cases, it has been edited, and grammar and spelling has been corrected. The same few editions are consulted again and again, and analyses have rarely strayed from the obvious.[72] As we will see, the *Chronicle* has typically been interpreted, even in sympathetic readings, as a tool for hegemonic control. Celebrations of its significance still frame it uncomfortably as the Commandant's

---

70 Thomas Brune, *Flinders Island Chronicle* Prospectus, 10 September 1836.
71 Thomas Brune, *Flinders Island Chronicle*, 10 September 1836.
72 Brune's 17 November 1837 edition is probably the most published, as two of the four drafts contain pleas to the King for removal from Flinders. This edition has gained interest due to being misinterpreted as an act of editorial subversion.

creation.⁷³ Penny Van Toorn's examination of religious currents in the *Chronicle*, while the most extensive to date, views Arthur and Brune as mediators of the coloniser's doctrine.⁷⁴ This is where the discourse sits.

In fact, the *Chronicle* is much more than a mouthpiece for the Commandant. Those editions dominated by religious indoctrination actually contain a great deal of information, if effort is invested in peeling back the layers of meaning. Contrary to many assessments, the *Chronicle* was by no means dominated by religion. In its later stages, religious exhortations are almost completely absent. The majority of known editions identified in this study are dense with day-to-day news of the settlement. Where the Commandant does speak, it is often as a third party, having his messages relayed. Looked at afresh, the *Chronicle* opens new windows of understanding into VDL life after dispossession. Most importantly, the forty-two editions and drafts⁷⁵ of the *Chronicle* show Wybalenna from a VDL point of view.

Written Sermons, Spoken Sermons and School Examinations

The second group of documents in this study is *Sermons and Examinations*. This comprises sermons handwritten by the young *Chronicle* editors, Walter George Arthur and Thomas Brune; sermons delivered by more senior, adult men which were recorded by Robert Clark, the settlement's catechist; and records of school examinations,

---

73 For example, see Greg Lehman, 'Reconciling Ruin: The transformation of Tasmanian Aboriginal culture', *Historic Environment*, 17, No. 1, 2003; Rose, *For the Record*, 2; Dammery, *Walter George Arthur*, 10-11.
74 Penny Van Toorn devotes a book chapter to the Chronicle in *Writing Never Arrives Naked: Early Aboriginal Cultures of Writing in Australia*, Canberra, Aboriginal Studies Press, 2006.
75 Fourteen of which have been located and transcribed for the first time as part of this study.

also recorded by Clark.[76] Taken at face value, these documents appear to be a continuation of the Christianising attempt at Flinders Island, and they have never been seriously analysed beyond this level. Penny Van Toorn's study views the sermons as ultimately an attempt to impose a 'grotesquely degraded version of an English way of life'.[77] This is a valid preliminary assessment, but it does little more than scratch the surface of meaning.

These sermons – especially the spoken ones delivered by senior men – are a rich and telling resource. Pioneering performances by the Commandant's favoured youths, Walter Arthur and Thomas Brune, were soon followed by others. The tradition of oration at these night-time services became more popular over time. Men from Western VDL nations seemed to have been the first preachers; then the famed Big River/Mairremmener; finally, all nations were represented. This participation by senior men from a number of nations indicates, at the very least, an acceptance and embrace of the communal act of sermonising. For some, there was genuine religious meaning; for others, it may have reflected their leadership roles in the community, or their ambitions. Sermonising could be a spiritual act of obligation, the consolidation of social currency, or a valid night-time amusement in a technologically different time. These sermons contain a wealth of data for reflection on the cultural lives of VDL people at Wybalenna.

The records from the Flinders Island School also contain invaluable information. Even more than the sermons, the School examinations have been derided as little more than evidence of attempted

---

76 Written sermons, spoken sermons and school examinations located in G. A. Robinson Letterbook 1838–39, ML A7045 (Vol. 24), SLNSW, photographed from QVMAG Microfilm Reel CY548.
77 Van Toorn, *Writing Never Arrives Naked*, 101.

cultural genocide. However, this study looks beyond the obvious. The 'school' was actually a number of small tutorial groups, usually numbering three to five.[78] These were led by the Commandant, his sons, and other officials and their families as a condition of their employment. Importantly, educated VDL boys and girls also acted as teachers. As a result of this more intimate approach to education and indoctrination, the examinations trace individuals reacting to the dogma served up to them, and to each other. The examinations also represent the only recordings of many individuals, who might otherwise just be a name on a historian's list. This part of the archive has been fundamental in reconstructing a biographical database.

The Sermons and Examinations genre of documents, read against the grain of obvious colonial intent, offer rich insights into language creation and diversity, the persistence of ritual, and the community's balancing of original and introduced spiritual beliefs. Through the sermons and examinations, and the manner of their delivery and recording, we can glimpse the complexities of conversion, and the changing nature of affiliations between nations. It is possible to identify those who resisted the imposition of European religion, language and culture, and witness the gendered nature of conversion and language acquisition. There is evidence of which types of Biblical narratives captured the imaginations of VDL people, and, most poignantly, glimpses of what a VDL version of Christianity – and even heaven – may have looked like. Far from grotesque and valueless, the sermons and examinations are enlightening, if approached in the right way.

---

78 The women's classes tended to be larger (groups of eight to ten women, as opposed to three to five men).

'ME WRITE MYSELF'

Communications *1842–47*

The third genre of original documents examined, *Communications*, comprises letters written by VDL First Nations people between 1843 and 1847. These clearly mark the point where VDL people step out from the shadow of apparent hegemonic control. There are multiple authors and a range of recipients, and these extend to the point where VDL people were successful in being repatriated to the VDL mainland.

These documents were physically created by seven different writers, but their authorship was in many cases more communal. This book takes its name from a joint letter by two Big River nation chiefs to the Governor in June 1846. They proudly sign their names:

> Me write myself King Alphonso,
> Me write myself King Alexander.[79]

In this archive there are individual and group letters, directed to friends, humanitarian contacts and colonial functionaries. Most studied among these documents is a petition to Queen Victoria, communally authored in February 1846. In European eyes – and certainly among historians – this petition appeared to be the zenith of their campaign. In terms of the archive, though, this was more an opening of the floodgates, as a remarkable series of letters from numerous authors was to follow.

The petition to Queen Victoria has spawned two very distinct discourses. The first, beginning soon after its creation, disputed its authenticity. This is why, several months later when they wrote to the Governor, Kings Alphonso and Alexander used the valediction

---

79 King Alexander and King Alphonso to Governor Eardley-Wilmot, 19 June 1846, CSO 11/26/378, AJCP Microfilm 280/195, Reel 544, SLV.

INTRODUCTION

'Me write myself'. While a commissioned enquiry in October 1846 found the petition authentic, satisfying the Crown, decades later the much-quoted colonial writer James Bonwick again contested its authenticity. This renewed doubt lingered through the 20th century with Plomley and, more recently, Keith Windschuttle.[80] These writers contended that any instances of political activism were the work of interfering Europeans, and, perhaps, Walter George Arthur, who is interpreted as an agitator and a puppet of troublemakers.

The second, more recent assessment of the petition awards it much more credibility. Henry Reynolds greatly increased the profile of the petition, heralding it as a significant political milestone.[81] Likewise, Van Toorn credits it as an important tactical document.[82] Yet questions of authenticity remain an academic constant.[83] Ironically, letters written in the wake of the petition – which categorically prove authenticity, and were seen to do so by the Government at the time – have received relatively minor attention, and no in-depth study.[84]

These *Communications* will be used in the final section to reconstruct the growing pan-VDL consciousness at Wybalenna, and the complex political campaign conducted by VDL people in the

---

[80] See, for example, Bonwick, *The Last of the Tasmanians*, 267; Turnbull, *Black War*, 224; Windschuttle, *Fabrication of Aboriginal History*, 233.

[81] See especially Chapter 1, Henry Reynolds, *Fate of a Free People*, revised edition, Camberwell, Penguin, 2005.

[82] Reynolds, *Fate of a Free People*; Van Toorn, *Writing Never Arrives Naked*; Penny Van Toorn, 'Indigenous Australian Life Writing: Tactics and Transformations', in Bain Attwood and Fiona Magowan (eds.), *Telling Stories: Indigenous History and Memory in Australia and New Zealand*, Sydney, Allen & Unwin, 2001, 1-20.

[83] Since embarking on writing this study, two questions regularly come up. The general public are interested in the extinction myth: academics are interested in authorship.

[84] Two letters (one each from Mary ann and Walter George Arthur) are reprinted in Heiss and Minter, *Macquarie PEN Anthology*; letters are also mentioned in Reynolds, *Fate of a Free People*; Ryan, *Tasmanian Aborigines*; Dammery, *Walter George Arthur*; Plomley, *Weep in Silence*; Van Toorn, *Writing Never Arrives Naked*.

tumultuous final year of their exile. This campaign was sophisticated, far-reaching, at times dangerous, and ultimately successful. This part of the narrative is greatly informed by testimonies to the official inquiry into the petition, and other charges, held at Wybalenna in October 1846. It will be clear that the goal of self-sufficiency and self-determination was a long-standing one, and pre-dated the celebrated petition to Queen Victoria by many years. There were campaigns over wages and property, and the abiding importance of VDL peoples' status as free people of their original Country. After all, the two Big River Kings Alexander and Alphonso, who so proudly asserted 'Me write myself', began their letter to Governor Eardley-Wilmot 'To good Father of the big river the own country'.[85] They were acknowledging that he was currently in control, but it was their *own* Country.

European Sources

Records made by colonial Europeans are usually the first port of call in histories of VDL. These are extensively consulted in this study, but chiefly as contextualising data, or to 'fill in the blanks' where accounts by VDL sources are unavailable. The importance of journals by George Augustus Robinson, as transcribed and published by Plomley and Ian Clark, cannot be overstated.[86] Another key source is the catechist Robert Clark, who spent more time with VDL people than any other European, both at Wybalenna and later back on the mainland. He was mourned many years after his passing by VDL

---

85   King Alexander and King Alphonso to Governor Eardley-Wilmot, 19 June 1836, CSO 11/26/378, AJCP 280/195, Reel 544, SLV.

86   Plomley's *Friendly Mission* (1966) and *Weep in Silence* (1987); Ian D. Clark (ed.), *The Journals of George Augustus Robinson, Chief Protector, Port Phillip Aboriginal Protectorate*, Vol. 1, January 1839–September 1840; Vol. 2, October 1840–August 1841; Vol. 3, September 1841–December 1843; Vol. 4, Jan 1844–Oct 1845. Melbourne, Heritage Matters, 1998.

INTRODUCTION

people, but remains in the historical shadows, due to Plomley's inexplicably low regard for him. Other sources include newspaper accounts, letters from Europeans on the island to various humanitarian figures (particularly the Quakers James Backhouse and George Washington Walker), and Colonial Office archives.

In consulting these sources, however, the hierarchy of credibility will be kept in mind. This history, on which we now embark, is one constructed, wherever possible, from VDL sources. The mantra will be *We do not need yet another European history of VDL people*. It is the simplest way of keeping the baggage in check.

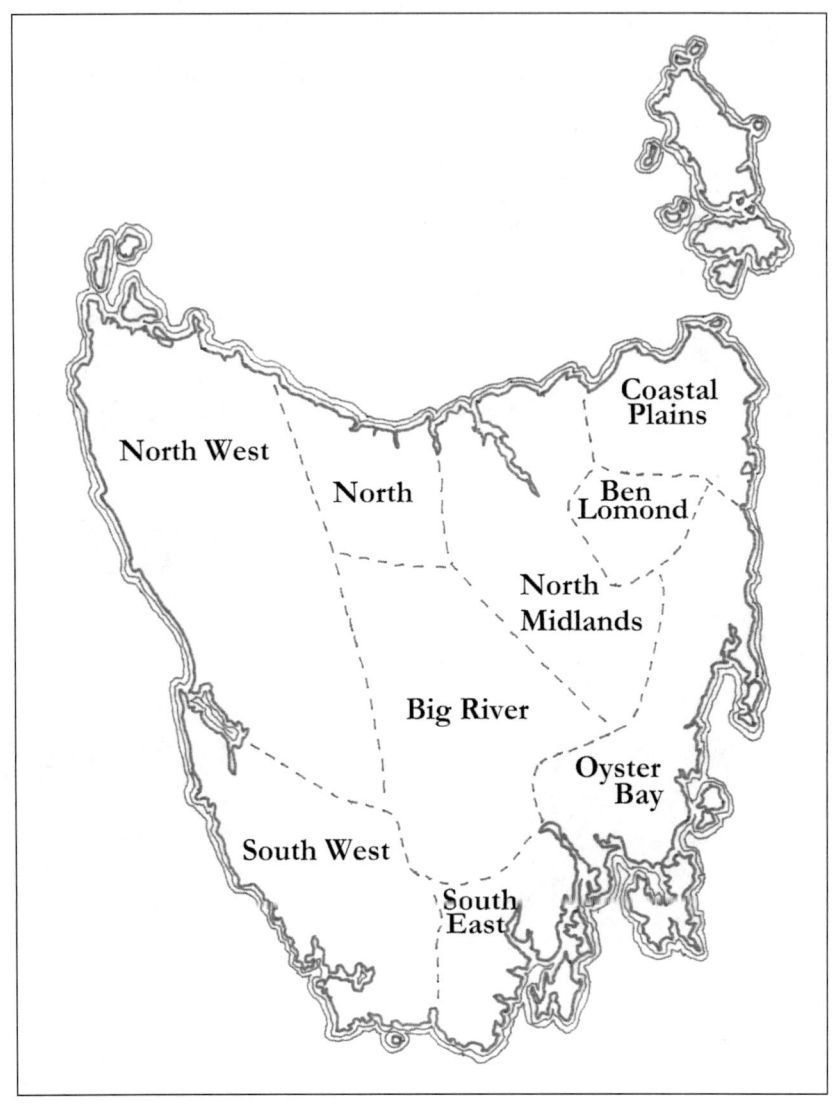

First Nations of Van Diemen's Land – approximate national boundaries.
A general guide only. © L. Stevens 2017

Chapter 1

40,000 YEARS TO EXILE

I will not engage in a history of the human settlement of Van Diemen's Land. The documentary evidence which exists is too heavily weighted by the post-European story to result in anything but a European history of colonisation, and detracts from the real focus of this study: the under-examined Wybalenna exile. Likewise, I will not attempt a detailed examination of pre-contact First Nations societies. Due to the complexities, and the contested nature of the record, even a cursory attempt becomes saddled with the multitude of issues arising from problematic historiography. It is outside the scope of this study to condense the histories and responses of a number of distinct cultures: this I leave to more detailed studies of the individual nations or periods.[1] This study is intended to be read in tandem with those works, and informed by more general histories.[2] What follows is but a brief summary of key events.

---

1 See especially Patsy Cameron, *Grease and Ochre*; the early chapters of Shayne Breen, *Contested Places*; Graeme Calder, *Levee, Line and Martial Law: A History of the Dispossession of the Mairremmener People of Van Diemens Land 1803–1832*, Launceston, Fuller's Bookshop, 2010; Ian MacFarlane, *Beyond Awakening: The Aboriginal Tribes of North West Tasmania – A History*, Launceston, Fuller's Bookshop, 2008.

2 See especially Henry Reynolds, *History of Tasmania*, Cambridge and Melbourne, Cambridge University Press, 2012; Lyndall Ryan, *Tasmanian Aborigines*; for the purely European story, James Boyce, *Van Diemen's Land*.

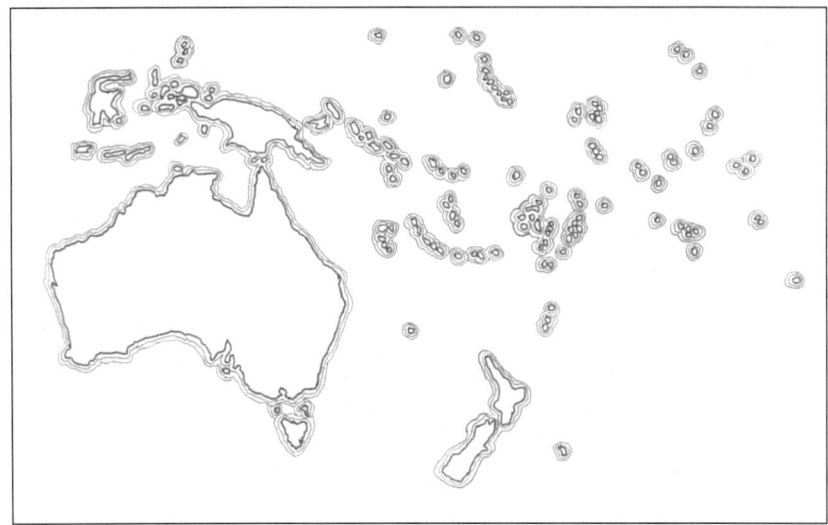

On Positioning

It's only an island when you look at it from the water.

Chief Brody, *Jaws*[3]

The idea that First Nations peoples have *always* lived in Australia is a passionately held and defended one. It runs through many origin stories, contending that the ancestors of the first peoples have been there since time began. From the beginning – *always*. This powerful and widespread historical narrative links land, people and time in a holistic concept called Dreaming.[4] A discipline like history, with its burden of evidence and reliance on archaeology where no written

---

3   Chief Brody, *Jaws* [Motion picture], Steven Speilberg (Dir.), USA, Universal Pictures, 1975.

4   'Dreaming' is used as opposed to 'Dreamtime', which locks concepts in a temporal space and is more suited to explain creation stories. For a useful conceptualisation of Dreaming, see Deborah Bird Rose's description of Dreaming as synchrony in 'Ned Kelly Died for Our Sins', *Oceania*, 65:2, 1994, 179-181.

CHAPTER 1

record exists, can be forgiven for being uneasy about concepts like *forever*. It is usually deftly avoided.

This study, however, is committed to privileging First Nations accounts and systems of knowledge where possible and appropriate. And to properly contextualise the writings of VDL people during their exile at Wybalenna, we must go back. *Way* back – past historiographical debates, shipping records and the wild cartographic imaginings of the Age of Exploration.[5] Anthropological categories and ideas about social evolution must be set aside, to venture to a place where European ideas of progress – and evidence – do not exist.

At the beginning of this story, the moon and the planets are still, roughly, in the same locations, but the observable transit of stars is different. The land is modified, with vastly altered shores and land masses. Volcanic and tectonic incursions write and rewrite the landscape. Alternately arid, moist and smothered by glacier, this is a world in flux. Mountains, deserts and river courses are different, as are the animals, fish and plants that populate them. The one striking thing which is thoroughly modern is the people.[6]

The first human cultures in Australia flourished in a temporal period before the continent – as we know it – physically existed. The lands, seas, plants, animals and climate were all different, and the first peoples literally witnessed the formation of what is now the Australian landscape. In this sense, First Nations people have been living on the Australian continent since time began – *always*.

---

5   Pierre Desceliers's 1550 'Chart of Australia' as one example. According to George Collingridge, an amalgam of Portuguese and Spanish maps, Marco Polo's descriptions of Java, and a great deal of imagination. See George Collingridge, *Discovery of Australia*, [1895 Hayes Brothers Sydney], facsimile edition, Silverwater, Golden Press, 192-193.
6   Modern humans as defined by Linnaean taxonomy.

The academy, from which this study originates, tells a similar narrative, which is no less fantastical-sounding in parts to many First Nations creation stories. The dramatic, currently-dominant narrative holds that human beings had been in Australia for at the *very least* 45,000 years. This assessment, which importantly posits the First Nations of Australia as the world's oldest continuous culture, is a conservative one, based on sound scientific data.[7] It is therefore the very minimum which is proven. 45,000 years is a very good first step on the way to always. But always, of course, is a very difficult quantity to measure.

Within a few millennia of arriving on the continent which encompassed the current-day Australian mainland as well as New Guinea and Tasmania, the first human colonists spread far and wide. By 45,000 years ago, people were well established, as the research into Lake Mungo proves, at the Willandra Lakes system in western New South Wales. By 30,000 years ago, there is abundant evidence of people living across the metaphoric four corners of the continent – from today's Pilbara to far north Queensland; from the Great Australian Bight to the contemporary Melbourne suburb of Keilor. People lived in caves, rock shelters, and built dwellings. They populated mountains, forests, lakes and deserts, and crossed vast distances in difficult circumstances.

When people first lived in Trowunna or Van Diemen's Land it was a peninsula of sorts. To gain access, people had to cross the Bassian Plain or desert, which according to research by John Taylor was part of an extensive and extremely arid valley that stretched from Shark Bay in Western Australia to the current Tasmanian land

---

7   The upper end of this current estimated date range for human occupation of Australia is 60,000 years.

CHAPTER 1

mass.[8] From around 42,000 years ago, people were successfully inhabiting much of the modern Tasmanian land mass.[9] It was a resource-rich environment, sustaining human life right through a number of major climate shifts. Although much evidence has been lost, due to the rising of sea levels submerging many sites of human occupation, inland evidence shows multiple locations with continuous occupation from at least 34,000 years ago, such as Parmerpar Meethaner.[10] Some sites were used at the height of the last Ice Age, then abandoned, such as the famous Kutikina Cave.[11] Other locations were used mainly in more temperate periods. Some areas, however, are thought to have been rarely used, due to a range of climatological and geographical features such as permanent rain shadow.

Around 12,000 years ago, a cycle of global warming began. People in what was soon to be VDL emerged from ice age cave-living and shed their clothing, preferring the use of seal and other animal fat mixed with ochre as insulation.[12] Other people began arriving, via

---

[8] John Taylor, *Cultural Evolution in Palawa (Tasmanian Aboriginal) Societies 40,000 BCE to 1803 AD*, PhD Thesis, University of Tasmania, incomplete, 44-45.

[9] A wealth of scholarship exists documenting human occupation of various regions. See especially the work of Richard Cosgrove, Sandra Bowdler, John Mulvaney, Rhys Jones and Jim Allen.

[10] Jim Allen dates Parmer Parmeethener between 33 and 39k, Warreen 36–41k. *Peer Review of the Draft Final Archaeological Report on the Test Excavations of the Jordan River Levee Site, Southern Tasmania*, Robert Paton Archaeological Studies, August 2010.

[11] An incredibly rich archaeological assemblage was excavated in 1982, which had a major influence on stopping the damming of the Franklin River, close to which it is located. Rhys Jones, Don Ranson, Jim Allen and Kevin Kiernan, 'The Australian National University–Tasmanian National Parks and Wildlife Service Archaeological Expedition to the Franklin River, 1982: A Summary of Results', *Australian Archaeology*, No. 16, June 1983, 57-70.

[12] Ian Gilligan, *Another Tasmanian Paradox: Clothing and Thermal Adaptations in Aboriginal Australia*, Oxford, Archaeopress, 2007; Sagona cites Backhouse (1843) and Davies (1841) as discussing the mixing of grease and ochre into a paste for insulation; Antonio Sagona, *Bruising the Red Earth: Ochre Mining and Ritual in Aboriginal Tasmania*, Carlton, Melbourne University Press, 1994, 23; see also Patsy Cameron, *Grease and Ochre*.

the desert land bridge. However, with global warming, the Bassian Plain began to submerge. Over several thousand years, a lake expanded until the western side of the land bridge disappeared completely. The total submerging of Bass Strait, and isolation from the north, would not have been a surprise. It did not happen overnight. For many centuries, there would have been warning, and northeast coastal people would certainly have had a choice, of sorts, on whether to stay on the island, or go north.[13]

Human settlement on the large, triangular island diversified and flourished. Communities that had survived the perils of the Ice Age consolidated language, land use patterns and cultural identities. These may have been challenged, and perhaps enriched, by contact with migrants from the north. By the time the seas rose to submerge the last link back to the main continent, the population which had been in place for tens of thousands of years was augmented by those who had ventured south in the post-glacial period. The newer arrivals probably settled towards the southern and eastern parts of VDL.[14] By six thousand years ago, there were no new arrivals. In this post-glacial period, VDL people organised themselves into a variety of socially, culturally and linguistically diverse societies. Henry Reynolds asserts that they 'were, in fact, small nations which had long traditions of complex "international" relations'.[15]

Diversity was a hallmark of the First Nations of Van Diemen's Land. Some nations were allies, such as the Big River and Oyster Bay people, and were fluent in each other's languages. Others such as

---

13   Patsy Cameron writes evocatively on this under-examined period in *Grease and Ochre*.
14   John Taylor used linguistic, archaeological and ethnographic evidence to locate the Nara speakers, who were the final migrants before separation. John Taylor, *Cultural Evolution in Palawa (Tasmanian Aboriginal) Societies*.
15   Reynolds, *Fate of a Free People*, 149.

CHAPTER 1

the North West people had no contact with those to the east, though they did share reciprocal hunting arrangements with the South West people. There were long standing animosities, such as between the Ben Lomond and Big River–Oyster Bay alliance. And while there is only scant evidence from the pre-European period, it is clear, from the evidence at Wybalenna, that many of the old alliances, and animosities, were retained. In many ways, it is the Wybalenna record of exile which can give many pointers to pre-war, pre-exile life.

Much has been made of the isolation in which the various First Nations of VDL presumably developed. Archaeologist Rhys Jones did much to expose the longevity of VDL occupation; he also framed VDL isolation pathologically. VDL people, he famously wrote, suffered a 'squeezing of intellectuality' and 'slow strangulation of the mind'.[16] As a backward and isolated people, so the story went, they were destined to fail. However, the only people talking about isolation were the Europeans.

Island life, of course, is no impediment to cultural progress, and the cultural worlds of the First Nations people of Van Diemen's Land were full. Patsy Cameron paints a compelling picture of traditional life ways of the Coastal Plains nation, with a rich cultural and spiritual life.[17] The work of Shayne Breen, Ian MacFarlane and Graeme Calder likewise present windows into pre-contact worlds of the Northern, North West and Big River–Oyster Bay nations. Van Diemen's Land might be seen in the same context as Epeli Hau'ofa's evocative depiction of the richness and complexity of Pacific island

---

16 Rhys Jones, 'The Tasmanian Paradox', in R. V. S. Wright (ed.), S*tone Tools as Cultural Markers: Change, Evolution and Complexity*, Canberra, Australian Institute of Aboriginal Studies, 1977, 203.
17 Cameron, *Grease and Ochre*, 20-33.

culture in *Our Sea of Islands*: 'Their world was anything but tiny. They thought big and recounted their deeds in epic proportions'.[18]

The issue of isolation will be rested with one final question. Is it reasonable to assume – as the discourse currently does – that VDL was *never* visited by Melanesian or Polynesian people? Given the dramatic and successful Pacific maritime expansions of the past millennia, it is difficult to imagine – even given the treacherous seas of Bass Strait – that Pacific mariners did not visit VDL. While there is currently no direct evidence of trade or contact with mainland Australian, Melanesian or Polynesian mariners, the possibility should not be discounted. Given the skill and tenacity of Polynesian mariners, it seems counterintuitive to hold too fast to ideas of hermetically sealed isolation. The Pacific had been a very busy waterway for hundreds of years before Europeans arrived. Absence of evidence is not evidence of absence.

Looking at What the White People Did

The European history of Van Diemen's Land is a familiar one, and its narrative of 'discovery' is writ large across VDL land and seas. It holds that the remarkable VDL isolation was interrupted in the 17th century, as a steady procession of European superpowers sent investigators. It was always a colonial affair: when Abel Tasman named the island Van Diemen's Land in 1642, it was in honour of his patron, then-governor of the Dutch East Indies. The coastlines, rivers, and towns of modern day Tasmania bear the names of the English and French mariners like Du Fresne (1772), who was the first European to make contact with Nuenonne/Bruny Island people; Englishman Tobias Furneaux who visited Adventure Bay in 1773, again meeting

---

18   Epeli Hau'ofa, 'Our Sea of Islands', *The Contemporary Pacific*, 6:1, Spring 1994, 152.

CHAPTER 1

with the Nuenonne nation; and Bruni d'Entrecasteax (1792) who also met the Nuenonne people at Adventure Bay, and whose name lives on in the D'Entrecasteaux channel, and Bruny Island.[19] Bass and Flinders circumnavigated VDL in 1798, lending their names to the strait they charted, and later what was initially called Great Island. Ann McGrath writes evocatively of these early encounters as, in retrospect, moments to cherish: 'moments of promising warmth and openness, of recognition and of our common humanity … rare times of mutual trust between indigenes and foreigners' because, importantly, the strangers would return permanently to their own lands.[20]

A VDL perspective of this exploration narrative is not unknown to us. VDL people watched and they waited. They spread the word and then they watched some more. We can look to the experiences of the Nuenonne/Bruny Island people, who had the most experience with investigators. The great negotiator and sage Doctor Wooreddy[21] would later tell the missionary G. A. Robinson: 'the natives went to the mountains, went and looked at what the white people did, went and told other natives and they came and looked also'.[22]

People watched and waited. On a mountainous island, there were many vantage points. At times, negotiations were entered into, such

---

19 The spelling of Bruny Island has often been varied. The same goes for the Nuenonne people who bear that name (Thomas Brune, David and Peter Bruny or, as used in this study for these individuals, Bruney).

20 Ann McGrath, 'Tasmania 1', in Ann McGrath (ed.), *Contested Ground: Australian Aborigines Under the British Crown*, St. Leonards, Allen & Unwin, 1995, 311-312.

21 Born around 1786, Bruny Island. Commonly known as Doctor, due to his status as a traditional healer and clever man. Spelling varies across the written record, e.g. Wooreddy, Woorady, Wooradeddy, Wooraddy. This study follows the spelling used by Mudrooroo/Colin Johnson in his novel *Doctor Wooreddy's Prescription for Enduring the Ending of the World*, Melbourne, Hyland House, 1983. Later known at Flinders Island as Count Alpha. See *Weep In Silence*, 834, 837, for detailed nomenclature.

22 Doctor Wooreddy to G. A. Robinson, 11 July 1831, from *Friendly Mission*, 408.

as the Coastal Plains nation's partnership with independent sealers and whalers on the Furneaux group islands. Cameron has established patterns of labour migration in the early years of the Coastal Plains nation's links to what she calls the Straitsmen, where women – the *Tyereelore*, expert sealers and birders – worked seasonally on the islands with the Straitsmen.[23] However, few VDL–European relationships would follow this collaborative pattern.

The British arrived in the south-east of modern day Tasmania in September 1803. The first encampment was in Mairremmener Country.[24] A permanent settlement was established at Risdon Cove, on the east side of what was called the Derwent River. In May 1804, this was the site of what would be known as the Risdon Cove Massacre, where it appears a large hunting party was attacked by nervous marines, with a large number reported dead.[25] This set the tone for future relations. The following year, the settlement was moved across the Derwent, and grew into Hobarttown. Hundreds of kilometres to the north, the river port of Launceston was established in 1804 on the Tamar River, and pastoral expansion flourished.

There was no attempt at treaty. The resource-rich corridor between the two initial port settlements of Hobarttown and Launceston sat squarely within the traditional lands of the powerful alliance of

---

[23] Patsy Cameron, *Grease and Ochre*, 79-111.

[24] Mairremmener is used by Graeme Calder and others, following the work of linguist John Taylor; it denotes both the Oyster Bay peoples, plus their close associates the Big River and North Midlands nations. See Calder, *Levee Line and Martial Law*, 17-20, fn. 254. In later times, the infamy of the Big River peoples ensured that all three allied nations were associated as 'Big River' people.

[25] As discussed by Henry Reynolds, this was a controversial incident at the time, and has been ever since. For the most recent discussions, see Henry Reynolds, *A History of Tasmania*, 20-24; James Boyce, *Van Diemen's Land*, 38-40; Lyndall Ryan, *Tasmanian Aborigines*, 49-51.

CHAPTER 1

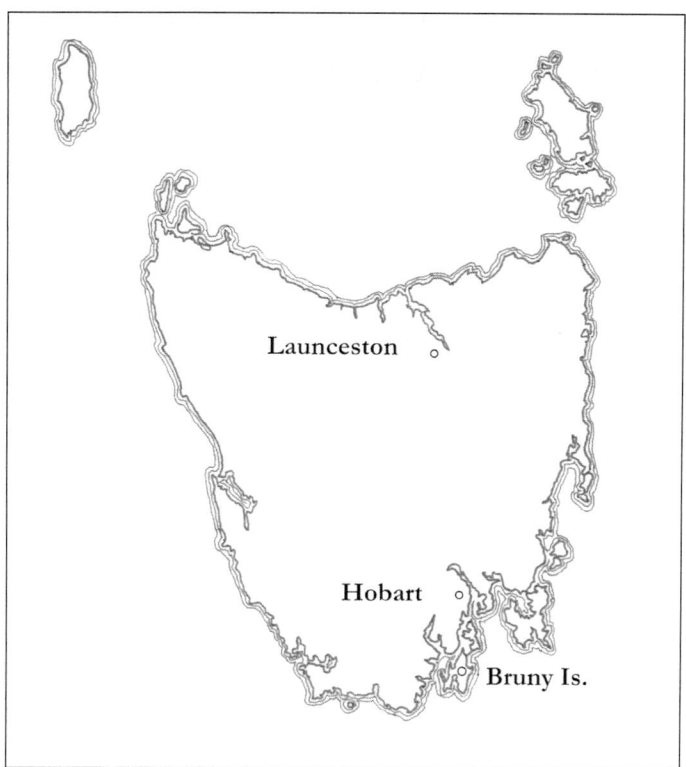

First major towns, Van Diemen's Land. © L. Stevens 2017

the Big River, Oyster Bay and North Midlands peoples, and their traditional enemies, the Ben Lomond nation. This region included lakes, waterways and land strategically modified over many centuries for hunting and cultural purposes. With the arrival of men, guns, fences and sheep, the Big River and Oyster Bay alliance was effectively invaded on two fronts. Within a decade, VDL people found themselves not sharing use of the land, but forced from it. During the 1820s, as land grants increased and the carefully-crafted kangaroo hunting runs became covered in sheep,[26] VDL people retaliated.

---

26 Sharon Morgan, *Land Settlement in Early Tasmania: Creating an Antipodean England*, first paperback edition, Cambridge, Cambridge University Press, 2003, 5-23.

The events of the so-called 'Black War' were surprisingly well recorded at the time, and have been a focus for historians ever since.[27] A number of nations – especially the Big River and Oyster Bay alliance – waged a determined, patriotic campaign in defence of Country. It was fought on a national or clan-based level, rather than nations joining together against the British. The fighting was stealthy, what we would call guerrilla-style, and very effective. Charismatic individuals, male and female, emerged as leaders, reacting strongly to the frontier violence they were experiencing at the hands of convicts, free settlers and roving parties with an eye to bounty. Cumbersome firearm technology, in the early days, was ably challenged by skilled hunters who could spear a target at seventy metres. By the time Sir George Arthur declared martial law in 1828, it is estimated that 369 settlers had been killed in frontier violence.[28] The number of VDL deaths was probably three times that.[29]

The war in Van Diemen's Land became a threat to successful colonisation. George Arthur considered the ongoing hostilities a 'heavy calamity upon the Colony' which 'wholly engrosses and fills my mind with painful anxiety'.[30] The administration's most desperate attempt

---

27 The most recent publication on this topic, Nicholas Clements's exhaustive *The Black War: Fear, Sex and Resistance in Tasmania*, Brisbane, University of Queensland Press, 2014.

28 Henry Reynolds quoting Plomley's estimate, in Reynolds, 'The Written Record', in B. Attwood and A. G. Foster (eds.), *Frontier Conflict, The Australian Experience*, Canberra, National Museum of Australia, 2003, 82. This number has been revised down to 250 by 1831, in Henry Reynolds, *Forgotten War*, Sydney, Newsouth, University of New South Wales Press, 2013, 10.

29 This is at odds with the general 10 to 1 ratio which has been applied in mainland studies – see Broome, 'The Statistics of Frontier Conflict', in Attwood and Foster (eds.), *Frontier Conflict*, 88-98. Henry Reynolds's most recent estimate is that the death toll from frontier violence in Tasmania may have been as high as 1000; *Forgotten War*, 133.

30 Lt Gov. Arthur, 20 November 1830, reprinted in Henry Reynolds, 'Genocide in Tasmania?', in A. D. Moses (ed.), *Genocide and Settler Society: Frontier Violence and*

CHAPTER 1

to gain control of the Big River–Oyster Bay rebellion was the failed 'Line' campaign of 1830.[31] All the able-bodied (white) men in the colony famously linked together in a human line across the landscape, attempting to drive VDL people onto the Tasman peninsula. It is usually reported that the Line was a failure, having only caught two people – an old man and a child. However, the Line brought enormous amounts of fear to VDL people still on the land, and while it may be viewed as folly, as an operation to engender terror it was a stunning success.[32]

Violence, however terrible, was probably not the main physical threat to VDL people associated with colonisation. Introduced diseases had a catastrophic impact, just as they had on mainland First Nations. Many deaths were by pulmonary causes, especially influenza, similar to the Victorian experience. For those VDL people who consorted with colonists, the adoption of clothing was also disastrous, as the change from the efficient insulation provided by grease and ochre to damp European fabrics also exacerbated pulmonary complaints. Alienation from traditional food sources led to greater reliance on a European diet, which also proved detrimental to VDL people.[33] VDL people were thus fighting a war on numerous fronts – they were meeting violence, dispossession, and loss of family

---

Stolen Indigenous Children in Australian History, New York and Oxford, Berghahn Books, 2004, 146.

31   Commonly known as the Black Line – something of a misnomer, as its constitution was overwhelmingly white.

32   G. A. Robinson used 'The Line' – and fear of soldiers – to great effect, to convince VDL people to retreat to Swan Island. Recounted in his journals of October–November 1830, *Friendly Mission*, 280-351.

33   Change from a lean, protein and grain base diet to stodgy English staples is known to be problematic, as was shown in the tragic case of the mainland Pintupi in 1963–64 that suffered a massive 40 per cent mortality due largely to the change from desert to Mission staples. See R. Folds, *Crossed Purposes: The Pintupi and Australia's Indigenous Policy*, Sydney, University of New South Wales Press, 2001, 21-24.

and clan, cultural liberty and means of subsistence. The only alternative – colonial charity in the form of clothes and staples – made them sick.

This is the fatal impact version of VDL history, and it has been an especially powerful model. Men came in ships with guns and disease, and other men came with pen, ink and paper. Sometimes they were one and the same, usurping traditional owners then agonising about it in their journals and letters home. They could act one moment with banal brutality, then pose as good citizens.[34] The settlers and officials knew they had brought the diseases and wrought the violence, but barely paused to reflect. When they did reflect, they fancied that the VDL people were fairly compensated by European advances. Writing in 1832, James Bischoff summarised the colonial narrative of the time of VDL people as 'degraded and wretched savages' formerly in 'a state of misery and precarious subsistence advanced to comfort and happiness'.[35]

This comfort and happiness was a fiction. Within three decades, the original VDL population, which is estimated conservatively at around 6000, but was probably higher, suffered a dramatic decline. Whole nations – such as the North Midlands and Ben Lomond – were dispossessed and to a large part scattered. Husbands lost their wives – highly destabilising in monogamous societies – and families lost their children. And children, tragically, lost their language. By the early 1830s, when our story really begins, the 'known' VDL population was around three hundred people.[36] This was a huge

---

[34] One clear example is John Batman; another is Edward Curr, head of the Van Diemen's Land Company operation.

[35] Bischoff, *Sketch of the History of Van Diemen's Land*, 36.

[36] This figure does not include the many VDL men, women and children who lived with and worked for settlers, nor those living on Bass Strait islands, nor those employed in

CHAPTER 1

reduction in pre-European numbers, foreshadowed with the Eora in Sydney, and soon to be echoed by a similar decline across Bass Strait in Victoria.[37] While it must be acknowledged that this figure of three hundred is probably a gross underestimate – there were certainly VDL people living in numerous other locations – there is no doubt, in any of the narratives about British settlement of Van Diemen's Land, that the result for VDL people was cataclysmic.

For most VDL people, by the end of the 1820s it was already too late. Their worlds had not been lost so much as stolen. Word of *bad white men* would have caused fear among those who had not yet met any Europeans. All VDL people who had heard the stories would have been on high alert. Some took up the armed struggle: others, as we shall see, sought a political solution. The novelist Mudrooroo characterised this period in VDL history in the title of his well-known novel *The Ending of the World*.[38]

However, we can also see when we turn our attention to the texts created by VDL people that this was not the end of *everything*. The characterisation of a people sinking into depression and wasting away might be true in part: what we now know of as post-traumatic stress disorder must certainly have been widespread. Yet we must also remember that VDL people were skilled adapters. Like all human beings, they were inherently geared towards survival. When weighing up their next step, they would have sought out the best option for themselves and their group. The VDL people faced with dispossession in the 1820s were not afraid to change to make this occur.

---

shore- and sea-based whaling industries. It also does not account for VDL people who were now on the Australian mainland, New Zealand, and further afield.

37 Broome, *Aboriginal Victorians*, 92.
38 Mudrooroo's fictionalised account (as Colin Johnson) is entitled *Doctor Wooreddy's Prescription for Enduring the Ending of the World*.

The Nuenonne Set the Agenda

In 1829, the Nuenonne people now located around Bruny Island secured the first significant concession from the empire which had invaded their land. In February of that year, a deputation had visited Hobart to seek assistance, and in response a mission was established on Bruny Island, affording the Nuenonne and other nations food and protection from violence.[39] The mission also represented a conduit for future political negotiations. The location – in close proximity to the Adventure Bay whaling station, and in easy reach of Hobart – was perfect for a people already well adjusted to the presence of Europeans.[40]

The Nuenonne and other VDL people at Bruny Island were not without a leader of great sagacity. Doctor Wooreddy, later known as Count Alpha at Flinders Island, was old enough to remember a time before Europeans. He could remember the shock of seeing the huge white sails on the horizon, and had been privy to many discussions among the Nuenonne about what this might mean.[41] As a young man, he would have been aware of the violence done at Risdon Cove, and seen his own people's side of the Derwent become infested with white people and their things. He would have witnessed vandalism of his environment, brutality against his own people, and the war raging to the north.

---

39   Lyndall Ryan discusses how, after a complaint from Nuenonne men (unnamed) about treatment of women by the sealer John Baker, the man was arrested and a ration station planned: *Tasmanian Aborigines*, 113. See also Reynolds, *Fate of a Free People*, 130.

40   At this time, an estimated 90 mostly European men were engaged in the onshore whaling operation at Adventure Bay. Susan Lawrence, 'Excavations at Kelly & Lucas' Adventure Bay Whaling Station', *Newsletter, Australasian Society for Historical Archaeology*, Vol. 28, 1998, 5.

41   Detailed in his discussions recorded in G. A. Robinson's journals. An evocative description, given in conversation on 11 July 1831, reproduced in Plomley, *The Friendly Mission*, 408.

CHAPTER 1

Yet amidst this calamity, characterised by Mudrooroo as the ending of the world, the Doctor maintained a pragmatism that would have far-reaching impact. He had his own family to provide for, which in 1829 included a wife and three children.[42] There was also a broader community of survivors, dispossessed and orphans who were now frequenting his land. In a bold move, which amounted to an act of resistance, the Doctor looked to a future for his people beyond the devastation around them: akin to the idea of Radical Hope explored by philosopher Jonathon Lear, Doctor Wooreddy pushed for a future 'that could not yet be grasped'.[43] This involved, in the first place, making strategic connections.

The advertisement for an administrator to run the mission on Bruny Island had attracted a number of respondents. Some, such as former sealer John Boultbee, were rendered ineligible. George Augustus Robinson was much more to Sir George Arthur's taste of what a missionary to natives or convicts should be – of lower rank, steady, Evangelical, and with a large family to share the workload. Already successful as an artisan and property developer, this position was something of a backwards step career-wise for Robinson; however, he leapt into action on receiving the appointment. While his first *named* contact was Trugernanner, four days after his arrival, it is probable that Doctor Wooreddy, as the acknowledged Chief, would have been among the first consulted.[44]

---

[42] At the beginning of the Bruny Island mission, according to Robinson's journals, Wooreddy had a wife and three children. He was also infatuated with sixteen-year-old Trugernanner, but their relationship would not be pursued until his wife had passed away.

[43] Jonathon Lear, *Radical Hope: Ethics in the Face of Cultural Devastation*, Cambridge, Harvard University Press 2008, 123.

[44] Robinson arrived on 30 March 1829, and 'had an interview with the natives'; met Trugernanner on 4 April 1829; in *Friendly Mission*, 55-56.

What happened next was observed by a six-year-old orphan boy. His name does not appear in the mission's records, but this boy would later assume a unique place in Australian history as Australia's first Indigenous journalist. Eight years later, known as Thomas Brune, he recalled his observations of events at Bruny Island in the *Flinders Island Chronicle*:

> ... when I was in that country which his called Brune Island I seen many of them together with the Commandant left all his Children and when into the woods and found them in the bush then brought them to Flinders Island[45]

Here, fourteen-year-old Thomas Brune is writing about what he witnessed as a young boy: his Countrymen joining forces with the missionary George Augustus Robinson.

The traditional narrative holds that in 1829, Sir George Arthur commissioned the intrepid lay preacher G. A. Robinson to traverse the island and convince the warring VDL nations to lay down arms and abandon their Country. This remarkable series of journeys, conducted between 1830 and 1834 with the assistance of VDL translators and intermediaries, was amply recorded in Robinson's journals.[46] His journals reveal a man acutely aware of his own myth-making.[47] The journeys led to the construction of Trugernanner as a Malinche-esque operative.[48] The VDL people accompanying Robinson were often characterised, in the eagerly-digested official narrative, as

---

45 Brune, *Flinders Island Chronicle*, 22 Sep 1837, QVMAG Plomley Collection CY825-67.
46 Plomley, *Friendly Mission*, 141-857.
47 See the discussions by various authors in Johnston and Rolls, *Reading Robinson*, including Patrick Brantlinger, 'King Billy's Bones: Colonial Knowledge Production in Nineteenth-Century Tasmania', 47; Cassandra Pybus, 'A Self-Made Man', 105; Henry Reynolds, 167.
48 A characterisation exploited by Rae-Ellis in *Trucanini: Queen or Traitor?*

CHAPTER 1

willing helpers to Robinson; they were apostles to him as saviour. The traditional view is illustrated perfectly by Thomas Brune eight years later as he writes for the *Flinders Island Chronicle*:

> The Natives would being so micerable if the Commandant did not take them the Commandant likes poor blacks and he save them from the white inccase that the whites shoot them.[49]

This was the story that Robinson, Governor Arthur, the Crown and the humanitarian lobby all wanted to tell, and it dominated the historical discourse for a century and a half. It gave the Crown success in a sea of guilt – an assuaging of responsibility for the havoc wrought by colonisation. The colonisers could be seen, finally, as offering some degree of rights to VDL people – though as Evans et al. remind us, these rights were generally based on paternalism not equality.[50] The narrative of Robinson as colonial agent and conciliator remains a rich source of critique for generations of historians and activists.

Few, however, have proposed a reading of events as radical as Henry Reynolds. He characterises the conception and performance of the first 'Friendly Mission' as a Nuenonne peace mission.[51] Reynolds contends that representatives of the Nuenonne, led by Wooreddy, *recruited* Robinson and through him, the Crown. Trugernanner, Dray and Pagerly – three young women who had extensive experience with Europeans at the Adventure Bay whaling station – had English

---

49　Thomas Brune, *Flinders Island Chronicle*, 10 September 1837, QVMAG Plomley Collection CY825-61.

50　J. Evans, P. Grimshaw, D. Philips and S. Swain, *Equal Subjects, Unequal Rights: Indigenous Peoples in British Settler Colonies, 1830–1910*, Manchester and New York, Manchester University Press, 2003, 34.

51　Henry Reynolds, 'Revisiting Risdon Cove', presentation at Tasmanian Historical Research Association Conference, University of Tasmania, 4 September 2010.

language skills, and functioned as chief interlocutors. The evidence fits Reynolds's suggestion: accompanied by Robinson and his European attendants, Wooreddy and the VDL diplomats were able to move beyond the confines of the so-called Bruny Island Mission under official protection. They set the course, and led Robinson. At times, they took him where he wanted to go. At other times he was well aware, and recorded in his journals, that they had deliberately led him off-course. There would have been no 'Friendly Mission' without the VDL diplomats; as Reynolds observes, Robinson was 'guided, fed, sheltered and, in all likelihood, managed by his Aboriginal companions'.[52]

The Crown's object was conciliation, and, if possible, bloodless dispossession. To this end, Robinson was clearly charged with offering a treaty to the warring nations. If they would vacate their lands for a short while – a season or two – they would receive everything they needed for their comfort, and protection from violence. The deal is inferred in Robinson's journals, Sir George Arthur's communications, and by the VDL people who were there. Seventeen years later, they reminded the monarch:

> … we were not taken Prisoners but freely gave up our Country to Colonel Arthur then the Governor after defending ourselves… Mr Robinson made for us and with Colonel Arthur an agreement which we have not lost from our Minds since and we have made our part of it good.[53]

---

52   Reynolds, *Fate of a Free People*, 136.
53   Walter G. Arthur, King Alexander, Augustus, John Allen, King Tippoo, Davey Bruney, Washington and Neptune to Queen Victoria, 17 February 1846, Colonial Secretary's Office, Corres. Records, Civil Branch, 1845–47, CSO 11/26/378, AJCP 280/195, Reel 544, SLV.

CHAPTER 1

Lt Governor Arthur, as the King's representative, made no secret of the Crown's commitment to giving VDL people a comfortable life elsewhere. As he told the Aborigines Committee in Hobart in early 1831, there was to be 'no restraint imposed on their amusements and sports of the chase'.[54] The VDL diplomats were vital to getting this message across the cultural divide. While VDL people who met Robinson in Country would have very good reason to be suspicious of the Governor's message, the presence of Wooreddy and an increasingly multicultural mission party gave the offer legitimacy.

Removal from the mainland was promised to last only a season or two. All across the island, the promise held appeal to VDL people who were lost, angry, traumatised and war-weary. Many – at least initially – went willingly. The Governor was later to tell the Select Committee on Aborigines of the Crown's 'humane and desirable objects', boasting 'Great exertions have been made to conciliate these natives, and to remove them from the mainland'.[55] Colonial hopes for VDL survival, though, were not high in 1831: Arthur wrote of the first proposed sanctuary on Gun Carriage Island, 'even if they should pine away … it is better that they should meet with their death in that way, whilst every act of kindness is manifested towards them'.[56] Arthur was not alone in his real and abiding concern. By 1831, removal from the VDL mainland was perceived as the only way to protect a people on the verge of extinction. Patrick Brantlinger describes this

---

54 Report of the Aborigines Committee, Hobart, 4 February 1831, in Bischoff, *Sketch of the History of Van Diemen's Land*, 251.
55 Sir George Arthur to Sir Thomas Fowell Buxton, 18 September 1834, in *Minutes of Evidence before Select Committee on Aborigines (British Settlements)*, Imperial Blue Book, 1836, nr VII, 538, facsimilie reprint, Cape Town, C. Struik Pty Ltd, 1966, 679.
56 Lt Governor Arthur to Secretary Murray, 4 April 1831, in Bischoff, *Sketch of the History of Van Diemen's Land*, 255.

European tendency as propleptic elegy: the mourning of a lost object before it is completely lost.[57] The lost world of the VDL people was lamented by the very people who were sending them into exile on a steady stream of government and hired vessels. It was, as Robinson noted numerous times in his journals, quite *affecting*.

It must be remembered, though, that not all VDL people were sent into exile. In the neat traditional narrative of VDL dispossession, this is commonly overlooked. Even as the supposed remnants were secure in their Bass Strait exile, many VDL First Nations people, taken as children and raised in European households as domestic servants, remained effectively as members of mainstream society. Others travelled more widely, following the whaling industry, to New Zealand and beyond.[58] As late as 1852, individuals known to the previously exiled community were in the Victorian gold diggings and whaling.[59] And of course there were the many Tyereelore – VDL women, and their children, living 'under the radar' with Straitsmen on outlying islands. The reality that the exiles who were to become the Wybalenna community were not the last of the VDL population was to become an important challenge to the extinction myth, so morbidly celebrated fifty years later. For now, however, we will follow the exiles.

---

57 Brantlinger, *Dark Vanishings*, 4.
58 See Susan Lawrence, *Whalers and Free Men: Life on Tasmania's Colonial Whaling Stations*, North Melbourne, Australian Scholarly Publishing, 2006; Nigel Prickett, 'Trans-Tasman Stories: Australian Aborigines in New Zealand Sealing and Shore Whaling', *Terra Australis*, 29, 351-366; Lynette Russell, *Roving Mariners*.
59 Walter George Arthur's 1852 letter to Thomas Thompson details VDL people in gold mining, whaling, and living in the community. See letter from Walter Arthur to Thomas Thompson, 16 January 1852, ML A7088, Robinson Papers Vol. 67 Miscellaneous Journals and Papers, 1839, 1843, 1850–52. Fred Cahir discusses the Briggs family in *Black Gold: Aboriginal People on the Goldfields of Victoria, 1850–1870*, Aboriginal History Monograph 25, ANU E-Press, 2012, 27.

CHAPTER 1

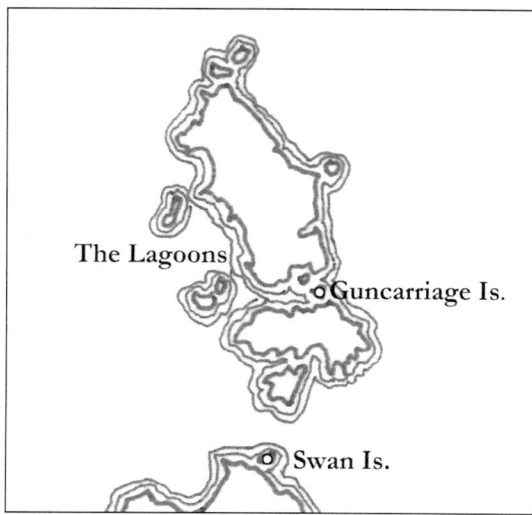

Bass Strait transit camp locations, 1830–32. © L. Stevens 2017

Three Camps to Exile

The first site of the exile of VDL people, Swan Island, is observable from the mainland. It was only ever conceived as a temporary step – in Plomley's words, a holding camp.[60] The first small group was delivered there by Robinson on 4 November 1830: he cynically exploited their fears of the Line operation, pretending to be afraid for his own life and assuring them that *bad white men* were coming and would shoot all of them.[61] Initially at least Swan had an abundance of bird life, eggs, snakes and rats, and by March 1831 it provided at least immediate safety from aggression for thirty-five people. And due to the successes of the mission, the numbers were growing. VDL people had been promised a return to their own Country once hostilities from whites abated. In truth, once they had agreed to walk off their land, the die was cast. From that point, as Plomley noted,

---

60 Plomley, *Weep in Silence*, 29.
61 Robinson's journal, 2 November 1831, *Friendly Mission*, 298.

the Government saw them as pensioners of the colony.⁶² Meanwhile, the search for a suitable permanent seat of exile continued. It occupied the thoughts of George Arthur, his colonial secretary John Montagu, George Augustus Robinson, and most of all VDL people.

Gun Carriage Island, now called Vansittart Island, was the next encampment en route to exile. Its organisation and execution was haphazard. There was no legitimate colonial representative to administer there, and it provided little protection for the first groups of VDL people who arrived. Archibald Maclachlan, a medical dispenser serving fourteen years transportation and lately of Maria Island penitentiary, arrived in March 1831 to act as temporary administrator.⁶³ One of his first tasks was to banish the Straitsmen and the Tyereelore from Gun Carriage to other islands in the Furneaux group. Their accommodation was appropriated, although Maclachlan told Robinson that the exiles preferred to sleep outside, refusing the huts for 'if they slept outside the devil would cure them'.⁶⁴ It seems that the leading couples of the Friendly Mission were not averse to sleeping inside: Robinson reports that he 'shewed the chief Mannalargenna and wife, Black Tom and wife, and Woorady and wife their houses and gardens, with which they were much pleased'.⁶⁵ We can only speculate on how they must have seen the irony of now being the usurpers of the Straitsmen and Tyereelore.

The population would fluctuate – VDL people were continually coming and going, with the Friendly Missions delivering new exiles, then absorbing others to act as interpreters. In May 1831, for

---

62 Plomley, *The Tasmanian Aborigines*, 93.
63 Maclachlan would later set up as a doctor in Hobart. From Plomley, *Weep in Silence*, 964.
64 Robinson's journal, 30 April 1831, in Plomley, *Weep in Silence*, 45.
65 Robinson's journal, 4 April 1831, in *Friendly Mission*, 369.

CHAPTER 1

example, Robinson took fourteen of the Gun Carriage Island exiles with him when he returned to the VDL mainland via Swan Island.[66] For the party who accompanied Robinson, it was a welcome chance to return to Country. For the group who were left behind on Gun Carriage Island, though, there was no such reward. They probably, we might speculate, have felt cheated: they had been promised the world by Robinson and the mission party, then left on a granite island without proper protection. They were war veterans who had negotiated a settlement, but they were now being treated like prisoners. There were others, such as the famed warrior Walyer, known as the Amazon, who was seriously ill.[67] It was during the uncertainty of the Gun Carriage Island establishment, in July 1831, that the first permanent superintendent arrived to relieve Maclachlan.

Alexander Wight was a career soldier. He had spent twenty-two years in the 63rd West Suffolk Regiment of Foot – known as the Bloodsuckers – and seen service in Portugal, Guadeloupe, and Ireland. Subsequently his regiment was transferred to New South Wales, then Van Diemen's Land. Wight was in his late forties and, ominously, had only recently had his rank of sergeant reinstated, after a demotion to private. Wight's transgression to earn this censure is unknown, but it appears the rest of his career stayed on a less-than-stellar path. In 1833 he would be jailed briefly, and discharged from

---

66 'Woorady & Trugernanner, Black Tom & wife Pagerly, Dick alias Pompy, Jock, Pung, Loetherbrah, Tunnerminnerwait, Davy and Dick (two children), Jumbo, Timme and Tib'. Robinson's journal, 4 May 1831, *Friendly Mission*, 381.
67 Walyer/Tarereenore/Mary Ann. Northern nation, famed for leading a band of resisters on armed raids against settlers. Multiple mentions in Robinson's Friendly Mission journals and in the colonial press; her illness noted here in Robinson's journal, 3 May 1831, *Friendly Mission*, 381. For discussion on Walyer's disputed fate, see Leslie Alderton, 'A Historical Overview of Tasmanian Aboriginal Women Who Co-Habited with Sealers and Whalers in the First Four Decades of the 19th Century', Honours Thesis, University of Ballarat, 2012, 57-61.

the regiment the following year, with the comment that 'his character had been indifferent'.[68]

A man of indifferent character was the last thing the VDL people arriving into exile needed. They would have been anxious, traumatised and most likely ill. They had been promised a haven, and instead they were faced with Wight, a corporal, and five privates.[69] His attitude was far removed from that of Robinson and Governor Arthur. To Wight, the VDL exiles were not the regrettably dispossessed who were entitled to all care and kindness, as the Aborigines Committee would have it: instead, he treated them as prisoners and 'used coercion, including using sealers against them'.[70] Tensions between the VDL exiles and Wight increased, as the haven they had been promised was becoming another open-air prison.

Another move followed in November 1831, northward, to what was then known as Great Island. The first community on what would soon be known as Flinders Island comprised a man of indifferent character, his troops, and at least sixty people who were angry with him, the Crown, and sometimes each other. This is where our story really begins.

---

68 Biographical information from Plomley, *Weep in Silence*, 794; Regimental information from James Slack, *The History of the Late 63rd (West Suffolk) Regiment*, London, Army and Navy Co-operative Society, 1884, online at http://www.archive.org/stream/historylaterdwe00slacgoog#page/n3/mode/1up, accessed 26 November 2016.
69 Plomley, *Weep in Silence*, 48.
70 Plomley, *Weep in Silence*, 36.

Chapter 2

EXILED TO GREAT ISLAND

Flinders Island was once a tall mountain range which encompassed today's smaller Furneaux Island chain. For ancient travellers, crossing the Bassian desert from the north, the approach would have been dry, cold, wind-battered, and probably devoid of vegetation even during the more moist climactic cycles. The peaks of Flinders would have served as a visual herald of a broad and sustaining environment. While much evidence has been lost due to rising sea levels, Mannalargenna and Beeton Caves – both located on modern-day Furneaux Islands – establish a human presence from 18,000 years ago.[1]

Over the millennia, as the desert turned to sea, the heights of the peaks were reduced, but they remained an important marker for people heading south along the isthmus. They were perhaps now even more significant, as the only major landmarks on the journey. With the other high formations in the Furneaux group creating a mountain pass, the Flinders area would have been a refuge for those completing the tenuous crossing, or about to set out. The mountain range, in this time period, was an oasis.

---

1   For an overview, see Josephine Flood, *Archaeology of the Dreamtime*, revised edition, Marleston, J.B. Publishing, 2004; John Mulvaney and Johan Kamminga, *Prehistory of Australia*, St Leonards, Allen & Unwin, 1999.

And then, as the seas rose further, the mountain range slowly became a series of islands. For generations, people travelled between the islands of what would become the Furneaux group and the main island of Tasmania to the south. As this became increasingly difficult, due to sea depths and currents, the populations again would have been faced with a choice. A permanent population decided to remain on Flinders Island, still making use of the adjacent smaller islands.

People lived on Flinders Island until around 4000 years ago. Archaeologists have suggested a number of possible fates of this population: Josephine Flood contends that isolation caused the decline, while Peter Hiscock points to an acute El Nino climate shift in this time period which likely caused starvation.[2] These assessments, however, may well be clouded with the dying race lens: Patsy Cameron argues convincingly that the Furneaux Islanders may well have migrated south to the mainland, bringing with them their watercraft technology.[3] Certainly, there is evidence of people visiting a number of offshore islands in this time period; within two millennia, boat-building technology had spread the length of the Tasmanian mainland. The treacherous seas around the Furneaux group, subject to the strong winds known as the Roaring Forties which proved so important to the age of sail, would be a barrier, but not an absolute one, to occasional visits. It is almost certain that the rugged, rich islands were visited seasonally for their plentiful resources of seals, birds and eggs. Flinders Island, in short, should not be considered necessarily a strange land, especially for the Northern and Coastal Plains nations. It shared the maritime climate of much coastal regions: mild temperature ranges, buffeted by strong winds. Much

---

2 Flood, *Archaeology of the Dreamtime*, 208-210; Peter Hiscock, *Archaeology of Ancient Australia*, London and New York, Routledge, 2008, 140-141.

3 Cameron, *Grease and Ochre*, 29.

CHAPTER 2

of the plant, sea and all-important bird life was similar. It was, to large degree, familiar territory; and one which the ancestors had traversed. The transfer of the community of exiles to Flinders Island in November 1831 can thus potentially be seen as a reoccupation.

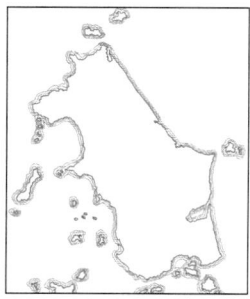

Taking Great Island

> I have been here from the first time of the Settlement.
>
> Frederick[4]

> I have been here since the beginning of the Settlement.
>
> Neptune[5]

> Mr Robinson brought me to the Island and I have been here ever since.
>
> Noemy[6]

---

4   Pallooruc/Tommy/Frederick, from Circular Head, North West nation (*Weep in Silence*, 842). Testimony given in October 1846. Friend Inquiry papers, AOT CSO11/1/27, C658.

5   Merappe/Rinehebigger/Drinene/Neptune (*Weep in Silence*, 848; Plomley asserts that Neptune is probably from the Northern nation, but it is clear, from repeated entries connected to the 1838 sermons, that he came from the West Coast). Testimony given in October 1846. Friend Inquiry papers, AOT CSO11/1/27, C658.

6   Bonenerveve/Marwerreek/ Peterlarrack/Nommi/Nomime/Noemy (*Weep in Silence*, 848). Testimony given in October 1846. Friend Inquiry papers, AOT CSO11/1/27, C658.

The first few months of the Flinders Island exile were a continuation of the war which still raged on the mainland. This particular battle, however, was conducted far from the eyes of colonial authorities, and went uninspected by humanitarian observers. The removal to the islands ensured a growing bounty for Robinson, and fewer sleepless nights for Sir George Arthur in Hobart: out of sight, back of mind. They were fixated on pacifying the Big River peoples who remained in Country. The VDL people, who had been shipped away on a promise of freedom from violence, were an afterthought.

It took Robinson and the Governor a leisurely twelve months to decide on a suitable, permanent site for the settlement – The Lagoons, on the south-east coast of what was then Great Island. This survey might have been accomplished in a matter of weeks, as it certainly would if it was to the benefit of the Crown. The Aborigines Committee in Hobart was, for some time, undecided about the nature and permanence of the island exile, or whether there would in fact be one at all.[7] The delayed confinement on Swan and Guncarriage Islands no doubt intensified resentment and the further breakdown of trust.

The VDL people who stepped from boats into the settlement site of The Lagoons in November 1831 had good cause to be on guard against Europeans. The soldiers treated them as prisoners, not veterans. The convicts attached to the settlement threatened the men and abused the women, seemingly with impunity. Sergeant Wight soon became too reliant on John Smith, the resident sealer. Instead of expelling him as instructed, Wight installed Smith into the day-to-day running of the settlement, which alarmed the community.[8]

---

7   See discussion in Boyce, *Van Diemen's Land*, 284-309.
8   Wight wrote to Arthur on 6 August 1831 that Smith was needed for his boat and for basics like tools – for example, the settlement had no axe of its own. Wight again spoke of Smith's usefulness on 15 November 1831. QVMAG Plomley

CHAPTER 2

An already strained community, operating under a perpetual cloud of threatened violence, was thrown into further tumult with the arrival of a new group by the *Opossum* in December 1831. Delivered by Robinson, the new group included several Big River warriors, most notably a young man aged no more than twenty named Maccamee.[9] With two others, Maccamee had recently been found guilty of the notorious killings of Captain Parker and the surveyor William Thomas.[10] He had escaped the noose, and was now in exile. He would come to be known as Washington.

Children also arrived on the *Opossum*. Friday was a boy around twelve who had no knowledge of his original name or language. Robinson had encountered him at John Batman's property, then later working for criminals in Launceston. When Friday arrived at The Lagoons, there was a rare moment of joy: he was reunited with his father, the esteemed Ben Lomond chief Rolepa. Friday would later be known as Walter George Arthur.

Amidst family and clan reunions, the fledgling community at The Lagoons remained tense. At the beginning of 1832, resentments surfaced in the face of threatened and actual violence from soldiers, convicts, sealers, and each other. The women, especially, were vulnerable to sexual abuse from the European men. Sergeant Wight was

---

Collection CHS 53 5/15.

9 Mierpunner/Ewunermanarer/Myapanna/Maccamee, later renamed Washington. Big River nation.

10 The three Big River men found guilty were Maccamee (later, Washington), Wowwee (later, King Albert) and Calamarowenya (later, Tippo Saib). The Parker-Thomas killings became a famous outrage, much discussed in newspapers at the time and feature in most 19th century histories. The event warrants a chapter in James Fenton's *Bush Life in Tasmania Fifty Years Ago* [1891], reprint, Devonport, C. L Richmond and Sons, 1964; more recently, Henry Reynolds opens *Forgotten War* with the story, 9-14; there is some discussion by Boyce, though he omits reference to any VDL perspective, in *Van Diemen's Land*, 289-290.

ill-equipped to deal with the complexity of the settlement: he was temperamentally unsuited and professionally under-resourced.

A large group of women at The Lagoons had been 'rescued' from sealers. Known as Tyereelore, or later on Flinders as the Sealing Women or Sealers' Women, they originated from a range of nations, usually to the north of VDL. They had formed the backbone of the sealing and birding economy of the Bass Strait islands through the 1820s, and some had travelled great distances.[11] They also bore the brunt of much frontier violence, often being kidnapped into servitude. The Sealing Women, as we shall call those at Wybalenna, became emblematic of the Bass Strait island cultures depicted as wholly barbaric, with Jorgen Jorgenson reporting women 'generally carried away by force or fraud',[12] and G. A. Robinson labelling conditions on the Bass Strait islands 'the African slave trade in miniature'.[13] Cameron, however, gives a more nuanced reading, attributing more agency to the women and complexity to the island economies, asserting that the Tyereelore 'did not consider themselves slaves, identifying themselves with a new title that summed up their new role and status as island wives'.[14]

From the beginning, the Sealing Women caused trouble for the Europeans – chiefly men – who sought to control them; they also generated mayhem among the VDL men. They were by far the most Europeanised of all VDL people, save the children who had

---

11 One woman, Menerletenner/Meelathinna/Blind Poll/Agnes. Born around 1797, she had been to Sydney and as far as Mauritius: *Weep in Silence*, 809, 857.

12 Jorgen Jorgenson's 'Concluding Remarks', in N. J. B. Plomley (ed.), *Jorgen Jorgenson and the Aborigines of Van Diemen's Land: being a reconstruction of his 'lost' book on their customs and habits and on his role in the Roving Parties and the Black Line*, Hobart, Blubber Head Press, 1991, 126-127.

13 Robinson's journal, 11 October 1829, in Plomley, *Friendly Mission*, 91.

14 Cameron, *Grease and Ochre*, 122.

CHAPTER 2

grown up on settler properties. Many had experienced violence and exploitation in conditions akin to slavery, and aligning themselves permanently with men – *any* men – was often not a high priority. They were much more comfortable with each other, and with their dogs. Other women – their friends and Countrywomen – remained on various islands with their euphemistic husbands, the Straitsmen. Some unions were consensual; others were initiated and maintained by force.

The Sealing Women at Flinders maintained contact with the other island women by the unofficial maritime network. While the Crown desperately wanted to rid the smaller islands of sealers – ostensibly to protect the women from further kidnapping, but also to have a semblance of control over the administrative periphery – on a day-to-day basis the sealers were a constant presence at Flinders. Sergeant Wight needed sealers such as John Smith to maintain order. Their continued visitations, however, undermined any sense of protection for the VDL people, or good colonial governance.

The Sealing Women presented, without doubt, the biggest security threat to Wight and the administration of the settlement. The male warriors were numerous, especially with the arrival of the Big River men, and were known to be excellent in combat. The decade-long VDL War is proof of this. However, through their often unwilling sojourns with the sealers and Straitsmen, the Sealing Women had become worldly. They knew English, and the nascent South Seas pidgin. They had met people from Africa, India, the Pacific and the Americas. They had intimate knowledge of the sealers and VDL women currently on each island, and they had grudges to settle. The sealer John Smith – who was now playing such an active role in the running of the settlement – was top of their list. It was looking increasingly like the Governor was reneging on his promise of protection, and the women decided to take matters into their own hands.

The first plans would have been laid soon after the community was transplanted to Flinders, in November. The collaborative nature of the plan can be traced through a series of statements taken after the event.[15] It began with Broomterlandenner, a woman known to the Europeans as Bet, probably Bet Smith.[16] According to another woman Flora,[17] Bet first raised the issue of killing the Europeans on Flinders and taking their boat.[18] The VDL men and women who wanted to join in would return to the mainland. Flora set about enlisting other women to join them. Another enthusiastic conspirator was Wild Mary,[19] whose role was to persuade the men to join the women's bid to return to the mainland.[20] Knowing that they might need more boats than just the settlement boat, which Bet had first

---

15 Recorded and witnessed by three sealers, Robert Gamble, Thomas Mason, and John Strange. QVMAG Plomley Collection CHS53 5/15.
16 There is confusion in identifying Bet/Broomterlandenner. 'Bet' was a common name given to Sealing Women, and there appears to be no Broomterlandenner in the census lists (this spelling of the name comes from Wight's reports and the statements witnessed by Gamble, Mason and Strange). She may be one of three 'Bet's known to have lived with sealers, probably 'Bet Smith' who was closely acquainted with or else (less likely) the woman later known as Queen Elizabeth, wife of the famed Oyster Bay chief Tongerlongeter (King William).
17 Plorermininer/Plownneme/Pelloneneminner/Panghum/Flora, said to be from the Ben Lomond nation, a Tyereelore who lived with John Brown. Cameron, *Grease and Ochre*, 135; Plomley, *Weep in Silence*, 858-859.
18 Flora's statement witnessed by Gamble, Mason and Strange, Jan 30 1832, QVMAG Plomley Collection CHS53 5/15, 12.
19 Pieyenkomeyenner/Pincomminner/Wild Mary, from the Big River nation. Plomley, *Weep in Silence*, 864.
20 According to a statement made by Wotycowwidyer/Wot/Harriet, witnessed by Gamble, Mason and Strange, Jan 30 1832, QVMAG Plomley Collection CHS53 5/15, 11

CHAPTER 2

proposed taking, Big Mary[21] suggested taking the boat from the sealers at Green Island.[22]

It is here that the plan broadened, and became more than just one of seeking immediate liberty. The women decided to act on behalf of other women still left on the islands. Ben Lomond woman Little Mary[23] would later testify that the women intended to make a sweep of the islands, taking other boats from sealers, rescuing their women and killing their children.[24] Angry at the broken promises, and even more so at the Straitsmen, they were determined to get some semblance of justice. Failing justice, they would extract vengeance. Wild Mary freely admitted:

> … they intended to call at other Islands and to take the females from the Sealers and also a Boat belonging to John Smith, and to Kill two Half Cast Children belonging to this man and take his woman also.[25]

The plan was one of resistance and vengeance. It involved violence towards Europeans and – most provocatively – the liberation of sex slaves and killing of children born by rape. The issue of infanticide is emotive and charged, and this is not the first time it has been raised. A Coastal Plains nation woman Pleenperrenner – also known

---

21 Tylerwinner/Tilaway/ThielewannA/Henrietta (Plomley, *Weep in Silence*, 864). Like Bet, the records on Tylerwinner aka Big Mary are incomplete and confused.
22 Big Mary's statement witnessed by Gamble, Mason and Strange, Jan 30 1832, QVMAG Plomley Collection CHS53 5/15, 12.
23 Nickerermargerer/Nickerumpowerer/Little Mary, from the Ben Lomond nation, was a Tyereelore who had lived with sealer Edward Thomlin (or Tomlin), who was himself the son of a Tyereelore. Cameron, *Grease and Ochre*, 135, Plomley *Weep in Silence*, 864.
24 Little Mary's statement witnessed by Gamble, Mason and Strange, Jan 30 1832, QVMAG Plomley Collection CHS53 5/15, 12.
25 Pincommininer/Wild Mary, Statement witnessed by Gamble, Mason and Strange, Jan 30 1832, QVMAG Plomley Collection CHS53 5/15, 13.

widely as Mother Brown – had lived with Smith, and had let it be publicly known that she had killed some of her own children. She is also credited by Robinson as having considerable influence over the other women, being older than them, and is noted as the inventor of the notorious 'obscene dance', the implications of which are discussed by Kate Merry in her study of the Tyereelore.[26] For a time, Pleenperrenner was located at the settlement, and her comments about killing her own children were made public by Robinson. Three major possibilities occur when examining the claims of infanticide: the story was a complete fallacy, and Pleenperrenner had never said such a thing; that she was making the story up to shock and provoke a European audience; or else she was deadly serious, and felt no qualms about 'putting away' the children.

In all likelihood, the women were serious. They were justifiably angry at their apparent abandonment by the Crown which had made great promises. Moreover, some of the Straitsmen were known to have carried out barbarous acts of physical and sexual abuse, including murder and a trade in 'slaves'. To kill the children would be to deprive the Straitsmen of a future generation of workers to exploit and abuse, and – possibly – take revenge. Infanticide, despite the awful connotations, was a legitimate strategy.

VDL men did figure in the women's plans, as they evolved by January 1832. They were enlisted to set fire to the hut the European men slept in, and take their weapons and kill them. They would also be on hand to help row the boats from island to island as they freed

---

[26] Robinson's journal, 31 March 1831, *Friendly Mission*, 366; Kate Merry, 'Dancing with Devils: The Aboriginal Women and the Sealers of Bass Strait and Kangaroo Island in the Early Nineteenth Century', in Giselle Bastin, Kate Douglas, Michele Macrea and Michael X Savvas (eds.), *Journeying and Journalling: Creative and Critical Meditations on Travel Writing*, Kent Town, Wakefield Press, 2010, 116.

CHAPTER 2

the captive women, though women were appointed to steer, making use of skills learnt while with the sealers. Even those not actively involved in the planned rebellion were privy to the conspiracy. Two women, it was decided by the others, would not take part in the rebellion. Kit[27] was told by the organisers that she and one other would remain on Flinders, as she would 'sooner live along with the whites, having done so for Many Years'.[28]

The plan was also known of further afield. At the beginning of January, a young Coastal Plains nation woman later to be known as Louisa was visiting from Preservation Island.[29] She was accompanying James Munro, the elderly unofficial constable who was her 'husband'.[30] Louisa went out hunting with the women, and was told a secret which she kept to herself.[31] She went back to Preservation Island and waited; to be rescued, perhaps: the revolt may well have been imminent. However, news from Hobart would complicate the situation even further. On 7 January, the *Hobart Town Courier* joyfully announced:

---

27 Nowlywollyger/Kit/Little Kit/ from the Mount Cameron area of the Coastal Plains people, was a Tyreelore who had lived with the sealer Robert Rew: Cameron, *Grease and Ochre*, 135. There is some confusion around Little Kit's identity in Plomley: he states that Little Kit is from Cape Grim/Mount Cameron West (*Weep in Silence*, 861), but lists another woman, Sabina, as having the same name Nolahallaker; McFarlane states that Little Kit and Sabina are the same woman in *Beyond Awakening*, 237.

28 Kit's statement witnessed by Gamble, Mason and Strange, Jan 30 1832, QVMAG Plomley Collection CHS53 5/15, 13.

29 Then known as Jumbo. Drummerlooner/Bullrer/Rumanaloo/Louisa, from Cape Portland, North East nation: *Weep in Silence*, 796, 862.

30 The terms 'husband' and 'wife' are used loosely in 19th century records relating to VDL people, especially the Tyereelore. A number of the women who were listed as 'wives' to sealers had in fact been kidnapped and traded, and many of the designations in Plomley's biographies of VDL people were very brief (i.e. just a few days), and do not indicate long-term attachment.

31 Statements witnessed by Gamble, Mason and Strange, Jan 30 1832, QVMAG Plomley Collection CHS53 5/15, 13.

> It is with no small pleasure we announce the gratifying news that the whole of the Oyster Bay and Big River tribes, the most sanguinary in the island, have surrendered themselves to Mr. Robinson, by whose conciliatory intervention the desirable event has been mainly brought about. They consist of 16 men, 9 women and 3 children, and may be expected in town today to join the Aboriginal Establishment at Great island, by the Charlotte, now in the harbour.[32]

The imminent arrival of a large Mairremmener group would have caused anxiety for Wight and the other Europeans, who were generally only able to maintain control by threatened violence or incarceration. And when the celebrity exiles did finally arrive, the tensions which had plagued the community for months flared dangerously. The Big River people already in exile would have been greatly bolstered by the arrival of their Countrymen. The Ben Lomond people would have been unsettled at the arrival of a group of their traditional enemies. The leaders of the nation most feared by whites were arriving into a community which was already planning a violent escape. The war had definitely come to Flinders.

On 22 January, the plan was put into action. The VDL men were dispatched to the Europeans' tent in the middle of the night to kill them. However, there had been a failure of security: the conspiracy had already been revealed to Sergeant Wight by an informant, and he and the Europeans were well prepared.

Wight's response was gendered and uneven. Twenty men were imprisoned with little food and water on Little Kangaroo, Mile and Chalky islands. In the middle of January, this had the potential to be deadly. However, the women – who had hatched the plot, and

---

32   *Hobart Town Courier*, 7 January 1832, 2.

CHAPTER 2

organised every detail among themselves – appear to have escaped punishment. Wight had their statements taken down and witnessed by a trio of sealers – Robert Gamble, Thomas Mason, and John Strange. Supposedly impartial witnesses, they were hardly Hobart's idea of steady citizens: they were exactly the kind of men that Wight was supposed to have banned from the settlement.

A very different story about the escape was heard by George Augustus Robinson, when he arrived on the island shortly afterwards. Of the events in January, he would advise the Colonial Secretary:

> The natives positively declared that they had never once thought of offering violence to the white inhabitants, but on the contrary complained very much of the treatment they had received from the men employed on the establishment.[33]

The women's role in planning is hidden, to suit Robinson's depiction of them as powerless, and in need of rescue – at a bounty, of course. Their testimonies are ignored, and only see light more than a century later, in N. J. B. Plomley's research. In his brief examination of this series of events, Plomley refers to the statements of the women, and there is a clear sense that he gives weight to their version of events.[34] This infers a departure from Plomley's common view of VDL people as pliable objects to whom things happen. In this case, the story told shortly after events by the men to Robinson was that it was all a misunderstanding. The men had gone to the European huts, they said, to look for their women, neatly sidestepping the women's role in planning the escape. Plomley unironically asserts that ultimately 'it

---

33   Robinson to the Colonial Secretary, cited in Plomley, *Weep in Silence*, 41.
34   Plomley, *Weep in Silence*, 39.

is not possible to exlain the forbearance of the Aborigines, except to suggest that the military show of force cowed them'.³⁵

It is a strange kind of forbearance, we might suggest, that plots in great detail the murder of one's captors!

The active role of sealers in subjugating VDL people in the early weeks of The Lagoons settlement illustrates Wight's misunderstanding of the charge that had been given him, and his lack of skill. There were other incidents involving the unhappy union of soldier and Straitsman. Several weeks after the escape attempt, and just before Robinson's arrival, a VDL man failed to return from a group hunting expedition. Louisa and Flora, who were key conspirators of the escape plan, again step to the fore, telling Wight that the missing man had been murdered (he was in fact lost, and would return some hours later). Perhaps concerned for the missing man, perhaps evening a score with the VDL men, or perhaps causing mischief as an act of resistance, Louisa and Flora named two VDL man as murderers.³⁶ In a search for the body, one of these supposed VDL murderers was shot by Edward 'Sydney' Mansell, a sealer, and received very poor treatment from Maclachlan, the convict medical attendant. Mansell was charged with the shooting and sent to Hobart, but it appears he never answered those charges. In assessing the actions of the women, Plomley admits their 'hatred of Europeans and suspicion of their motives'.³⁷ This is a long way from inexplicable forbearance.

The situation at The Lagoons was proving untenable. Both harbour facilities and drinking water had proved unsatisfactory, and Wight's poor administration kept morale low. Robinson was dispatched to

---

35   Ibid., 42.
36   The names of these two innocent VDL men are not known.
37   Plomley, *Weep in Silence*, 42.

CHAPTER 2

clean up the mess, and he undoubtedly alerted the Hobart Press, who announced 'his presence we learn is required to organise and domesticate that interesting colony, now amounting to nearly 100 blacks'.[38] Robinson's arrival at The Lagoons in mid-February probably helped to defuse the situation, as he became the figure of authority.

By the beginning of March, Sergeant Wight's reign was over. He was relieved by a young officer from his own 63rd regiment, Ensign William Darling (soon to be Lieutenant). This young man – born in Nova Scotia, barely twenty-two years old, and brother of former New South Wales governor Sir Ralph Darling – was to usher in a new era on Flinders Island. Finally, the Crown was to make good on at least part of its promise to the people of VDL: that their needs would be met, and that they would be free from intimidation.

William Darling was a progressive young man, respectful of both his orders from the Governor, and the exiles who now numbered seventy-five he was to protect. He seems to have had the necessary interpersonal skills to gain an element of trust from the VDL exiles. He reported to Hobart, 'I allow no restraint of any sort to be put on them; they go out hunting whenever they like and as long as they like'.[39] In June, Darling began scouting for a better location for the settlement.

In August, the community suffered a blow when the first children were taken away. We do not have any record of the VDL exiles' reaction. Among those transferred to the King's Orphan School in Hobart was the young son of Ben Lomond chief Rolepa, known later as Walter George Arthur. Aged around twelve or thirteen, he was

---

38   *Hobart Town Courier*, 11 February 1832, 2.
39   Darling's report to Lt Governor Arthur, 4 May 1832, reprinted in Plomley, *Weep in Silence*, 991.

still listed as 'Friday' in the census. He was most likely sent with David and Peter Bruny, whose father Wooreddy was currently on mission duties on the mainland. The children's transfer was noted in the colonial centre, with the *Hobart Town Courier* reporting that Captain Jackson of the *Charlotte* 'has brought up with him 3 pretty little boys to be educated in Hobart town'.[40] Their removal had been recommended by Darling in May 1832, as these 'fine intelligent lads', he feared, 'by remaining here will only grow up in ignorance'.[41] Darling's belief was symptomatic of the humanitarian rationale that the children's future would be more secure if they could be educated and then integrated into a new proletariat. This was a policy which was later to become institutionalised across British colonial strongholds. It would take two years of lobbying to get the children back.

To the colonial public, Flinders Island was now a source of fascination. Newspapers constantly lamented the lack of interesting news of the settlement. Such had been the terrible impact of the war, and the relief at its apparent ending, that there was a constant appetite for stories about life on the island exile. In August, the *Hobart Town Courier* was happy to be able to report:

> There are now about 80 of the aborigines at the establishment on Great Island. They are all, we rejoice to learn, happy and contented in their new situation, and are daily acquiring a relish for industrious and civilised habits …[42]

In August 1832, the new settlement site had been decided upon, though it would be several months, before the community was moved

---

40   *Hobart Town Courier*, 24 August 1832, 2.
41   Darling to Lt Governor Arthur, 4 May 1832, reprinted in Plomley, *Weep in Silence*, 991.
42   *Hobart Town Courier*, 31 August 1832, 2.

from The Lagoons. In October, a further twenty-seven exiles were added to the community. Combined with those already there, The Lagoons now had a permanent population of over one hundred. It was about to undergo its final transformation.

The Establishment of Wybalenna

In early 1833, the community of exiles was moved once again, this time several kilometres to the north, to a spot known as Pea Jacket Point. This spot was less swampish than The Lagoons, and very close to Green Island, which the best harbour in the islands. That said, harbouring was still a problem, and would remain so for the history of the settlement. Boats might sometimes be anchored at Green Island for days, in full view of the community, but unable to discharge their cargo across the small channel due to rough seas. The new location had an improved water supply, and, it was thought, was a more conducive situation. There was good arable land, abundant bird life, and easy access to other parts of the island. Pea Jacket Point, however, was not an auspicious title.

The name of Wybalenna did not come about by accident. The colonial state wanted to be seen to be conferring a degree of VDL ownership of the settlement, at least in its name. Back in June 1832, when William Darling first wrote to Hobart recommending Pea Jacket Point as a potential permanent site, the Governor wrote in the margin, 'I hope Mr Darling will find some native name for it'.[43] In February 1833, Darling obliged, advising the name 'Wybalenna' had been conferred, meaning 'Black Man's Houses' in the Nuenonne/Bruny Island language. It is noteworthy that even though Nuenonne

---

43   Arthur's comments on Darling's report of 25 June 1832; cited by Plomley, *Weep in Silence*, 65.

numbers were very low on Flinders Island, their language was chosen. Use of his own language highlights the degree of seniority that Wooreddy – now commonly known as Doctor – had achieved in the VDL–European cultural exchange.

There is little evidence during this period of the nature of intranational VDL relationships. Most of the records we have are from Europeans, and discuss the issues that concerned Europeans. George Augustus Robinson was often in the field, tracking down the remnant VDL population on the mainland, and the archive is lacking his compulsive record keeping and ethnographic eye. Census information is infrequent, which is surprising given the rising cost of the settlement. Deaths were recorded, but not always the names. The colonists on the whole did not inquire much into VDL language, culture or worldview. It is telling that it took three decades of settlement, and the depositing of the VDL nations together into exile, for this following fact to be reported as news:

> It now clearly appears, from the evidence of Mr. Robinson and others that the different tribes of the Aborigines in this island are not only distinct, but that they do not even understand each other's language.[44]

In trying to piece together what life at Wybalenna might have looked like for VDL people in this early period, we have to rely chiefly on the writings and actions – sometimes shenanigans – of the settlement's white staff. The European population at Wybalenna had expanded to Darling and his officers, plus a resident convict population including boatmen, a cook, baker, tailor, clerk, brick makers, a bricklayer, carpenter and labourers. Yet due to the scale of

---

44   *Hobart Town Courier*, 22 January 1831, 4.

CHAPTER 2

the infrastructure needed to accommodate the community, Darling asked for even more staff.[45]

Perhaps the most significant new arrival in the middle of 1833 was Thomas Wilkinson, the first catechist. This was an important appointment, given the Crown's commitment to Christianising the VDL population. Aged thirty-four and with a wife and four children, Wilkinson leaps from historical record as an enthusiastic, deeply Evangelical man with the best interests of VDL people at heart – his own version of their best interests, that is. He started a school soon after arriving, and by September reported to the Governor that 'three are able to read easy lessons, and nine fine youths are learning to put letters together'.[46] It appears that at least some VDL people saw him as a useful ally. Wilkinson also took the trouble to learn their language – or at least, the lingua franca of the settlement – and began translating the Bible. This was not an uncommon approach: by 1829 at the Lake Macquarie mission, Lancelot Threlkeld wrote to NSW Governor Sir Ralph Darling (the elder brother of William Darling) to say he had translated the first fourteen chapters of Luke into Awabakal.[47] Two years later, Threlkeld was in communications with the British and Foreign Bible Society, who were keen to publish his work.[48] Missionaries were fervently translating the Old and New Testaments from English to First Nation languages in

---

45 Cited in Plomley, *Weep in Silence*, 65.
46 Wilkinson to Arthur, 17 September 1833, ML A2188 Arthur papers Vol. 28, 1825–1837.
47 Letter from Lancelot Threlkeld to L. G. Darling, 26 October 1829, reprinted in Niel Gunson (ed.), *Australian Reminiscences and Papers of L. E. Threlkeld, Missionary to the Aborigines*, Australian Aboriginal Studies No. 40, Ethnohistory Series No. 2, 1974, 247.
48 Letter from William Greenfield to Lancelot Threlkeld, 26 July 1831, in Gunson (ed.), *Australian Reminiscences and Papers of L. E. Threlkeld*, 254.

New Zealand, Hawaii, Fiji, and Samoa. In New Zealand alone, the Church Missionary Society (CMS) produced 3.5 million printed pages of Maori language Biblical text between 1835 and 1840.[49] It remains a vibrant Pacific industry to this day. As Robert Kenny writes, 'Christianity is the religion of translation'.[50] It was reasonable for Wilkinson to assume his translation would meet with favour, and be encouraged – especially when his contemporary, Threlkeld, had received such support from the brother of his own Commandant.

Lt Governor George Arthur, however, came from a different school. He insisted that the Bible be taught in English. When he then read Wilkinson's report and the translation of the first four chapters of Genesis, he was horrified.[51] His hopes for a VDL future hinged on loss of their own language and culture. In Plomley's opinion, 'Arthur simply could not understand that the only way to enter the hearts and minds of the Aborigines was through their own language'.[52] Arthur annotated Wilkinson's report, 'The perusal of this leads me deeply to regret that a person who can be so useful should have, unfortunately, acted so imprudently'.[53]

---

49 Tony Ballantyne, 'Christianity, Colonialism and Cross-Cultural Communication', in John Stenhouse (ed.), *Christianity, Modernity and Culture: New Perspectives on New Zealand History*, Adelaide, ATF Press, 2005, 43-44.

50 Robert Kenny, *The Lamb Enters the Dreaming: Nathanael Pepper and the Ruptured World*, Carlton North, Scribe, 2007, 103. See general discussion of translation in Kenny, 100-106.

51 A fragment is reproduced in N. J. B. Plomley, *A Word-List of the Tasmanian Aboriginal Languages*, N. J. B. Plomley in association with the Government of Tasmania, 1976, 42-43; see also Wilkinson to Arthur, 17 September 1833, ML A2188 Arthur papers Vol. 28, 1825–1837.

52 Plomley, *Weep in Silence*, 69.

53 Arthur notation on Wilkinson's report, 17 September 1833, ML A2188 Arthur papers Vol. 28, 1825–1837.

CHAPTER 2

Wilkinson had also alienated his commanding officer, William Darling. Emerging as perhaps a serial complainer, and accused of lacking social graces, Wilkinson frustrated Darling to such an extent in his first months at Wybalenna that by October Darling gave an ultimatum: if Wilkinson did not go, he would. Darling's report to Sir George Arthur set in motion the early removal of Wilkinson.[54]

Arthur enlisted James Backhouse and George Washington Walker, the influential, well-travelled Quaker humanitarians and social commentators. Their opinions held great sway in colonial Hobart, as well as the other British colonies of New South Wales, New Zealand, and Norfolk Island. They visited Wybalenna twice in this period, in October and then December 1833, ostensibly to enquire into the tensions between Darling and Wilkinson. Their observations provide some evocative glimpses of life on the island.

In October, the VDL people occupied the 'breakwind' – three 'rude' dwellings or huts, each housing twenty to thirty people.[55] This kind of housing would have been seen as crude by the Europeans, but it would have served a real purpose at Wybalenna. The main huts would have been occupied by the three main remaining nations – the Ben Lomond, the Big River–Oyster Bay alliance, and West Coast. The Sealing Women – that independent group who tended to inspire trouble by picking partners at will, from one nation then another – usually lived a distance away from the main camp. Backhouse and Walker speak glowingly of the good-tempered, intelligent and lively

---

54 Darling to Arthur, 25 October 1833, ML A2188 Arthur papers Vol. 28, 1825–1837. See also Anna Johnston, 'The "Little Empire of Wybalenna": Becoming Colonial in Australia', *Journal of Australian Studies*, 28:81, 2004, 17-31.

55 James Backhouse and George Washington Walker, October 1833, Reports of Visits to Penal Settlements at Port Arthur and Norfolk Island and Aboriginal Settlements at Flinders Island, 1833–35, Royal Commonwealth Society relating to Australia Letters, AJCP M1693, SLV.

character of the VDL people, and of a 'general feeling of goodwill which seems to pervade the settlement'.[56]

The Quakers' first visit in October left the Wilkinson situation unresolved. Wybalenna was a hotbed of bickering colonial administrators and frustrated war veterans. Meanwhile in Hobart, a significant event was taking place. Benjamin Duterreau was allowing public viewing of some of his sketches. These included portraits of Wooreddy, Trugernanner, Mannalargenna and others, and preliminary sketches for 'The Conciliation'. These were described in great detail by the *Hobart Town Courier*, which also acknowledged the drastic situation in which VDL people now found themselves:

> Great praise is due to Mr. Duterreau for his thus fixing on canvass which may commemorate and hand down to posterity for hundreds of years to come so close a resemblance in their original appearance and costume of a race now all but extinct.[57]

In stark contrast to twelve months ago, when the VDL exiles had been left in the incompetent control of Sergeant Wight, the colonial machine was now fully focused on ameliorating their conditions – or at least giving that impression. In December 1833, Backhouse and Walker again visited the settlement. Backhouse's description of their arrival gives a colourful sense of the reception they received:

> We reached Wybalenna soon after sunset. On approaching this place, we were discovered by some women who were cutting wood: they recognised us as old acquaintances, and gave us a clamorous greeting, which brought all the people and dogs out of their huts, with such a noise as, had we not known that it was

---

56   James Backhouse Walker, 'Notes on the Aborigines of Tasmania, extracted from the manuscript journals of George Washington Walker', from *Early Tasmania, Papers Read before the Royal Society of Tasmania during the Years 1888 to 1889*, Tasmania, H. H. Pimblett, Government Printer, 1950, 252.

57   *Hobart Town Courier*, 20 December 1833, 2.

CHAPTER 2

the expression of friendship on the part of the people, would have been truly appalling.⁵⁸

Backhouse and Walker's visit and inquiries were to have lasting implications. They would recommend Wilkinson's removal, thus alleviating Darling's personnel problem. In addition, their positive assessment of the character of VDL people was to become important in the ongoing campaign, by Robinson, Arthur and Montagu the Colonial Secretary, to either return VDL people to the mainland, or shift the whole community to New Holland. The Quakers also opened up economic ties between the exiles and small business people on the VDL mainland. They had brought donations from Launceston shopkeepers, which inspired a trade in skins. Darling was later to place a notice in the *Launceston Advertiser* thanking the good citizens:

> … on behalf of the Aborigines at the Establishment of Flinders Island, for the contributions lately made for them, through the medium of Messrs. Backhouse and Walker; and to inform the public, that a repository is opened at Mr. I. Sherwin's, where skins, and other articles, will be occasionally sent in by the Aborigines, for barter.⁵⁹

This was the first of many actions by Backhouse and Walker to attempt to integrate the exiled community with the colonial economy, society, and religious life.

On the recommendation of Backhouse and Walker, Thomas Wilkinson was removed from his position of catechist. It was agreed by all commentators, including the Quakers, Darling, the Governor, and more recently Plomley, that Wilkinson lacked the social graces

---

58   30 Dec 1833. From Backhouse, *A Narrative of a Visit to the Australian Colonies*, 180.
59   *Launceston Advertiser*, 3 April 1834, 2.

to work harmoniously with Darling. Plomley was blunt, painting Wilkinson as uneducated and a religious bigot.[60] However – most importantly, but obviously not taken into account – Wilkinson was popular among the VDL people, with Backhouse and Walker reporting:

> … it is admitted on all hands that both himself and his valuable wife have conducted themselves with uniform kindness to the aborigines, who resort daily in considerable numbers to their house.[61]

The loss of the Wilkinsons, then, would be felt most keenly by the community. However, another would soon arrive, who was to have a lasting impact on the VDL exiles. In many cases, they would spend the rest of their lives together.

King Will Keep Them

In August 1834, the community received its second catechist, a man who was to have abiding links to the VDL people for decades. Robert Clark had been a teacher and a school inspector in his native County Cork. He had travelled to the colonies with his wife and children and, reminiscent of Wilkinson, received the catechist appointment after being in the colony barely three months. Plomley, whose reading of Clark's personality and motives is unrelentingly negative, introduces him as 'a man who was to have a long and disruptive association with the Settlement and who harmed it immeasurably'.[62]

The community that Robert Clark and his family joined was very vibrant and fluid. The addition of forty-six new exiles raised the

---

60   Plomley, *Weep in Silence*, 70-71.
61   Backhouse and Walker report, December 1833, cited in Plomley, *Weep in Silence*, 70.
62   Plomley, *Weep in Silence*, 71.

CHAPTER 2

overall number to between 150 and 200 people.[63] People still organised themselves along national or language lines, but due to practical demands needed to communicate. Robert Clark noted on his arrival 'eight or ten different languages or dialects spoken by about two hundred people': however, in a testament to VDL adaptability, 'I found them instructing each other to speak their respective tongues'.[64] Plomley also remarked on the adaptability and inventiveness of VDL languages and their speakers.[65]

A lingua franca evolved, which was to serve for the life of the settlement. According to linguist Terry Crowley, it was a blending of an emergent VDL pidgin and a South Seas pidgin used by the women who had lived with sealers on Bass Strait islands.[66] The settlement's vocabulary was dominated by Eastern and North Eastern words, reflecting the dominance of those nations, according to Plomley.[67] R. H. Davies, master of the *Shamrock* and then the *Eliza* who regularly visited Flinders Island from 1832 to 1837, also noted VDL exiles and Europeans alike using a mixture of English, various VDL and Australian languages, and 'even Negro words'.[68] However, while there are numerous word-lists created in VDL since the 1820s, there was not one systematic study, such as that undertaken by Threlkeld at Lake Macquarie, where a grammar was printed by early 1835.[69] Sir George Arthur's edict that English be the language of civilisation

---

63   Ibid., 75.
64   Letter from Robert Clark, quoted in James Bonwick, *Daily Life and Origins of the Tasmanians*, [1870], first reprinting, New York and London, Johnson Reprint Corporation, 1967, 153.
65   Plomley, *A Word-List*, xiv.
66   Crowley, 'Tasmanian Aboriginal Languages', 63-64.
67   Plomley, *A Word-List*, xv.
68   R. H. Davies, 'On the Aborigines of Van Diemen's Land', *Tasmanian Journal of Natural Science, Agriculture, Statistics &c*, Vol. II, 1846.
69   In Gunson, *Australian Reminiscences*, 256.

limited those records. While glimpses of the Flinders Island lingua franca can be gained through recorded testimonies and in letters, there is at present no detailed record. The language of the settlement remains an enigma.

In the latter part of 1834, illness was endemic. When the young surgeon James Allen arrived in September, he found a quarter of the VDL people sick. Within three years, a half became ill.[70] New arrivals fared the worst, many not surviving the trip to Flinders. As with the frontier, the most damage was done by common contagions like influenza, to which the VDL people had no resistance.

In September 1834, William Darling was recalled to his regiment. The 63rd was leaving Van Diemen's Land for India. The Governor's plan all along had been for Robinson to take over administration of the settlement, once he had pacified all of the VDL nations. Due to the success of the Friendly Mission, and the exertions of Wooreddy and the other translator/diplomats, that total banishment would soon be accomplished. Yet Robinson was still busy travelling between Flinders, the centres of Hobart and Launceston, and the countryside of VDL with his mission team, looking for VDL people who had so far avoided capture.

An interim administrator was needed, and Henry Nickolls was sent to Wybalenna to assume control from Darling. An agricultural agent and farmer prior to assuming the position on Flinders, he had worked a large land grant on the South Esk River near Launceston. Unlike Darling, who was a young single man, Nickolls came with a large family and a career outside the army. His vision for the future for Wybalenna – and by extension, its exiled population – was an

---

70 Allen's official report, 20 September 1837, quoted in Bonwick, *The Last of the Tasmanians*, 266.

CHAPTER 2

agricultural one. To progress, Nickolls believed, VDL people had to work. They needed to be civilised to be saved. As we will see, this view ran counter to Governor Arthur's view that Christianity was the only saviour. It harkened back to the nostalgic ideal of the yeoman farmer, and was a variant on other plans for proletarianisation of VDL people, such as was currently being enacted in the King's Orphan School on Friday and the Bruny brothers. On Flinders Island, though, the concept of work had a much deeper meaning than Nickolls could have known: Broome has noted of mainland First Nations that labour 'reflected the deepest meanings of life and one's place in it'.[71] This was certainly the case at Wybalenna, where the issue of work cut to the core of the exile, and Nickolls's plans met with instant resistance.

To Nickolls's frustration, he found that the men – especially those from the Big River and Ben Lomond nations – flatly refused forced work. He had probably expected VDL people to behave as convicts or assigned servants did, but instead he met with a proud refusal, and reminder of the terms of treaty. In his report to the Colonial Secretary eight weeks after taking office, Nickolls's vexation is palpable as he relays their matter-of-fact assertion:

'King will keep them, white men work and not they'.[72]

What Nickolls failed to understand is that VDL people were actually not adverse to work at all. On the contrary, when it was in their interests, or when they were paid fairly, both women and men were

---

71 Richard Broome, 'Aboriginal Workers on the South Eastern Frontier', *Australian Historical Studies*, 103, October 1994, 204.
72 Nickolls to Colonial Secretary, 27 November 1843, cited in Plomley, *Weep in Silence*, 85.

highly industrious.⁷³ Their objection, of course, was to any suggestion of obligation to work for their keep. As a people, they held strongly that they were not convicts or slaves, but free subjects of the Governor and the Queen. The only real problems at Wybalenna arose when administrators disrespected this status as free people. This happened in 1832, with Sergeant Wight, and as we shall see it would happen again most spectacularly in 1846, with Henry Jeanneret. Henry Nickolls was at risk of falling into this dangerous assumption.

In February 1835, ten more children were removed from Wybalenna and placed in the King's Orphan School. The idea of removal of children for their supposed improvement was a widely held one, not restricted to orphans. A similar program was pioneered by Governor Lachlan Macquarie at the Parramatta Native Institution, the intent to redeem children from 'their state of abjection'.⁷⁴ However, in Van Diemen's Land there were dissenting voices, with the *Hobart Town Courier* writing movingly of the injustice of removing children against the wishes of their families or guardians. Importantly, it added:

> These people are or ought to be as free as our selves ... This was the great and laudable principle on which the government all along went, in the mediations of Mr. Robinson with all the tribes which brought about the present happy arrangement unprecedented in the annals of man ...⁷⁵

This is a clear reference to the unwritten treaty which VDL people – and clearly, part of the colonial public – held in their minds. The following month, a public meeting in Brighton celebrated that, unlike other colonies where there was rampant barbarity, VDL Aborigines

---

73   This is later attested to constantly in the *Flinders Island Chronicle*.
74   *Sydney Gazette*, 17 April 1819, 2.
75   *Hobart Town Courier*, 20 February 1835, 2.

were well protected, and 'every pains is taken to inure them to habits of industry and civilization, and to instruct them in the truths of the Christian faith'.[76] The good people of Brighton were certainly rewriting their own history, just three years after the end of the war waged in the area they now called home.

At Wybalenna, VDL people were turning their attention to writing. In the first record of the VDL commitment to literacy as political action, Henry Nickolls informed the Colonial Secretary, in July 1835, of a new trend. A number of the adult men, he said, had expressed the strong wish to 'become scholars like white men', and had volunteered for classes with Robert Clark, the catechist.

> ... their object is to write to their 'Governor Father in Hobart Town' that is the Lieutenant Governor whom they are anxious to induce to remove them to their native land. They all ardently wish to be removed, which delusion has been practised upon them I conclude for the purpose of keeping them quiet.[77]

Nickolls is here expressing the same patronising disbelief in VDL agency which has characterised the writing of their history. The 'delusion' of removal, which Nickolls hints has been encouraged to ensure amiability, was in fact a policy which was being actively discussed by the Colonial Secretary Montagu, Robinson, and the Governor. The plan – which Robinson freely shared with his VDL friends, and probably anyone who would listen – involved removal to New Holland (particularly the Spencer Gulf/Adelaide region). It appears most of the VDL community were in agreement.[78]

---

76 *Hobart Town Courier*, 20 March 1835, 2.
77 Henry Nickolls to Colonial Secretary, 9 July 1835, cited in Plomley, *Weep in Silence*, 85.
78 Evidenced in Robinson's journals, plus a petition submitted to the NSW Legislative Council in August 1838, signed by all adult VDL men at Wybalenna.

The identification of writing as a tactic is an important step in the evolution of VDL political activism. Previous VDL literacies such as petroglyphs, scarification and shell-work had long served cultural, political, social and spiritual needs. However, after a bitter war, and three years of exile, literacy – as Marie Battiste writes, functioning both as 'a shield of cultural transmission and as a sword of cultural assimilation'[79] – became central to the campaign to return to the mainland. This same tactic was repeated many times by First Nations people in colonised situations.[80] Led by the adult men, VDL people were self-organising to attain the relevant skills, and had actively recruited Robert Clark to teach them. This evidence of an early adoption of writing challenges views that only a few young agitators were literate, and that the older generation were removed from literacy.[81]

This forward-thinking activity was conducted, however, in a community which was at times still deeply traditional. In the same report remarking on the desires for education, Nickolls reported 'determined hostilities' between the Ben Lomond and Big River peoples, brought on by their enforced close proximity. Nickolls advised the Colonial Secretary of the mayhem this had caused:

> The Western natives have attached themselves either to one or the other of the two tribes as their inclination has led them, this virtually making the whole body for the purpose of war

---

79   Marie Battiste, 'Micmac Literacy and Cognitive Assimilation', paper presented to *Mokakit Indian Education Research Association*, London, Ontario, July 26 1984, 1.
80   See, for example, Battiste on the Micmac; also Sequoyah's development of the Cherokee Syllabary c.1820, widely used within a few years, standardised in 1827, used in *The Cherokee Phoenix* from 1828: Ellen Cushman, 'The Cherokee Writing Syllabary', 255-281; John B. Davis, 'The Life and Work of Sequoyah', 149-180; Theda Perdue, 'Rising from the ashes: The Cherokee Phoenix as an Ethnohistorical Source', *Ethnohistory*, 24:3, Summer 1977, 207-218.
81   Plomley asserted that only four or five VDL people, at the very most, were capable of reading and writing: *Weep in Silence*, 990.

CHAPTER 2

to consist of only two tribes. It requires very great vigilance to prevent their breaking out into open hostilities.[82]

On the ground at Wybalenna, Henry Nickolls was having trouble keeping order.

Meanwhile in London …

The Select Committee on Aborigines (British Colonies), convened in 1835, was charged with finding what could be termed a global solution to the 'native question'. Their charter sought to recommend measures to ensure First Nations peoples 'where British Settlements are made' received justice, civilisation, and Christ.[83] What eventuated was at times a critical self-examination of the colonising process, chaired by a panel of humanitarians and evangelists, including Sir Thomas Fowell Buxton, anti-slavery campaigner and founder of the Aborigines Protection Society.

Reports were heard from across the British Empire, including the Cape Colony, Sierra Leone, Australia, New Zealand and Canada. A large percentage of those testifying were missionaries, as Christianity travelled with empire, and sometimes preceded it. The voices of First Nations people were rarely heard, with two notable exceptions from the Cape Colony. Written evidence was tabled on behalf of Boesack Tamoer, and the Xhosa leader TzaTzoe famously addressed the Committee.[84]

Written evidence was also submitted by the Lieutenant Governor of Van Diemen's Land, Sir George Arthur. He advised the Committee,

---

82 Henry Nickolls to Colonial Secretary, 9 July 1835, cited in Plomley, *Weep in Silence*, 88.
83 Report (introduction), August 1836, *Minutes of Evidence before Select Committee*, iii.
84 Boesack Tamoer's testimony was tabled by Colonel Wade, 25 March 1836, *Minutes of Evidence before Select Committee*, 302-303.

among other things, that the VDL exiles who had put up a resistance infamous across the empire now: 'appear to be very happy in their new abode, and are exceedingly tractable and docile'.[85]

Henry Nickolls, struggling at Wybalenna to maintain peace between the Ben Lomond and Big River people, might have disagreed. But as it was, George Arthur – aside from James Backhouse, who also wrote a brief letter – was the most knowledgeable informant on Van Diemen's Land to address the Committee.

A number of churchmen and gentlemen-about-empire gave evidence to the Select Committee on the New South Wales colony. Very few, however, had direct experience of Van Diemen's Land. Archdeacon William Grant Broughton, who had assumed ecclesiastical charge of the colonies in 1829, was among the first to testify. His closest brush with Wybalenna was when he interviewed Wilkinson and his wife, prior to their appointment to the settlement in 1833.[86] However, in early 1830 he had temporarily chaired the Aborigines Committee at the request of Arthur, to lend it integrity and the appearance of independence.[87] When asked by Buxton whether he credited VDL people with equal intellect and power of comprehension, Broughton observed:

> The craft and design which they display in attacking the houses of the settlers and effecting their mischievous purposes were so great, that they cannot be considered deficient in power of contriving and laying a plan.[88]

---

85 Sir George Arthur to Sir Thomas Fowell Buxton, 18 September 1834, in *Minutes of Evidence before Select Committee*, 679-680.
86 Archdeacon Broughton, 3 August 1835, *Minutes of Evidence before Select Committee*, 23-24.
87 Ryan, *Tasmanian Aborigines*, 120-121.
88 Archdeacon Broughton, 3 August 1836, *Minutes of Evidence before Select Committee*, 24.

CHAPTER 2

Saxe Bannister, in his testimony to the Committee, also admitted only limited experience of Van Diemen's Land.[89] Although his recommendations for *new* Australian colonies was to 'make treaties with the natives before proceeding further', for NSW and VDL he was fixated on the moral character of the colonies, focusing more on the evils of convict transportation.[90]

One moment in particular highlights the complexity of the concerns of the Select Committee, which, after ten months of questioning, had been exposed to a litany of abuses from around the British colonies. Captain David Bucham was being questioned regarding the apparent total demise of the Beothuk First Nation in Newfoundland – an extinction myth which directly parallels that which evolved in Tasmania. After Bucham's evidence that no attempt had been made to conciliate or Christianise, and instead violence was endemic, Buxton asked him:

> Q. Then the effect of the visitation of civilised and Christian men, as far as Newfoundland has been concerned, has been the entire extirpation of the whole body of the natives?
>
> A. It has had that effect, I have no doubt: in fact it was considered a meritorious act, at one time, to kill an Indian.[91]

Buxton's frustration is almost palpable. While focused here on events in Newfoundland, it has much broader resonance, especially for Van Diemen's Land. Brutality on the colonial frontier was something that other people did. These evangelical Christians – with their cast-iron commitment to spread the Word, whether recipients

---

89 Saxe Bannister, 31 August 1835, *Minutes of Evidence before Select Committee*, 174-178.
90 Ibid., 177.
91 Captain David Bucham, 18 May 1836, *Minutes of Evidence before Select Committee*, 478.

asked for it or not – only very reluctantly admitted that they, too, were perpetrating a kind of violence. The catastrophe that colonisation unleashed onto First Nations people was seen as a regrettable side-effect – something like the cliché about not making omelettes without cracking eggs. As Andrew Porter observed of the Select Committee Report, 'The introduction of Christianity and "social improvement" was itself referred to … now as a "fair remuneration for the loss of their lands."'[92]

Back in Van Diemen's Land, there were changes afoot. Henry Nickolls's tenure as administrator of Wybalenna was drawing to a close, and the new, true Commandant was about to take the reins. And in Newtown, just out of Hobart, Friday and the Bruny Brothers prepared for a move. As always, the shipping news kept a watchful eye:

> The *Tamar* proceeds to Launceston on Monday with the remaining sixteen aborigines, namely nine adults seven children to Flinders Island, under the care of Mr. G. A. Robinson, to whose charge the establishment at that station is now, we learn, wholly confided.[93]

Wybalenna was about to welcome two very different personalities, both of whom would have a profound effect on the direction of the settlement, and the future of VDL people themselves. One was a colonial official from London's East End, self-made and still ambitious, about to take on a strategic promotion. The other was a Ben Lomond youth of serious nature and sharp intellect, who would emerge as a leader of VDL people. They represented a new beginning.

---

92 Andrew Porter, *Religion versus empire? British Protestant Missionaries and Overseas Expansion, 1700–1914*, Manchester and New York, Manchester University Press, 2004, 146.

93 *Hobart Town Courier*, 18 September 1835, 2.

CHAPTER 2

The Light Comes to Wybalenna

In October 1835 – as the Select Committee was sitting – the cutter *Isabella* dropped anchor at Green Island. Among the passengers awaiting transfer across the strait to Pea Jacket Point, and the community of Wybalenna, was the 'conciliator' George Augustus Robinson, and members of the diplomatic team who had led him around VDL and persuaded their Countrymen to leave. The Friendly Mission party was now quite extensive – over twenty-five VDL people from various nations had taken part – and they were now, finally, coming out of their own Country and into the community they had helped to create. Wooreddy, who as we have seen was one of the key instigators of the whole 'Friendly Mission', had been reunited with his sons David and Peter, and they sailed 'down' to Flinders together.[94]

George Augustus Robinson was assuming the role of superintendent (or, as he would have it, Commandant). With the financial and ideological support of the Crown, he was to institute a range of experimental programs on the island during his four year tenure, and exert a significant and sometimes very positive influence on the younger exiles. Yet by the time Robinson arrived at Flinders Island in December 1835, the zenith of his goodwill to VDL people had noticeably passed. His journals, once abounding with religious conviction and evangelical zeal, were now largely concerned with his career advancement.

To the exiles on the island, who over three years had dealt with a series of superintendents, threats and anxieties, the arrival of Robinson as permanent Commandant undoubtedly added a sense

---

94 There is a clear geographical hierarchy between Flinders and Hobart. All correspondents (VDL and European) talked of going 'up' to Hobart, or 'down' to Flinders.

of security. Most of them had had dealings with him. While he was probably far from universally trusted, important leaders seemed happy to negotiate with him on a day-to-day basis, and this brought much of the community into the agreement.

The second significant arrival – travelling with Robinson, in fact – was fifteen-year-old Walter George Arthur. In December, he was still known as 'Friday'. Four weeks later, he was known as Walter – or specifically Prince Walter in deference to the status of his father Rolepa.[95] He had spent the last two years at the King's Orphan School, since being sent there by William Darling: this, combined with spending at least part of his childhood with Europeans of the criminal classes, had given him both education and some degree of worldliness. The terms most commonly used to describe him at this time were shrewd and very intelligent.

If Robinson's arrival added a sense of security, then the return of the community's children was a sign of hope. Walter Arthur, the Bruny brothers and the other children would have brought, in a sense, *The Light* to Flinders. A light of hope, and also of literacy. This was a cause for great celebration, and – it was hoped – an easing of the ever-present tensions between the Ben Lomond and Big River nations. The return of Robinson and the children was relayed to the *Hobart Town Courier*, which announced:

> By the last accounts from Flinders Island there are now in all 135 Aborigines at that station. Mr. Robinson had given them a grand entertainment on the accession of those he brought with him, which had the effect of making them all friends,

---

[95] The Island census of January 1836 shows him as Walter George Arthur, not Walter Juba Martin (his first editorial name), although it must be noted that this census was reconstructed from several sources by Plomley, and may not reflect what Walter was actually named at this time.

CHAPTER 2

and drowning all the national differences which were still alive amongst them.[96]

The celebration was not complete, however: not all the children were returned straight away. As Walter and the Bruny Brothers were being reunited with the families and Countrypeople, other VDL children remained in the King's Orphan School. Conditions there were austere, and the young inmates resided eighty to a dormitory, sleeping in hammocks. A report from the *Colonial Times* in April 1839 described cold, comfortless and ill-arranged quarters, with two hundred boys exhibiting 'abjectness and squalor'.[97]

Still remaining in this penitentiary-like establishment was the young orphan boy we last met at Bruny Island six years earlier, who witnessed the beginnings of the 'Friendly' or Nuenonne Peace mission. His name, unrecorded in 1829, became Thomas Brune. It is clear that he was at the Kings Orphan School, but we have no information on how he came to be there, how long he stayed, or even precisely when he left for Flinders Island. We only know that by May 1836 this studious thirteen-year-old had been brought to Wybalenna.

After seven years of institutionalisation, to be suddenly on an island with scores of his Countrypeople, but knowing no people or the language, must have been an intense culture shock. Unlike Walter and the Bruny brothers, who had loving family, Thomas Brune was alone. He was possessed of a skill, however, which was going to cement his place in the community. His literacy rapidly earned him positions of educational and religious responsibility. He taught in the

---

96 *Hobart Town Courier*, December 4 1835, 2.
97 *Colonial Times* report, April 1839, cited in Morgan, *Aboriginal Education in the Furneaux Islands*, 95.

school, served as a clerk for both the Commandant and the catechist, and was soon to assume an even more significant position.

The First Incarnation of the *Flinders Island Chronicle*

Thomas Brune's great skill – beside his literacy, and extraordinary penmanship – was in knowing exactly what the Commandant wanted him to say. In an exquisite hand, given his age and training, young Thomas Brune wrote a Prospectus and an edition of the *Chronicle* on 10 September 1836. The Prospectus served as a mission statement, and the first edition relayed news. While signed by Brune and his co-editor, Walter Juba Martin,[98] there is little doubt that the content of the Prospectus and first edition were dictated to Brune by the Commandant. As such, both documents reflect Robinson's ambitions for himself, and the settlement.

The Prospectus set out the terms and conditions of the *Chronicle*, including 'to promote christianity civilization and Learning amongst the Aboriginal Inhabitants at Flinders Island'. Promising to be a weekly journal, its size, price and distribution of profits was clearly stated, as was the hope that it 'may induce Emmulation in writing excite a desire for useful knowledge and promote Learning generally'. The *Chronicle* was thus a product and a tool of the prevailing ethos of self-improvement, which Robinson lived and championed. The Prospectus finished with a broader audience in mind: 'Persons out of the colony may Subscribe'.[99]

The first edition of the *Chronicle* proper begins with a call to set history aside. The war and dispossession – undoubtedly still fresh in everyone's minds – was to be forgotten. From the very first line,

---

98 Soon to be renamed Walter George Arthur.
99 Prospectus, *Flinders Island Chronicle*, 10 September 1836.

CHAPTER 2

Thomas Brune advised his fellow exiles, 'we cannot look back on the Events connected with our history'. Instead, they should:

> ... date our history of Events from the Month of October 1835 when our beloved father made his appearance among us ...
> we had been in a deplorable state.
> we looked for a better day and it has arrived
> what a contrast between the present and the past.[100]

Robinson is typically centre-stage, with his dramatic bringing of light and hope. Through his youthful scribe, the Commandant cast himself as the 'beloved father'. Penny Van Toorn argues that Robinson was discursively placing himself 'into the same position as God',[101] but the representation seems more Messianic than divine. This first edition was all about rewriting history and heaping platitudes upon the Commandant. Reading it, one can almost envision the 'beloved father' leaning over Brune's young shoulder, choosing the superlatives with which to further his own career.

This first foray into journalism – comprising a Prospectus and one edition – although purporting to be for the edification of the exiles on the island, was squarely aimed at Hobart, and further, London. In fact, Robinson brought the *Chronicle* to the attention of the Government *before* it was even written, mentioning it in his report to the Colonial Secretary on 8 September 1836 – two days before the first edition was created.[102] Understandably, there is almost universal agreement among modern commentators that the *Chronicle* was devised and enacted as a performance of civilization. In Mudrooroo's

---

100 Thomas Brune, *Flinders Island Chronicle*, 10 September 1836.
101 Van Toorn, *Writing Never Arrives Naked*, 107.
102 Report cited in Plomley, *Weep in Silence*, 648.

words, this was writing 'for the Governor's pleasure'.[103] It was to be written proof that the regrettable removal of VDL people from their Country was for their own good. On a symbolic level, the editorial control exercised by Robinson can be seen as metaphorical for the British Empire's hegemonic domination of a colonised and exiled people.

Thomas Brune, though penning Robinson's words, was a willing accomplice. His position as writer of the *Chronicle* set him apart from the other children, with whom he still lived in a dormitory at Robert Clark's house. Thomas's command of the English language earned him a position and a place: he had power. His only rival was his co-editor, who had been long-favoured and often called Prince Walter. As the writer of the earliest editions of the *Chronicle*, however, Thomas Brune's legacy is important. Although Walter Juba Martin's name is listed on most of the surviving copies, they are all in Thomas Brune's hand.

While Robinson's propaganda dominates the Prospectus and first edition, there is also a glimpse into island life. The only real piece of reportage concerns the arrival of the *Eliza* at Green Island. As an island community, people in Wybalenna – just like Hobart, and other colonial ports – lived by the shipping news. It was on the front pages of newspapers, the issue of central importance. The coming and goings of ships would always be a major talking point at Wybalenna. The exiles had all been passengers on at least one of these ships, and knew them well. Importantly, the ships carried supplies of food and other goods which were sometimes desperately needed. Maritime activity was also a very tangible link back to the

---

103 Mudrooroo Narogin, *Doin Wildcat*, Melbourne, Hyland House, 1988, 113.

CHAPTER 2

VDL mainland, and the various nations' own Country. VDL people, through the course of their exile, kept a very close watch for ships. That said, the *Eliza*'s mention in this first edition of the *Chronicle* in September 1836 was quickly related back to Robinson, who was to travel in her to Hobart. This focus on Robinson's departure reveals his editorial hand, as his trip to Hobart was foremost in his mind.

On a pragmatic level for Robinson, in September 1836, the *Chronicle* was armour in his application for a Chief Protector role on the Australian mainland, a pension, or both. This explains why, with the ink barely dry on numerous copies of the *Chronicle* and Prospectus, Robinson bundled them up, and sailed for Hobart aboard the *Eliza* – 'as smart a little cruiser as ever bore the King's flag', according to Fenton.[104] Within two days of arriving in Hobart on 21 September, Robinson's report to the Colonial Secretary was printed almost verbatim in the *Hobart Town Courier*. A glowing account of Robinson's administration, it claimed, extraordinarily, that sickness was wholly unknown, and continued:

> The greatest cordiality and mutual good feeling prevails throughout the whole establishment – a fact which our readers in Hobart town will, we fear, scarcely be able to credit, as Mr. Robinson has been the means of establishing a weekly newspaper among them. It is entirely written by the Aborigines, and is published under the name of '*The Aboriginal Flinders Island Chronicle*', on half a sheet of foolscap every Saturday, price 2d each, and the profits arising from the work are equally divided among the editors.[105]

The *Flinders Island Chronicle*, plus the reports published in the *Courier* and submitted to the Governor, were ammunition in Robinson's

---
104   Fenton, *Bush Life in Early Tasmania*, 78.
105   *Hobart Town Courier*, Friday 23 September 1836, 2.

battle for recognition as he fought a financial contest for himself and his sons over the next seven weeks. His journal shows a man consumed with anxiety over the Governor's avoidance of him. Governor Arthur, though, was embroiled in his own controversies.[106] Public dissatisfaction with the Governor was so high that, according to Reverend Robert Knopwood, when his vice-regal appointment ended in late October 1836, Sir George Arthur was escorted to the port by a guard of soldiers, two deep, to protect him from angry crowds.[107]

With Arthur gone, Robinson's claims for future employment and compensation for work done by his sons remained unresolved. He had fully expected to be offered an appointment as Protector of Aborigines on the mainland, and take the VDL community with him, but that discussion was frozen. He had also lost his greatest ally, Arthur, and would now have to cultivate a relationship with the new, as-yet-unknown Lieutenant Governor. For a man of humble beginnings in a society with deeply entrenched class divisions, this was a fraught affair. Robinson's journal reflects great frustration, but little reference to Wybalenna. From September to December 1836, we have few glimpses of life on the island at all.

Robinson's focus on his career and his family is understandable, but casts a poor light on his supposed commitment to VDL people. Four years earlier, George Washington Walker had expressed concerns about Robinson's abilities as Commandant, doubting he

---

[106] See, for example, A. G. L. Shaw, *Sir George Arthur, Bart: Superintendent of British Honduras, Lieutenant-Governor of Van Diemen's Land and of Upper Canada, Governor of the Bombay Presidency*, Carlton, Melbourne University Press, 1980, 135-176.

[107] Knopwood's diary, 29 October 1836, in M. Nicholls (ed.), *The Diary of the Reverend Robert Knopwood, 1803–1838*, Launceston, Tasmanian Historical Research Association, 1977, 655.

CHAPTER 2

possessed 'the requisite qualifications, either as regards to his judgement or his principles'.[108] In the years since first joining forces with Wooreddy and the Nuenonne to find a political solution to the VDL war, Robinson had become highly ambitious. We might once imagine him being 30 per cent ambition and 70 per cent goodwill: by December 1836, those percentages were reversed. At times, it was only ambition.

It would be remiss, however, to paint Robinson in 1836 as a cold hearted man. The journals of his early Wybalenna appointment reveal a man deeply concerned for the welfare of the people he helped to exile. His care and concern, especially for certain individuals, was genuine and was reciprocated. But VDL people had been an important social vehicle for him, and would remain so into at least his immediate future. As such, his dealings with them had become pragmatic.

After seven weeks away from the settlement, Robinson's affairs were resolved. The claims on behalf of his sons for land, as reward for their efforts during the Friendly Mission, were finalised to his satisfaction. His hopes for the Protector of Aborigines position were dashed, however, by a salary offer which was insultingly low. Robinson's only option was to return to Flinders Island, and continue to build his own legend. In December 1836, he sailed across Bass Strait to Boonwurrung Country on the Australian mainland to investigate, among other issues, women who had been kidnapped by sealers. On this brief venture, his chief guide and interpreter was the ex-Tyereelore Matilda, who had arrived at Wybalenna some

---

108 G. W. Walker's journal, 3 November 1832, reprinted in W. M. Oats, *Backhouse and Walker: A Quaker View of the Australian Colonies 1832–1838*, Hobart, Blubber Head Press, 1981, 44.

months earlier.[109] On his return to Flinders Island, Robinson began work to ensure his administration matched his glowing reports of it. The *Flinders Island Chronicle* – already heralded in the Hobart press and beyond, through colonial syndication – appears to have been abandoned after just one issue.[110]

---

109 Maytepueminner/Mathabelianna/New Maria/New Matilda/Matilda. Born around 1805, possibly Swanport, Oyster Bay nation but unclear. Kidnapped at a young age by sealers, forced to help kidnap Bunwurrung women from Port Phillip before arriving at Wybalenna in June 1836: Plomley, *Weep in Silence*, 808, 865.

110 If any copies were written, their existence is not known, and Robinson is silent about it in his journals.

Chapter 3

THE PROMISE OF WYBALENNA

It was the best and the worst of times. By January 1837, the situation of the VDL exiles on Flinders Island was markedly improved from the chaotic, brutal days of Sergeant Wight. For the first time, the Crown looked like delivering on at least part of its promise. VDL people were finally, comparatively, safe from harm. Their children had been returned to them. They were free to come and go as they pleased, though they did pay strategic tribute to the Commandant with the fruits of the hunt. Traditional rituals were still performed and new ones were invented, albeit with increased secrecy. The basics of tea, flour, sugar, meat, tobacco and more were provided free of charge at the settlement, along with fruits and vegetables from the gardens. Work was not compulsory, and those who did work received wages. There was medical care, education, and religion if people wanted it. VDL people were not enslaved or imprisoned, and Wybalenna might very well have been an exemplary settlement, the poster child for how a colonial government might make restitution for damages done. It might have been a haven, by 1830s standards.

However, there were two major impediments to Wybalenna being a showcase humanitarian paradise. The first is freedom – an idea which came to be redefined at Wybalenna. VDL people steadfastly maintained and proclaimed their status as a free people. From early observations by Backhouse and Walker, and to the chagrin of more than one superintendent, the concept of freedom was paramount. VDL people told anyone who would listen that they were not prisoners or convicts, but a free people.

Yet, obviously, they were confined to an island and unable to leave. Their home Country, which was within sight on a clear day, lay across a treacherous, wind-battered strait. Many had been promised a return to their homeland after a season, but by 1837 this would have been seen through as gammon. This steadfast claim to freedom, in the face of their obvious predicament, should be viewed as an act of courage. Philosopher Jonathon Lear suggests 'At a time of radical historical change, the concept of courage will itself require new forms'.[1] Holding on to the idea of being a free people points to VDL people's ability to see beyond the present catastrophic situation: the essence of what Lear calls radical hope. The concept of freedom was vital for VDL people, even in exile – *especially* in exile.

The second major impediment to the ultimate success of the Wybalenna venture was death. The mortality rates of VDL people were devastating. Despite the best attentions of VDL kin and community, and the genuine care of the administration team (if not the soldiers and convicts), death was ubiquitous. At least seventy VDL people had already died on Flinders Island since the community was moved there in 1832.[2] And the coming year, 1837, was to be among the worst.

---

1 Lear, *Radical Hope*, 118.
2 Figures taken from Plomley's painstaking research – in 1832, 3 deaths; 1833, 32; 1834, between 14 and 18; 1835, 14; 1836, 4. *Weep in Silence*, 938-941.

CHAPTER 3

In the face of this death, estrangement from land, and cultural loss, it would not be surprising for the surviving VDL population at Wybalenna to feel beaten. Certainly, the vast majority of assessments of Wybalenna have taken this line.

This study gives authority to the words of VDL people. In the absence of words, actions can be 'read', in the tradition of E. P. Thompson's studies of the English crowd, as acts of legitimation and consensus, 'informed by the belief that they were defending traditional rights or customs'.[3] By entering from this angle, a very different world is revealed. We find a Wybalenna that is vibrant, energetic and busy, and peopled by strong-willed war veterans and fiercely independent women. It is a cornucopia of languages, traditions, alliances and enmities, with a clear sense of itself and inner boundaries. It is a far cry from a mere graveyard: VDL people were not the types to waste away, and certainly not in silence. They retained culture, freedom and hope for the future, with a loud and distinctive voice.

The World of Wybalenna

> *What form is the world?* Round
> *How is it divided?* Into four parts
> *What are they called?* Europe Asia Africa and America
> *What part are we living in?* Asia.[4]

The colonial world was watching Wybalenna, in its distanced, complicated, 1830s way. News travelled slowly, despite the eagerness

---

3   E. P. Thompson, 'The Moral Economy of the English Crowd in the Eighteenth Century', *Past & Present*, 50, Feb 1971, 78.
4   Thomas Brune, Flinders Island school examination, 9 May 1837, George Augustus Robinson Letterbook 1836–1838, ML A7044, Vol. 23, accessed at QVMAG Plomley Collection Reel CY548 (hereafter Robinson Letterbook, QVMAG CY548).

of writers, messengers and consumers. If the seas were inclement, it might sometimes take weeks for mail written at Wybalenna to make it to Hobart. From Hobart to the administrative centre of New South Wales, transit might also take weeks, and from the antipodes to the colonial centre of London would take months. By the beginning of 1837, the glowing reports in the Hobart colonial press, and the *Flinders Island Chronicle*, about improvements at Wybalenna would not yet have reached England.

If intelligence travelling to the colonial centres was slow, then information flowing back to Wybalenna was even more torturous. News of the death of the King – surely the biggest news story of 1837 – took six months to arrive. Mail packets delivered by a regular series of government and private vessels were the source of great excitement – a lifeline for administrators, and a source of keen interest for the VDL exiles. Every aspect of their arrival was noted, from speculation about the many glimpses of sails which could be seen from Mount Franklin, to excitement when supply ships finally dropped anchor at Green Island. The winds which circled the southern ocean, broken only by the VDL coast, the Furneaux Islands and, to the east, New Zealand, often caused delay. Sometimes it would take days for the seas to be safe enough to send out the settlement boat to retrieve mail and supplies, and amidst this excitement, officials such as the Commandant had to make sure their outward mail was ready. Many, many colonial letters were penned in haste so as to be despatched to a waiting boat.

VDL people were well aware of the impact of squiggled ink on paper. Henry Nickolls had already written of their quest for literacy, so they could write to the Governor. And as will be illustrated by events to come, they became adept at negotiating the sometimes

CHAPTER 3

frustrating official mail systems, for their own political purposes. They also made strategic use of unofficial channels, such as sealers and other mariners who made clandestine visits to the island.

In early 1837, however, VDL people were not writing letters. They were not even, it seems, writing the *Flinders Island Chronicle*. But they still maintained a keen interest in what was delivered, especially news from Hobart and further afield. They would have paid special attention to events in Port Phillip, where they expected to be moved in the near future.

If viewed from the machine room of the British Empire, the Aboriginal Establishment on Flinders Island was as geographically isolated from the colonial nerve centre as it was possible to be. It was an outpost of the distant colony of Van Diemen's Land, which was itself distant from the administrative hub of New South Wales. Yet the concept of distance was very different in the colonial world. Isolation was the rule, rather than the exception, and the idea of empire maintained a sense of connectedness which defied distance and time. The VDL First Nations people and the Europeans on Flinders Island would have felt the effects of isolation, but for many this was normal. As we have earlier noted, it is only an island if you look at it from the sea.

The community's focus was often outwards, to the sea: to their own Country on the VDL mainland, and to possible new homes. On this aspect of the future, the community of exiles were receiving mixed messages. On the one hand, there were continuing discussions about moving the entire community to the Australian mainland. These discussions were being conducted from the colonial headquarters in Sydney down, leaving a long paper trail involving Governors, secretaries and of course Commandant Robinson. The opinions of prominent VDL men were continually canvassed about the prospect of moving across Bass Strait, and what they might expect there.⁵ Robinson's claim to moral authority with the VDL people was in part predicated on his close connection with the Crown, and there is little doubt but that he would have made clear to the VDL leaders that the Governor and the Colonial Secretary supported this idea of migration. Consequently, while the move to the Australian mainland looked inevitable, it would be reasonable to assume that Wybalenna would have taken on a temporary aspect. Flying in the face of this apparently impending move was a paradoxical sense of increased permanency. The Wybalenna settlement was fast evolving from transit camp to village.

A mass renaming of individuals had already taken place in January 1836. Robinson diarised, 'The natives were highly pleased with the change: it was what they desired'.⁶ David Davies criticised renaming as an 'irritating habit' of the Commandant, where 'he tried to complicate the simple and leave things that should be done alone'.⁷ However, Henry Reynolds writes that this bestowal of new – and to Robinson, less barbarous – names is one of Robinson's 'most misunderstood actions. His list of new and old names makes it clear that what he was doing was replacing the colonial demotic, often derisive names already in use and not original tribal ones'.⁸ As discussed earlier, many people already had numerous names which varied according to age, marital status and location; as Lyndall Ryan notes,

---

5   Robinson's journals make multiple mentions of his conversations with leaders about removal to either Spencer Gulf or Port Phillip, and this was a regular topic of ongoing discussion at all levels of administration.

6   Robinson's journal, 15 January 1836; Plomley, *Weep in Silence*, 336.

7   Davies, *The Last of the Tasmanians*, 196.

8   Reynolds, 'George Augustus Robinson in Van Diemen's Land', 168.

CHAPTER 3

acknowledging a new name for a new Country at Wybalenna was in keeping with cultural traditions.[9] The names awarded were often poetic and spectacular, based in classic literature or military leaders of the past, such as Napoleon, Neptune, Alexander, Tippoo Saib and Augustus. Trugernanner became Lalla Rookh, and Wooreddy became Count Alpha – although it is interesting that he was still most often referred to as Doctor in Robinson's journals. National leaders and their wives became Kings and Queens, and one promising youth – already renamed Walter George Arthur, after the erstwhile Governor – also became Prince Walter in deference to his father, King George. Such noble names were, according to Nicholas Cree, 'grand and ridiculous' or just 'unsuitable', but this probably speaks more to the author's low regard for VDL people than issues of nomenclature.[10]

In February 1837, the Commandant instituted a flurry of progressive endeavours, many of which seem to have been embraced, at least to some degree, by the community of exiles. A VDL constabulary was established – naturally, under the guidance of the Commandant and the Kings – with each of the three main national groups (Big River, Ben Lomond and Western) represented with constables. Transgressions were heard by a court of VDL elders. Again, these officers were strategically hand-picked by Robinson, but it is unlikely the community would have abided anyone without proper authority in their eyes. A Wybalenna currency was instituted – coins stamp-marked for use only on the island, 'F.I'. on one side and 'A.E'. on the other.[11] There was a weekly market where luxuries, tools

---

9   Ryan, *Tasmanian Aborigines*, 225.
10   Nicholas Cree, *Oyster Cove: Last Home of the Tasmanian Aboriginal*, Toorak, Cree, 1979, 35.
11   F.I. = Flinders Island, A.E. = Aboriginal Establishment.

and non-essential supplies could be purchased.[12] A close account was kept of all work done and wages paid.[13] Flocks of sheep were maintained on nearby islands; some were owned collectively by the community, and others were individual property of either Friendly Missions participants, or awarded as tribute to senior leaders. Profits from the industry of VDL people – such as potatoes taken to Hobart for sale, wool, or the seasonal mutton-bird barrelling – went back into the VDL account.

Yet it was never truly equitable. The Commandant perpetuated a distinctive hierarchy of nations at Wybalenna. The Big River nation, who had alternately terrified and impressed colonial officials and settlers alike, was the most favoured, as demonstrated in the use of space: at a festival late in February 1837, members of the Big River nation were positioned next to the officers, with the other nations and clans more distant. As the year progressed and a major building works program began, the Big River–Oyster Bay people were also the first to be housed in the new cottages. This undoubtedly caused tensions with the Ben Lomond people, as traditional enmities between the Big River and Ben Lomond nations continued well into exile.

At the beginning of March 1837, word was finally received at Flinders regarding the appointment of a new Lieutenant Governor, to replace Sir George Arthur. Sir John Franklin already had a name

---

12 The accounts list each exile and their purchases on set dates. For example, on 31 January 1837, King William purchased plates and tobacco; Henrietta purchased rice, sugar and plums; Hannibal purchased pipes and marbles: Flinders Island Accounts, Robinson's Letterbook, QVMAG Reel CY825.

13 For example, on 6 November 1837, financial tribute was paid to the Kings, plus wages were paid to those in the offices of constabulary, clerical work, singing, teaching, cooking and stores. Wages were also paid by the load for work such as carrying wood (men) or grass (women) – see entries for 16 October 1837. Road making was paid by the day – see entries for 19 February 1838, Flinders Island Accounts, Robinson Letterbook, QVMAG CY548.

CHAPTER 3

as an intrepid (if not always successful) Arctic explorer. Accompanying him was his redoubtable second wife Lady Jane Franklin (nee Griffin), and a private secretary, Alexander Maconochie. All three, in their own way, were to have an impact on the lives and fortunes of the VDL exiles. Commandant Robinson's journals from this point forward regularly speculate on if and when the new Governor might visit Wybalenna, an honour which the former Governor – despite his role in its establishment – never bestowed.

The social organisation of Wybalenna continued. Education and Christianisation – often one in the same – were of paramount importance to the Commandant and the Crown. They were also embraced by at least some of the VDL exiles. The nightly school and church meetings were an important part of the social fabric, providing the main chance for parents to interact with their children.[14]

The church meetings also afforded the VDL people who embraced Christianity the opportunity to proselytise. The most enthusiastic of the VDL preachers was Noemy of the Western nation, noted for his characteristic sermons.[15] Noemy was also a constable, and responsible on more than one occasion for seizing ochre used in frowned-upon rituals. On 7 April, impounded ochre was thrown into the sea, in yet another ultimately futile attempt to convince VDL people to abandon tradition.

---

14   Children normally lived in a dormitory at the catechist's house, usually with the parents' express permission

15   Bonnerveveve/Nommy Merewick: *Weep in Silence*, 848. Noemy first appears in Robinson's field journals on 28 April 1833, one month later Noemy, his wife Wonghowrum (later Catherine), child, and a portion of his clan forced by threat of firearms to follow Robinson. Sent on the *Shamrock* to Flinders on 6 June 1833, Noemy does not appear in Robinson's records for another two and a half years, when he is present at a luncheon in Robinson's house at Wybalenna with other significant leaders: in this entry, he is named as Maywodick. Robinson's journal, 15 January 1836, *Weep in Silence*, 336. Noted for sermons in Robinson's journal, 29 April, 6 May 1837.

The settlement's church also afforded an important role for favoured youths such as Thomas Brune and Walter George Arthur, who often read prayers and, increasingly, wrote and delivered their own sermons. Arthur had been apprenticed to the carpenter back in December 1836, but this appears to have been short-lived, as he was clearly more suited to clerical and even missionary work. The church meetings also seem to have held genuine appeal to a wide range of VDL people through the act of singing. There was an official choir, which Arthur was paid one shilling per week to lead, and a general enthusiasm about singing. Even those who were known to regularly perform ceremonies in the bush enjoyed singing hymns. Singing took place in church, in their own homes, and in the bush. This should hardly be surprising, as song and performance were already important to VDL cultures.

The school was based on smaller tutored groups. The women's classes tended to be larger, at least ten students in each one, due to a lack of female teachers. They were led by the wives of administration staff plus seventeen-year-old Mary ann, whose mother Sarah[16] had been rescued from sealers. Mary ann would later occupy a central role in future political activism on Flinders, but for now she lived with the Commandant's family, and appeared to be on very close terms with the Commandant's wife Maria and daughters Maria and Eliza.[17] Unusually for VDL women, a large amount of trust and responsibility was placed in Mary ann's hands.

---

16   Tarenootairer/Jackanoothara/Tibb/Sarah. Had lived with the sealers John Smith and George Robinson. Said variously to be from Cape Portland (*Weep in Silence*, 869) and Mussel Roe (ibid., 825). Aligned at Wybalenna with Ben Lomond nation. Mother of Mary ann (whose father was a Straitsman), plus Fanny (later Fanny Cochrane Smith) and Adam (whose father was Eugene/Niccermanic.

17   Maria Robinson (nee Evans) had four sons and three daughters living: George (born around 1815), Charles, William and Henry; Maria (England around 1820), Eliza (born in Hobart in 1927) and Cecelia (born in 1835).

CHAPTER 3

The schooling of the men and boys was performed in much smaller groups, sometimes of only three or four. This allowed for much closer personal interaction and attention. Walter George Arthur and Thomas Brune were appointed as teachers, as were several other literate youth who had been educated in the King's Orphan School. This method of the young tutoring their elders has been criticised by Penny Van Toorn as culturally inappropriate, with a broad generalisation that in 'Indigenous Australian societies' the asking of direct questions, especially by the young of the older, is offensive.[18] However, the evidence suggests that at Wybalenna the VDL adults were much more enthusiastic about gaining literacy skills than has been previously assumed. Official records, skewed as they were towards evidencing Christianisation, indicate that many of the adults were slowly gaining literacy skills. Education at Wybalenna had only been in genuine effect for eighteen months; prior to Robinson's tenure, it received only lip service. Even after this short time, many of the adult VDL exiles already had knowledge of the alphabet, numeracy, and were beginning to read.

Examinations were conducted over twelve days between 9 and 21 May 1837, to gain a benchmark of the skills possessed by VDL people, to which future assessments could be compared.[19] Not all VDL people were included: at the time of the May 1837 examination, the Commandant's most trusted diplomats were not at Wybalenna, but on the mainland with his son Charles.[20] A number of other key

---

18 Van Toorn, *Writing Never Arrives Naked*, 109.
19 Detailed records of the examinations are contained in Robinson's Letterbook, Mitchell Library, A7044 V. 23 (here listed as Robinson Letterbook, QVMAG CY548); copies were also undoubtedly sent to the Colonial Secretary for the information of Lt Governor Sir John Franklin.
20 This party included Doctor Wooreddy, Trugernanner, Tunnerminnerwait (recently renamed Napoleon), Maulboyheener (Robert), Planobeena (Fanny), and

individuals also on the island at the time – such as the famed Big River chief King William[21] – were not recorded. This indicates that the school was not compulsory, just highly encouraged.

The examinations which took place in May were recorded responses to set questions. This mode of teaching at Wybalenna has been roundly condemned, with Van Toorn summarising the critiques as 'suggesting that the Aboriginal pupils neither internalised nor utilised nor retained what they had learned at the Flinders Island school'.[22] Plomley was forthright in his assertions that education and Christianity had not made 'the least impact on the life and thought' of the exiles, and that the exiles 'submitted to the force-feeding because they had no choice'.[23] Robert Travers agreed that the 'aborigines knew how to please their superintendent if they knew little else', and, even more derisively, David Davies commented that Trugernanner was not examined, 'her talents being more of a sexually athletic nature'.[24] This last comment – from a British academic – speaks volumes for the credit shown to VDL people, and their story. It is also ill-informed: during the 1837 examinations, Trugernanner – and a number of the Friendly Mission party – were actually on the mainland, seeking a group known to be at large in the North West.

This study does not dispute critiques of the inadequate education offered at Flinders Island, or the fact that the examinations were

---

 Richard aka Cranky Dick.
21 Tongelongeter/Putumpatecher/Pyreparnner/King William/Governor. Oyster Bay nation Chief. Renowned warrior, arm amputated after battle. Detailed in Friendly Mission journals: *Weep in Silence*, 829, 852.
22 Van Toorn is summarising Plomley, Ryan and Rae-Ellis. From *Writing Never Arrives Naked*, 112.
23 Plomley, *Weep in Silence*, 103-104.
24 Robert Travers, *The Tasmanians: The Story of a Doomed Race*, Melbourne, Cassell Australia, 1968, 207; Davies, *The Last of the Tasmanians*, 199.

effectively a performance of civilisation with which to assure the colonial public that attempts were being made to better the VDL people. The evangelical character of the school examinations is plain, as the vast majority of questions, for most of those quizzed, relate to religion and the Bible. What previous critiques have failed to acknowledge, however, is the wealth of data contained in the school reports: they simply have not seen the wood for the trees.[25]

When read for the *people* who sat down in the school house to be quizzed, these records are a rich and valuable resource, unique among the large archive on VDL history. Certainly, many VDL people were mentioned by Robinson in his copious journals, and there were census lists of varying detail kept at regular intervals. On occasions like deaths or other milestones, various individuals were described – sometimes in very touching detail – by the Europeans who knew them. Yet these school examinations are the only place where a large body of the exiled community were surveyed at the same time, offering information on lesser-documented VDL people, as well as new insights into those already known.

One such example is Walter Arthur's father Rolepa, or King George, the important Ben Lomond leader. King George is mentioned numerous times in Robinson's Friendly Mission and Flinders Island journals as an informant on Ben Lomond language and culture. In the May 1837 school examinations, it is noted that he is 'imperfect in his letters': in other words, there was little progress towards literacy. King George is asked only six questions in total:

---

25 Most writers have not even looked at the examinations in detail. The study by Anne Therese Morgan on education in the Furneaux Islands does not appear to have closely consulted the archives, for she claims women were not examined. See 'Aboriginal Education in the Furneaux Islands (1788–1986): A Study of Aboriginal Racial Policy, Curriculum and Teacher/Community Relations', Thesis, Centre for Education, University of Tasmania, 1986, 98–104.

Who made you? God
Where is God? In Heaven
Who made the trees and the salt water? God made them all
Do you like to hear about God? Yes sir
Do you like to tell your countrymen about God? Yes sir
Do you like to learn about God? By & by I will learn plenty.[26]

The first two questions were a given: every single VDL person interviewed was posed the same ones, and gave the same response. On the face of it, the other questions are also unchallenging, and without doubt leading. The low number of questions may suggest that King George is not one of the most successful students: however, in the comments which accompany his examination, it is noted that he is 'very intelligent'. This was not a description given lightly, as only four VDL males were described as intelligent in these examinations – King George, William Robinson,[27] Walter Arthur and the youth Adolphus. This is not to say that VDL men were considered stupid by people who had dealings with them. In the 1830s, virtually all reports of VDL people – from the humanitarians Backhouse and Walker, to the erstwhile Governor, to a wide variety of Europeans who had regular contact – held that VDL people had roughly the same potential as Europeans. It was just a matter of education through Christianisation. However, during these examinations, only these four VDL males – and, as we shall see, eight women – were singled out as remarkable in this respect.

In addition to his notable intelligence, King George's brief examination is also distinguished by hints of religious commitment. The questions posed to him mention spreading the word among

---

26   School examinations, Robinson Letterbook, QVMAG CY548.
27   Pannabuke/William Robinson, from Sandy Cape, West Coast nation. Probably In his early 30s at this time: *Weep in Silence*, 816, 852.

CHAPTER 3

Countrymen. This is a leading question, asked of only six people in total, all men.[28] From this we might confidently suggest that King George had played some part in being seen to spread the Word. His further response 'by & by I will learn plenty' – different to the customary responses of 'Yes' or 'Yes sir' – suggests an assurance. Or, at the very least, it suggests the strategic appearance of it. His language also gives us a small taste of the lingua franca – the Flinders Island pidgin – at work.

There are many other examples of the school examinations shining light on neglected individuals, who had previously been a mere name and area of origin in the copious historiography of VDL. Clara, who answered eighteen questions, was noted as perfect in the alphabet and as a Collect or prayer reader during services.[29] According to the notes, Clara 'possesses considerable aptitude to learn, but is very indolent'.[30] Daphne also answered numerous questions and knew the alphabet but, in contrast to Clara, 'is very intelligent and industrious'.[31] Flora, also known as Panghum and one of the conspirators in the attempted uprising against Sergeant Wight, had been recently bemoaned by the Commandant in his journal for

---

28 Noemy, Alexander, Frederick, Augustus, King George and Thomas (not Thomas Brune).
29 There is some confusion over Clara's identity, with contradictory information across Plomley's *Weep in Silence* biographies. Clara's name is listed as Teddeheburer/Taneeberrick/Princess Clara/Clara. Daughter of Wyne, Chief of Pieman River. Born c.1820 (855-856). The entry for Teddeheburer states that she died of pneumonia on 9 February 1837 (826), but the only death on that date appears to be Lynoongar (Appendix II:C, Record of Deaths, 941).
30 Robinson's observations on Clara, May 1837 school examinations, Robinson Letterbook, QVMAG CY548.
31 Dromedeener/Cranky Bet/Daphne, 34 years old in 1837, probably from Swanport and associated with Big River–Oyster Bay nations: *Weep in Silence*, 856. Robinson's observations on Daphne, May 1837 School examinations, Robinson Letterbook, QVMAG CY548.

'conduct reprehensible'.³² This troublesome woman answered thirty-four questions, could spell simple words, and it was noted, 'This is a very intelligent woman, speaks the English language fluently and is assiduous and industrious'.³³ Likewise, insight is gleaned from the interview of former Sealing Woman Louisa, who displayed a detailed knowledge of Genesis, could read and write, spoke English fluently, and displayed 'the manners of a European'.³⁴ Like the other women noted above, Louisa was also praised for being industrious.

Industriousness in this age of self-improvement was a highly sought-after quality, followed by the trait of being well conducted, which spoke to self-control which underpinned self-improvement. Of the men, many were lauded for their industriousness and good, steady conduct. Some were noted for just being well conducted, and there is a small group who receive neither of these accolades. Romeo answered only two questions, and was noted as inattentive at his lessons.³⁵ Despite receiving no comment on either his industriousness or good conduct, he was 'a good husband and kind father'.³⁶ Phillip was a good husband, perfect in his letters and with conduct noted as *generally* good.³⁷ Achilles was also noted as a good husband and

---

32   Robinson's journal, 4 March 1837, *Weep in Silence*, 429.
33   Robinson's observations on Flora, May 1837 School examinations, Robinson Letterbook, QVMAG CY548.
34   Louisa had previously lived with 'Constable' James Munro. Plomley lists Louisa as married to Tippoo Saib, but this was much later, and a temporary relationship. At the time of the examinations, Louisa was a single woman: *Weep in Silence*, 862. Robinson's observations on Louisa, May 1837 School examinations, Robinson Letterbook, QVMAG CY548.
35   Towterrer, aged in his late 30s at this time, had been Chief of the Port Davey people: *Weep in Silence*, 830, 849.
36   Robinson's observations on Romeo, May 1837 School examinations, Robinson Letterbook, QVMAG CY548.
37   Bung's Jacky; no other name for Phillip recorded by Plomley: *Weep in Silence*, 848. Robinson's comments in the examinations list Phillip as being a Ben Lomond man. Robinson's observations on Phillip, May 1837 School examinations, Robinson

CHAPTER 3

orderly, although 'imperfect in his letters' and 'fond of the chase'.[38] Achilles was posed the question 'Do you like to sing about God?', which hints at his choir membership, and, given that he was in the class of the youngest of the tutors, Prince Adolphus, we might assume that little hope was held for this Ben Lomond man's advancement. As in many texts of this kind, we can tell just as much from what is left out than what is stated.

The school examinations of the women reveal a great deal. As we have already seen, eight of them were noted for their intelligence (as opposed to two men and two youth). Jemima was noted as 'young and interesting … most domesticated and speaks the English language fluently. Is very intelligent and an industrious wife'.[39] Rose is described as a 'shrewd intelligent woman';[40] Helen (also known as Ellen) as a 'remarkably industrious well conducted clever woman';[41] and Bessy as 'shrewd and industrious'.[42]

Interestingly, the only VDL male described as shrewd was Walter George Arthur. As a whole, the women answered more questions than men, and seemed to have a much more detailed knowledge of

---

    Letterbook, QVMAG CY548.

38 Trowlebunner/Rowlepanna/Parumgmunermooner/Drowlepuner/Achilles: *Weep in Silence*, 836. Robinson's observations on Achilles, May 1837 School examinations, Robinson Letterbook, QVMAG CY548.

39 Nurnepattenner/Cranky Poll, aged in her late 20s at this time. From the Big River nation, said to be involved in the famed Parker-Thomas murders: *Weep in Silence*, 860. Jemima was posed 30 questions, among the highest of all the women, and was also noted as perfect in her letters. Robinson's observations on Jemima, May 1837 School examinations, Robinson Letterbook, QVMAG CY548.

40 Myhermenanyehaner/Gooseberry/Joanna, from the Big River nation. Had lived with the famed bushranger Musquito: *Weep in Silence*, 867.

41 Nunneatheganner/Ellen/Corrobery/Twopence. Born around 1810, Big River nation: *Weep in Silence*, 850.

42 Pangernowideic/Pignaburg/Bessy Clark, 12 years old, from Port Davey: *Weep in Silence*, 853.

Genesis – or at least, an appreciation for what might be seen as the unfolding family drama of Adam and Eve and their sons, Cain and Abel. The women were also more often posed the question 'What is the soul?', eliciting the answer 'That which thinks', and more likely to be noted for their expertise in the English language skills and European-style conduct. These English language skills undoubtedly relate to the fact that many of the women had lived with Straitsmen.

The examinations of the VDL youth on Flinders Island display at times a deep understanding of both Biblical and general knowledge. Thomas Thompson, aged about eleven, answered fifty-four detailed questions, recited fourteen hymns, could read and had 'knowledge of numerals'.[43] He was a teacher in the school, and was also learning the trade of carpenter. In addition to a wide range of questions regarding events in Genesis and broad Christian knowledge, he answered questions about the Julian calendar and British currency.

Peter Bruney, one of the sons of Doctor Wooreddy, answered fewer questions and repeated fewer hymns than Thompson, but it is noted that he was excelling in his apprenticeship as a tailor, having 'made his own garments for some time past'.[44] His brother David, about two years older than Peter, spoke English 'fluently and with a perfect English idiom', and was being trained as a carpenter.[45] Thomas Brune, apparently no relation to the brothers, except from Country of origin, and who penned the first *Flinders Island Chronicle*

---

43 Thomas Thompson, born around 1828. Mother: Harriet (Wottecowidyer); father: James Thompson (sealer). *Weep in Silence*, 850, 859.
44 Droyerloinny/Peter Bruney, also spelt Brune, Bruny and Bruni. Born around 1825, Bruny Island. Father: Wooreddy; mother deceased. Born circa 1827: *Weep in Silence*, 834, 848.
45 Myungge/David Bruney, also Davey, Brune, Bruny and Bruni. Born around 1823, Bruny Island. Father: Wooreddy; mother deceased. Born circa 1825: *Weep in Silence*, 834, 841.

CHAPTER 3

back in September 1836, answered a staggering 123 questions. He displayed a broad range of Biblical and general knowledge, had acquired boot making skills to the point of recently making his own shoes, and was already working as a clerk in both the Commandant's and catechists' offices. Interestingly, despite Thomas's obvious thirst for knowledge, he is not recognised by the Commandant for his intelligence: instead, it is noted that 'he has committed to memory a good many hymns and possesses other general information'.

Walter Arthur is listed in the examination records as 'Prince Walter'. Significantly, there is no mention of a trade for Walter Arthur, even though there were earlier attempts to apprentice him to the carpenter. Yet his considerable intelligence and shrewdness is noted, as is the fact that he is a clerk in the catechist's office and a teacher in the school. Young Walter's close contact with Robert Clark, the catechist, was to have significance for both of them, and lead to a lifelong friendship and collaboration on behalf of VDL people. For now though, like Thomas Brune he answered a wide range of questions, from scripture to science, including:

> *What is the difference between eternity and time?* Eternity last forever, has neither beginning or end, time has a beginning and will end
> *Does the earth stand still?* No it goes around the sun
> *How is day to night occasioned?* By the world turning on its own axis.[46]

These school examinations have been largely ignored by historians, discounted as being of little importance. However, from just the brief sample we have taken above, we can see the richness of observation

---

46　'Prince Walter', May 1837 School examinations, Robinson Letterbook, QVMAG CY548.

which can be garnered. The examinations provide census data, complete with personal observations of the individuals, in much greater detail than the general name and origin lists made by Robinson and other administrators. These school examinations – and those which would follow nine months later, in February 1838 – afford us the best and only view of many of the VDL exiles.

Further, what is left out is just as interesting as what is actually said. The silences, the questions not posed, the individuals barely quizzed, all provide tantalising indications of who was eschewing the Commandant's teachings, and who was accommodating them on their own terms. Most interesting of all, perhaps, is the strong performance of many of the women. Considering they had much larger classes, and probably lower expectations placed on them by a society still deeply entrenched in a Christian, patriarchal ideal, their success is even more significant. These examinations prove the point – if the women's role in earlier subversive acts has not already done so – that they were far from the cowed, vulnerable victims usually depicted in traditional histories.

As the winter of 1837 wore on, life became exceedingly difficult on Flinders Island for VDL people. Already enduring exile from home Country, they were also adjusting to a changed living, dietary and cultural landscape. More and more, the people left the Wybalenna settlement on hunting forays which stretched, from the hours desired by the ever-watchful Commandant, to days then weeks. The Commandant's journals reveal a man constantly frustrated by his inability to keep the VDL people on the settlement. And, continuing the tendency for Europeans at Flinders to be constantly embroiled in power disputes, the catechist Robert Clark and storekeeper Loftus

CHAPTER 3

Dickenson (effectively the Commandant's two proverbial right hands) were constantly bickering.

Death was a constant visitor to the island through this period. Robinson's journals, our main source of information of this period in the absence of VDL texts, paint a harrowing picture of a man genuinely worried about the level of illness among the VDL people, but also concerned about how this would look to authorities.[47] On the Australian mainland, Lancelot Threlkeld was also reporting a devastating mortality; in September 1837, he reported a population of only thirty four, down from sixty four in 1828.[48] Mission life, as has been widely observed, proved deadly to the first generation.

The seemingly unstoppable illness at Wybalenna culminated, on 20 June 1837, with the death of Oyster Bay chief King William. The esteemed leader's passing left the entire community traumatised, amply illustrated by Robinson's own personal reflection of shock and grief:

> I was distressed. It appeared like a dream. I could scarcely believe or credit it real. Can it, said I, can it be possible that King William, he who the other day was jocose, and he dead who scarcely ever was ill whilst on the settlement, a strong hale and robust man? Oh yes, it is true, it is too true.[49]

King William's passing threw 'a halo over the settlement', and the loss to the community of such an esteemed leader had immediate consequences. Shortly after the news spread through the settlement,

---

[47] On 15 June, Robinson received word that Lt Governor Franklin intended to visit: *Weep in Silence*, 451.

[48] Threlkeld to E. Deas Thomson, 22 September 1837, in Gunson, *Australian Reminiscences and Papers of L. E. Threlkeld*, 262.

[49] Robinson's journal, 20 June 1837, *Weep in Silence*, 453.

Coastal Plains woman Rebecca came to see Robinson and, on behalf of herself and three other women, announced her intention to shift to the Ben Lomond group, and into the protection of King George. They obviously felt less secure without King William. This would only be the beginning of a realigning of the pathways of power on the island, brought about by the sudden and unexpected loss of a leader of unquestioned sagacity and authority. And those testing the traditional boundaries – and forging their own independent networks – were the women.

The Incorrigible Women

> ... some of the woman are industrious and strong women they goes and gets the gras every morning and then goes to their schools and then go home to their own houses.[50]

The Sealing Women of the Wybalenna community already had experience with Europeans. Publicly, they were the most victimised of all, suffering apparently at the hands of both their VDL men, who, as was often erroneously reported, had sold them into slavery, and from the callous, brutal sealers and whalers who exerted despotic control over them. The misery of these women before their rescue and transfer to Flinders is a continuous theme through VDL history which remains the chief depiction of them to this day.

However, this characterisation of the Sealing Women as only victims demands to be challenged. Historian Patsy Cameron argues that many of the sealer–VDL alliances had an economic base, and that the women 'were equal partners with the Straitsmen in the development of this new way of life, which comprised a blend of clan

---

50   Brune, *Flinders Island Chronicle*, 10 September 1836, QVMAG CY825-63.

CHAPTER 3

and European traditions'.[51] Once on Flinders Island, these women 'rescued' from slavery on the smaller islands refused to submit to a passive, gendered role. As Lyndall Ryan notes, they 'emerged as a significant dissident group, critical of the Establishment and resisting both Robinson's authority and that of the Aboriginal men'.[52] As has already been shown, in 1832 they instigated an attempted uprising against Sergeant Wight and the other Europeans guarding them. By 1837, despite acquiring the genteel arts of sewing, knitting and crocheting under the tutelage of Catherine Clark, the catechist's wife, the women persisted in frustrating all attempts to control them. They eschewed the control of men – *any* men. The Commandant's journals continually lament their going bush as a group, and especially their use of ochre body decoration – barely disguised code for continuity of traditional culture and ritual.

In addition to refusing to have their movements controlled by either VDL or European men, the women actively used humour and rumour – gammoning – in a subversive manner. It appears that at times they deliberately gave the impression of being more unruly than they actually were. In August, Robinson reported that a number of them drank beer and became drunk (or pretended to be drunk). Loud and unruly, they caused a fracas, then, once reported to Robinson, denied being drunk, and blamed the Ben Lomond women for gossiping about them.[53] On many other occasions, recorded in both the *Flinders Island Chronicle* and in Robinson's journals, the women actively spread false stories, apparently to create chaos, and for their own amusement.

51　Cameron, *Grease and Ochre*, 122.
52　Ryan, *Tasmanian Aborigines*, 134.
53　The 'drunken' women episode in Robinson's journal, 7 August 1837, *Weep in Silence*, 469.

Gammoning – that is, the stretching of truth, playing of tricks, pranks and general creation of mischief can be seen as a genuine mode of resistance. Anthropologist James C. Scott famously wrote about these smaller, less obvious acts of disguised rebellion in his influential *Weapons of the Weak*, describing:

> ... ordinary weapons of relatively powerless groups: foot dragging, dissimulation, false compliance, pilfering, feigned ignorance, slander, arson, sabotage, and so forth ...[54]

The actions of the Sealing Women fall into this category, and they remained a constant concern for the Commandant. Their uncontrollable behaviour, independence from men and reluctance to marry caused friction among the men in the community, and challenged the image Robinson wanted to promote to Governor John Franklin, who was expected on a visit any day. On a deeper level, headstrong Indigenous women, who even more than men needed to be seen as in need of paternal protection, were a very real threat to the process of Christianisation and civilisation. Robinson's journals reveal a man continually obsessed with the women's movements and conduct, an anxiety about the female body which Antoinette Burton and Tony Ballantyne say demonstrates 'how crucial its management was believed to be for social order and political stability'.[55]

In August 1837, it was the Sealing Women's choice of celibacy which alienated the VDL men, and consumed the mind of the Commandant. To populate the cottages which were under construction,

---

54   James C. Scott, *Weapons of the Weak: Everyday Forms of Peasant Resistance*, New Haven, Yale University Press, 1985, 29.

55   Tony Ballantyne and Antoinette Burton, 'Introduction: Bodies, Empires and World Histories', in Tony Ballantyne and Antoinette Burton (eds.), *Bodies in Contact: Rethinking Colonial Encounters in World History*, Durham and London, Duke University Press, 2006, 5.

CHAPTER 3

the Commandant needed families. Stable 'married' couples would show the Governor that, despite the terrible loss of population, a new VDL social fabric was being woven at Wybalenna. To achieve this, Robinson tried forcing the single women into a series of unwanted marriages. One woman, the 'inexorable Emma'[56], was sought after by a number of VDL men but flatly refused all comers. Another, Clara, was almost physically forced into marriage but violently refused. One of the Commandant's forced 'marriages' was between Flora and young Walter Arthur, who was a decade her junior at only seventeen. Their marriage, along with the five others performed, or rather ordered, by the Commandant on 10 August, did not last. Four days later, the women left their 'husbands' *en masse*.

The Commandant was furious. His journals detail his retaliatory actions: he instantly stopped their flour rations and reproved them and the 'instigators' (presumably, other Sealing Women). They returned the next day, but within a week the 'incorrigible' women had again left their men, threatening to take their dogs and go into the bush. There is only Robinson's account of this, from his journals, but it is not hard to envision those proud, resolute women drawing a line in the sand. Their threat to leave the settlement was an open challenge to the authority of the Commandant, and through him, the Crown's civilising mission. Frightened that Governor Franklin could arrive at any time and witness this mayhem, a beaten Robinson relented. The women were told they did not have to live with their 'husbands' – a truth that they, through their own actions, knew to be self-evident.[57]

---

56 Purlurrepennener/Meethecaratheeanna/Little Tuery/Emma, born c.1808. Plomley lists as former Sealing Woman, and 'Big River native (?)', *Weep in Silence*, 857-858.
57 The marriage saga covered in Robinson's journal, 10 to 19 August 1837, *Weep in Silence*, 469-473.

The Commandant's capitulation was a resounding victory for the women, but it does not necessarily represent an acknowledgment of their rights. Robinson's surrender came only one day before he recorded, in his journal on 20 August, receipt of an appreciative letter from Governor Franklin, who promised a visit. It was, in a very real way, a capitulation by Robinson in order to keep the peace. In later years, several of the women involved in this incident would take husbands of their own choosing from the available pool. These relationships would be genuine and long-lived. However, many of the Sealing Women remained single, preferring each other's company, or that of men only on their terms, for the rest of their days.

By the beginning of September 1837, Wybalenna was more like a supply depot for the VDL exiles than a permanent home. The nightly prayer meetings continued, with Noemy taking a leading role. Robert Clark recorded in great detail one of his animated sermons, which apparently had a great effect on all those present, VDL and European, and this deserves to be quoted in full:

> God noracoopa he coethee us, you coethee God – coethee a plenty big one you taplady weethicallee God send Jesus Christ to save us to parraway the Devil, potheae you coethe the Devil parraway, coethe God coethe Jesus Christ the son of God – you taplady lutha you coethe you noracoopa God make you a good man you go top weekthiekatha.[58]

This is one of the rare occasions when the language of the settlement is recorded. As was the tradition, Noemy initially addressed the congregation in his first language, then used the lingua franca, quoted above. It reminds us that there was a complexity of communications

---

58 Recorded by Robert Clark in a letter to Robinson dated 2 September. Printed in Plomley, *Weep in Silence*, 707.

which often goes unstated in the official record, for fear of the campaign of education being deemed a failure. Seen as barbarous and usually hidden by the Commandant, the language in this passage proves that there was always much more going on at Wybalenna than the official accounts would have us believe. And it was in this climate of complexity – with the cloud of illness and death lingering, the Commandant frantic that the new Governor might arrive at any time, and a settlement all but abandoned due to VDL recalcitrance – that the *Flinders Island Chronicle* was reborn.

The Great Flourish of the *Flinders Island Chronicle*

It is impossible to say exactly when the *Flinders Island Chronicle* leapt back into production. Prior to this study, the earliest edition was thought to date from 28 September 1837. However, a careful search of the archives has rendered six earlier editions and drafts, and there may well be more. We will enter the world of Wybalenna through the eyes and the pen of the young orphan scribe from Bruny Island.

On 10 September 1837, Thomas Brune was hard at work. He produced two editions of the *Flinders Island Chronicle* that day. One features the Commandant, and a theme that was to become regular: the fulfilment of the promises made to VDL people in their own Country. The other edition is very rich in detail about events at the settlement. Beginning, 'I cannot say that the black people are laize their working at cutting the bushes and then they gets Money for it', Brune provides an almost breathless summary of activity on the settlement. He details the weekly market, again mentions wages being paid, the planting of strawberries, convicts working the paddock, the presence of disease and Doctor Allen's role, the building of the new houses, new blankets, rugs and bedding being issued, road-making, the men sawing and then carrying firewood, and the myriad activities of the women, who carried grass, went to school, and also went out hunting but returned again in a short time. The community Brune represents in this one edition of the *Chronicle* is dizzyingly industrious. However, not everyone meets with his approval:

> The Aboriginal youths Augustus and Walter what are they do I cannot see them doing anything they plays where they pleases I do intend that the Commandant will set them to their work for their run about the Settlement like Dogs.[59]

This is the first hint that there was tension between the two young writer-editors of the *Chronicle*. Thomas Brune is clearly frustrated, and perhaps with good reason: up until this point, Walter Arthur's role in the production of the *Chronicle* is hearsay. There are no early *Chronicle* editions written in his hand. It may well have been galling for Brune, who had no family or connections, to see 'Prince Walter' obviously fawned over by the Commandant, praised for his intellect and enjoying himself with another youth while he – Thomas – worked hard at his clerical duties. In addition, Arthur now considered himself a man, and no longer lived with Brune and the other children at the catechist's house. The three year age difference between the two editors would have represented a massive gulf.

Not surprisingly, this edition contains no reference to the sombre news of the death by pneumonia the previous day of South West man Milton.[60] He had arrived at Flinders via the *Tamar* in September

---

59   Thomas Brune, *Flinders Island Chronicle*, 10 September 1837, Robinson papers, QVMAG CY825-65.
60   Pennemeroe/Milton: *Weep in Silence*, 846. From Birches Rocks, South West nation, Milton had met Robinson in June 1833 in Country, and is mentioned as having lost an eye due to a slug fired by a soldier (15 July 1833): Plomley, *Friendly Mission*, 794. When they reunited shortly afterwards, nine members of Milton's eleven-strong Pieman River clan had died (24 July 1833): *Friendly Mission*, 805.

CHAPTER 3

1833, yet left little trace in the settlement record, being ill for much of 1837, and therefore not taking part in the May school examinations. Shortly before he died, Milton told Robinson's son Charles that the devil had burnt his throat with a firestick. The only entry in Robinson's usually copious diaries that day was '12pm, Milton died of pneumonia'. The following day, a post-mortem was carried out and Milton's head was removed before burial, presumably for a collector. The Commandant's journal contains the bitterly ironic entry:

> A report was made that Milton had died: my clerk immediately placed a ruler to his name and was about to blot it out, I corrected him as I had no official notice from the medical officer. About midday the notice came when instantly up went the ruler and the pen run cross the name and out went the name ... The subject is a lesson; yet a little while and our names will be blotted out with as little ceremony. What a lesson.[61]

The fate of Milton was not unusual, either in the cause of his death, the banality with which he was disposed, or his scarce presence in the colonial record. The winter of 1837 had been a terrible one for illness, and Milton would not be the last.

The next edition of the *Chronicle*, produced one week later on 18 September, gives a very strong clue as to the motivation behind reviving the newspaper. After again detailing that the VDL people had new houses, blankets, rugs and bedding, plus go to school and church, Brune advises:

> ... and the governour his coming down from Hobart town very soon and he exceps that people will be clean and dresst up and be nice and tide

---

61   Robinson's journal, 10 September 1837, *Weep in Silence*, 477.

> And look at them and might say to them can you tell me who made you And stand up right and not be stand as they alway do governour do not like the people stand that a way
> When they stand upright it is sufficient.⁶²

Standing upright for the Governor, neat and tidy, was obviously a key concern for the Commandant, for it seems he has been quoted verbatim here by Brune, 'When they stand upright it is sufficient'. One wonders how poor the posture of VDL people might have been in the Commandant's eyes to elicit such a suggestion. We also see a hint that the common question asked at the school examinations – 'Who made you?' – could be asked.

Just days later, Brune produced yet another edition, proving that the *Flinders Island Weekly Chronicle* – as it was originally called – was never going to work to such a timetable. Existing only in a fragmentary nature, undated and unsigned, it is identifiable as the work of Thomas Brune by handwriting and punctuation style, and was probably written on 20 September. It begins with a reference to an earlier piece of writing, perhaps the *Chronicle* of 18 September, and again an acknowledgement of work performed by the VDL people, including men carrying wood, and women carrying grass. Then, the following event is noted:

> The New Holland woman and a Sealers boat man and two Children and he came to the commandants office and ask the Commandant for Some tar to mend his boat and he had to sleep at one of the prisoners huts and then he had to go away.⁶³

This undoubtedly refers to the visit, noted in Robinson's journal on 20 September 1837, of the recidivist convict John Strugnell. Brune

---

[62] Thomas Brune, *Flinders Island Chronicle*, 18 September 1837, Robinson papers, QVMAG CY825-65.
[63] Thomas Brune, *Flinders Island Chronicle*, undated, ML A7073, Vol. 52, part 4, 20.

CHAPTER 3

reminds us that many nearby islands were still inhabited by sealers and women from VDL and the Australian mainland, some willing companions, many otherwise.[64] Strugnell was deliberately kept away from the VDL people, and although there is no word on where the women and children slept, we can safely assume it was not with the convicts.

In this undated draft, Thomas also mentioned the various trades performed in Hobart to which Robinson was endeavouring to apprentice the VDL youths, including shoemaking, carpentry and blacksmithing. Here the *Chronicle* depicts colonial attempts to assimilate Aboriginal people into a new working or peasant class: for, as Henry Reynolds noted, 'Civilisation meant proletarianisation'.[65] The constant references to work performed – which would be a trademark of the *Chronicle* – also speaks to this framing of VDL people as a race civilised, in part, by work. Brune relates the important news about the arrival of the *Tamar* with a large supply of flour, and the robustness of the people's flock of sheep. The issuing of fresh meat and its superiority to salt meat is also discussed – an important issue on both nutritional and gastronomical accounts. This draft contains no attempt at religious indoctrination, save for the comment:

> … the native people of Van Diemen,s land
> are well off in there situation where they are
> and I hope God will protect them in every place were ever they go.[66]

---

64 The situations of these women were the source of great moral outrage at the time, among First Nations and European people. New research by Patsy Cameron and Lynette Russell also looks at the nature of economic and domestic arrangements between First Nations women and European Straitsmen.
65 Henry Reynolds, 'Aborigines and European Social Hierarchy', *Aboriginal History*, Vol. 7, 1983, 124.
66 Thomas Brune, undated, *Flinders Island Chronicle*, ML A7073, Vol. 52, part 4, 20.

Another undated *Chronicle* appears around this time, in draft form, and cross-scored across the sheet. Again, the writer is Thomas Brune, and again the efforts of Noemy are lauded at the very beginning:

> I know the Black people are learn the ways of God his Native Noemy he tells them about God and bout Jesus Christ and about the way we should believe in the Lord …[67]

Brune goes on to discuss work done by the VDL people, both illustrating and lauding their industriousness. He then returns to the regular theme of how in their own Country they knew not God, and how now at Flinders the Commandant was instructing them. This draft is quite rough, and parts of it will appear in a subsequent edition, dated September 22. It also contains the observation,

> When I was in my Country I seen many of them in the bush for there was Natives their Country but not many of them I seen.[68]

Detailing how the Commandant went into the woods and brought the VDL people to Flinders where they were receiving the word of God, Brune adds 'The Natives them knows all this seins they been on Flinders Island they did not know these things in their heads until they came on Flinders now they did not have these words in their own Country'. For a second time in one edition, Noemy is singled out for his church performance – 'Aboriginal Noemy shout out to them as it were a minister'.

Some of this language was corrected in the more polished edition of 22 September.[69] 'Did not have these words' becomes 'We ought to learn these words'; 'When I was in my Country' becomes 'When I

---

67 Thomas Brune, fragment of *Flinders Island Chronicle*, 22 September 1837, QVMAG CY825-27.
68 Thomas Brune, undated, *Flinders Island Chronicle*, QVMAG CY825-65-29.
69 Thomas Brune, *Flinders Island Chronicle*, 22 September 1837, QVMAG CY825-67.

CHAPTER 3

was in that country which is called Brune Island'; and 'Noemy shout out' becomes 'Noemy spoke out'. Noemy, as we have already seen, was clearly marked as an exemplary convert. As such, he is the most mentioned man in the *Chronicle* – besides, of course, the Commandant.

Thomas Brune was still the chief writer of the *Flinders Island Chronicle* – at least going by the editions of it which are currently known. On 28 September 1837, he produced a copy which was completed, polished, dated and signed. Until this study, this was thought to be the first edition. It displays a significant shift to the style of reportage which marked the *Chronicle*, and begins:

> The Native people of Van Diemen,s Land is gone out huntting
> and some of their men his got some books out with them
> and they are sunging and reading out in the bush
> and praying to God every night I suppose.[70]

This intelligence, about the absentees praying in the bush, came from a reliable source. Doctor Wooreddy had observed the newly elected Big River nation's King Albert[71] singing what he called 'Sunday corrobbery' and reading 'the Book'. To Robinson, undoubtedly instructing Brune in what to include in this edition, this was a significant victory in his campaign of Christianisation. It is also a powerful, evocative image, given credibility by the way it was related voluntarily by Wooreddy. This report about people being away in the bush further testifies to the exiles' freedom of movement, despite the constant entreaties to return or remain at the settlement.

Wooreddy's other report to the Commandant on that day – that the women used ochre and grease on the Sabbath – was suppressed, and

---

70   Thomas Brune, *Flinders Island Chronicle*, 28 September 1837, ML A7073, Vol. 52, part 4, 17.
71   Wowee/Warwe/Wawme/Albert, from Port Sorrell/Big River nation, one of the Parker-Thomas killers: *Weep in Silence*, 835, 837.

did not make it into the *Chronicle*. This flouting of Christian instruction by the women led Julia Clark to speculate that perhaps they 'had thrown in their lot with the Biblical Devil, against God and the white invaders'.[72] It is interesting to further ponder whether the 'Sunday corrobbery' and the use of ochre and grease by the women might have taken place as part of the same event. They refused to abandon traditional culture: in early August, ochre was once again seized. Antonio Sagona noted that with no source on Flinders, ochre must have been brought in.[73] The latest stash of ochre was likely smuggled in by the mission party who had returned from the mainland in late July.

The remainder of the *Chronicle* of 28 September was devoted to what were to become regular themes: the progress of the VDL people's education, exhortations to learn about and love God, and promises of a better future in heaven: 'always sunging in heaven no hungeree no thirst we well have every thing that is good in heaven'.[74] It seems, though, that those who were still out hunting in the bush preferred to eat in *this* life. Even though basic rations were available on the settlement, hunting – and the continuation of culture that it offered – remained an important part of life. By the end of the month, Robinson recorded that the 'greater part of the natives' – men and women – had gone hunting.[75] Despite his constant entreaties that the Governor would visit any time, VDL people insisted on doing things their own way.

---

72   Julia Clark, 'Devils and Horses: Religious and Creative Life in VDL Aboriginal Society', in Michael Roe (ed.), *The Flow of Culture: Tasmanian Studies*, Occasional Paper No. 4, Canberra, Australian Academy of the Humanities, 1987, 62-63.
73   Sagona, *Bruising the Red Earth*, 24.
74   Thomas Brune, *Flinders Island Chronicle*, 28 September 1837, ML A7073, Vol. 52, part 4, 17.
75   Robinson's journal, 27 September 1837, *Weep in Silence*, 480.

CHAPTER 3

Walter Arthur Takes Up the Pen

If Walter Arthur had written any editions of the *Chronicle* before October 1837 – and it seems reasonable to assume he did, given the constant linking of his name to the venture – then those editions are currently not known to us. On 2 October 1837, however, he enters the documentary record in tandem with Thomas Brune. Curiously, both scribes produced an edition of the newspaper on the same day. The timing hints at a competition between the two, and each made references to the other in their contribution. While both editions were concerned with sermonising, personal issues began to infiltrate. Brune wrote of 'the Aboriginal Youths Walter and Thomas Bruney assisting Mr Clark in the Church on Sundays': in naming themselves, he was cementing their social position.[76]

Walter Arthur's *Chronicle* of 2 October – his first currently known – began with what was to become his characteristic 'Now my Dear friends'. After exhorting his Countrymen to continue learning to read, and praising the fact that 'some of you … now can read and can spell words for four or five siylaibles', Walter turned his attention to his co-editor:

> And when I am in school I always see Mr Thomas Brune Laughing and playing away in the middle of school.[77]

This is not the first instance of naming and shaming in the *Chronicle*. As we saw in an earlier edition, Brune had already chastised Walter and Augustus[78] for running around the settlement 'like dogs'.

---

76 Thomas Brune, *Flinders Island Chronicle*, 2 October 1837, ML A7073, Vol. 52, part 4, 21.
77 Walter George Arthur, *Flinders Island Chronicle*, 2 October 1837, ML A7073, Vol. 52, part 4, 23.
78 Thermanope/Ben/Augustus/Augustus Clark. Born around 1821. From Macquarie Harbour, had been at Orphan School before going to Flinders Island: *Weep in*

However, despite Arthur's observation about 'Mr Thomas Brune Laughing and playing away' constituting an obvious criticism, it is important to note the respect with which Arthur nonetheless views Brune. He is the only VDL man or youth who warranted the title of 'Mr' from Arthur. Despite the rivalry, Arthur obviously differentiated between Brune and the greater VDL population, perhaps due to their shared literacy. In acknowledging Brune's position as editor, even silently, Arthur also inflated his own status.

The industriousness of the VDL people was again highlighted. Arthur described gardening, sowing of trees and fencing, and recounted a curious meeting on the road home from the Sisters, at the north of the island, with two women. He formally distanced himself from them – 'their Names were Flora and Louisa' – which raises some questions. Just six weeks earlier, he had been 'married' to Flora during Robinson's wholesale attempt to control the women by forcibly wedding them. Their union, like the others performed that day, was short-lived. In the *Chronicle*, he wrote as though he barely knew her. Walter was perhaps slighted, like some of the other men, at the women's preferred independence. Again, we get a sense of the complexity of interpersonal relations, and of a community which was constantly mobile. People were always coming and going, and meeting on roads between.

The young writers were full of energy and verbose, and therefore the *Chronicle* was never a weekly publication. Four days later, on 6 October, Thomas and Walter had each written another issue. Both, as was usual, were chiefly concerned with sermonising. Thomas, importantly, recorded:

Silence, 838.

CHAPTER 3

> The Aboriginal Male Noemy has got the love of God … in his heart
> he tells them about God and Jesus Christ and
> every thing that is good for them and for every body.[79]

Again, Noemy is publicly heralded for piousness. Noemy's moral position in the community was certainly being cemented: he was a constable on the settlement, and several times had been responsible for confiscation of ochre used in rituals. He had been noted on numerous occasions by Robinson for his striking addresses to the church congregation, and for 'reading books' in his home.[80] Noemy's active embrace of Christianity challenges the view espoused by Penny Van Toorn that the Bible and the English language were mere tools to shape the VDL people into 'a grotesquely degraded version of an English way of life'.[81] As we saw earlier from Noemy's sermon in the settlement's lingua franca, the Wybalenna version of Christianity – like the English language – was not set in stone, but a cultural influence which certain people at the settlement accepted and shaped to their own ends, and others rejected.

Walter Arthur's *Chronicle* of 6 October carried several recurrent themes. The women had apparently complained of being overworked at digging and carrying grass, leading him to respond, with a touch of sarcasm, 'thats to much carry a little Graſs'.[82] He also chastised those who had gone bush, linking this to becoming unwell. Illness, at this time, was widespread: Robinson's journal recorded a report from

---

79　Thomas Brune, *Flinders Island Chronicle*, 6 October 1837, ML A7073, Vol. 52, part 4, 25.
80　Robinson's journal, 29 April 1837, 6 May 1837, 3 Sep 1837, 3 October 1837, 21 Oct 1837, *Weep in Silence*.
81　Van Toorn, *Writing Never Arrives Naked*, 101.
82　Walter George Arthur, *Flinders Island Chronicle*, 6 October 1837, ML A7073, Vol. 52, part 4, 27.

Constantine,[83] who had just returned from the east coast Lagoons, where many were unwell. Interestingly, he reported that attempts were made to phlebotomise or bleed Frederick with broken glass. It appears from other comments in the Commandant's journals that VDL people enthusiastically adopted the practice of bleeding, then a common European treatment for many medical issues. The embrace of phlebotomy is not surprising, given the importance of scarification in pre- and post-European VDL culture.[84] It was an imported medical treatment which aligned with traditional practice.

Illness was widespread and deeply worrying for the whole Wybalenna community in October 1837. While Walter Arthur berated his Countrymen for going bush in his *Chronicle* of 6 October, he also engaged in a kind of question-and-answer, with the questions undoubtedly coming from Robinson, and perhaps his own suggested explanation:

> … and now my dear friends what was it keept you out so long a time
> my friends cant you tell what it was keept you out so long
> why I think they were looking out for the sick.[85]

The situation was dire. VDL people camping at The Lagoons and Badgers Corner were sick. There was also an encampment of Sealing Women, many of whom were gravely ill. At the settlement, 'Old' Kit[86] had been ill for weeks, attended by other former Tyereelore. On

---

83   Mokerminer/Makeadru/Big Jacky/Big Jack/Constantine, probably born before 1800: Weep in Silence, 841.
84   Discussed in some detail in N. J. B. Plomley's *The Tasmanian Tribes & Cicatrices as Tribal Indicators among the Tasmanian Aborigines*, Occasional Paper No. 5, Launceston, Queen Victoria Museum and Art Gallery, 1992, 39-50.
85   Walter George Arthur, *Flinders Island Chronicle*, 6 October 1837, 27.
86   Warkernenner/Wonginner/Worekenna/Kitty/Old Kit. From Tomahawk River, Coastal Plains nation, a Tyereelore who had lived on Hunter Island: *Weep in Silence*, 832, 861.

CHAPTER 3

9 October, people from the Western nation returned from the bush, and a Western Nations woman Nomerrucer died. Like many of the VDL exiles, there is precious little about Nomerrucer in the written record. She was tended in death by her clanswoman Tarramaneve,[87] while her son William Robinson was away hunting.[88] Her son's absence may well be the reason that, according to Robinson's reports, the exiles 'did not lament in their usual fashion'.[89]

Thomas Brune and Walter Arthur's *Chronicles* of this period were deeply focused on death and the afterlife. This was a time of great distress. On 10 October Robinson visited the encampment of seriously ill Sealing Women, and recorded a touching scene of the women sitting in a hut and others nearby, tending to them and cooking birds. It was here that Trugernanner (known as Lalla Rookh in Robinson's journals) made her oft-quoted remark to Robinson that soon there would be no blackfellows to live in the new houses.

On 11 October a new medical attendant, Doctor Walsh, arrived to relieve James Allen, who had a strained relationship with Robinson. In his *Chronicle* of the same day, Thomas Brune depicted a tragic slice of life which was all too common:

> When I was standing at Mr Clarks house
> I saw corfin carrying along the settlement
> we will all be like that, My friends just in the same way we must go.[90]

---

87 Like Nomerrucer, little is known about Tarramanever/Toinneburer. Both women appear to come from Sandy Bay in the Western nation.
88 Robinson's journal, 9 October 1837, Plomley, *Weep in Silence*, 484.
89 Ibid.
90 Thomas Brune, *Flinders Island Chronicle*, 11 October 1837, ML A7073, Vol. 52, part 4, 31.

This was undoubtedly linked to the death of Nomerrucer: Brune noted, 'do you see there was one of our sisters die she died on Monday 9th October which is I hope gone to glory'.[91] He chastised the people who remained in the bush – 'what busineſs they stooping out there long in bush' – and records the departure for Badger Corner at the south of the island of Henry to retrieve the sick.[92]

Yet amidst the melancholy cloud of sickness and death, mundane matters occupied the young writer's thoughts. There was a survey of the stores, and the receipt by the community of kettles, crockery and cutlery. At the market people bought tobacco, pipes and threads. A meal of mutton and plum pudding was shared after the market, and the only bush sojourner to return in time to partake was Alexander.[93] Thomas ended this edition with a customary exhortation to pray and praise God – 'if you do not God will cut you off from the face of the earth' – and at the bottom of the sheet, after signing off, he drew an exuberant flourish. This adornment – like the elaborate 'W's sometimes drawn by Walter Arthur – hint that, despite the anxieties at the time, Thomas Brune was proud and enjoying his position of authority as a scribe.

The sickness at the settlement continued, as it did in Hobart, where Reverend Knopwood diarised that much of the general population was suffering from influenza.[94] On 13 October, West Coast girl, Mohanna, died of pneumonia.[95] Robinson's journal contains a moving

---

91 Ibid.
92 Lerpullermenner/Henry. Aside from wife, Lucy, very little biographical information in Plomley, *Weep in Silence*, 844.
93 Moomereriner/Druemerterpunner/Long Billy/Count Alexander/King Alexander. Born around 1802, Big River nation. 'Thin man': *Weep in Silence*, 810, 837. Portrait painted by John Skinner Prout, printed in *Weep in Silence*, fp. 322.
94 Knopwood's diary, in Nicholls, *The Diary of the Reverend Robert Knopwood*, 670.
95 Mohanna/Moarna/Moouner/Moyhenung/Moyhenny. Born around 1828. Mother Naydip, father Wyne (Pieman River Chief), sister Clara: *Weep in Silence* 809, 810-11.

CHAPTER 3

tribute to Mohanna, followed by a paradoxically scientific observation of her post-mortem examination. As Inga Clendinnen noted of Robinson's journals, he ranged 'From horror to banality in a single breath'.[96] Mohanna was buried the following day. Shortly afterwards, the catechist Robert Clark sat with another desperately ill VDL exile, Hector.[97] Robert Clark recorded the following conversation with this young man, son of the famed leader Mannarlargenna:

> *Are you very sick?* Yes me plenty manaty.
> *You coethee God?* yes me coethee plenty.
> *You coethee Jesus Christ?* Yes me coethee Jesus Christ the son of God.
> *Do you pray to him?* Yes me pray to him plenty, me pray last night our Father which art in heaven plenty.
> *You very sick you krakabuka by and bye?* Yes me tabletee werthickathe to God, me coethee.[98]

Hector smiled after uttering these words and, according to Clark and Doctor Walsh, died a short time later.[99] Such a scene complied with what Pat Jallard called the evangelical Protestant model of the good Christian death – dignified, witnessed and documented.[100]

There was an especially tense meeting that night at the school, where 'upwards of a dozen' VDL men spoke. Robinson endeavoured to 'support their minds under the calamity they were labouring'.[101]

---

96 Inga Clendinnen, 'Reading Mr Robinson', in M. Fraser (ed.), *Seams of Light: Best Antipodean Essays – A Selection*, Sydney, Allen & Unwin, 1998, 77.
97 Neerhepeererminer/Kartitteyer/Hector. Son of Mannalargenna, and aged in his early 30s at this time. According to Plomley, of the Oyster Bay people (but Mannalargenna is known to be from the Coastal Plains nation): *Weep in Silence*, 812, 843.
98 Plomley, *Weep in Silence*, 714-715.
99 Robinson's journal has him dying early the following morning, on 15 October: *Weep in Silence*, 487.
100 Pat Jallard, *Australian Ways of Death: A Social and Cultural History, 1840–1918*, Melbourne, Oxford University Press, 2002, 51-52.
101 Robinson's journal, 14 October 1837, *Weep in Silence*, 487.

Sadly, we have no documentation of exactly what was said by the VDL men at this meeting, but the mounting death toll on the island was almost certainly a central issue. There had been three deaths within one week, and the following afternoon, a fourth: 'Old' Kit, lovingly tended to by other Tyereelore, passed away in the home of King George. As with Hector, the cause was listed as pneumonia. Although the weather was unseasonably hot, pulmonary complaints were wreaking havoc with the exiles.

Late in the day, Napoleon and Robert,[102] who had been away hunting on the far north of the island, returned to the settlement, reporting that many were sick at Killercrankie Point. They asked for flour and sugar to take to them.

The Commandant's response was, as was increasingly usual, pragmatic. Control over VDL people, so he could present the right image for Sir John Franklin when he arrived, was foremost in his mind. He refused to allow supplies to be taken to the sick, thereby forcing their return. Also on this day – after refusing the request for food supplies – he noted in his journal with clear annoyance that Dr Walsh had dissected Hector without informing him. The Commandant's pragmatism continued the following day when, on 16 October 1837, Kit and Hector were buried in the same grave, which had been dug double-deep. This was certainly culturally inappropriate, but was the Commandant's macabre solution to the rampant mortality. There were now simply too many graves: this would give a very

---

102 Maulboyheener/Timme/Big Tuery's Jemmy/Timmy/Smallboy/Robert/Bob. In 1837, aged around twenty. Featured throughout Robinson's Friendly Mission journals. There is some confusion over his origin, as Plomley equates his father as Rolepa (King George), hence brother to Walter Arthur – though is known to come from Coastal Plains nation, not Ben Lomond: *Weep in Silence*, 849; Patsy Cameron, pers. comm.

CHAPTER 3

poor impression to the Governor, whose impending visit occupied Robinson's thoughts.

Walter Arthur's edition of the *Chronicle* dated 16 October was silent on these particular deaths. However, he discussed the deaths of many good people, which he hoped had 'gone to Glory', and with whom in death he hoped to be reunited. Much of this edition, which was uncharacteristically low on sermonising, observed life at the settlement. Arthur reported the arrival of the *Tamar*, and promised 'by and by we will hear about what things have occurred in the Neaghbouring lands'.[103] Again, this illustrates the importance of news transfer, and the paradoxical connectedness of the island to Hobarttown and, through it, other nodes of the colonial network.

VDL people refusing to 'come in' from the bush remained a very big issue. Walter Arthur again criticised those who were staying away from the settlement, and gave a dramatic account of the moment of return of some absentees:

> Thomas Brune sang out and said haillow here comes four Copper Bushmen comeing in from the Bush.[104]

The term 'copper colour native' is repeated later in the same edition, but nowhere else in the *Chronicle*; or, it seems, in any other VDL writing. We might speculate that it was a term used by a European, or someone else, on that particular day or around that time, which was picked up on by the sharp young scribe. We do not know exactly who these Copper Bushmen were, but it was important to Arthur to inform them that due to their delay they had missed plum pudding. And there was more:

---

103 Walter George Arthur, *Flinders Island Chronicle*, 16 October 1837, ML A7073, Vol. 52, part 4, 35.
104 Ibid.

> I went out side of the Commandant Office and I looked towards Mount Franklin and I behold the men aploughing a field in the direction of Mount Franklin … you did not know nothing at all about these ploughing the Ground or any thing at all.[105]

Arthur then took aim at his co-editor, telling how Brune 'hast Got a way of Bringing Dogs to the Commandants Office' and was always making a mess. Robinson had noted in his journal that both Brune and 'Prince Walter' were working in the Commandant's office that week. As Brune generally wrote in the catechist's office, which was separated from the Commandant's office by fields, a small wood and what was called the Native Square, this forced proximity was obviously causing conflict. Arthur's perceived seniority over Brune – he was three years older, and son of an important Chief – is palpable as he recounted:

> And I saw Mr Thomas Brune come this morning to get a wheel Barrow and I asked him where was he agoing too boy but he would not take a thing at all he was sulky.[106]

Here, Brune is 'Mr' but he is also 'boy'. Arthur continued, in a testifying manner, to recount the things he had seen. There were group dramas, such as the scene of consternation on the road to the sawpit, when impatient VDL exiles waited on the sawyer, who did not have wood prepared for their beds. This event was considered important enough to be relayed in some detail. There were smaller reports as well: two unnamed men went shooting, and Neptune was seen scrubbing his bed tick. Arthur advised the VDL community not to sleep on the ground, but up on beds so the warmth from their

---

105 Ibid.
106 Ibid.

CHAPTER 3

fires could circulate, and then added, somewhat abruptly, 'may people out of the colony subscribe'. This reminds us of the Prospectus of the *Chronicle*, produced thirteen months earlier, which announced that the *Chronicle* would be sold, and the profits shared by the editors. Given the abiding interest in the goings-on at Flinders from the VDL mainland, it is not beyond the realms of possibility that people outside Wybalenna and even outside the Australian colonies would subscribe. However, we have no information on this. Walter Arthur finished his action-packed *Chronicle* of 16 October with an ornate 'W'. It was an echo of Brune's flourish from his 11 October edition, and in practising his signature Arthur was in a very real way asserting his identity as a young literate man. His literacy – and position as editor – gave him authority.

Walter Arthur and Thomas Brune were unafraid to assert this authority over other members of the community. On 17 October, Robinson recorded in his journal that the pair visited the people's cottages and warned the women that, if they did not clean up, they would be named in the *Chronicle*. Here, the writers were revealing themselves, as Reynolds noted, as 'confident, even self-righteous young men'.[107] According to Robinson:

> Several of the women begged they would not put them in the paper, said they might KARNY speak but not write.
> They seem to have a great abhorrence of being put in the newspaper.[108]

---

107 Reynolds, *Fate of a Free People*, 17.
108 Robinson's journal, 17 October 1837, *Weep in Silence*, 489. Lyndall Ryan incorrectly attributes this reference to the *Chronicle* editors threatening the women with the resolution of the recalcitrant brides episode, which actually occurred months earlier, in August 1837 (see 'The Incorrigible Women' above).

Shaming was a recurrent theme in the *Chronicle*, from the competitive asides between Brune and Arthur, to constant references to the women and, occasionally, lazy men. While there is little information on the role of shaming in VDL cultures, it is possible to draw tentative links to mainland practices of shaming or public ridicule as tools of negative sanction. Shaming now plays an important part in many restorative justice programs across Australia, and, on a traditional level, ridicule is commonly linked to neglect.[109] In threatening to name the women in the *Chronicle* for untidiness, the writers may thus have been conforming to mainland practices; however, it is important to keep in mind, as Jean Harkins notes, that the very word 'shame' contains semantic and cultural differences between Indigenous and Anglo-Australian usage.[110] And shaming the women, in particular, may have involved issues of nakedness, which Irene Watson has linked to white supremacy and extinguishment.[111]

The editors were obviously beginning to fulfil the role the Commandant had envisioned for them as moral police. Their entreaties to their fellow exiles to come back to the settlement appeared, also, to be paying off, though we cannot attribute the returns to the constant mentions in the *Chronicle*. Illness was a much more likely explanation. On the same day of the young editors' inspection of the houses and threat to put names in the paper, a group of Big River people returned to the settlement, many of them unwell. In an epic act of

---

109 B. Debelle, 'Aboriginal Customary Law and the Common Law', in E. Johnston, M. Hinton and D. Rigney (eds.), *Indigenous Australians and the Law*, Sydney, Cavendish, 1997, 86.

110 J. Harkins, 'Linguistic and Cultural Differences in Concepts of Shame', in D. Parker, R. Dalziell and I. Wright (eds.), *Shame and the Modern Self*, Melbourne, Australian Scholarly Publishing, 1996, 84.

111 Irene Watson, 'Naked Peoples: Rules and Regulations', *Law/Text/Culture*, Vol. 4, No. 1, 1998, 10.

CHAPTER 3

communal care, they had carried Oyster Bay man Tippo Saib[112] for many kilometres through the bush.

This was not the only group suffering sickness. To the north at Killercrankie Point, a group remained who had been refused supplies by Robinson. He instead despatched Achilles and Napoleon (Tunnerminnerwait) to retrieve the sick, expressing the view in his journal that the prevailing sickness was 'the consequence of their hunting and roaming unattended'.[113] However, the civilising triumvirate of housing, clothing and soap was much more responsible. As Ian Gilligan's recent study into the VDL peoples' post–Ice Age abandonment of clothing concluded, they had greater morphological adaptations to cold and used only what was needed.[114] The use of grease on the body had been essential, but was now discouraged. Likewise, the promotion of a sedentary lifestyle was cited by erstwhile settlement doctor James Allen as a cause of their decline. Now in Hobart, he told Backhouse and Walker:

> ... their remaining very constantly on the Settlement (which they are encouraged to do, in order to promote more rapidly their civilization) instead of making frequent excursions, for a few days together, into the bush, also tends to deteriorate their health.[115]

This view was also related to James Bonwick years later by Doctor Story, a Quaker, who said 'the deaths at Flinders Island and the

---

112 Calamarowenye/Calerwarrermeer/Jacky/Tippo Saib/King Tippoo. Born around 1810, from Kangaroo Point, Oyster Bay nation: *Weep in Silence*, 850-851. Was taken into custody around the time of the Parker-Thomas murders. Graeme Calder lists as Kallerromter, one of the Parker-Thomas killers: Calder, *Levee Line and Martial Law*, 245.
113 Robinson's journal, 17 October 1837: *Weep in Silence*, 489.
114 Gilligan, *Another Tasmanian Paradox*, 102.
115 Backhouse, *A Narrative of a Visit to the Australian Colonies*, 491.

attempt at civilizing the Natives were consequent on each other'.[116] Commandant Robinson, however unknowingly, pushed on relentlessly.

As October 1837 wore on, the Commandant was busy superintending public works, leaving the *Chronicle* editors with a greater degree of freedom. An increasing sense of agency and authority is reflected in Thomas Brune's *Chronicle* of 18 October, which was packed with news. Some was days old: he marked the arrival of Doctor Walsh on the cutter *Vansittarte*, and the departure of Doctor Allen, who was already in Hobart, visiting Backhouse and Walker. He also discussed the return of two men from the bush (presumably Tunnerminnerwait and Maulboyheener) and the deaths of a sister and brother (Kit and Hector). He observed the minutiae of life on the island: two men carrying wood, another carrying flour to the stores with the bullock cart, and 'Mr Walter' chopping wood at the Commandant's office. Further, Brune placed himself front and centre, recording walking from the Commandant's office and seeing Davy Bruney walking along to the breakwind, seeing Walter holding the paint pot while the Commandant painted numbers on the cottage doors, and seeing Mr Clark, Dr Walsh and 'G. A. Robinson' walking to the stores. This is one of only two times through the entire *Chronicle* that the Commandant was referred to by name, not as 'The Commandant'. One can hear their discussion retold through Thomas: 'it appears to me that the black population of this island is not in a regular order but the Commandant will put them to right by and by wen the houses is made'.[117]

---

116 Bonwick, *The Last of the Tasmanians*, 266.
117 Thomas Brune, *Flinders Island Chronicle*, 18 October 1837, ML A7073, Vol. 52, part 4, 37.

CHAPTER 3

This edition of the *Chronicle* also sheds light into the ongoing tensions in the community, when it depicted the funerals for Hector and Kit. Brune wrote:

> … on the 16th October I saw two corfins carrying
> one by the prisoners and one by the Natives
> and were put into the grave and I saw Isaac stamping on one of the graves
> and he began to laugh at me it is not right to laugh when any person is put into the grave [118]

We might speculate on the behaviour of Isaac.[119] Brune reported that Isaac stamped on *one* of the graves, but Robinson's journal clearly stated that both Kit and Hector were buried in the same grave. Isaac was not, apparently, related to either of the deceased. Perhaps, instead, he was celebrating the death of Hector, or else traditionally marking it. Two years earlier, at the death of famed Coastal Plains nation Chief Mannalargenna, Robinson noted that members of the Big River nation had danced with impropriety.[120] However, a Christian Englishman's 'impropriety' might well be a VDL exile's ceremony. This may have been an act of honouring. Or perhaps this entire incident might just be a case of Isaac goading Thomas Brune, to ridicule the very upright young man. In a place so culturally entangled, each action has a multitude of possible explanations.

The Commandant's journal of late October 1837 reveals the settlement as a hive of activity. Some absentees returned, bringing presents to placate, and Washington brought the first eels to the settlement

---

118 Ibid.
119 Probelattener/Larcurkenner/Lacklay/Jemmy/Isaac. Born around 1817, north of Great Lake, Big River nation: *Weep in Silence*, 844.
120 Robinson's journal, 4 December 1835, *Weep in Silence*, 313.

from Stony Castle. To Robinson's delight, Ajax[121] invited two other Big River men to dinner in his cottage, and they used knives and forks 'with dexterity'.[122] At a prayer meeting on 20 October, Robinson observed:

> Noemy's harangue was quite characteristic. He had a small book in his hand, a primer, on which his eyes occasionally dwelt as a relief while he collected his thoughts …Said heaven was a fine place, plenty black men and women in heaven a long time ago. Said plenty to eat in heaven, fine place, fine whaleboat in heaven …[123]

In his *Chronicle* of 24 October, Walter Arthur recorded a conversation with Washington during a walk around a field. Washington asked him 'why is it that the wheat rise up it selve' and Arthur answered 'it dont up by it selve jump up no': he attributed the growth of the wheat – and themselves – to God.[124]

This pairing – Walter Arthur and Washington – was a significant one. They had first arrived at Flinders Island together five years earlier, when Washington had just escaped the death sentence for his role in the Parker-Thomas killings, and Arthur had been plucked from an apparent life of crime in Launceston. They came from nations that were traditional enemies – Ben Lomond and Big River – whose animosities had continued right up to the current day. However, they were both young men – Arthur seventeen, Washington probably in his early to mid-twenties – and the camaraderie they would develop

---

121 Maleteherbargener/Titterrarpar/Jacky/Count Ajax/Ajacks. Born around 1790, Stoney Creek (Mid-North) nation: *Weep in Silence*, 807, 837.
122 Robinson's journal, 20 October 1837: *Weep in Silence*, 490.
123 Robinson's journal, 21 October 1837: *Weep in Silence*, 491.
124 Walter George Arthur, *Flinders Island Chronicle*, 24 October 1837, ML A7073, Vol. 52, part 4, 39.

CHAPTER 3

would help set the Wybalenna exiles on a course towards a pan-VDL nationhood. For now, though, they passed conversations about wheat.

Arthur also reported a number of events he had seen at the settlement, giving us the sense of a community brimming with activity. There was a running race between two young boys, Johnny Franklin[125] and the often-naughty Teddy Clark,[126] who two days earlier had been sentenced by the Native Court to wear a log chained to his leg for stealing.[127] Ten or eleven men were seen at work gathering thistles in the garden, and a man was seen carrying a ringtail possum. Women were observed walking around the stock yard, and another group of women caught Arthur's eagle-eye, 'what they was doing I cant tell'. There was an undertone of disapproval here, which was overt when he also reported seeing 'some women carrying woods upon a Sunday'. He described consulting the catechist over the appropriateness of working on the Sabbath. The observation that young Charles Clark[128] killed a redbreast inspired a discussion on the morality of killing birds; there was also talk of leaving soap lying about. The soap issue was recorded in a conversational tone:

> And also another thing you should not throw about the soap they have to much Mr Clark … and yet they dont care for it no they would sooner put on that there clay stuff.[129]

---

125 The son of Charlotte, a woman from 'New Holland' (probably Spencer Gulf region) rescued from sealers. Aged around seven at this time.
126 Edward Clark/Teddy, orphan, parents and origin unknown. Born circa 1832: *Weep in Silence*, 850.
127 Robinson's journal, 21 October 1837, *Weep in Silence*, 491.
128 Pennemoonoopcr/Rawee/Drunteherniter/Charles Clark/Charley Clark. Mother: Toinneburer (Arthur River, North West nation). Had spent time at Orphan School in Hobart. Born circa 1825: *Weep in Silence*, 829, 840.
129 Walter George Arthur, *Flinders Island Chronicle*, 24 October 1837.

Later, when talking about how the houses would soon be finished and 'then you will all be playing at all sorts of Games and then you will be amusing yourselves every day', Arthur remarked that the people would no longer need to collect wood and grass and stated, 'you will like that yes you will like that'. In an apparent aside to Robert Clark, or perhaps the Commandant, he added, 'they will I know that well'.

Thomas Brune's *Chronicle* for the same day also mentioned seeing soap lying about the settlement. This was obviously an important, symbolic issue. Rather than criticise though, Brune noted that 'some of them is very fond of soap'.[130] Like Arthur's *Chronicle* of the day, Brune cited many such events in the community: collecting, carrying items and also playing duckstones. This traditional game, the object of which was to hit a stone off a rock, was popular: the young boys Thomas Thompson and Charles Clark played it at the catechist's quarters, as did a group of older men at an undisclosed location.

In another example of naming and shaming of the Sealing Women to assert power over them, Brune recounted an interaction between young Thomas Thompson, who was kneeling on the ground, and the often-named Flora, who went up and looked at him, then went away laughing. This depiction sounds innocent enough, but given the editors' previous threats to name women in the paper, and Flora's demonstrated previous bad behaviour, it is likely she was ridiculing Tommy, and this reference was designed to castigate her.

This edition of the *Chronicle* also contains a sign of the ongoing discussions on removal to Port Phillip. Brune writes:

---

130 Thomas Brune, *Flinders Island Chronicle*, 24 October 1837, ML A7073, Vol. 52, part 4, 41.

CHAPTER 3

> ... if you was going to new Holland you would asked what sort of place it was and there you would go on and ask each other what sort of place it was.[131]

It reminds us yet again that the ultimate aim of the key Europeans involved was to move the community to the Australian mainland, and integrate with mainland nations. Yet as we have already observed, despite the plan to move to the Australian mainland – which was obviously being discussed by the VDL community – Wybalenna was taking deep root. A large-scale program of public works was underway, with twenty cottages almost completed in what would be known as the Aboriginal Square. Even as Brune was composing his *Chronicle* with the mention of the move, 20,000 bricks were being prepared for firing. It was a massive undertaking, and would provide housing which was of a very solid quality, by a humble 1830s workers-cottage standard. The completion of the houses was close, Brune assured the community, adding, 'The Commandant will put them to rights some day or another'.

One of the most fascinating events depicted in the *Chronicle* was a special lecture delivered by the Commandant on pneumatics. Thomas Brune was greatly impressed, and devoted his entire next edition of the *Chronicle* on 27 October to what was, for him, a major event:

> The people were dresst up as in the same as we was going to church the white people also they were dresst up as well as them and the Officers and the militaries and they were all afsemble together in the school house. Then the Commandant took a shilling and a feather was put on a ruler and Commandant let them down and one fell down [not] as quick as the other and

---

131 Ibid.

what caused the feather swim so long in the air because the
feather is much lighter than the shilling …¹³²

Thomas Brune's enthusiasm for the lecture is palpable through his writing. He has a keen, inquiring mind. He copies his mentor the Commandant, using the *Chronicle* to discuss basic aerodynamics, and while we will never know what the general VDL congregation made of the lecture, we know without doubt that Brune, at least, was hungry for knowledge. Interestingly, in his conclusion 'and you knows who made all these things', he does not mention God by name – perhaps recognising the general knowledge of God and his omnipotence among the population.

The pneumatics lecture, while obviously exciting for Brune, seems to have left no impression on Walter Arthur at all. His edition of the *Chronicle* also dated 28 October made no mention of the lecture. Instead, he reported on the usual activities around the settlement, particularly movements of the women – walking down by the lumber yard, also by the side of the hill, and carrying wattles in from the bush. Arthur described a group of men climbing the flag staff – perhaps a formal structure, or the small hill to the north of the settlement – and Achilles coming down from the hill carrying wood on his shoulder. The arrival of the whaleboat from Green Island was reported, carrying as it did five hundred mutton-birds. Arthur also told the community:

> And now look here and when I want to tell you all that
> the Commandant Give you many things
> you ought to thank the Commandant for it
> and not tak it without thank the Commandant for it.¹³³

---

132   Ibid.
133   Ibid.

CHAPTER 3

Gratitude towards the Commandant was becoming more of an issue for the young writers of the *Chronicle*. Three days later, on 31 October, Thomas Brune also chastised people who did not thank the Commandant when he issued the mutton-birds, singling out the 'Native Women' as chief ingrates. He described other activities of the women – going to Mrs Clark's house to make their gowns, plucking the mutton-birds and carrying grass – and the arrival of the boat from Green Island with sheep and even more mutton-birds for consumption. Brune also guardedly chastised people for not paying greater attention to the Commandant when he spoke at the evening school, foreshadowing the soon-to-be delivered next instalment of the Commandant's pneumatics lecture.

There is no *Chronicle* to report the reception of Robinson's second pneumatics lecture on 3 November, but according to his journal it lasted almost three hours, with a break in the middle for wine and other refreshments, and some flute-playing by Robert Clark. Walter Arthur's next edition of the *Chronicle*, dated either 6 or 8 November, was concerned with ensuring the VDL people asked permission before leaving the settlement. He even gave the example of Mr Clark asking permission to go on an outing to the Grass Trees Plain. This is probably a sign that, with warm weather coming, people were beginning to leave the settlement when they wished.

This edition of the *Chronicle* also contains arguably the most poetic, moving passage in the entire newspaper. Describing how the people were 'always swimming' and how the Native Women played a prank, telling everyone there was a brig coming when it was only a rock, Arthur wrote:

> … and the Native men was playing and singing about God and Jesus Christ

and they were asinging bout there own country song and some of the Native people was shooting swans and Duck and Pelilcans. And Native men was singing Godly song.[134]

This provides an idyllic vision of life at the settlement, a combination of playing, hunting and joyful singing about old Country and new Gods.

However, three days later on 9 November, Thomas Brune's edition of the *Chronicle* had a worried edge. After describing the usual activities, he declared 'I say that the people is very well off on the settlement they get every thing and what more can they want'.[135] He then warned people not to steal, nor fight each other ('it is the Devil that makes you fight'), and stated that while the 'people is very good', they are 'not good in Jesus Christ'.[136] As an example, he cited Edward (Leepunner), who came in to the Commandant's office, and was given pen and paper. Edward began to write and then, according to Brune, laughed at him. The same thing – being mocked for writing – was done by Achilles. Brune also reported seeing the men playing spears, and some people putting on red ochre and grease 'which is very bad work'. This edition proves conclusively that ritual activity was still being performed at Flinders Island.

One of the paradoxes of life at Flinders Island, however, was that people were apparently embracing Christianity – or some ritual aspects of it – contemporaneously as they adhered to traditional ways. This is brilliantly illustrated by an observation by the Commandant, made on an evening stroll with his wife and

---

134 Walter George Arthur, *Flinders Island Chronicle*, 6 November 1837, ML A7073, Vol. 52, part 4, 49.
135 Thomas Brune, *Flinders Island Chronicle*, 9 November 1837, ML A7073, Vol. 52, part 4, 51.
136 Ibid.

CHAPTER 3

daughter on 12 November. They were visiting a South Western woman Ponedimerneep, who was very ill, when they heard hymns being sung in Washington's cottage. The singing was so perfect that the Robinsons suspected that their sons must be there, leading the singing, but, as Robinson wrote:

> ... what was our surprise to find on entering the cottage that none but natives were there, about twenty to twenty-five in number, men and women, all seated round the fire and singing praises to the Almighty.[137]

This evocative image of the Big River nation, singing fireside hymns in the new cottages, shows a community of complex identities. As with Walter Arthur's observations one week earlier of the people singing about their own Country and Godly songs, we see clear indications of religious syncretism. The *Chronicle* shows that some – like Noemy – had a genuine commitment to Christianity. Others, like Thomas Brune in his pneumatics edition and Washington in his conversation with Arthur about wheat, showed scientific enquiry. The Big River people, as always, maintained their national identity. The Sealing Women enjoyed sewing, eschewed housework, and largely rejected attempts at civilisation and Christianisation. The *Chronicle*, at this stage, shows a varied set of responses from the VDL community to the range of opportunities and pressures confronting them.

As the summer of 1837 approached, the young editors of the *Chronicle* were at the forefront of this cultural tug-of-war. In the warm evenings of November 1837, the cottages at Wybalenna continued to resound with hymns. Walter Arthur noted this phenomenon

---

[137] Robinson's journal, 15 November 1837, *Weep in Silence*, 497.

in an incomplete, unsigned *Chronicle* of 13 November.[138] Observing that 'The people had prayers in their houses every night last week and the week before and singing hymns', he also relayed the tale of a man who, after shooting ducks at The Lagoons, came home sulky. He waited until the other men were at the school, then fired at a dog and, angry that he missed it, deliberately spilled the people's tea. Arthur added, 'when Native men came home the Native women told it to the men he would not have done it when the Native men were at home'.[139] Could this perhaps have been Napoleon (Tunnerminnerwait), who, Robinson's diary showed, had recently attacked Washington's dogs? This event shows that, despite the communal prayers and hymn-singing, tensions – likely inter-national – could still boil over.

Arthur also reported that the storekeeper, Mr Dickenson, went to Green Island 'to see about the people wool'. The community were well aware of their ownership of the sheep at pasture on Green, Chalky and other islands of the Furneaux group, the wool of which was sent to Hobart and the money credited to them. The sheep were tended by convicts – such as 'Black Pierre', the flagellator[140] – and occasionally VDL people. Walter Arthur, in following years, was assiduous in keeping track of his and his father King George's sheep. His first dispute with a subsequent superintendent, Doctor Jeanneret, which eventually led to the petitioning of Queen Victoria, was over the people's access to their earnings from wool and potatoes. This edition of the *Chronicle*, however, closed with a lecture about too much

---

138 Michael Rose dates this entry as 6 November. Handwriting and date formatting style are Walter Arthur's.
139 Walter George Arthur, *Flinders Island Chronicle*, 13 November 1837, ML A7073, Vol. 52, part 4, 53.
140 John Pierre, from Grenada; arrived in Van Diemen's Land on the Elphinstone in September 1836 (SLV AJCP Microfilm Roll 90, HO11/10, 230); convicted of larceny, claimed harbouring a slave, *Weep in Silence*, 988.

CHAPTER 3

game-playing – 'They are to fond of playing marbles too much and will not mind their Books'.[141] This chastisement is in stark contrast to the claim, made several weeks previous, that once the cottages were done, the people would be free to play games to their hearts' content.

Marbles must have overtaken Duckstones as the game of choice in mid-November, because Brune's next *Chronicle*, one day later on 14 November, opened with an almost identical complaint, 'Native men play to much at marbles they don't attend to their books'.[142] The authors echoed either Robinson or each other. The importance of marbles – as either a game of acquisition, or display of skills – is borne out in the archaeological record, with marbles located from a number of the excavated VDL cottages.[143] The VDL men also seemed to be shirking their wood-carrying duties, although Brune noted that he did see the women carrying grass and going to make their gowns. There were obviously rumblings of discontent in the community, perhaps a continuation of the dog-shooting tensions that Arthur had noted the previous day. Brune wrote:

> I heard a noise on the Settlement
> it seems to me that the people were growling at one another
> it is the Devil that makes you fight
> God don't like those that fight.[144]

---

141 Walter George Arthur, *Flinders Island Chronicle*, 13 November 1837, ML A7073, Vol. 52, part 4, 53.
142 Thomas Brune, *Flinders Island Chronicle*, 14 November 1837, ML A7073, Vol. 52, part 4, 55.
143 Marbles are an archaeological feature not just at the Wybalenna, but at most Australian colonial sites. See Judy Birmingham, *Wybalenna: The Archaeology of Cultural Accommodation in Nineteenth Century Tasmania*, The Australian Society for Historical Archaeology, 1992, 117-119.
144 Thomas Brune, *Flinders Island Chronicle*, 14 November 1837, ML A7073, Vol. 52, part 4, 55.

The South West woman – who Robinson visited on the night of the glorious singing – died on 13 November. Named variously Ponedimerneep by Robinson, 'the Native female Pondammireep' by Brune[145] and 'the Native Aboriginal female Pondanarip' by Arthur,[146] her case highlights the difficulty faced in attempting to trace individuals due to variations in the record. Even her post-mortem report by Doctor Walsh confuses her with another recently deceased woman, Pillah.[147] Still, Ponedimerneep, her passing and her funeral, was significant enough to make her the only individual named, at death, by both *Chronicle* writers.

Walter Arthur's *Chronicle* of 15 November recorded a new game being played, Bull in the Ring.[148] Unusually, Arthur also described the activities of Europeans, presumably prisoners (although these are never referred to as such in the *Chronicle*), putting stakes around the barley field to make a fence. He also recorded seeing the constable – probably not the Aboriginal constable, Noemy, who he would have positively named – and his wife 'taking a saw and Began to saw down a large tree'. Both of these events were of obvious interest to the community. Also noteworthy was young Teddy Clark's continuing misbehaviour. Arthur recorded, 'And now you all see that little Teddy is Got the old man in him. And what is the reason of that because the Devil is in his heart',[149] giving no indication of the activities of Teddy on this occasion. The comment about having 'the old man

---

145 Ibid.
146 Walter George Arthur, *Flinders Island Chronicle*, 15 November 1837, ML A7073, Vol. 52, part 4, 57.
147 Matthew Walsh to Deputy Inspector General of Hospitals, 25 October 1837, CSO 1/325/6578, 188-189, reprinted in *Weep in Silence*, 931.
148 Possibly a touch football game (aka 'Kill the Man' or 'Kill the Carrier').
149 Walter George Arthur, *Flinders Island Chronicle*, 15 November 1837, ML A7073, Vol. 52, part 4, 57.

CHAPTER 3

in him' might mean he was just like his father, but in the official records at least, Teddy (or Edward Clark) was listed by others as an orphan, his parentage, nation and original name unknown. Perhaps this 'old man' was the colloquial devil, dovetailing with the belief among some VDL nations that the devil resided in their breast, as the source of ill-feeling toward each other.

Deaths continued at Flinders Island. On 15 November, the Commandant plotted a map of the burial ground, and two influential Big River women became seriously ill. Arthur's *Chronicle* of 16 November, given the circumstances, could reasonably have been expected to contain comments on prayer, God and the hereafter. However, despite encouragement to read, and praise for Robinson and Clark (by their office, not name) who were 'always down to see you', Arthur was silent on the distress which was permeating the community. He opened with the frequently-made observation that the houses would soon be finished, and noted that the fencing work of the white men in the barley field was continuing. Arthur saved most of his criticism for Ajax, who had gone hunting after rats and mice, because 'he think that there is not a enough to eat at the Settlement to fill his belly'.[150] Ignoring the hunger issue, Arthur suggested that if Ajax took up God's book 'he would not be so fond of hunt as he is liking'.

One day later, Thomas Brune produced probably the only well-known and controversial issue of the *Chronicle*. Four drafts of his edition of 17 November exist, clearly showing the usually masked hand of the Commandant-censor. Through the variations, it is possible to see Brune's earliest draft in a looser hand and with the editing in Robinson's writing; a second draft, with just a few corrections; a third

---

150 Walter George Arthur, *Flinders Island Chronicle*, 16 November 1837, ML A7073, Vol. 52, part 4, 59.

draft, with no corrections and 'copy for report' in Robinson's writing at the top; and a fourth draft, with no corrections or annotations at all.[151]

All four drafts recount the heroic tale of the Commandant going into the bush, saving the VDL people from bad white men, then bringing them to Flinders Island 'where you get everything', including medical attention. All four drafts then moved on to repeat the oft-cited observation, 'You have got fine houses I expect you will not vexte one another'. This is the first appearance of the word 'vexte', which, spelt differently, became important in Brune's next edition. As the drafts continued, there was a short mention about a market being held, and more platitudes towards the Commandant. The distress around the settlement is echoed in the comments 'There is many of you dying my friends' and entreaties to pray to God or suffer eternal punishment.

The arrival of the brig *Tamar* was featured in all four drafts, with hope of hearing news from Hobarttown. The first draft then observed, 'I saw Adolphus and Davy carrying fish to the Commandant quarters',[152] a slice of life not repeated in the other drafts. Instead, the three later drafts – after the hope of hearing news from Hobarttown – stated:

> Let us hope it will be good news
> and that something may be done for us poor people
> they are dying away
> The Bible says some of all shall be saved
> but I am much afraid none of us will be alive by and by
> as there is nothing but sickneſs among us.[153]

---

151 Running in apparent reverse order in the Robinson papers: ML A7073, Vol. 52, part 4. I suggest they were written in the order 67, 65, 61 then 63.

152 Thomas Brune, *Flinders Island Chronicle*, 17 November 1837, ML A7073, Vol. 52, part 4, 67.

153 Thomas Brune, *Flinders Island Chronicle*, 17 November 1837, ML A7073, Vol. 52, part 4, 61, 63, 65.

CHAPTER 3

The key line in this edition follows, the insertion and deletion of which has attracted the attention of many modern writers:

> Why dont the black fellows pray to the king to get us away from this place.[154]

This line appears in two of the drafts, the second and third written, but not the last.[155] It has been suggested by numerous writers that this line escaped Robinson's initial censorship.[156] This is certainly a seductive image, young Thomas Brune subverting the authority of the Commandant to sneak out a message of rebellion. However, this is almost certainly not the case.

Firstly, the notion of petitioning the highest office was not a new one. It was no secret that Robinson had been agitating for the removal of the VDL people for a number of years, with the support of Colonial Secretary John Montagu, and he claimed the verbal assent of the VDL people.[157] Sir George Arthur was also vocal in supporting this plan.[158] Support for removal to the new colony at Port Phillip continued under Governor Franklin, and on 12 August 1838 – only nine months after this edition of the *Chronicle* – a petition was signed

---

154 Ibid.
155 Ibid., 61, 65.
156 Rose, *For the Record*, 208; Penny Van Toorn, 'Indigenous Life Writing: Tactics and Transformations', in Bain Attwood and Fiona Magowan, *Telling Stories: Indigenous History and Memory in Australia and New Zealand*, Allen & Unwin, Sydney, 2001, 8; Van Toorn, *Writing Never Arrives Naked*, 119; Katherine Russo, *Practices of Proximity: The Appropriation of English in Australian Indigenous Literature*, Newcastle, Cambridge Scholars Publishing, 2010, 181.
157 Montagu to Robinson, 7 February 1835; Robinson to Montagu, 7 February 1835; Robinson to Montagu, 11 February 1835, in M. Cannon, M. (ed.), *Historical Records of Victoria, Foundation Series, Vol. 2A, The Aborigines of Port Phillip 1835–1839*, Melbourne, Victorian Government Printing Office, 1982, 8-12.
158 Lt Governor Arthur to T. Spring Rice, 27 January 1835; Arthur to T. Spring Rice, 10 March 1835, in *Cannon, Historical Records Of Victoria, Vol. 2A*, 6-12; also in Sir George Arthur papers regarding Aborigines, 1825–1837, Mitchell Library, SLNSW, Sir George Arthur Papers, 1821–1855, Vol. 28, MAV/FM4/ 3680.

by all the adult men in the community, asking to go to Port Phillip.[159] Robinson's submission to the Committee on the Aboriginal Question held in Sydney in October 1838 also addressed the plan, and assured the VDL people's continued good behaviour.[160] Robinson's journals throughout his tenure as Commandant make references to his efforts to remove the Community to Port Phillip, and ten days after this *Chronicle* was written the new hospital assistant Lewis, on his arrival, told Robinson that there were reports around Hobart that the settlement was to be moved to New Holland.[161] The subject of removal to Port Phillip was well known to the Community: many of the Sealing Women had already been there, and one, Charlotte, was a native of New Holland. The evidence suggests that Thomas Brune's plea was not subversive at all.

There is a second, more probable explanation for the removal of the line about petitioning the King. This edition of the *Chronicle* may not have been written on 17 November, but over a number of days, with some stunning news in the intervening time calling for a change of wording. Brune wrote in the *Chronicle* that the 'Tamar' arrived at Green Island 'this morning', and they were yet to have any news from Hobart. In fact, the brig was first seen on 20 November, and – much to Robinson's chagrin – the Tamar's boat did not reach the settlement until the next day, 21 November. It brought the news from home that the King was dead, and Victoria was on the throne. This information – many months after the event – shows the far-flung nature of the Flinders Island Settlement, both geographically and

---

159 Reprinted in *Weep in Silence*, 751.
160 'Report from the Committee on the Aborigines Question with Minutes of Evidence, Ordered by the Council to be printed 12th October 1838', Votes and Proceedings of the Legislative Council, Sydney, J. Spilsbury (microfilm, La Trobe University Library).
161 Lewis quoted in Robinson's journal, 27 November 1837, *Weep in Silence*, 504.

CHAPTER 3

temporally. The death of the King goes a long way to explaining the editing out of this possibly inappropriate line about petitioning him.

None of these explanations are designed to detract from the power of Thomas Brune's writing. The words, coming from the hand of a young Aboriginal man, 'I am much afraid that none of us will be alive by and by as there is nothing but sickneſs among us', would have packed a massive humanitarian punch to the colonial authorities, many of whom were genuinely concerned at the plight of the VDL people and the catastrophic mortality rates. Whether these words were suggested by or controlled by Robinson, Clark or others is, in many ways, beside the point: they were in the educated script of a young, literate VDL man. That made them impossible to ignore. This edition of the *Chronicle* once and for all abandoned the precept that everything was fine at the settlement and, for the first time, truly exposed the hopelessness of the situation.

These were the settlement's darkest days. The deaths of the two very popular women, Queen Elizabeth[162] and Jemima, on 17 and 18 November respectively, were a devastating blow to the community. Even Robinson, for all his stoicism, shed an 'involuntary tear' at the death of Queen Elizabeth, and said 'I did all I was able to suppress my feelings'.[163] The 'universally respected' Jemima – who six months earlier had been described as young, interesting and very intelligent – was attended in her final hours by up to thirty people who sat around her in rows. These important women warranted a new type of funeral, and on 18 November Queen Elizabeth was buried in a spectacular night-time service in which all the VDL males – men and

---

162 Hurlanerhener/Drierlergenerminner/Big Bet/Waterloo Bet/Queen Elizabeth. Born around 1798, Big River nation. Widow of famed King William/Montpelierata: *Weep in Silence*, 857.
163 Robinson's journal, 17 November 1837: *Weep in Silence*, 498.

boys – held torches. Apparently designed by Robinson to echo regal funeral rites, he wrote, 'My mind was seriously impressed with the solemnity of the occasion'.[164] The following night, Jemima was buried in the same manner. These would seem to be the only two funerals of this kind at Wybalenna.

Illness was widespread. A number of other women were seriously sick, including the famed diplomat Trugernanner, former Tyereelore Louisa, and young Western Nations wife and mother Deborah.[165] They asked to be bled, although the new doctor put little stock in phlebotomy. Many of the sick left the settlement for Stony Castle and other locations. The frustrated Doctor Walsh told Robinson he was looking for causes to the great mortality, but had to 'grope his way in the dark' due to his predecessor not leaving adequate records. These were desperate times.

It was in this climate that Walter Arthur wrote his final *Chronicle*. Echoing a sermon given by Robert Clark three days earlier, which talked about the VDL people's reluctance to hear about death, Arthur wrote:

> Now my friends I should like to tell about something
> what yourselves to not like to hear it mension to you
> that is you have got to die some time or another
> yes you must all die we have not got to stop in this world
> where there is haveing no peace and where there is always sickneſs.[166]

---

164 Robinson's journal, 18 November 1837, *Weep in Silence*, 500.
165 Larmoderick/Mangbopeer/Deborah, born around 1812. Sister of Neenhonic/Jacky McCracky, d. 25/2/37. Wife of Pendowtewer/ Rodney: mother of Robert b. 16/4/36: *Weep in Silence*, 803, 856. 'Captured' in September 1832, associated with North West nation: *Beyond Awakening*, 236.
166 Walter George Arthur, *Flinders Island Chronicle*, 23 November 1837, ML A7073, Vol. 52, part 4, 69.

CHAPTER 3

This is not the first time Arthur had taken this line in his *Chronicle* writings, but given the context of the deaths of Queen Elizabeth and Jemima, and the community's general sickness, his words were and are intensely powerful. He also alluded to tensions among the community:

> whould you like stoop here this wicked and sinful world
> where there is always fighting and Growling.[167]

Robinson's journal relayed two small incidents that are perhaps indicative of a community under stress, hence the resultant 'growling'. An irate Trugernanner, furious about thefts, confronted Leonidas.[168] Again displaying a dry wit which leaps from the pages of the archives, she asked this convert to Christianity, who preached at the community's church, whether God told him to steal pipes from the women. In another example of small, lingering tensions, Robinson recorded an altercation where Ajax derisively called a woman 'black'. Offended, the unnamed woman asked Ajax if *he* was a white man.[169] These glimpses hint at issues of theft, religion, race and gender, behind the ever-present 'growling'.

Walter Arthur had one more observation in his final *Chronicle* on day-to-day events at the settlement. He described how he and Thomas Brune – not 'Mr', or 'the clerk', just Thomas Brune – went for a walk up to Mount Franklin, which overlooked the settlement. Thomas said to him 'Behold', because the younger boy Adolphus 'got lost in the bush and then he began to cry out for one of us'. Adolphus, aged about

---

167 Ibid.
168 Dowwrunggi/Leati/David/Leonidas. Born around 1810. Birthplace unclear, but associated with the Big River nation; one of the famed Parker-Thomas killers, who according to Maccame (Washington) shot Parker with his own gun: *Weep in Silence*, 797, 841, 847.
169 Robinson's journal, 22 November 1837, *Weep in Silence*, 503.

nine, was orphaned three months earlier at the death of his mother Andromache.[170] However, unlike other orphans like Thomas Brune or Teddy Clark, 'Prince Adolphus', as the Commandant often called him, was clearly favoured, being the son of renowned Western Nations leader Wymerric, who had died five years earlier. Robinson had personally adopted the boy, in honour of his father's 'sagacity and manly bearing'.[171] Later, Adolphus would find a home, temporarily at least, with Sir John and Lady Franklin, with Robinson describing him as 'a shrewd and intelligent lad'[172] and still recalling his father 'as much celebrated for hunting as for his skill and prowess in battle'.[173] On this day, in helping the little boy lost in the bush, Walter Arthur and Thomas Brune appear to have played a protective role. This is the last time that the two Editors are mentioned in each other's *Chronicle*.

It would be two weeks before another *Chronicle* was published – that is, according to the information currently available. But a momentous event took place which was to forever change the dynamics between the Commandant, George Augustus Robinson, and his two obedient scribes. On 2 December 1837, one week after what currently stands as his final edition, Walter Arthur was found in bed with Mary ann Cochrane, fellow teacher at the school and the most promising, in the Commandant's eyes, of all the VDL women. She

---

170   Larratong/Larretung/Larhertounge/Eastbynown/Narthebynoune/Tureweek/ Queen Andromache. Born around 1792, Robbins Island, wife of renowned Western Nations leader Wymerric. Mother of Adolphus: *Weep in Silence*, 803, 853.
171   May 1837 school examinations, comments regarding Adolphus. Robinson Letterbook, QVMAG CY548.
172   G. A. Robinson to Lady Franklin, 10 February 1839, Robinson Letterbook, QVMAG CY548.
173   G. A. Robinson to Lady Franklin, 15 July 1839, Robinson Letterbook, QVMAG CY548.

CHAPTER 3

occupied a position of great intimacy with the Robinson family, and was on very close terms with the Commandant's wife and daughter.

The illicit relationship between his family's favourite, Mary ann, and the young man earmarked by Robinson as a future leader of his people, came as a terrible shock. To compound the dismay, the couple were discovered by Robinson's own daughter Maria.[174] The former high regard in which both Walter and Mary ann were held, plus their flouting of the Christian moral code in front of his own daughter, made this a double calamity, and in Robinson's eyes a clear betrayal of trust. Robinson notes that Mary ann was reproved, but remained silent about his reaction towards Arthur, until three days later, when he simply stated, 'Put Walter in gaol 11 am'.[175] The *Chronicle*, for Walter Arthur at least, was at an end. But Thomas Brune still had three editions to write.

De-friending George Augustus Robinson

Thomas Brune was under immense pressure. The Commandant was vexed, his co-editor was in jail, and Brune was being threatened with punishment himself if he did not work harder. His edition of the *Chronicle* dated 7 December 1837 is one of the most illuminating of the series. There is talk of a boat going to Prime Seal Island containing Dr Walsh, two of Robinson's sons and some unnamed VDL men, probably to collect mutton-birds. Brune also describes an inspection he conducted with Mr Lewis of the people's cookware and crockery stores. A boat was also reported, arriving with

---

174 As his eldest daughter, named (by convention) only as Miss Robinson. Then probably aged around sixteen or seventeen.
175 Robinson's journal, 5 December 1837, *Weep in Silence*, 507.

wool. These issues all paled in comparison with the biggest issue of the day: cows getting into the potato paddock.

The people, it seems, were aware of this bovine intrusion but did not act. One can almost picture them looking on, greatly amused. There would have been conjecture and opinions, but – frustrating the Commandant – no action. It seems the community stood and watched. This was another clear example of the kind of resistance James C. Scott spoke of in *Weapons of the Weak*: inaction. Brune chastised them in the *Chronicle* – 'you would not take and drive out of the garden no you would not. Commandant then seen the cows in the garden and he began to speak to you on the subject'. None of the onlookers are named in the *Chronicle*, but it is clear that the Commandant was enraged by the situation. Brune warned:

> My friends you must not fixed the Commandant any more
> he has got every thing for you
> you would get nothing at all the Commandant
> the only thing I got to say to you
> you must not fixed the Commandant.[176]

'Fixed' here undoubtedly means vex, and has been translated this way by Michael Rose in his reproduction of the issue.[177] Brune reiterated the same warning – 'do not fixed the Commandant' – a third time at the end of his edition. Brune's nervousness seems well justified, for Robinson was clearly in a martial mood that day. His journal records a bizarre scene where he conducted an experiment on the Cape Barren geese. Armed with the dried skin of an eagle, wings extended, Robinson went among the geese and waved it about, causing

---

176 Thomas Brune, *Flinders Island Chronicle*, 7 December 1837, ML A7073, Vol. 52, part 4, 71.
177 Rose, *For the Record*, 17.

CHAPTER 3

them 'the greatest possible fear by screaming and crowding together. Their feathers were all erect and they were so terrified that they had no courage to run off but crouched on the ground screaming and making a noise'.[178] This behaviour was undoubtedly, in Robinson's eyes, a scientific experiment. Fourteen-year-old Thomas Brune, though, was nerve-racked, a fact he even discussed in the *Chronicle*:

> ... hear this I got rittes to you the same things over and over again
> Commandant has directed me to work
> and if I dont attend to it I must be put in to joal.[179]

This is probably the most extraordinary statement in the *Chronicle*, for it confirms just how far the humanitarian dream of Wybalenna had deteriorated in just one year. It illuminates Robinson's abuse of power, and gives a real glimpse of how stressful life was for Thomas Brune. The honeymoon period of journalistic empowerment was over, and Brune was working in fear. He could be in no doubt that Robinson would make good on the threat of jail if he so desired, for Walter was still imprisoned. Robinson's journal recorded visiting Walter in jail with 'parson' – undoubtedly Robert Clark. While there is no insight into Walter's response to incarceration, it appears Mary ann – in Robinson's eyes, Walter's partner in moral depravity – was unrepentant: he simply recorded, 'Mary Ann very saucy to me today'.[180]

Robinson's abuse of Thomas Brune continued. Brune's next edition of the *Chronicle* dated 9 December was full of encouragement to read

---

178 Robinson's journal, 7 December 1837, *Weep in Silence*, 507.
179 Thomas Brune, *Flinders Island Chronicle*, 7 December 1837, ML A7073, Vol. 52, part 4, 71.
180 Robinson's journal, *Weep in Silence*, 7 December 1837,

the Bible – 'you better read it at onest'[181] – and to pray, believe in Jesus Christ, and prepare for death. Significantly, 'Jeovah' was named. The only reference to Settlement life was the observation of women carrying grass, and a market being held where pipes, hooks and tobacco were sold. There was no encouragement to praise the Commandant or warnings not to vex him. Thomas Brune was walking a fine line.

Two days later, his fears of 7 December appear to have been realised. Robinson's journal noted 'Discharged Walter from gaol, and sentenced Brune to two hours in the stocks'. There was no explanation of Thomas's offence – if, it must be said, it definitely was Thomas Brune. Occasionally, Wooreddy's sons Davy and Peter were simply called Brune or Bruney in Robinson's journals. Given the threats Thomas recorded just a few days earlier, however, it is reasonable to assume that the young editor suffered this indignity.

The final edition of the *Chronicle* was not produced by Thomas Brune until 21 December 1837, close to two weeks later.[182] Events important to this edition, however, occurred in the interim. On 12 December – the day after the release from jail of Walter Arthur, and incarceration of Thomas Brune – Robinson gathered together a group of VDL people, some of whom had been his most loyal companions through the conciliatory missions of years gone by.

In what must surely have been an attempt to recreate the goodwill of their halcyon days, Robinson led the group in an exploratory mission across Flinders Island. In blistering heat, the group fought through scrub and forests of dead, burnt wood which had recently

---

181 Thomas Brune, *Flinders Island Chronicle*, 9 December 1837, ML A7073, Vol. 52, part 4, 73.

182 There is one other possible edition in the Robinson papers, in the handwriting of Thomas Brune, dated 'January 1838'. This is an extremely rough draft, quite different to the other editions, and, as it appears to be a sermon, is not considered here.

CHAPTER 3

been fired by unnamed VDL people, a continuation of the burning practices which had been used for generations to modify VDL land for hunting. Walter Arthur, recently released from jail, had been included in the party, not as a reward for previous loyalty, but, as the Commandant said plainly, 'to punish him by making him carry a pack as well as to keep him out of further mischief in my absence'.[183]

The journey was laborious, and the Commandant pushed the party on relentlessly. If the first day was hard, with the heat and charred landscape, the second day was worse. They reached the east coast of the island, after a river crossing almost drowned one of the men, Richard, also known as Cranky Dick.[184] The party went on a 'devious and circuitous' route through 'impervious scrub and deep lagoons'. This land was alien to Robinson, but well known to the VDL community, especially the women. That second night, as on the first, the party camped and enjoyed the fruit of the hunt.

Robinson's journals of the expedition, which go into remarkable detail, are strangely silent on what transpired during the third day. By the third night, however, at a location the Sealing Women called Sally Lagoon, a crisis developed. The VDL party, which included his most loyal and longstanding guides Doctor Wooreddy and Trugernanner, turned on Robinson – in their own, very passive way. Complaining that on the previous day the group had been 'inattentive to my wants', even though they had given him food at every previous encampment- he wrote:

---

183   Robinson's journal, 12 December 1837, *Weep in Silence*, 509.
184   Teengerreenneener/Roonthadauna/Dick/Cranky Dick/Brumby's Dick/Pompy. Born around 1810, Ben Lomond, said to be 'imbecile of mind' or 'halfwitted' (perhaps suffering seizures), but entrusted on multiple Friendly Missions as guide. Often worked as shepherd on smaller islands during Wybalenna period: *Weep in Silence*, 849.

> ... tonight they were worse than heretofore. They had four swans, an abundance of kangaroo, ducks, teal, etc. and never prepared me a morsel nor made me a shelter wherein to sleep nor made my tea nor damper bread. These I did myself. I was exceedingly displeased at their negligence, at their careless indifference and their ingratitude.[185]

Whatever Robinson's motivation in gathering together the Friendly Mission group, it appeared to have backfired. The refusal of even his most loyal attendants to share their food with him is striking. Yet again, we may refer to James C. Scott's list of tactics employed by powerless people unable or unwilling to display outright defiance – 'foot dragging, dissimulation, desertion, false compliance, pilfering, feigned ignorance'.[186] To this, we might add, refusing to share food. The following morning, Robinson appears to have finally admitted to himself that his moral standing with this important group of VDL leaders and diplomats was at an end.

The Commandant abandoned the trek altogether. He gathered the five men who he still considered loyal, or who had no say in the matter – Walter, Isaac, Richard, Edward,[187] and Albert[188] – and the group began the arduous walk back to Wybalenna. Walter Arthur again served as the Commandant's unwilling pack-horse. The other ten men and women who comprised the party remained in the bush, at their leisure.

The two-day trek back to the settlement was severe. The heat was oppressive, and their route through the burnt forest yielded no water.

---

185 Robinson's journal, 14 December 1837, *Weep in Silence*, 511.
186 Scott, *Weapons of the Weak*, xiv.
187 Leepunner/Little Billy/Edward. From Macquarie Harbour, South West, born around 1817, confusion as to his original identity (Plomley lists three possibilities): *Weep in Silence*, 842.
188 Warwe/Wowwee/Albert, from either Big River or Port Sorrell, born around 1810. One of the Parker-Thomas killers: *Weep in Silence*, 835, 837.

CHAPTER 3

They were plagued by mosquitos, sand-flies and stinging insects. The dogs belonging to the VDL trekkers refused to go on in such conditions, and remained in the bush. The following day, 16 December, was even hotter. In Hobart, Reverend Knopwood remarked that it was 108 degrees in the shade, and the heat had destroyed many fruits and vegetables.[189] For the Commandant, leading his reduced party through the rough Flinders Island scrub after a disastrous mission, it must have been almost unbearable. Robinson, Arthur and others suffered frequent nosebleeds. Their clothes were torn and their skin and throats were coated with charcoal from battling through the burnt forest. Robinson's dog remained in the bush, unable to continue, its tongue lolling out of its mouth and foaming.[190] On every level, the trip was a disaster.

Robinson, Arthur and the four other men arrived back on the settlement late on 16 December. The slighted, furious Commandant told all and sundry about the greediness of the ingrates, and when the quietly defiant party eventually returned, three days later, he reproved them yet again. It is no surprise, then, that the edition of the *Chronicle* that was produced in the wake of this debacle, dated 21 December but also depicting events from 22 December, would feature the injustice perpetrated by those who would not share their food.

Tellingly, in his *Chronicle* Thomas Brune took aim at Doctor Wooreddy (calling him by his endowed name, 'Alpha'). He was openly chastised for taking a swan away from Richard, roasting it in the fire, and then only giving Richard a bone. Wooreddy, due to his age and position, had long been a confidante of Robinson, and it was

---

189   Knopwood's diary, 16 December 1837, in Nicholls, *The Diary of the Reverend Robert Knopwood*, 673.
190   Full account in Robinson's journal, 12–16 December 1837, *Weep in Silence*, 509-514.

probably his betrayal that stung the most. Brune detailed the generosity of the Commandant and the greed of the VDL party in tones approaching the feverish:

> ... why dident you give the Commandant a pice of kangaroo
> No you would not because you was so greedy
> you was like hogs eating away as fast as you could
> you throwed it on the fire as quick as you can
> incase that the Commandant should wanted a pices of it ...[191]

This was followed by a threat: if they did not improve their behaviour, the Commandant would be angry. He would not give them anything anymore, and would leave so they would have to get another Commandant. The issue of the cow in the garden which had so enraged Robinson was raised again, and the people chastised for playing marbles and games. One moment, Thomas encouraged the people to love the Commandant: the next, he commanded fear:

> The Commandant his majistrate over this Island
> he dont let the people be master over him while he his on the island and he certainly will not be given them any things any more ...[192]

We can only speculate on the issues that inspired the great food rebellion, which incensed an already vexed Commandant. It is very likely linked to issues of protocol, or what Broome calls right behaviour, and sovereignty. This trip had been an invasion: Robinson had forced them to bring him into their own VDL space, uninvited. These areas of the island were well known as hunting spots by the exiled VDL people, and retreats from the surveillance of the settlement. They were bush places where traditional lifestyle and business

---

191 Thomas Brune, *Flinders Island Chronicle*, 21 December 1837, ML A7073, Vol. 52, part 4, 75.
192 Ibid.

were conducted: places to heal, experience privacy, conduct ceremony, and access food. They were places of last resort. After all the deaths and broken promises, the Commandant's encroachment represented a very real infringement on VDL rights over land. And because most of the group had accompanied him on the Friendly Missions, it must have seemed like history repeating itself.

Finally, this issue of the *Chronicle* raised the issue of forced work. Robinson was certainly in a mood to punish the people. Thomas Brune described some women who had carried grass for several mornings and received payment for it, then added:

> … when the peoples work they will get money for it and if they dont work they cant have nothing if they dont work at all they cant have any things
> No they cant at all.[193]

As we will see from events which would take place eight years later, this attitude – that VDL people must work for their keep – is the same sentiment which would spark a rebellion against superintendent Henry Jeanneret. But Thomas Brune, in 1837, was too young and powerless to openly challenge a furious Commandant. In this angry, resentful and potentially volatile atmosphere, the *Flinders Island Chronicle* was at an end.

Summary

The *Flinders Island Chronicle* was all but ignored by scholars for one hundred and fifty years, and has still had relatively little serious attention. N. J. B. Plomley was the first historian to publish several issues of the *Chronicle*, and commented that although it was a mere

---

193   Ibid.

vehicle for Robinson, 'Nevertheless a little of the Aboriginal peeps through occasionally'.[194] Michael Rose brought the *Chronicle* to wider attention in 1996 in his survey of Indigenous print journalism, *For the Record*, highlighting the 'many very valuable and revealing elements of straightforward reportage'.[195] Penny Van Toorn's analysis of the *Chronicle* finds it 'ventriloquised by Robinson' for a colonial audience, and Lyndall Ryan's brief assessment draws attention to its revelations of the determination of the adult exiles to retain culture.[196] Greg Lehman positioned the authors, quite rightly, as writing 'from the ruins of a culture'.[197] Elizabeth Burrows's recent media study highlights self-censorship, suggesting this may be an act of resistance.[198] Murray Johnson and Ian McFarlane even more recently deride the *Chronicle* as 'substandard by any measure'.[199] Elsewhere, the *Chronicle* is dismissed as 'an admirable idea, theoretically sound but useless in practice', and its writers 'mouthpieces of Robinson's propaganda'.[200]

The most evocative interpretation of the *Chronicle* is by Mudrooroo, in his novel *Doctor Wooreddy's Prescription for Enduring the Ending of the World*. The reader joins Doctor Wooreddy as he finds a quiet spot and sits down, a copy of the *Chronicle* in his hand. He looks at the script and makes out some words – partly by his own recognition,

---

194 Plomley, *Weep in Silence*, 990-991.
195 Rose, *For the Record*, 2.
196 Van Toorn, *Writing Never Arrives Naked*, 103-111; Ryan, *Tasmanian Aborigines*, 230-232.
197 Lehman, 'Reconciling Ruin', 1.
198 Elizabeth Burrows, 'Resisting Oppression: The Use of Aboriginal Writing to Influence Public Opinion and Public Policy in Van Diemen's Land from 1836 to 1847', *Media History*, 2014. Published online, DOI: 10.1080/13688804.2014.925684.
199 Johnson and McFarlane, *Van Diemen's Land: An Aboriginal History*, 244.
200 Rae-Ellis, *Black Robinson*, 126; Morgan, *Aboriginal Education in the Furneaux Islands*, 104.

CHAPTER 3

and also from hearing the young writer repeat the phrases as he copied them from Robinson's draft. It is the edition from 17 November 1837, with the plea to the King:

> He stared down at the black marks and his eyes went through them to the twenty-nine people that had recently died, leaving the sick behind to suffer and recover listlessly.[201]

Mudrooroo's reading, through the Doctor's eyes, illustrates the paradox of life at Wybalenna in 1837 which is revealed through the *Flinders Island Chronicle*. The fictionalised Doctor ruminates on the document's content, which highlights the prevailing mortality at the settlement. This part is clear, and indisputable.

However, he needed to find a quiet spot to do it. In spite of the ongoing tragedy, the bold and visionary undertaking which was the *Chronicle* illustrates that Wybalenna was a busy, noisy and complex place. It offers a greater depth of knowledge of what might have been occupying Doctor Wooreddy's thoughts as he looked down at the black marks. Through the *Chronicle*, we can almost begin to imagine the cacophony of people and languages, work and games, unions and enmities, and gossip and gammoning which surrounded him. The *Chronicle* illuminates this poorly understood period, affording a vivid and invaluable window into everyday life on the island.

---

201 Mudrooroo, *Doctor Wooreddy's Prescription*, 145.

Chapter 4

THE BATTLE FOR VDL SOULS

By January 1838, the battle for the physical Country of VDL Nations had been fought. The British colonisers – for a time at least – had won. The VDL mainland had largely been ethnically cleansed. There was at least one family group known to be living in the North West, in the lands occupied by the Van Diemen's Land Company's pastoral lease. Many VDL people still lived and worked within the colonisers' homes, farms and businesses, often having done so since childhood. Others, too – mainly women and children – lived on Bass Strait islands and further afield with European men. Some individuals, including children, had left VDL for the Australian mainland and beyond, in the busy maritime industry, and as part of colonising families. Others established careers and even businesses for themselves within the whaling industry. The homelands, however – where a complex range of cultures and languages had developed over tens of millennia – appeared lost to British control. For the victors, ruling the land was not enough. As we have seen by the recommendations of the Select Committee in London, there was still an important battle to be waged. To fully complete the imperial mission – though couched as compensation for the devastating loss – the next battle was for souls.

CHAPTER 4

Sin, Damnation and the Gnashing of Teeth: The Written Sermons

> ... there is black men in other Countries they know about God and Jesus Christ they dont have more instructions than what You have they can read the Bible and understand it.[1]

By the dawning of 1838, the *Flinders Island Chronicle* was history. Its two scribes had disappointed the Commandant to the extent of temporary incarceration. Walter George Arthur – in proclaiming himself as a man in the most obvious (and, in the Commandant's eyes, immoral) sense – was no longer as pliable a vessel as he once was. Thomas Brune, who emerges through the historical record as an earnest young man but perhaps lacking the confidence and sense of identity held by Walter Arthur, was clearly still a willing servant of whatever cause the Commandant wished of him. In a very real way this was Brune's only option: not having Arthur's family links, shrewd intellect or new masculine status, Brune's allegiance to the Commandant was much more vital to his social security.

These were days of transition at Wybalenna. It had grown to be much more than a mere staging point of exile, or temporary encampment. Yet some of the revolutionary social experiments undertaken over the last eighteen months had begun to unravel. Wybalenna was no longer the community which boasted its own newspaper, and an ostensibly friendly relationship with its Commandant. The falling-out of important Friendly Mission leaders and the Commandant – so simply but dramatically illustrated with the failure to share food on the 'Unfriendly Mission' just weeks previous – showed a fracture of trust. Yet some of the old institutions remained. The literary

---

1   Thomas Brune, Sermon, 28 January 1838, QVMAG CY825-77.

productions of January 1838 function as a kind of bridging series to a new type of text, and community.

Throughout the first week in January, the two young scribes Arthur and Brune kept up their usual, almost competitive, writing. In 1838, however, their medium was written sermons. This was not a new genre: these documents began appearing around the same time the *Chronicle* was revived in September 1837, and bear a striking physical resemblance to the handwritten newspaper. But for the headline – now, simply 'Sermon' or 'The Sermon' – at first glance they appear identical. Both sermons and *Chronicles* were signed off with the author's name, either Thomas Brune or Walter George Arthur, then 'Aboriginal Youth, Editor and Writer'. However, while the *Chronicle* encompassed daily life on the settlement as its main subject matter in later 1837, the concerns of the sermons were entirely religious.

This reflects a trend began around October 1837, when the program to culturally colonise the exiled VDL population diversified. During the vice-regal reign of Sir George Arthur, the Christian and civilising mission were one in the same thing. In the erstwhile Governor's mind, civilisation could *only* follow Christianisation. He would not broach any other possibility. However, in September 1837 a new, more secular, Lieutenant Governor, Sir John Franklin, was in power. Franklin was certainly less imbued with a sense of humanitarian responsibility than Sir George Arthur. He was also no Evangelical Christian. Perhaps in response to this change of vice-regal direction, the two heads of the colonial beast began to splinter.

If the *Chronicle* can be seen as symbolising the civilising mission, then the sermons represent the Christianising mission. The *Chronicle* initially featured heavy sermonising, but quickly became focused on daily settlement life. This was a period of frenetic activity on

CHAPTER 4

Flinders Island: VDL people were getting sick, dying, going hunting for extended periods, and spontaneously adopting Christian and 'civilised' habits where desired. The unmarried women were the source of a moral panic for both VDL men and the Commandant, and it is around this time that more written sermons appear in the record. The spiritual concerns were now separately recorded.

Walter Arthur and Thomas Brune were seventeen and fourteen respectively when the first sermons were produced, and at times their testaments, like the *Chronicles*, brim with youth and zeal. The sermons were written at first in tandem with the *Chronicle* – sometimes on the same days – but with divergent concerns. On 14 November 1837, for example, Thomas Brune wrote a short, very matter-of-fact *Chronicle* which chastised men for playing marbles instead of working, and detailed general comings and goings on the settlement. In contrast, his sermon for that day was concerned primarily with Christ's interceding role, and the omnipotence and invisibility of God, the King of Kings:

> And now my friends you know that there is a God over you but where is God you cannot see him No my friends you cannot see him God all over ble∫sed forever more.[2]

Two days later, Brune wrote of Christ as 'our mediator and redeemer which was crucified on the tree for our sins'.[3] This sermon might have been written in November 1837, or March 1838, because, without any external temporal markers – for example, noting events at the settlement – the messages were all essentially the same. VDL people had to fear God, love God, love Christ who had died for them, learn to read the Bible, and pray. God's country was good, and

---

2   Thomas Brune, Sermon, 14 November 1837, QVMAG CY825-119.
3   Thomas Brune, Sermon, 16 December 1837, QVMAG CY825-73.

the Devil's country was bad. Salvation was in the Book. The sermons were almost certainly an adjunct, or supporting device, to the key themes raised week to week in Robert Clark's services. The sermons, then, remain roundly the same from late 1837, when they were written parallel to the *Chronicle*, through to early 1838, when they were the only production.

The main change was what VDL people were hearing. No longer were their own affairs seemingly worthy of being reported: now, it was only Christianity. It is as if, from the final *Chronicle* – that stinging rebuke of those who refused to share food with the Commandant – the community was being punished by not having its own news reflected. From that date forward, there was only indoctrination.

Only twice, in the first week of January 1838, was news from the settlement reflected in the written sermons. Both Thomas Brune and Walter Arthur noted two deaths which had occurred. Brune wrote, 'There is two of our brothers died and we shall die very soon ourselves God will cut us off if we go on in our wickedneſs'.[4] From a sermon written around the same time, Walter Arthur also wrote, 'And now my friends you all see that there are two of our Brothers which have died within this week which I hope is gone to Glory'.[5] The deceased were the young Western Nations man Benjamin,[6] and older man Constantine.[7] They both passed away on 29 December 1837, of meningitis and tuberculosis respectively.[8]

---

4   Thomas Brune, Sermon, 2 January 1838, QVMAG CY825-123.
5   Walter George Arthur, Sermon, undated (January 1838), QVMAG CY825-117.
6   Pendewurrewic/Pendemurrernuic/Corinpardune/Ben/Benjamin. Born around 1817, Macquarie Harbour, *Weep in Silence*, 838-839; North West nation: *Beyond Awakening*, 238.
7   Mokerminner/Makeduru/Big Jacky/Big Jack/Constantine. Very little information on record: *Weep in Silence*, 841.
8   Dr Walsh's records lack detail, but Robinson's journals hint at these causes. Robinson's Letterbook QVMAG CY548.

CHAPTER 4

Walter Arthur's sermon from this first week in January – one of his last – is also one of the final examples of the specific shaming of women. He writes:

> … that work that some of you women was going on with the other night was most abominable in the way that you was going on the other night do you think you will go to heaven when you die no my friends you need not to think of that fine place after you have been offended God who was so kind to you after all see how the way you are agoing on in you wickednefs.[9]

'That work' to which he refers is almost certainly the series of events detailed in the Commandant's journals. It was yet another episode on the long-running saga of the women who refused to be married – or at least, to one man at a time. Robinson reported, in somewhat guarded language, how Flora, Emma, Matilda and Rebecca[10] had been the centre of trouble because one of them (he does not specify) had been chosen as a wife by Alphonso,[11] a Big River man:

> This lady complained of the hardship of her being compelled to confine her favours to one VIBER when the other three women were left to the liberty of their choice.[12]

A protracted series of negotiations ensued, with a complexity to rival any modern soap opera. One eligible young man, Isaac, was being sought in earnest by Ann, to the extent that he had taken refuge in another man's house, and even hiding in the bush, to

---

9   Walter George Arthur, undated Sermon (January 1838), QVMAG CY825-117.
10 Meerterlatteenner/Meterlatteyar/Big Sally/Thomson's Sall/Sally/Rebecca. Born around 1803, Coastal Plains nation. Ex-Tyereelore: *Weep in Silence*, 867; *Grease and Ochre*, 135.
11 Neernnerpatterlargener/Meenerkerpackerminer/Mannapackername/Meenabaekamenna/Big Jemmy. Born around 1807, Big River. 'Knife scar on belly': *Weep in Silence*, 838; listed as Native of Port Sorell, wife Jemima: *Friendly Mission*, 1019.
12 Robinson's journal, 6 January 1838, *Weep in Silence*, 518-519.

escape her. It was decided he should instead have Matilda, one of the recalcitrants, as he had 'sighed long for her'. The overlooked Ann, irate and demanding a husband, was at first 'given' Frederick. However, Rebecca – another one of the reluctant brides – insisted Ann have Edmund, who she had been allotted but did not fancy. Various complicated transactions ensued, with King George and the Commandant offering suggestions, but the key deciding parties being the women themselves.

The women demonstrate a remarkable degree of agency in deciding who they wanted to marry, if at all. This high level of consent was a far cry from the forced marriages of August 1837, and seems the only way to avoid the 'abominable' behaviour noted by Walter Arthur in his sermon which, in all likelihood, was lewdness and adultery. Underlying the discussions on morality and female sexuality was European frustration at continuity of culture: ochre was still getting to Wybalenna, and practices such as the 'obscene dance', invented years earlier by Mother Brown, were still conducted. The 'wickedness' of the women, and their determination to control their own affairs, are a constant of both VDL and European records at Wybalenna.

This glimmer of insight into daily life – where the writings of VDL people work to corroborate European accounts – become all too rare after January 1838. In an undated sermon, but certainly from this time, Walter Arthur hints at unrest among the women with his advice, 'don't be Growling and Fighting and tearing each others frocks'; then, in the language of the day, adds, 'and when you at Hell you will always Tormented in the land that beneath with fire and Brimstone for ever and ever'.[13] Thomas Brune also raises a similar fate, advising,

---

13 Walter Arthur, undated Sermon (January 1838), QVMAG CY825-109.

CHAPTER 4

'The Devil will take you to hell and after You will be crying and weeping and nashing of teeth and be in pain for ever and ever'.[14] The written sermons were, on the whole, focused on the key concerns seen fit to impart in a religious context of that time: God, Christ, sin, suffering, heaven and hell, death, condemnation and prayer. Familiar and terrifying imagery was constantly repeated, as Thomas Brune again told his Countrypeople:

> ... he will come again to call us to account for all the things that we have done in our bodies whether they we good or bad ... if you are good you will have eternale life if you are bad you will have eternale punishment there you will be burning for ever and ever crying and weeping and nashing of teeth.[15]

As the month of January wore on, with no *Chronicle* and few hints in the sermons as to events at Wybalenna, Robinson's journals supply the only sense of events on the ground. In one instance, the catechist Clark tells him of a herb the women have been using to induce miscarriage. This significant information – which may go a long way to explain the very low birth rates at Wybalenna over the course of its history – is dismissed out of hand by the Commandant as 'Fudge!'[16] On 11 January, there was yet another 'fracas' regarding marriages, and on the following night yet another death, that of William Robinson in cottage 18.[17] One week later, Walter Arthur – once the Commandant's great hope – was charged with stealing knives from the store, and sentenced on 22 January by the VDL court to wear leg irons for four days. However, it is unlikely he served the entire

---

14 Thomas Brune, undated Sermon (January 1838), QVMAG CY825-87.
15 Thomas Brune, Sermon, 4 January 1838, QVMAG CY825-127.
16 Robinson's journal, *Weep in Silence*, 520.
17 William Robinson (Pannabuke) was one of the four 'intelligent' men, noted at the May 1837 school examinations.

sentence, as a long-awaited and celebrated event occurred before his sentence was over.

On 25 January 1838, two ships – the *Shamrock* and the *Eliza* – anchored off the settlement. Among the *Shamrock*'s key cargo was a man who would have a profound effect on the spiritual and social future of the settlement – its first official minister, Reverend Thomas Dove. Until now, the exiles had made do with untrained evangelicals of the frontier missionary variety, such as Wilkinson and Clark, at the former Governor's direction. The new Governor, Franklin, had seen fit to send an ordained man. The letter advising Robert Clark that he had been made redundant would not arrive for another week. This in itself would have caused a sensation, but for the illustrious cargo in the *Eliza*: the new Governor, Sir John Franklin, complete with his wife Lady Jane, his secretary Machonochie, and a large, auspicious party.

The visit was recorded in minute detail in the Commandant's journal. As is to be expected, this information is chiefly concerned with his own interests. However, it is possible to trace the participation of the VDL exiles, and speculate on what might have been significant for them. From first light – when reports of the *Eliza's* imminent arrival began to circulate – the community went into a frenzy of activity. The VDL cottages were thoroughly cleaned, and the fronts of them tidied. It is not clear who performed this work, but given the very regular chastisements in the *Flinders Island Chronicle* for the VDL people to clean their houses, we might assume that Europeans took responsibility, under the orders of the Commandant. If there is one thing we can be almost certain of at Wybalenna – besides the fact that people could not be stopped going bush – it is that people could not be forced to clean their houses.

CHAPTER 4

As the evening progressed, Robinson waited at the beach for the vice-regal party. Perhaps to avoid a scene of total chaos at the arrival, he had decided not to have the entire population attend, 'although they were all in their new attire and only required the attendance of the three kings in their full dress ... on landing the Governor was met by the three kings George, Alfred and Alpha, and by them welcomed to the settlement'.[18] The party then walked to the settlement, and due to the brevity of the Franklins' visit, an exhibition was arranged immediately:

> They were highly gratified by the various dances of the natives, and the natives were equally pleased with their visit. The Governor and Lady Franklin asked a variety of questions relative to the aborigines and their customs and amusements and seemed to heartily participate in their hilarity ... The natives exhibited their war dance, kangaroo ditto, emu ditto, horse ditto, and a variety of others.[19]

The Commandant's journal records, in minute detail, the domestic arrangements for the visit, his impressions of each of the party, and the shock which the Reverend Dove's unexpected arrival had caused Robert Clark. However, he does not give us any real indication of how the VDL exiles viewed the visitors or, indeed, how the visitors viewed the exiles, save for amusement. His record of the following day, likewise, is heavy on domestic comings and goings and the naming of European actors, but quite sparse with individual VDL people.

The following morning, 26 January, meetings, reviews and a series of inspections of the settlement occupied the time of the visiting party. This culminated in a visit to the school, where the exiles were

---

18   Robinson's journal, 25 January 1838, *Weep in Silence*, 524.
19   Ibid., 525.

assembled in their newly-issued clothing. Again, despite Robinson's detailed descriptions of the visit, only rarely do VDL individuals step out as protagonists. He records Thomas Brune (as only 'Brune') reading the roll call in the school: then, after a number of hymns were sung:

> … several of the natives exhorted their countrymen partly in their own and partly in the English language. Nome excited the greatest attention.[20]

Yet again, Noemy was singled out above all the other VDL men. Other VDL people are mentioned directly as having met, or been brought to the attention of the visitors, include Peter Bruny, son of Wooreddy, whose skills as an apprentice tailor were extolled; young Johnny Franklin, whose name caused 'a little risibility' in the party; and Ajax, who joined the visitors on a walk up Mount Franklin to see the sunset (and was used as a messenger). There were exhibitions such as a large mock war dance and battle, and, on the second night – a very warm and still one – a spontaneous torch-lit outdoor concert. It had begun in the schoolhouse, and gathered more numbers as it reached the square, where, according to Robinson, the singing:

> … was now a complete medley; some were singing, others were bawling, others talking, adding to what were the monotonous notes of the harmonicas which the native performers considered as sounds of sweetest melody. All this was certainly characteristic of the people and was what might have been expected from a number of savages and remnants of different tribes.[21]

The Franklins and their companions spent barely twenty-four hours at Wybalenna. They left in the evening on January 26, fifty

---

20   Ibid., 526
21   Ibid., 529.

CHAPTER 4

years to the day of Europeans first arriving on Eora land. This anniversary was nowhere mentioned. According to Robinson's journal, all visitors praised his administration of the settlement. They left as they arrived – in the evening, and in haste, with many administrative edicts, and several requests. Lady Franklin wanted a child or two, and the Governor, Lady Franklin and Captain Machonocie all wanted skulls of VDL people. These requests were certainly not bizarre by 1830s standards, and would, as we will later see, be fulfilled.

The Governor's visit does not seem to have excited any great interest on the VDL mainland, with the Launceston press later announcing:

> Sir John Franklin and suite returned to Launceston from his visit to Flinders on Sunday last, in the Government schooner yacht Eliza. We learn that His Excellency expressed himself much pleased with the aboriginal establishment, under the management of Mr. Robinson, the minutiae of which he personally inspected.[22]

While we do not have a VDL First Nations perspective of this significant visit, we can read certain behaviours – especially the cacophonous singing so vividly described by Robinson above – as signals of genuine excitement. This would certainly have been the biggest event to happen at Wybalenna for a long, long time. From the exiles' point of view, they had new clothes, cleaned houses, gifts, feasts and parties. While none of this was to make up for the exile they were enduring, the break in monotony would, at least, have been welcomed, as it was for the Europeans. For the three Kings, getting to officially greet the Queen's representative would also have been an important procedure. They also would have spent some time

---

22 The *Cornwall Chronicle*, 3 February 1838, Vol. 4, 18 (p. 2 of edition). This report was, however, syndicated and repeated on the Australian mainland.

watching the new Governor, to gauge his character. In welcoming Franklin to Wybalenna, they were establishing a complex relationship with the Governor, who represented their symbolic father, and was now tied in to expectations of reciprocity.

It was not such a good visit for Robert Clark, the Wybalenna catechist. With no warning, he had discovered his position no longer existed, as the Reverend Thomas Dove had been appointed to look after the spiritual needs of the VDL exiles. To make matters worse, there was no time to adjust, as Dove and his wife had arrived with the vice-regal party. For Clark, who in his four years had developed close personal relationships with the VDL people, as well as language awareness second to none, this came as a shock. Without doubt a man on a mission, he had imagined spending many more years, or perhaps the rest of his life, with VDL people. Although assured by Franklin that he may remain at Wybalenna for now, the future, for this Irish schoolteacher who had heard the missionary call, remained uncertain.

The replacement of Robert Clark, the untrained catechist, with Thomas Dove, the ordained Presbyterian minister, is a pivotal moment in Wybalenna history – certainly of more long-term significance than the vice-regal visit. It marks a departure from Sir George Arthur's maxim that a common-bred, roughened missionary was preferable to a gentlemanly minister for work on the moral frontier. In being sent a 'proper' minister, the Wybalenna community was being told it was no longer on the frontier, or an uncouth penal settlement. It had, to a degree, been civilised: the heathen minds had been cultivated to enough of an extent to accept more civilised words.

This was a first for the VDL community. The religious onslaught which had so far confronted and attempted to convert them had

CHAPTER 4

been strongly evangelical, and untrained. From the 1829 mission by then-lay preacher Robinson at Bruny Island, to their now-erstwhile catechist Robert Clark, the VDL people who were under official 'protection' had almost exclusively dealt with the unordained. To these men, and their often redoubtable wives, the Word was much mightier than the institution of the church. They were gathering souls for God, not exclusively for any one specific denomination.

Thomas Dove represented a very different culture and approach. A Glaswegian in his mid-thirties, he studied at the University of Glasgow, and emigrated to Van Diemen's Land in 1835. There he met his wife Dora, who he married in 1837, before taking up a position at Oatlands, and then accepting the Wybalenna role.[23] As an educated, presumably gentleman preacher, he would initially have been welcomed by Robinson. However, from the outset, the Doves alienated all those around them. The VDL population likely looked forward to his first service, as any new face was a talking point in an isolated community. However, Dove's first scheduled morning service, on 28 January, was to disappoint at least the Commandant, as the Reverend did not attend. His preaching in the evening service of that day did not excite any comment at all, but Robinson's journals were soon marked by disapproving comments about the new Chaplain. Reverend Dove flatly refused to undertake the schoolmaster role, or to have the children live with him. He rarely, in the early months, had contact with the VDL exiles.

Robert Clark remained physically at the settlement, only receiving word on 31 January of losing his job. Over the next few months, the insecurity of his situation clearly began to affect the former catechist's

---

23   R. S. Miller, *Thomas Dove and the Tasmanian Aborigines*, Melbourne, Spectrum Publications, 1985.

activities. This in turn eroded the social standing of the young VDL scribes Thomas Brune and Walter Arthur. While the Commandant and the catechist had served as mentors to them, the new Chaplain seemed to encourage no such relationship. With no more *Flinders Island Chronicles* to monitor the influence of a new spiritual guide, we can perhaps still see the exhortation style of Robert Clark (said by the Commandant to, at times, be a ranting strain)[24] reflected in Thomas Brune's written sermon from this period: a sermon committed to paper, but certainly, with its interrogative style, designed to be read aloud:

> Do you think my friends that God his very good
> yes my friends
> and dont you think that Jesus is very Good
> yes and my friends dont you know that there is three persons in the Godhead
> perhaps you might say who are they
> why I should say the Father Son and Holy Ghost these are all one the Father his equal to the Son and the Son is equal to the Holy Ghost and these three all agree in one.[25]

One of the new Chaplain's first activities was to preside over school examinations. Beginning on 9 February 1838, these took place over several days, and reflect a different mode than the previous tests recorded. Most of the interrogations were conducted in groups, with questions being put to individuals at random. Only a few individuals – most noticeably Leonidas and Neptune – received questioning at length. In the earlier examinations, people were questioned individually, and the records give personal reflections on each participant. Here – undoubtedly as the new Chaplain had not yet

---

24   Robinson's journal, 28 January 1838, *Weep in Silence*, 531.
25   Thomas Brune, Sermon, 7 February 1838, QVMAG CY825-81.

CHAPTER 4

developed these personal relationships and estimations – there is much less information on each person.

Leonidas is one individual whose examination goes against this trend. Nine months ago, only six questions had been put to him, and the only comments on him had been 'This man is well conducted and attentive in his work'.[26] This may well have been caution on the Commandant's part, as Leonidas, a former Big River warrior, was one of the infamous Parker-Thomas killers of 1831. Seven years later, and now aged in his mid-twenties, Leonidas had clearly embraced Christianity, and answered over seventy of Reverend Dove's questions. There is a rare hint of VDL language with the questions, *'Where was Jesus Christ Born?* In Bethlehem. *In what place?* A stable. *What is a stable?* Pacarthene Librunny, a horse house'.[27]

As with many of the other VDL people, the Genesis foundation stories resonated, and Leonidas demonstrated knowledge of deluge, Noah's tribulations, heaven and hell, the importance of the Bible, plus the unquestioned VDL favourite story of Cain and Abel. Perhaps through the Cain and Abel story, VDL people – whose cultural practice, as far as is known, did not feature blood sacrifice – may have identified with Cain. The Christian God's rejection of him for not offering a blood sacrifice when ordered may have inspired sympathy. Cain's eternal exile had the potential to relate to VDL peoples' life experiences, where they were forced into the position of being fugitives in their own land. VDL people may alternatively have identified with Abel, who was wronged despite being an innocent. The Edenic archetypes of Adam and Eve may also have resonated with VDL creation or traditional stories which remain unknown to us.

---

26 May 1837 school examinations. Robinson Letterbook QVMAG CY548.
27 Leonidas, 12 February 1838, Robinson Letterbook QVMAG CY548.

Leonidas's examination, while confirming a VDL interest in those previously important stories of family, kin, adversity and cataclysm, also contains indications of a new ideological trend likely introduced by Reverend Dove. The question is put to Leonidas, 'Who crucified Jesus?' And he responds, 'The Jews'. This same question – eliciting the same response – was also put to Neptune, Noemy and others, and the theme further carried with the boy Thomas Thompson, who was asked 'What did the Jews do to Jesus before they crucified him?' to which he answered, 'Put a crown of thorns on his head'.

This clear line of questioning was new. In the May 1837 examinations, 'The Jews' were noted as God's favourite people, the Children of Israel, who were protected by God and led from bondage by Moses.[28] Theirs was clearly a heroic story, and perhaps served as an allegory for the VDL people being led to safety by the Commandant. Wybalenna was, after all, a Promised Land. Less than a year later, Jewish people were not the dispossessed and long-suffering heroes who VDL people might relate to, but villains. This dramatic change might be attributed to Dove's influence; a man recently arrived to the colonies from a Europe rapidly becoming more anti-Semitic. It also, importantly, absolves the occupying Roman colonists, personified by Pontius Pilate, of responsibility – an ideological turn with important ramifications for a people, such as the VDL exiles, dispossessed by a colonial empire.

Neptune is another young man who, like Leonidas, appears to have flourished in the months between the May 1837 examinations, and those of 1838. In the previous test, he answered only seven questions, and was described by Robinson as 'a young man, tall and well made

---

28 Questions put to Walter Arthur and Thomas Brune in the May 1837 examinations.

CHAPTER 4

… well conducted and industrious'.[29] Eight months later, when examined by Dove, Neptune answered over seventy questions, showing a wide-ranging knowledge of Genesis, plus New Testament texts; he was the only VDL exile posed the question, 'Who was struck dead for telling a lie?' to which he replied 'Ananias & Saphira his wife'. As we will later see, Neptune also took on a leading role in delivering sermons to the VDL community.

Other men demonstrate a clear increase in their ability to answer questions, including Washington, Peter Pindar, and Alexander. Oyster Bay man Tippo Saib evidences a detailed knowledge of the story of Noah, exemplifying the interest shown in this particular story by the VDL community in general. In addition to the basics of the story – God's warning to Noah, his instructions regarding the ark and the length of the deluge – he also cited the names of Noah's three sons.

Another interviewee of note was Napoleon (Tunnerminnerwait), a Friendly Mission veteran who had been absent, on the VDL mainland with Charles Robinson, during the 1837 examinations. This enigmatic young man from Cape Grim, on the North West coast, had already been immortalised in a portrait by Thomas Bock, and was notable for being the only VDL exile, among those already well known portraits, depicted broadly smiling. Later to become relatively famous in Port Phillip, his answers to the twenty-five questions put by the new Chaplain reveal a broad, basic knowledge of the key ideas presented to VDL people at Wybalenna. He is the only person asked 'Who was the strongest man?' to which he replied 'Samson'.

The examination of the women under Reverend Dove seemed to be fraught with problems. Instead of being interviewed separately, as

---

29   Robinson Letterbook QVMAG CY548.

previously, they were seen as a group, and generally only answered one or two questions each at a time. There are nowhere near the detailed, individual glimpses we were able to achieve in the earlier examinations, and so prohibits any definitive estimation as to whether they had gained the increase in general Biblical knowledge that some of the men seemed to display. Certainly, the brief comments about their literacy gains seem to imply that many of them knew the alphabet and some could read with a basic proficiency. Interestingly, while the same stories of Adam and Eve, Cain and Abel, and the deluge were clearly well known, the women also mention, among those saved, the wives of Noah and his three sons.

There were clear issues with the women's willingness to participate. The large classes led by Mrs Clark, wife of the recently deposed catechist, were for one session very compliant, but at a later questioning were 'very sulky' and refused to answer questions.[30] The students led by Mary ann, affianced to Walter Arthur, deliberately avoided their first examination on 15 February, and only reluctantly partook on the following day. This hints at a number of problems which were building. Mrs Clark had been insulted by the behaviour of Reverend Dove's apparently difficult spouse, and, like her husband the former catechist, was very influential with the VDL exiles. Any insult to her would have been keenly felt by the people.

More generally, it appears that the Reverend Dove himself had not taken steps to ingratiate himself with the community, either VDL or European. He had already upset some of the Europeans at the settlement with 'strong and disrespectful allusions to the Catholic

---

30   This was noted by Dove in his comments, and by Robert Clark in his record of the examination: Robinson Letterbook QVMAG CY548.

CHAPTER 4

church',[31] so much so that the Catholics had been excused, by the Commandant, from attending further services. Mrs Dove had already insulted the Robinsons to the extent that Robinson's wife and daughter would not speak to her, and the Chaplain had created ill-feeling with Robinson's sons. There are hints of poor relationships developing with the VDL people too: the examinations record the new Chaplain addressing himself 'very feelingly' to individuals who had, in his eyes, neglected their instruction.[32] He also expressed annoyance that they were otherwise occupied, building a road, when expected for examinations.[33]

Dove's alienation from the community was self-imposed. He had refused to teach at the school, or house the children as the catechist had, and the Commandant's journal contains frequent complaints about him not visiting the sick. Tellingly, it would be several *months* before he visited VDL people in their homes. On 23 February, the Commandant records asking the VDL exiles (he does not record their gender or age) if they had enjoyed the examinations, and they fervently replied to the contrary, that 'they did not like the "damnation"'.[34] It is impossible not to compare this very poor early relationship with the close bonds developed with Robert Clark.

The questioning of the boys in the February examinations was similar to that of the women: they were quizzed in groups, rather than as individuals. Whereas in the previous examinations several of the boys had answered over one hundred questions, in quite astonishing detail, they were now only asked one or two questions at a time. This speaks

---

31 Robinson's journal, 17 February 1838: *Weep in Silence*, 534.
32 Dove to Achilles, recorded 16 February, Robinson Letterbook QVMAG CY548.
33 Work for which they were paid 'a considerable sum'. Detailed in the Flinders Island account books, in Robinson Letterbook QVMAG CY548.
34 Robinson's journal, 23 February 1838, *Weep in Silence*, 535.

to the new Presbyterian Chaplain's very patriarchal focus, and disinterest in young people. Tellingly – as with the previous examinations – the girls were not examined at all. When the examinations were finally presented to the Commandant in late February, he expressed pleasure with them in his journal, and then seems to have filed them away. These were the last, wide-scale surveys of their kind on the island. However, the Christianising mission at Wybalenna had one more very dramatic, and illuminating, genre of testimony to deliver.

'Put away your corroberries': The Spoken Sermons of the Men

> … you will not be old in Heaven you will always be young men there – there are no old men there you will never die there never sick never hungry never meet no bad people there no bad white men there …[35]

The night-time prayer meetings at Wybalenna are one of the least understood aspects of life on the island during the exile. As is clear by now, the Van Diemen's Land exiles exercised a great deal of control over their own movements, and they simply would not attend the school, the chapel, or the settlement itself, if their interests or affairs were engaged elsewhere. Therefore, it behoves us to take the records of these events seriously. Far from the characterisation by Robert Travers, which holds 'They probably just listened, much as do those poor derelicts of today, who pay for a bowl of soup by sitting through a Salvation Army service',[36] the VDL exiles were active and dynamic participants and leaders of the meetings.

From as early as 1836, the Commandant's journals made clear that VDL men were delivering spontaneous sermons at prayer meetings

---

35 Neptune, Sermon delivered 31 March 1838. Robinson Letterbook QVMAG CY548.
36 Travers, *The Tasmanians*, 208.

CHAPTER 4

in the chapel/school-house. Robert Clark had occasionally made records of these speeches, and Robinson himself had also regularly quoted several memorable lines or incidents. The Commandant's notes at these times were congratulatory, evidence of the apparent progress of the Christianising mission. However, in late February 1838, the recording of these sermons went from ad-hoc to formalised, and a new and short-lived program of committing them to posterity was initiated. This has bequeathed to us a rich, surprising and illuminating set of documents which, while not handwritten by VDL people, are most certainly as close to their own words as it is possible to be. We can glimpse how Christianity was interpreted, which aspects were important, and gain a more nuanced reading of an aspect of life at Wybalenna which has previously been derided as, in Plomley's words, 'a disaster, because it took away from the natives the whole basis of their being, without substituting anything which they could understand and which could give direction to their lives'.[37] What follows clearly contests that assessment.

The prayer meetings were held at night, and after an opening sermon by either the catechist or, lately, the new chaplain, one of the two young scribes – either Thomas Brune or Walter Arthur – would read from a written sermon. The floor would then be opened to men of the community. The records beginning in February 1838 show a range of men adopting this practice. This may well reflect traditional practice of elders speaking at meetings.

Speakers invariably addressed first their own Countrypeople in their own language, which was translated to Clark by female interpreters. They then spoke in what was euphemistically called 'the language of the settlement' – what linguist Terry Crowley called

---

37   Plomley, 'Robinson's Adventures in Bass Strait', 41.

the Flinders Island dialect. This was then interpreted by Clark into English, and written up as a report. These reports were usually given to Dove for his approval that they were correct. A newcomer to the settlement, Dove would have lacked experience with the lingua franca, so this is likely to have been a vetting process. These reports were then forwarded to Robinson, who stored them with his papers.[38]

Noemy was without doubt the most enthusiastic VDL preacher. His efforts had been noted since late 1836, and by February of 1838 he was a veteran. On 24 February 1838, as was the custom, he first implored his Countrymen not to steal from, lie to, or scold each other, his words translated by Bessy Clark. He then, according to Clark, told the general assembly:

> Women you should not scold one another clean your houses early in the morning, do not be sulky, put your bad tempers away from you. Love God. Love Jesus Christ. Do not remain so long in the bush when you go forever doing what is bad.[39]

Here, we have yet more proof of cultural continuity: the women 'doing what is bad' is likely code for some traditional ceremonial activity involving the use of ochre.

Neptune, another regular speaker, was more concerned with attendance, both in the school and at the settlement in general. He told the general assembly not to be lazy, and not to remain 'out there' (the bush). His attention was on the more senior figures:

> Why do not the old men come to school? I do not stay at home. I come to school … You people why do you like to walk about

---

38 These documents are now located within Robinson's Letterbook, Mitchell Library, Robinson Papers, MLA7044, Vol. 23. Cited here as seen from Robinson Letterbook at QVMAG, microfilm reel CY548.

39 Noemy, Sermon delivered 24 February 1838, Robinson Letterbook QVMAG CY548.

CHAPTER 4

at night. It is very bad. I remain in my house. Why don't you remain at home?[40]

These two glimpses echo similar earlier pleas in the *Flinders Island Chronicle*: the constant reminder to stay at the settlement and not in the bush. This indicates that despite the constant entreaties, bribes and stern warnings, the community was still very mobile – and defiant.

The next two weeks on the settlement were marked by two deaths. On 26 February, Ben Lomond man Christopher died of tuberculosis.[41] One of the many VDL people about whose identity there is some confusion, he had not taken part in the recent school 'damnations', but eight months ago, in the May 1837 examinations, Robinson had identified him as 'a quiet inoffensive man, a good husband and industrious'.[42] The following day, after his post-mortem, his head was removed and sent as a gift to Captain Machonochie, the Governor's private secretary – fulfilling the request made on his recent visit.[43] On 3 March there was another death, of the young woman Deborah, of pneumonia. The Wybalenna population continued to be slowly depleted by pulmonary diseases.

At the Saturday night meeting on 10 March, Noemy and Neptune were joined by Big River man Leonidas. Leonidas beseeched the community not to be lazy and to read the Bible, learn and pray. A more censorious tone was taken by Noemy, who chastised the women

---

40   Neptune, Sermon delivered 24 February 1838, Robinson Letterbook QVMAG CY548.
41   Metterluerurparrityer/Metatalyrerparrelcher/Dick/Christopher. Born around 1798, Ben Lomond nation: *Weep in Silence*, 840.
42   May 1837 school examinations. Robinson Letterbook QVMAG CY548.
43   This skull would have been defleshed and prepared before sending. Plomley suggests that this skull, as at 1987, was in the British Museum, listed under the collection of Lady Franklin.

for 'continuing to do which is improper when you go to the bush … God may take away your lives very soon for your wickedness. You go about the settlement some of you living like dogs'. Neptune implored his own people not to continue with 'these bad things, after a little time you will all die'. He then told the general community how they should always love God, and how:

> We do not know God at first. God made the white man come to tell us of Jesus Christ the Son of God. He came from Heaven to save sinners. God made man first of the dust of the ground and breathed into his nostrils the breath of life and man became a living soul.[44]

This line – from Genesis 2:7, about God breathing into nostrils and man becoming a living soul – recurs numerous times in the written sermons of Thomas Brune and Walter Arthur. It is a visual, visceral image, undoubtedly carried over from sermons also delivered by Robert Clark and probably the new Chaplain. The idea of a creator breathing into the nostrils of a man sits comfortably with other imagery which also proved very popular among the VDL people, such as the form of Adam being created from the dust (or, as commonly repeated, the 'dirt on the ground'), and Eve created from Adam's rib. We might speculate that this concept of life coming from the earth resonates with mainland creation stories such as the stories recorded by William Thomas of Bunjil creating man from bark and clay, and breathing life into the nostrils of man.[45]

Between this prayer meeting and the next, there was a major event at Wybalenna. It hosted its very first Christian wedding,

---

44 Neptune, Sermon delivered 10 March 1838, Robinson Letterbook QVMAG CY548.
45 Richard Cotter (ed.), *A cloud of hapless foreboding: Assistant Protector William Thomas and the Port Phillip Aborigines 1839–1840*, Sorrento, Nepean Historical Society, 2005, 73.

CHAPTER 4

between Walter George Arthur, son of King George of the Ben Lomond nation, and Mary ann Cochrane, daughter of Sarah, a former Tyereelore now settled at Wybalenna with a new husband, former warrior Eugene.[46] The wedding between Walter and Mary ann was a far cry from the euphemistic 'marriages' which had taken place many times, over the months and years, at Wybalenna. This was the first one to be presided over by an ordained minister, and became a very elaborate, symbolic affair.

A large feast was held, rivalled only by those held for the King's Birthday celebrations six months earlier, and the one held during the Governor's visit. The entire community, VDL and European, attended, dressed in their finest clothes. All present were regaled with food, wine, music and amusements. Boards were laid out in a forest clearing, and a procession was formed, led by the Chaplain and the Commandant, who wrote a very detailed account. They were followed by the eighteen-year-old bride Mary ann, who wore 'a headdress of ribbons and ostrich feathers and a gilt chain around her neck and other garish ornaments'.[47] She was escorted by Big River leader King Alfred who was, in the settlement's hierarchy, the senior man and the symbolic father. Then, a procession of a large number of VDL women followed, their hair adorned traditionally with flowers. A Presbyterian wedding ceremony ensued, and then a large banquet, where the VDL community were encouraged to drink to the couple. Robinson records the resulting scene:

---

46 Nicermenic/Nickamanick/Eugene. Born around 1810, from Circular Head, North West nation. Said to have a club foot or 'no toes'. Was a member of Walyer's renegade band: *Weep in Silence*, 812, 842.
47 Robinson's journal, 16 March 1838, *Weep in Silence*, 542.

> Four bottles of port wine was given to them to drink the health of the happy couple, and this part afforded much amusement especially as each party drank to the health of all present. Some said one thing, some said another, but as the natives find it difficult to pronounce the 's', the whole appeared to say instead of 'good health', 'got to hell', and in conclusion, 'go to hell all of you'.[48]

Given what we know about the love of gammoning at Wybalenna, and the sense of humour of many of the women which might be described as saucy, this apparent mispronunciation may well have been deliberate. This is exactly the kind of small act of resistance that James C. Scott referred to in his *Weapons of the Weak*, here playfully planted in an otherwise celebratory day. The wedding celebration included music, dancing in the European and VDL styles, feasting and games, all in 'mutual good humour and hilarity'. Sadly, there is no direct record from either of the happy couple of their reflections on the event. Walter Arthur was no longer producing the *Flinders Island Chronicle* or, apparently, writing sermons.[49] Clearly, this was an attempt to solidify the pair as a young, exemplary Christian couple in the community's eyes: a symbol of what they all might strive to be.

However, it is also possible – and quite tempting – to read a more pragmatic reasoning behind the Commandant's enthusiastic 'blessing' of the young couple with this elaborate event. Four days later, the couple were shipped across the channel to take up residency on Chalky Island. Ostensibly to function as shepherds, it is curious that the Commandant would thus segregate his most promising youth: if the welfare of the community and the couple themselves had been

---

48   Ibid., 543.
49   The final, securely dated written sermon penned by him is dated 6 February 1838, although some of his undated sermons may have been written at a slightly later date.

CHAPTER 4

foremost in Robinson's mind, he would have been better served, surely, to have them remain as a good example. As his usually detailed journals are curiously silent on his motives for effectively exiling them, we can only speculate that he was worried about exactly what kind of influence this young, literate, confident and clearly rebellious young couple might exert.

Shortly before their departure, the newlyweds would have heard Noemy preach at the weekly event 'for prayer and mutual instructions'. According to Robert Clark's translation, Noemy reminded the community that God had made them all – white and black men, and white and black women. But, revisiting a regular theme that in the pre-Christian wilds they knew no God or salvation, only the Devil, Noemy lamented:

> The Devil can not make you good no never the devil is very bad and black men and black women have bad hearts very bad
> and the Devil makes them worse.
> But God is good Gods Country is a good country Heaven is a happy place put away the Devil and do not love the Devil
> Do not make bad things – Hell is the Devils Country.[50]

The depiction of heaven as God's Country and hell as the Devil's Country is an important one, and representative of the language commonly used both by Europeans trying to convey the abstract ideas of these places, and by VDL people spreading the Word. The following week, Noemy's sermon again focused on VDL people who followed the Devil too much, and did not read the Bible, pray or love God enough. These are familiar admonishments, expressed in many of the early *Flinders Island Chronicles* and written lectures by Thomas

---

50   Noemy, Sermon delivered 17 March 1838. Robinson Letterbook QVMAG CY548.

Brune and Walter Arthur, and probably heard by the VDL exiles regularly from their European religious instructors.

The following Saturday, before the prayer meeting, Robinson's journal reports that he visited 'Mary ann and her husband' on Chalky Island. His reticence to even mention Walter Arthur by name again points to his ongoing issues with the young man – either disappointment that he had not fulfilled the high hopes imbued in him, or annoyance at his refusal to do so. That night, a spirited prayer meeting was held in the chapel. Proceedings were opened, as had become usual, by Noemy. In his preamble to his own people in the Western language, he 'told them how he was first married to a little girl that he then did not know anything about God in his own Country'. Then, preaching to the whole congregation in the Flinders Island dialect, he told them:

> You show that you love the Devil for you do the Devil's work. God does not like that. You all dead people soon and where will you go to then. Is it to the Devils Country there is much burning there many hungry & sick and crying a great deal Oh it is a bad place Why are you not like me I do not scold or fight I don't tell lies I love God a little and love him a big one by & by I pray to God & sing hymns to God every Evening in my house.[51]

In this excerpt we see hints of Noemy's often-remarked-on style of harangue. Known to speak with a Bible in his hand, and pounding it for effect, in his 'Oh, it is a bad place' we can almost feel his characteristic, emotional delivery. His comment 'You all dead people soon' can be taken two ways – it may well have referred, on a local level, to the level of sickness and death which had visited the community in recent times; or it may be a deeper, spiritual allusion to

---

51   Noemy, Sermon delivered 31 March 1838. Robinson Letterbook QVMAG CY548.

CHAPTER 4

the evangelical focus on the second coming of Christ, and the end of days. For a people who have just undergone a brutal colonisation process, these two interpretations are not mutually exclusive.

On this particular evening, deep feeling was certainly in the air. Neptune, who had been bedridden with a severe eye infection, insisted on speaking. Covering his face with a cloth to shield his eyes from the candle-light, he delivered a remarkable and deeply moving entreaty to his fellow exiles to learn to love God:

> You did not know God in your own Country You were wild man there the white man hunted you and shot you there are a great many white men bad and a great many black men bad too God sent the white man Parson and he has instructed us about God and Jesus Christ the Son of God we now know that Jesus Christ made the Trees the Salt Water the Sun and moon and the Kangaroo and the Emu and everything …

Here, the colonial narrative of frontier violence finds a salve in Christianity. With great difficulty given his painful medical condition, Neptune continued to speak about the benefits of studying the Bible and gave a poetic and moving depiction of heaven – God's Country – as a place where everyone was young, and there were no bad white men. Instead of focusing on the terrors of hell, he urged his Countrypeople to love God, pray every night, and he would take care of them.

The final speaker on that night was Alexander, a Big River man. He began in the usual manner – chastising his fellow exiles for not being good or learning the Bible. And then, taking hold of the Bible from the desk, Alexander continued the theme of Christianity offering transcendence from their colonised condition. He told them learning the good book would teach them about heaven, where there was:

... no hunger there no thirst there no sick no bad people all are good there you like it there ... Jesus is there God is there Plenty of Good men are there you will never die there never be old you will love God always there.[52]

Alexander then turned to the women in the congregation and put a series of questions to them:

> To Rebecca – Where is God? In heaven everywhere
> To Harriet – Who is Jesus Christ? The Son of God
> To Jane – Who made you? God
> To Flora – What did Jesus Christ do for you? He died for my sins according to the scriptures
> To Juliet – What will you do to be saved? Believe in the Lord Jesus Christ.[53]

He was clearly here adopting the mode of interrogation used in the school examinations, and some of the most universal questions (such as 'Who made you? God') verbatim. This performance had a profound effect on the Europeans present. Reverend Dove, in his comments of appreciation to the congregation which were added to the record, did not cite Alexander by name, but he was certainly referring to him when he stated that the addresses were 'both eloquent and elegant and their gestures particularly graceful'.[54] The Commandant, also, was keenly struck by Alexander's address, and noted in his journal, 'Had any person told me that this man would have made such a pleasing exhibition and breathed such sentiments I could not possibly have given the least credence hereto'.[55]

---

52 Alexander, Sermon delivered 31 March 1838. Robinson Letterbook QVMAG CY548.
53 Ibid.
54 Comments appended to report, written by Robert Clark, quoting Reverend Dove. 31 March 1838. Robinson Letterbook QVMAG CY548.
55 Robinson's journal, 31 March 1838, *Weep in Silence*, 548

CHAPTER 4

One week later, the prayer meeting was also addressed by a number of men. This time, however, the record written by Robert Clark also gives a sense of the whole structure of the weekly event. He mentions the pivotal role of a 'Native youth' who commenced the service, repeating the confession of the Church of England and the Lord's Prayer, which the VDL community joined in. This native youth was almost certainly Thomas Brune. Once a frenetically busy journalist and sermon writer, his sermons – in the existing record at least – were now seldom, though he seems to have still been working as a clerk on occasion. Clark then records how he himself read from the Book of Matthew (passage unknown), translating some of it into the lingua franca, and then a hymn was sung. Then, the VDL speakers commenced.

Noemy, as usual, was first, and began by addressing his own people, claiming their continuing practice of being lazy and walking about too much at night was making them sick, and entreating them to remain at home, work and learn. His message to the entire congregation followed a similar line to his previous harangues: unless they learnt to love God, they would end up in hell. Neptune, who followed him, had quite clear instructions for his own Countrypeople in their language:

> Lazy woman should mend her own home and not be going to other peoples houses Keep your blankets clean carry plenty of wood to your houses for your fires take care of your clothes and sew them when they are old & torn do not throw them away when you go to the bush hunting as you want to do. You men ought to work do not be idle do as much good as you can and God will love you.[56]

---

56   Neptune, Sermon delivered 7 April 1838. Robinson Letterbook QVMAG CY548.

This constant criticism of the women is a key characteristic of the writings and sermons of VDL men. However, as we saw through the *Flinders Island Chronicle*, their busy movements were certainly monitored on a daily basis, and they were consistently praised for being hardworking. This hard physical work, which included making roads, carrying grass, sewing, gardening, curing birds and diving for fish, does not, however, seem to have continued into their own domestic situation.

The criticism of the women's housekeeping skills is almost a universal one. European observers such as Robinson, Clark and others were constantly frustrated at the level of cleanliness within the cottages. While obviously unafraid of toil, the women often display a general (though not total) abhorrence of domestic, indoors work, both at Wybalenna and later at the Oyster Cove station. Patsy Cameron has noted a similar recalcitrance regarding domestic cleaning among the Tyereelore on the smaller Bass Strait islands, where married women who worked extremely hard in the sealing and mutton-birding trade refused, point blank, to keep a tidy house.[57] While there was a clearly gendered division of work, it does not equate to a European public–private dichotomy. There was thus an obvious willingness to perform both menial outdoors work, perhaps often seen as men's work, and more traditionally female roles such as dressmaking – but not housework.

The refusal to perform housekeeping chores – such a regular focus of the VDL texts and sermons – illustrates the refusal of the women, culture-wide, to succumb to European standards of female behaviour. Housework is only one of the theatres of recalcitrance

---

57   Cameron, *Grease and Ochre*, 107-108.

CHAPTER 4

and steadfast independence of the women, but it is possibly the most universal. It would come up again, regularly, in the sermons delivered at Wybalenna.

Having discussed issues specific to his own people – and probably within the realms of his authority – Neptune then turned to the general congregation and spoke in the Flinders Island dialect. Opening with 'Gentlemen and Ladies', he reminded them of the terrible events which had brought them to their state of exile:

> In your own Country you did not know Jesus Christ No you were like kangaroos you rush about every place. The white man came to your country they Kill your Countrymens a great many of them, you then came to live in this place and good white men came to teach you about God about Jesus Christ you are not bad men the white man does not kill you now.[58]

This is a powerful narrative of events in the living memory of all the adults present, describing the political history of their exile, in religious guise. It is also a clear reminder of the trauma under which much of the community still laboured. Interestingly though, while there are clear allusions to frontier violence, there is no mention of the resistance of VDL people to the invasion – only the spectre of bad white men, a constant feature of the early *Chronicle*, sermons and, undoubtedly, community discussion. The patriotic defence of their lands was already being written-out.

The next speaker on this night, Big River man Alexander, provides an illustration of cultural continuity. Obviously, many in the community refused to abandon traditional cultural practice and ceremony, despite the years of concerted attempts to dissuade, sabotage and threaten. He pleaded:

---

58 Neptune, Sermon delivered 7 April 1838. Robinson Letterbook QVMAG CY548.

> Put away your corroberries put away your bad things your wicked doings ... You don't love Jesus Christ enough like me. I love God. I love Jesus Christ. I will go to Heaven when I die. No old man there all young boys there no sickness ...[59]

Leonidas spoke next, and, like Neptune, began with 'Gentlemen and Ladies'. His speech, however, is rich with hints of the Flinders Island dialect. After admonishing the congregants for playing too much and telling lies of each other, and for 'putting away' God, he implored them to:

> Let Jesus Christ jump up in your heart ... God made every thing we see the Sun the moon the Kangaroo the Emu the whale the wombat the pacalla the pacoothene all God made very good.[60]

The final speaker on this night was a very significant one. Doctor Wooreddy – cited in Robert Clark's record of the event as Alpha – spoke to the meeting in his own language, that of the Bruny Island nation. His delivery was interpreted by Wild Mary, and later confirmed by himself to Clark. This senior and highly respected man, who had played such an important role in bringing them all from the mainland to Flinders Island, told them:

> My brothers in our own country a long time ago we were a great many men a great number but the white man killed us all they shot a great many. We are now only a few people here and we ought to be fond of one another. We ought to love God. God make every thing the Soul go to him by and by.[61]

---

59 Ibid.
60 Leonidas, Sermon delivered 7 April 1830, Robinson Letterbook QVMAG CY548; Pacalla – cow or ox; Pacoothene – horse: Plomley, *A Word-list of the Tasmanian Aboriginal Languages*, 34, 297.
61 Wooreddy (Alpha), Sermon delivered 7 April 1838. Robinson Letterbook QVMAG CY548.

CHAPTER 4

Interestingly, it is noted on the record of this address that the Commandant 'stated why Alpha was not so advanced as the others having been occupied with himself and his Sons in the bush from the commencement of the Mission'. This explanatory note would certainly be for the benefit of Reverend Dove, who, we might suppose by this note being added at all, might have been critical of Wooreddy's perceived lack of advancement in Christianity. This was certainly to inform a newcomer, with little knowledge of the history of the conciliatory missions conducted during the worst of the times of war, of the significance of this elder.

Later on this very night, 7 April, the terrible mortality which had characterised the previous twelve months at Wybalenna struck again. Pneumonia claimed King Albert, the Big River man who, the previous year, had sung 'Sunday Corroberry' and read 'the Bible' in the bush. He was genuinely mourned by the Commandant as a 'fine young man, extremely intelligent, kind and affectionate. He was a favourite with my family … was far advanced in his studies, was an apt scholar and a good singer, and he was very industrious'.[62] Albert's wife was Wild Mary, who had played such an active role in the attempted rebellion against Sergeant Wight in 1832, and just this evening had translated Wooreddy's sermon for Robert Clark. The Commandant recorded that she had paid Albert every attention through his illness – unlike the Chaplain.

Reverend Dove's ministrations to the VDL people were coming under constant criticism from the Commandant. On the evening of Albert's death, he complained that the Chaplain never visited the VDL people. Three days later, he aired the same complaint, and noted that another one of the regular teachers – Loftus Dickenson – had

---

62 Robinson's journal, 7 April 1838, *Weep in Silence*, 549-550.

abandoned the school. With no *Chronicle* or written production, infrequent markets, morale among the teachers eroding, the new Chaplain refusing to superintend the children or take responsibility for the school and many of the Europeans now refusing to go to Reverend Dove's services, the once model community was crumbling.

As April 1838 wore on, morale at Wybalenna deteriorated even further. The Reverend Dove's services were now so unpopular among the Europeans that very few attended, and another of the schoolteachers – Mrs Lewis, wife of the dispenser – now also refused to teach her class of women. On 21 April, a prayer service was held, and the record which exists is the final in this series which appears to have been recorded. This was a remarkable session, in that two men who had never spoken before – Tunnerminnerwait and Maulboyheener (Napoleon and Robert) – took an active role in the proceedings.

In a break from tradition, the first speaker at this meeting appeared to have been not Noemy, but Alexander. As was the usual process, he first addressed his own Big River people, translated to the scribe Robert Clark by Oyster Bay woman Daphne, adjuring them 'not to go to the bush a long way to corrobery'. Instead, they were to come to the prayer meetings to sing and pray. Then, he addressed the general congregation in the local dialect on the regular themes – to take note of God's teachings in the Bible – and, in another rare taste of the dialect:

> me die go to Heaven Good people always crackney to heaven
> Mr Clark tell me & you Jesus Christ die was crucified –
> He die a little one not a long one then he jump up and went to Heaven by & by He bring you & me to Heaven if you are good people.[63]

---

63   Alexander, Sermon delivered 21 April 1838. Robinson Letterbook QVMAG CY548.

CHAPTER 4

This is perhaps one of the more authentic recorded sermons, as Clark himself notes in the preamble, noting the use of 'broken English'. In retaining words and phrases such as 'crackney', 'a little one', 'a long one', 'jump up' and 'by and by' – which were ordinarily edited out, and slipped through only rarely – we can see clear markers of the emergent Australian Aboriginal pidgin.[64]

Neptune spoke next on this evening. His opening comments to his own Western nation people, translated by Clara, are highly directed and critical, and again suggest some resistance among the congregation:

> Do not laugh do not talk whilst I am speaking you should not laugh in this house God does not like it You are a lazy people – don't love work. I tell you again look out your things made them and mend them and take care of them.[65]

Neptune then went on to urge his fellow exiles to learn about God and Christ, who had come to save sinners. Again, he repeated the common entreaty to learn to read and love the Bible. The civilising and Christianising mission, as one, continued. The following speaker was the veteran Noemy, who after briefly addressing his own people, spoke to the whole community on themes which had now become familiar:

> In your own country you did not know there was a God – all that you knew was to make spears and waddies and to kill one another by & by you came here Mr Clark read to you plenty. No waddy no spear in heaven a fine country white men black men there they are always singing about God ... if you go to Heaven

---

[64] The evolution of the lingua franca is discussed in greater detail by Terry Crowley, 'Tasmanian Aboriginal Language', 57-66.
[65] Neptune, Sermon delivered 21 April 1838. Robinson Letterbook QVMAG CY548.

you will not die any more You will be there little boys. Angels little girls for you old women. There always young forever.[66]

There is a poignant beauty in this image of heaven. As these sermons have repeatedly hinted, two of the key ideas which VDL people held about heaven, or God's Country, was that it was free from violence – no bad white men or bad black men for that matter, hence no need for spears and waddies; and also, most enigmatically, that it was a place where they would, eternally, be young children, and cheat death.

The next speaker on this night appears to have spoken very briefly. Tunnerminnerwait (Napoleon) was one of a group who, like Doctor Wooreddy, had missed much of the Wybalenna version of education due to being constantly employed on the VDL mainland in helping to round up the last remaining VDL people at large. In the February 1838 school examinations – his first – he had shown quite a remarkable knowledge, considering the small amount of time he had effectively spent on the island, between visits with Robinson and his sons. He had undoubtedly acquired knowledge of Christian ideas and stories during the Friendly Missions, when Robinson often held informal Sunday services. On this April evening, Tunnerminnerwait had one general statement for the assembled group: 'Blackmen Blackwomen Why do you fight God Jesus Christ came into the world to save sinners'.[67] He then put questions to the 'natives around him', according to Clark's record, but only one of these is listed: his charge to Harriet, 'What shall we do to be saved?' to which she replied – as they had all been well trained to do – 'Believe in the Lord Jesus Christ'. It is almost certain

---

66 Noemy, Sermon delivered 21 April 1838. Robinson Letterbook QVMAG CY548.
67 Napoleon, Sermon delivered 21 April 1838. Robinson Letterbook QVMAG CY548.

CHAPTER 4

that he posed more questions, and perhaps delivered a more detailed sermon, but regrettably – as our record of this man's own words are tragically thin – this appears to be the extent of Clark's record.

The next speaker was one of the regulars, Leonidas, of the Big River nation. Like Alexander's sermon from earlier in the same night, there is a sense of a more authentic language, and ideas, coming through as he says:

> Jesus Christ may spring up in your hearts you go to Heaven a good place that you die and make Heaven God made it God make the Trees the Salt Water the Sun the moon the Stars the Kangaroos the Porky the Pacathers the Sheep the Wallaby God make every thing – sing plenty to God in your house pray to him every night to parraway the Devil.[68]

Wooreddy then spoke to the group on a theme that was all too regular in both the spoken sermons of the men, and throughout the *Flinders Island Chronicle* – the monitoring of the behaviour of the women. His message, which was translated by Sophia,[69] was short and pointed:

> You make your persons too filthy by putting grease & red ochre on yourselves – you dirty your clothes you dirty yourselves – put it away you woman.[70]

This was, of course, more than an issue of cleanliness. Grease and ochre was code for performance of traditional rituals, the persistence of which was a clear threat to the Christianising mission. In singling out the women, Wooreddy, as a senior man with intimate

---

68   Leonidas, Sermon delivered 21 April 1838. Robinson Letterbook QVMAG CY548.
69   Dray/Drayduric/Redhica/Sophia. Born around 1800, Port Davey. On first Friendly Mission, spoke English fluently. Sent to Flinders Island September 1833: *Weep in Silence*, 798, 869. See also multiple mentions in *Friendly Mission*.
70   Alpha (Doctor Wooreddy), sermon, translated by Sophia, recorded by Robert Clark, 21 April 1838. Robinson Letterbook QVMAG CY548.

connections to the Commandant, is clearly positioning himself as on the side of the civilisers. The focus on their use of grease and ochre speaks to the centrality of the Indigenous female body, discussed by Ballantyne and Burton, as 'raced, sexed, classed, and ethnicised … sites through which imperial and colonial power was imagined and exercised'.[71]

The final speaker on this night again directed comments to the women, but saved his most important message for the community as a whole. Robert of the Coastal Plains nation[72] was another young man who had spent years traversing the VDL mainland in the various Friendly Mission campaigns. In his first sermon – and apparently only one, as the record currently stands – he encouraged the community to learn about God, telling them:

> You knew nothing in your own Country but to fight plenty. You learn plenty of good things from the white man. You could not make a house no you made a breakwind not a warm house. The Commandant make fine house for blackmen – you can't make glass for a window. You wild people all every one. When you came here you know nothing you went about naked but you kill kangaroo you no make stone houses you only make breakwind all round.[73]

This is a damning indictment of VDL culture indeed, perhaps the most severe of all the criticisms levelled at the community by one of

---

[71] Tony Ballantyne and Antoinette Burton, 'Introduction: Bodies, Empires and World Histories', in Tony Ballantyne and Antoinette Burton (eds.), *Bodies in Contact: Rethinking Colonial Encounters in World History*, Durham and London, Duke University Press, 2006, 6.

[72] Robert (Maulboyheener/Timmy/Smallboy) is sometimes incorrectly attributed to the Ben Lomond nation, and as a son to King George (Rolepa) and brother to Walter Arthur, perhaps due to an incorrect reading of a later Port Phillip journal entry by Robinson. However, he is known to originate from the Coastal Plains nation, not Ben Lomond.

[73] Robert, Sermon delivered 21 April 1838. Robinson Letterbook QVMAG CY548.

CHAPTER 4

their own. Many previous sermons from a range of speakers had bemoaned the lack of a concept of God before the white man came, and even warlike practices. However, in this statement, Robert is deriding his people for their apparent backwardness. This echoed some of the worst criticisms of them, and what would later evolve into aspects of the Social Darwinist paradigm. It is hardly surprising that this particular sermon from Robert was very warmly received. The Commandant made a special note about it in his journal, and at the bottom of the record Clark also recorded the delight of all those present.[74]

This was the last prayer meeting of which, it appears, a systematic record was kept. The Commandant's journals reveal a man plagued by problems with his own staff, especially the new Chaplain. The community was also continually haunted by illness. Two individuals lay mortally ill that night. Francis was a Big River man, noted as the only adult 'captured' during the famed Line operation.[75] In the May 1837 school examinations, he had answered few questions, but received the Commandant's stamp of approval as 'a good husband kind parent and well behaved'. He had been too ill to attend the February examinations. He lingered until May 10, when he was claimed by tuberculosis. The other sufferer was also from the Big River nation: Ellen, who had been noted in the 1837 school examinations as a 'remarkably industrious well conducted clever woman', had been ill for some time with pneumonia.

On 13 May, three days after Francis's passing, the Reverend and Mrs Dove had visited the Native Square for the first time. It was barely one hundred metres from where they had been domiciled, yet

---

74 Comments by Robert Clark appending sermons, delivered 21 April 1838. Robinson Letterbook QVMAG CY548.
75 Weltepellemeener/Parpemelenyer/Big Mary's Jemmy/Francis. Born around 1792, Big River nation, 'Big Man': *Weep in Silence*, 833, 842.

it took almost four months to venture there. This speaks volumes for the level of their comfort with, and commitment to, the VDL people, and the terrible error that Dove's appointment had been.[76]

Thomas Brune had now almost disappeared from the Wybalenna record. There are a number of undated sermons which may date from the period between March and June 1838, and it is highly probable that Thomas was still writing sermons – the indications from the prayer meetings held in March and April suggest he was at least still opening them and leading the hymns – but there is no meticulous record keeping. On 1 June 1838, he is recorded by the Commandant as 'T Brune writing in my office', yet it is unclear exactly what he was producing. By now, he was probably serving mostly as a clerk for Robinson, copying his voluminous and constant letters. On 8 June, a beautifully rendered copy of the hymn 'O'er Those Gloomy Hills of Darkness' is dated and signed by Thomas Brune. There is no personal comment, or individual trait to it, save for his signature at the bottom, reading 'Thomas Brune, Editor and Writer at the Commandants Office'.[77] Sadly, Brune is almost invisible from this point.

On 13 June, as the worst of winter began to envelope Flinders Island, Ellen died. Her lingering demise had been the source of great angst for the Commandant and the settlement's doctor, but again, the Chaplain seems to have paid her little mind. Robinson's journal movingly records, 'The deceased was a young woman of the Big River tribe, an excellent temper, a facetious disposition. Risibility was very powerful with her'.[78] Her subsequent post-mortem examination, held

---

76   By contrast, Robert Clark and his family – despite no longer officially employed – remained at Wybalenna, albeit with reduced activities, until May 1839, when officially dismissed.
77   Thomas Brune, Sermon, undated, QVMAG CY825.
78   Robinson's journal, 13 June 1838: *Weep in Silence*, 567.

CHAPTER 4

the following day, is uncharacteristically low on description from Robinson. There is no comment at all about any removal of body parts, but it is not unreasonable to assume that her head, like that of Francis who had passed away weeks earlier, was removed, cured and sent to the illustrious vice-regal party who had requested skulls.

On 16 June, Thomas Brune's situation as scribe at Wybalenna appears to have been finalised. The Commandant's journal simply states, 'T Brune went to Green Island and where he remains'.[79] The only explanation seems to be that some of the VDL exiles' sheep, which were based on Green Island, were lambing, and perhaps needed tending. The Commandant had now divested himself of his two most loyal and promising – and importantly, most literate – VDL youths. Their obvious talents were being squandered – we can only assume deliberately – in the isolated positions of shepherds.

Over the following months at Wybalenna we only have the Commandant's journal as proof of events. Further tragic deaths followed. On 20 June, Charlotte the two-year-old daughter of ex-Tyereelore Harriet, died of pneumonia. The following day, the Commandant began a survey of the older graves on the island, where people were interred, or cremated, before his more methodical burial system was introduced. On 29 June, he received a report from Chalky Island that Mary ann and Walter had 'burnt their hut'. The fire was most likely accidental, given the time of the year (mid-winter), and the safety problems associated with often unsound huts on the smaller, unprotected, wind-prone islands. The following day, on 30 June, there was another death of a child – this time that of seven-year-old Eliza Robinson, beloved daughter of King George and half-sister of Walter Arthur. She had long been ill, and her passing caused great

---

79 Robinson's journal, 16 June 1838: *Weep in Silence*, 567.

distress on the island, including to the Commandant, who was by now mostly hardened to the constant losses. His journal depicts the tragic scene of her devoted father, lying beside the dead child on the bed for many hours, with the square engulfed by the lamentations of the women.[80] Like most of the other recent deaths on the island, Eliza's was attributed to tuberculosis.

In mid-July, there was a further 'fracas' among the VDL people, which appears to have been related to – or resolved by – the 'marriage' of Eveline to Hannibal. On 18 July, there is the simple record of 'Walter and wife to Prime Seal Island' – the exemplary couple were again seemingly condemned to a further exile. On 4 August, there was yet another death – of Rodney, described in May the previous year as 'a well conducted industrious man from the West Coast'.[81] He had apparently been ailing for some time, as he had been too ill to attend the February 1838 examinations. Again, this is an individual about whom little is known, and the historical record, as presented by Plomley, is unclear;[82] and again, another VDL exile lost to pulmonary causes. Tragically, the following month, Rodney's young son Robert would also die. Yet the Commandant would not be at Wybalenna to preside over his post-mortem examination.

On 10 August, sensational news reached Wybalenna. More than a month previously, Sir John Franklin had addressed the NSW Legislative Council on the proposed future of the Wybalenna settlement. The Commandant learnt of the changes from an extraordinary edition of the *Hobart Town Gazette*, which 'made me acquainted with the intentions of the home government to remove the Flinders Island

---

80   Robinson's journal, 30 June 1838: *Weep in Silence*, 570.
81   May 1837 school examinations: Robinson Letterbook QVMAG CY548.
82   Plomley lists his identity as Pendowtewer, but this confuses him with another man, the brother of Napoleon (Tunnerminnerwait) who was known to have died in 1832.

CHAPTER 4

aborigines to Port Phillip, and of the offer to me of the appointment of Chief Protector of Aborigines in New South Wales'.[83] The Commandant sprang into action.

The following day, a petition was drawn up and signed by all of the adult men on the island, testifying as to their support, on behalf of their families, for the move to Port Phillip. It was signed by them all as marksmen, witnessed by the Commandant, Clark and medical attendant Matthew Walsh.[84] A report was also produced, which affords a full census list of the names of all of the eighty-two VDL exiles then living at the settlement, plus Europeans.[85] Robinson's overall census affords us a comprehensive snapshot into the population at Wybalenna at this time:

VDL Exiles		
Male	Adult	30
	Youth and Children	12
Female	Adult	35
	Youth and Children	9
Military	Officers	5
	Families	12
Free	Males	12
	Females	9
Convict	Male	32
	Female	3
Stock	Sheep	1300
	Cattle	62
	Pigs	30
	Goats	50

---

83   Robinson's journal, 10 August 1838: *Weep in Silence*, 576.
84   Original handwritten copy of the petition in Robinson's Letterbook, ML 7045 Vol. 24. Was also printed by order of the New South Wales Legislative Council, 5 September 1838. A copy of this printed order viewed in the Plomley Collection, CHS53 2/10-2/13.
85   Plomley Collection, CHS53 2/10-2/13

The census, Return, petition signed by the men, plus letters by Robinson and Clark, were quickly dispatched to Hobart, and then on to Sydney. Accompanying them, naturally, was the Commandant, soon to be Chief Protector.

Robinson would not return for five months, leaving a long gap with very little sense of events at Wybalenna. Plomley's detailed history of the settlement, as is to be expected, follows Robinson's travails. We know from Matthew Walsh's records that during this period, three women had died – Old Maria,[86] Susan[87] and Paulina[88] – all of tuberculosis. There is no clear idea of day-to-day life, including whether our two erstwhile scribes, Walter Arthur and Thomas Brune, were allowed to return from their exile on the smaller islands.

When Robinson did return, in January 1839, it was not to organise the removal of the whole community to Port Phillip, as hoped. Instead, over a long and sometimes tortuous visit to Sydney, the plans were quashed by powerful colonial forces in the NSW Legislative Council.[89] Although Robinson received some support, including from Lancelot Threkeld,[90] politics and capriciousness ensured that the plan failed. Charles La Trobe later told Robinson that Archbishop William Brougham opposed the move to annoy Sir George Arthur,

---

86   Bowle/Teldredmoorer/Maria/Old Maria. Born around 1987, Stony Creek, Oyster Bay nation: *Weep in Silence*, 863.
87   Maniyercoyertutcher/Lockjaw Poll/Mary[?]/Susan. Born around 1800. Wife of James [?]: *Weep in Silence*, 869.
88   Narlarrernilare/Little Sally/Little Salle/Paulina. Born around 1807, Big River nation: *Weep in Silence*, 866.
89   James Boyce gives some indication of proceedings, in Boyce, *Van Diemen's Land*, 310-312.
90   Threlkeld told the Committee that the VDL people, if transferred to Port Phillip, would not leave the Protectorate 'as they will be in terror of the neighbouring blacks': Threlkeld to the NSW Legislative Council, 21 September 1838, Report for the Committee on the Aborigines Question, in Gunson, *Australian Reminiscences*, 272.

CHAPTER 4

with whom he had quarrelled.⁹¹ Sir John Franklin – who had originally proposed the move – showed himself to be disinterested in the affairs of the VDL exiles.⁹² After some negotiation, Robinson – now operating under the title of Chief Protector – was officially permitted to take one 'family' with him to his new post at Port Phillip. He returned to Wybalenna on 10 January 1839, already with a clear idea of who would accompany him to Port Phillip. The community was about to be rent asunder.

The Dark Ages: Wybalenna and Port Phillip, 1839–42

The mixture of feelings among VDL people in January and early February 1839 is barely imaginable. Unfortunately, we have no VDL texts to illuminate this difficult period. A large group were to accompany the Commandant in his new posting as Chief Protector of Aborigines in Port Phillip, and, for them, parting from the island of their exile most certainly held promise of a better future.

Two orphans, Adolphus and Mathinna, were sent to live with the Franklins in Hobart. This move has been interpreted by historians and other commentators as the height of paternalism, but in 1839 it posed a genuine opportunity for the children, with greatly increased living standards. Robinson's letter to Lady Franklin introducing Adolphus speaks of his great admiration for the boy's father, years after his death, and his palpable hopes for the boy's future.⁹³ Mathinna, the orphan girl whose portrait by Thomas Bock would later inspire

---

91   Recounted in Robinson's Port Phillip Journal, 22 August 1840, in Ian Clark (ed.), *The journals of George Augustus Robinson*, Vol. 1, 363.
92   Lancelot Threlkeld, NSW Legislative Council, Report for the Committee on the Aborigines Question, quoted in Gunson, *Australian Reminiscences*, 272.
93   Adolphus was sent to Hobart with the visiting naturalist John Gould on 17 January 1839. Mathinna was also sent around this time, and two other boys, Teddy and Charley Clark, were also eventually sent to the Orphan School in Hobart.

a legend based on flimsy evidence, also stood to benefit greatly by improved housing, food and educational opportunities.[94] They were leaving, it should be remembered, a community which no longer provided either education or any chance of spiritual improvement, since the arrival of Thomas Dove.

January appears to have been a time of frenetic planning, as Robinson organised his affairs for his new appointment, and management arrangements were put into place for the community. The government ships *Tamar* and *Vansittart* arrived at Flinders Island on 3 and 8 February respectively, bringing a fresh contingent from the 51st regiment, to relieve the men of the 50th regiment. This military presence, of course, was for the *protection* of the VDL exiles against the convicts and sealers, and not to subdue them. Wybalenna was to be administered temporarily by Charles Robinson, the Commandant's eldest son, who had also arrived on the *Tamar*, with a large supply of flour, tea, sugar and sheep. The Doves – who were leaving for a spell in Hobart – smuggled one of the VDL girls, Mary Ann Thompson, away with them to act as a servant. The Commandant was busy packing, and loading the cutter for Port Phillip. Aside from Robinson's journals, there is little insight into the events in the VDL community during this time. However, it is clear that a hidden passenger, which had arrived aboard either the *Tamar* or the *Vansittart*, made its insidious way through the island.

During mid-February 1839, an epidemic of influenza swept the settlement. Its passage was indiscriminate, affecting Europeans and

---

94 For excellent discussion of the historical construction of Mathinna, see Penny Russell, 'Girl in a Red Dress: Inventions of Mathinna', *Australian Historical Studies*, 43:3, 2012, 341-362; for more on the Franklin period of Mathinna's life, see Alison Alexander, *The Ambitions of Jane Franklin*, Crows Nest, Allen & Unwin, 2013, 129-134.

CHAPTER 4

VDL people alike, but its effects were felt most devastatingly by the VDL community. Robinson recorded on 21 February that 'three parts of the aborigines are afflicted, several dangerously so'.[95] He had no time to ruminate, though.

Three days later, George Augustus Robinson – once Commandant of Flinders Island, now Chief Protector of Port Phillip – left Flinders Island, with part of the contingent of VDL exiles who he had claimed comprised a 'family'.[96] The rest would arrive in Port Phillip several weeks later with his wife Maria.[97] In his excitement over his own future, he spared little thought for the ravages of the epidemic back at Wybalenna. In the weeks between his departure and that of the rest of the contingent, the epidemic would exact a terrible toll.

In the space of five days – between 28 February and 4 March – eight of the remaining VDL population at Wybalenna would die. This represented a catastrophic loss – from 82 back in August, the remaining community was now down to 58.[98] The first fatality was Semeramis, a young woman intended to go to Port Phillip and whose husband Robert would later travel there.[99] She was followed, on 1 March, by two Ben Lomond men: Phillip, said to be 'a good husband and conduct generally good', and George Robinson, 'an industrious

---

95 Robinson's diary, 21 February 1839: *Weep in Silence*, 616.
96 'Wooradedy and wife, Napoleon, T. Brune, Walter, T. Thomson'. Robinson's journal, 25 February 1839: *Weep in Silence*, 617.
97 Mary ann Arthur, Peter Bruney, David Bruney, Charlotte (Kalloongoo, a New Holland woman), her son Johnny Franklin, Matilda, Isaac, Robert, Rebecca and Fanny sailed with Mrs Robinson on 30 March: *Weep in Silence*, 786.
98 3 deaths in late 1838, 14 to Port Phillip, 8 to influenza.
99 Numbloote/Semeramis/Jenny. Born around 1815, North of Great Lake, Big River/Nth Midlands. Portrait painted by Thomas Bock, smiling warmly. First husband shot by armed party; second husband Robert (Maulboyheener/ Timmee). Slated to move to Port Phillip but died in influenza epidemic: *Weep in Silence*, 814, 869.

man rather inattentive is fond of the chase'.[100] Edward, who had been one of Robinson's few loyal companions after the disastrous Unfriendly Mission tour of Flinders Island in December 1837 also died on that day, as did a child named Sarah, of whom we have no other information.

Wybalenna was in a desperate state. Two days later on 3 March, there were two more deaths. Sabina (or Little Kit) was a West Coast woman in her late thirties.[101] A former Tyereelore, she had previously told Robinson that the West Coast people believed 'when they die that they go to PONE.DIM, i.e. a country a long way off to England and that they appear as white people'.[102] The other death was a very significant one: Jane, also known as Boatswain, was an Oyster Bay woman and former Tyereelore who had been originally kidnapped by the hated John Smith.[103] She had played an active role within rebellious Sealing Women at Wybalenna: it was to Jane that the younger women turned when retreating from unwanted marriages. She may also have been the initial focus of the unsuccessful rebellion of 1832. The following day, the final death due to the influenza outbreak, on

---

100 Kolebunner/Koonerpunner/George/George Robinson. From Port Dalrymple, North Midlands nation. Brother of famed resistance leader Eumarrah: *Weep in Silence*, 801, 843; February 1837 school examinations.
101 Noluollarrick/Nolahallker/Tylo/Crook/Sabina/Little Kit (?). See earlier entry from January 1832 on confusion over this woman's identity. Plomley is unclear between Sabina's identity and that of 'Little Kit', who is also listed as Nolahallaker, and coming from Mt Cameron West/Cape Grim, Western nation: *Weep in Silence*, 813-814, 861, 868. McFarlane lists as the same woman, though this is not clear: *Beyond Awakening*, 237. Sabina and Little Kit are probably two separate women – Sabina from the Western nation, and Little Kit from the Coastal Plains. See Cameron, *Grease and Ochre*, 135.
102 Cited by Plomley in *Weep in Silence*, 868; no date given when this information was obtained.
103 Leenererkleener/Looerryminer/Boatswain/Jane. Born around 1795, Swanport, Oyster Bay nation, former Tyerleelore, abducted by John Smith: *Weep in Silence*, 860.

CHAPTER 4

4 March, was of another significant woman: Queen Adelaide was the aged widow of the famed Oyster Bay leader King William.[104]

For a community already reeling, the impact of these deaths – in addition to the losses of the Commandant, those who had already left, and those soon to depart – cannot be imagined. This was the deadliest week in Wybalenna's history.[105]

Thomas Dove, who was vacationing in Hobart with his wife and the purloined girl Mary Ann Thompson, now penned his Second Despatch.[106] His reports – the only direct and sometimes personal reflections on his interactions with VDL people – were treated with suspicion in Hobart even at the time of their first receipt, as his position was already under review for poor performance.[107] Dove does, however, provide several very telling anecdotes to help us build an impression of how he might have been received by the VDL people.

The Chaplain's interactions with Big River man Alexander, then in his late twenties, provide an informative window into his relationships. In February 1839, he wrote how, when he first knew the man, he was 'led to entertain a very sanguine expectation'. Alexander had answered detailed questions on John 3:16,[108] leading Dove to

---

104 Droomteemetyer/Narrerneckerbunnyer/Governor's lubra/Queen Adelaide. No information on her origin, but was the widow of famed King William, important Oyster Bay chief. Born around 1790–95: *Weep in Silence*, 798, 852.
105 Mercifully, there would only be two more deaths in the next twelve months. However, due to poorly kept records during this period, caused in part to lack of permanent superintendence, these names cannot be determined. See Plomley's comments, *Weep in Silence*, 942.
106 The first appears untraceable in the Tasmanian Archives, as at 1976. See notes in R. S. Miller's *Thomas Dove and the Tasmanian Aborigines*, 38.
107 Dove's reports consistently contradicted themselves, e.g. the regularity of his classes, his wife's interactions with the exiles.
108 'God so loved the world, etc' – the explanatory line Dove used.

believe that this man had 'a mind open to moral impressions'.¹⁰⁹ In his report, Dove does not acknowledge the fact that Alexander was a regular speaker at the settlement's prayer meetings. He leads the reader to believe that this discussion is Alexander's first. Dove then goes on to discuss how, at a later meeting, when trying to elicit interest in a passage from 1 John 1:7, Alexander displayed 'not only a dullness which staggered my hopes, but an evident desire to stir up noise and disorder among those who were present'. Alexander sank, Dove lamented, to 'this child of the forest … taking his place among the most careless and petulant of my charge'.¹¹⁰

As we have already seen from the observations of Robinson and others regarding Dove's interactions with VDL people, Dove certainly sought minimal contact with the people under his spiritual charge. His depiction of Alexander placed the responsibility for the failures of Christianisation squarely on the unimprovability of the VDL people themselves. In framing Alexander (a grown man, and former Big River warrior) as a wild child, and not crediting Alexander's demonstrated commitment to spreading the Christian message, Dove is working effectively to prove the hopelessness of his task. This explanation – that he could do virtually nothing for them – was his stock response until, two years later, he was criticised by the Governor for it. 'The Case of Alexander', as he put it, is more a testament to Dove's lack of commitment – and obfuscation of the facts – than Alexander's unwillingness to learn.

In his Second Despatch, Dove also included excerpts from his journal which testify to one of the time-honoured traditions of

---

109 'The Case of Alexander', Dove's Second Despatch, cited in Miller, *Thomas Dove and the Tasmanian Aborigines*, 45.
110 Dove, cited in Miller, *Thomas Dove and the Tasmanian Aborigines*, 45-46.

CHAPTER 4

Wybalenna: the non-conformity of the women. Some time in his first year of tenure, between January 1838 and February 1839, when faced with the absence of the women at his Sunday service, he decided to go in search of them. He waylaid a woman who happened to be passing, and ordered her to lead him to the group. This woman was the former Tyereelore and Friendly Mission diplomat, Fanny.[111] Dove describes how Fanny was vague about the women's location, and – in a tactic unknown to him, but reminiscent of Friendly Mission days – she continually called ahead, to allow the women to evade discovery.[112] When Dove finally came upon them – a party of fourteen women, enjoying a leisurely time together at a breakwind – he made it the scene of a religious service, where he 'pointed out to them as affectionately as I could the folly and wickedness of their conduct, as it was obviously their purpose to elude my intention of addressing to them the words of Eternal Life'.[113] He makes no comment about the reception this received. Again, this telling passage perhaps says more about Dove's lack of any genuine connection with the women than their attitudes towards religion. They did not like the 'damnation': they clearly did not like Dove. Yet they would be saddled with him – and his inappropriate, alienating approaches – for another two years.

---

111 Plorenernoopenner/Planobeena/Jock/Fanny. Born around 1805, Coastal Plains nation, from George Town/Piper River. Former Tyerleeore, joined the Friendly Mission, wife of Napoleon (Tunnerminnerwait). Portrait painted by Thomas Bock. Plomley says is sister of Ajax (unclear). Went to Port Phillip with Robinson and others in 1839: *Weep in Silence*, 821, 858. Ryan asserts that Plorenernoopenner and Fanny Hardwick, also abducted by sealers but taken to Kangaroo Island, are one and the same, but these are almost certainly two separate women; nowhere in the Wybalenna or Port Phillip records is the name Hardwick mentioned relating to this Fanny.
112 Robinson's field journals record his suspicions on multiple occasions that he was being misled, and that his guides were deliberately alerting those in the bush – by lighting fires, and by calling out – so that they could evade the conciliator.
113 Dove, cited in Miller, *Thomas Dove and the Tasmanian Aborigines*, 49-50.

There were some VDL exiles who, for a variety of reasons, would never have to endure the Reverend Dove again. Across Bass Strait in Port Phillip, the party of VDL exiles who Robinson had hand-picked to accompany him were settling into a range of new roles. They had been framed, initially at least in Robinson's official reports, as a family, but in their alien surroundings they were effectively a new tribe or nation. Headed by the acknowledged wise-man elder, Wooreddy (or 'the doctor'), his wife Trugernanner and Wooreddy's two sons David and Peter, the group also comprised the juveniles Thomas Thompson and Johnny Franklin, and Franklin's mother Charlotte, who originally came from the Spencer Gulf area of New Holland. Thomas Brune had also been recalled from his exile tending sheep to make the trip. There were also three young couples: Walter and Mary ann Arthur, also returned from exile; Tunnerminnerwait and his wife Fanny; Isaac and his wife Matilda; and Robert, whose wife Semeramis had also been intended to join them but had been the first to succumb to the influenza outbreak. This party clearly represented Robinson's most loyal allies from the Friendly Mission days – in the opinion of Ian McFarlane, 'their policy of guarded resistance paid off'.[114] In also boasting the young, exemplary trio of Brune and the Arthurs, Robinson was perhaps, as Cassandra Pybus suggests, choosing those 'most likely to survive and adapt in a new environment'.[115]

The removal of this particular group had, crucially, stripped the Wybalenna community of its most Europeanised members. The key Friendly Mission personalities, such as Wooreddy, Trugernanner and Tunnerminnerwait, had convinced many of those remaining to

---

114 Ian McFarlane, 'Pevay: A Casualty of War', *Tasmanian Historical Research Association Papers and Proceedings* 4: 84, 298.
115 Cassandra Pybus, *Community of Thieves*, Melbourne, William Heinemann Australia, 1991, 148

CHAPTER 4

abandon their lands and come to Flinders Island. With those charismatic diplomats gone, along with the literate youth, the remaining community was arguably a more hard-core, non-Europeanised grouping. Notably, none of those who made the trip to Port Phillip were from the Big River, Oyster Bay or Western nations, save for Tunnerminnerwait, a young Western man, whose upbringing had been decidedly multicultural for many years. The key holders of power at Wybalenna – the Big River and Ben Lomond nations – might actually have remained largely unaffected by the absence of the Friendly Mission party, if not for the ravages of the influenza outbreak of February and March.

Across Bass Strait ...

There is a wealth of scholarship on the events that transpired when the group of Wybalenna exiles went to Port Phillip. These form one of the foundation stories of the Port Phillip Protectorate, and Melbourne itself, and – like the Friendly Mission, Patriotic Wars and the Line Operation – it is beyond the scope of this study to cover them fully. For the sake of future events at Wybalenna, though, the experience of those who went to Port Phillip, and lived to tell about it, deserves a brief examination.

On arrival, in March 1839, the white population of Melbourne was already – after only a few short years – almost 5000. The lands of the Wurundjeri and Boonwurrung people were already under threat and, in many places, completely overrun. Robinson had proposed using his trusted VDL confidants in a similar diplomatic role as they had performed during the Friendly Missions on VDL, but in Port Phillip this was a very different proposition, not in the least because of the language barriers.

As the NSW Legislative Council had predicted, the feared Van Diemen's Land Aborigines were most certainly viewed by some of the colonists with mistrust and fear. But it must be said that the Protectorate itself was probably more loathed by the settlers, who saw it merely as an encumbrance to their free acquisition of land. Robinson's journals clearly describe the hostility his role encountered during his entire time at Port Phillip. As Chief Protector, he was responsible for overseeing the work of his four assistant Protectors – good Christian men recruited by Sir George Arthur in England, whom Robinson had met during his stay in Sydney four months previously. Robinson ordered his Assistant Protectors straight to work, to acquaint themselves with the nations in their Protectorate area.[116]

The Port Phillip Protectorate was an extraordinary undertaking for four individuals and one overseer. Even if they had been well equipped, with a staff of assistants of their own, they would have been hard pressed to fulfil their duties to the First Nations people they were charged with protecting. Yet in Port Phillip, problems of funding and bureaucracy – and, at times, inappropriate recruitment – constantly hampered the Protectorate's activities. It is clear from many events depicted in Robinson's Port Phillip journals, reports by the Assistant Protectors,[117] sympathetic government figures, and settlers that the Protectors were effectively powerless to enact the role to which they had been assigned. They were unable to alleviate intense

---

116 William Thomas was responsible for the Melbourne and Westernport areas, Charles Sievwright for the West, James Dredge for the East, and Edward Parker for the North and Northwest District.

117 Especially the papers of William Thomas, who remained in Port Phillip after the collapse of the Protectorate. See Thomas's papers at La Trobe Library, Public Records Office Victoria and Mitchell Library; summary in Richard Cotter (ed.), *A Cloud of Hapless Foreboding*, 8-68.

CHAPTER 4

violence on the colonial frontiers.[118] The law was as ineffective to protect the Victorian nations as it had been to protect the New South Wales or Van Diemen's Land nations before them.

Historiographical criticism of and animosity towards George Augustus Robinson, as the Chief Protector, has often led to an impression that the Protectors themselves were to blame for the perceived failures of the venture.[119] However, as Alan Lester observes, these historians 'perpetuate the very settler discourse which ultimately proved so successful at undermining humanitarian intentions'.[120] Lester tends to excuse the Crown (in the form of Governor Gipps and Charles La Trobe) from responsibility, by claiming that Gipps was fearful of a repeat of the post-Myall Creek trial backlash.[121] However, vice-regal apathy, lack of genuine commitment and a class-based resentment of Robinson the man were, in fact, the major contributing factors in undermining the Port Phillip Protectorate.

The immense scale of the challenges faced by the Protectorate took much of Robinson's time, minimising the attention that he could give to the members of his domestic and extended family. At first, his family and the VDL party seemed to be a fairly cohesive unit, going on grand picnics together and holding corroborees. For much of 1839, the experiment looked promising. This all changed with the arrival of the first superintendent of the Port Phillip colony.

---

118 See Broome's *Aboriginal Victorians;* Ian Clark's *Scars in the Landscape: A Register of Massacre Sites in Western Victoria, 1803–1859*, Canberra, Aboriginal Studies Press, 1995; Jan Critchett, *A Distant Field of Murder: Western District frontiers, 1834–1848*, Carlton, Melbourne University Press, 1992, for more on intensive frontier violence in Victoria from 1830 to 1860.
119 This theme is summarised well by Kenny, *The Lamb Enters the Dreaming*, 79-81.
120 Alan Lester, 'George Augustus Robinson and Imperial Networks', in Johnston and Rolls (eds.), *Reading Robinson*, 39.
121 Lester, 'George Augustus Robinson and Imperial Networks', 41.

Charles La Trobe's assumption of the role of superintendent on 1 October 1839 marks an intensification of Robinson's battles with authority, especially over his VDL charges. The first full meeting between the two men on the following day was heated, and it seems likely that La Trobe had arrived with his mind set against both Robinson and the values of the Protectorate. The VDL party arguably became collateral damage.

In an acrimonious discussion over funding for the VDL party's provisions several weeks later – a funding clearly promised by the VDL administration – it appears the tone of La Trobe's treatment pushed Robinson over the edge. He railed against what he saw as the Lieutenant Governor's ungentlemanly addresses and 'said I should not keep him and requested to be relieved of them [the VDL group]'.[122] Robinson was deeply affected by La Trobe's intensely negative attitude towards him from their very first meeting, and this was to impact much of his Port Phillip stay. Robinson had expected to be treated with respect, at least by another gentleman, if not the land-grabbing and hostile colonial public. Yet instead of the generosity promised by Franklin, where his VDL companions would be accommodated and financed by the Crown, it rapidly became clear that every allowance for both his VDL and Port Phillip charges – down to the last blanket – would involve a battle. The status he had enjoyed in VDL now accounted for little. For Robinson, this realisation would have left him personally and professionally shattered.

Indicative of the mythologising that has surrounded the VDL experience in Port Phillip, many histories incorrectly depict Robinson as abandoning the VDL party to their own devices, or at least tiring

---

122 Robinson's journal, 18 November 1839, in Clark (ed.), *The Journals of George Augustus Robinson, Vol. 1*, 105.

CHAPTER 4

of them very quickly. Archival sources – and a reading of events – dispute this interpretation. It is clear that Robinson did *not* try to divest himself of his responsibilities immediately on arriving, and they did not immediately abscond upon arrival in Port Phillip.[123] Further, the VDL visitors were not so neglected from the beginning that, as Fels claims, they took to 'theft as a means of subsistence'.[124] The former Friendly Mission ambassadors, and exemplary young 'civilised' people, found roles in a range of situations but remained connected to Robinson and his household for some years.

Rather than being abandoned in Port Phillip, the VDL 'family' who travelled with Robinson were actually provided for and, unless they removed themselves, closely supervised. All of the VDL men and boys, aside from Wooreddy who was now ailing, were set on the path to proletarianisation. As outsiders they were, in the early days of the colony, more attractive as candidates for employment than Victorian Aboriginal people, who were still seen as uncivilised. By 1840, the VDL men were working either for the Robinsons on properties, or gainfully employed by other private employers. This employment of VDL men was a practice criticised by Assistant Protector James Dredge, perhaps because of the potential for exploitation.[125] Nevertheless, Robinson's early Port Phillip diaries show a man genuinely trying to find a good station for the VDL people in his care, or at least giving the appearance of doing so. However, by the end of 1841, the situation would greatly deteriorate.

---

123 Vivienne Rae-Ellis's rendering of these events in *Black Robinson* – at best selective, and at worst mendacious – has proved influential on subsequent writers.
124 Marie Hansen Fels, *Good Men and True: The Aboriginal Police of the Port Phillip District, Melbourne*, Melbourne University Press, 1988, 42.
125 James Dredge, 'The Hanging of Two Aboriginals, 1842', *La Trobe Library Journal*, no. 7, April 1971, 77.

The disaster which befell the VDL party is well known, and has been documented by a large number of historians and other commentators.[126] In late 1841 – eighteen months after arriving – Tunnerminnerwait, Maulboyheener, Trugernanner, Fanny and Matilda murdered two whalers.[127] They had garnered an arsenal of weapons, and were now 'on the run'. The resulting chase, arrest and trial caused a sensation in the colonial press. Tunnerminnerwait and Maulboyheener – known as Napoleon and Robert at Wybalenna, and Jack and Bob in the Melbourne press – were convicted, and the all-white jury pleaded for mercy. Justice Willis disagreed, and pushed for the death penalty, to serve as an example to the Victorian First Nations. While the women were released into Robinson's custody, a death sentence for the men was announced on 3 January 1842. Tunnerminnerwait and Maulboyheener, who had played such an important role in the Friendly Missions, and both sermonised at the Wybalenna prayer meetings – were publicly executed before a crowd of thousands, in a spectacle well recorded elsewhere.[128]

The three women involved in the murders – Trugernanner, Tunnerminnerwait's wife Fanny, and Matilda – were sent back to

---

126 See among others, Jan Roberts, *Jack of Cape Grim: A Victorian Adventure*, Melbourne, Greenhouse Publishers, 1986; Ian McFarlane, 'Pevay: A Casualty of War', 280-305; Robert Cox, *Steps to the Scaffold; The Untold Story of Tasmania's Black Bushrangers*, Pawleena, Tas, Cornhill Publishing, 2004, 105-155; Leonie Stevens, 'The Phenomenal Coolness of Tunnerminnerwait', *Victorian Historical Journal*, 8:1, June 2010, 18-40; Marie Hansen Fels, David Clark and Rene White, 'Mistaken Identity, Not Aboriginal Resistance', *Quadrant*, Vol. 58, No. 10, Oct 2014, 74-83; Kate Auty and Lynette Russell, *Hunt Them, Hang Them: 'The Tasmanians' in Port Phillip 1841-42*, Melbourne, Justice Press, 2016.

127 The two whalers were probably known to the women, from the Adventure Bay whaling station, located near the former Bruny Island Protection station. They may also have been known to Tunnerminnerwait after his trip to the Western districts with Robinson in early 1841, when the story of the Convincing Ground massacre became known. See Clark (ed.), *Journals of George Augustus Robinson, Vol. 3*.

128 See especially James Dredge, 'The Hanging of Two Aboriginals, 1842'; Jan Roberts, *Jack of Cape Grim*, 90-94; *Port Phillip Herald* accounts.

CHAPTER 4

Flinders Island in May of 1842 along with Wooreddy who, tragically, died during the voyage. The man who had done so much to help build the career of Robinson, and arguably to save the lives of his VDL Countrypeople, was buried on Green Island. Several months later, Walter and Mary ann Arthur and their friend David Bruney bid a fond farewell to the Robinson family, with whom they were still on very good terms, and returned south, first staying in Hobart, and then returning to Wybalenna. David's younger brother Peter, who for a brief time turned to a life of crime, remained in contact with the Protector Robinson until his untimely death, at the age of 19, in 1843.[129] Isaac, aged around twenty one, was according to La Trobe's official report, 'taken by a Western Port settler in a small veſsel which is reported foundered at sea & all on board perished'.[130] Thomas Thompson found work on a property in Dandenong, and remained on the mainland, retaining contact with his VDL friends well into the 1850s.[131] Johnny Franklin was last heard of working for a Mr Bond on the River Plenty.[132]

Finally, the orphan Thomas Brune – the boy with no family or connections, who had begun the tradition of VDL writing with the first editions of the *Flinders Island Chronicle* and gone on to pen many written sermons – found work in Westernport with the settler Mr Jamieson. In January 1841, Brune reportedly fell from a tree 'in the act of getting an opossum'. Seriously injured, he survived for

---

129 Robinson's journal, 8 December 1843, in Clark, *The Journals of George Augustus Robinson, Volume 3*, 219.
130 C. J. La Trobe to Sir George Gipps, Return of VDL Aborigines in Port Phillip, 24 December 1841, SLV MS 8454 Box 650/17.
131 Walter George Arthur was in communication with Thompson, and his family, in 1852. See letter from Walter Arthur to Thomas Thompson, 16 January 1852, Mitchell Library Robinson Papers Vol. 67 Miscellaneous Journals and Papers, 1839, 1843, 1850–52, ML A7088 Parts 1–5.
132 La Trobe to Gipps, 24 December 1841, SLV MS 8454 Box 650/17.

three days, but then, according to Governor La Trobe, 'is reported to have died with the Bible in his hand'.[133] It was a tragic but somehow comforting end for the young man who found genuine solace in the Bible, and so many times spoke of the glories of the hereafter. Thomas Brune was nineteen.

Meanwhile at Wybalenna …

George Robinson Junior took over administration of Wybalenna, until the arrival of the next appointed administrator, Malcolm Laing Smith, three months later. Smith had been granted land at 'Avenue Plain' in the Northern Districts in the 1820s, a reward for his role in the hunt for bushranger Matthew Brady.[134] He brought his wife and seven adult children. Due to Robinson Senior's removal of most of the settlement records – which now exist in the Robinson papers at the Mitchell Library – Smith's early administration was confused and problematic. Robinson Junior also apparently was obstructive.

Smith's first report to the Colonial Secretary, dated 27 April 1839, was highly critical of the behaviour of Robinson Junior, the doctor Matthew Walsh and Robert Clark. More pertinently to our interests, he also raised very familiar complaints regarding the progress towards civilisation of the VDL exiles living there:

> I fear that the debased and vicious habits of most of the women taken from the sealers tend much to retard the moral and religious improvement of the mass of the people.[135]

---

133 Ibid.
134 Breen, *Contested Places*, 1.
135 Smith to Colonial Secretary, 27 April 1839, CSO 5/197/4720 227-34, cited in Plomley, *Weep in Silence*, 122.

CHAPTER 4

Clearly, the grease and ochre had still not been put away. In the month following this report, Matthew Walsh's replacement, Edward Fosbrooke, arrived at the settlement in May 1839, to assume the dual role of medical attendant and storekeeper. At this latter role he proved inefficient, and in the time-honoured Wybalenna tradition, there was soon considerable dissent between Smith, Fosbrooke and the Reverend Dove, who had also recently returned to the settlement despite a board of enquiry recommending his removal.

Dove supplies some of the only direct anecdotal glimpses of life on the settlement during this period. His Third and Fourth Despatches to the Colonial Secretary – dated October 1839 and July 1840 – are certainly of dubious integrity. Both carry the general line that the VDL population lacks the interest and capability to be educated, either in literacy or Christianity.[136] His Fourth Despatch carries some sample diary entries which, at the very least, place individuals within the documentary record. On 29 November 1839, Dove writes glowingly of a successful prayer session held the previous night where the atmosphere was marked by 'decency and cheerfulness', and adds that 'Alexander, Leonidas and Henry'[137] were particularly apt in their replies'. However, the following night:

> A very different scene awaited me. Not one of the male adults could be induced to quit their sports, and join me in the place of meeting. Alexander stood at the door, smoking his pipe, and apparently disposed to create disorder among the half dozen females, who were within.[138]

---

136   There are other fictions, such as his wife being the first ever to teach the women needlework, and that the community has no interest in being removed from Flinders Island.
137   'Henry' is almost certainly a mistranscription (by Miller) of 'Noemy'. The only other Henry (Leerpullermener) is nowhere else connected with delivering sermons.
138   'This entry also likely relates to Dove's previous reference to 'The Case of Alexander' in his Second Despatch. From Dove's diary, reproduced in Miller, *Thomas Dove and*

This is almost certainly the anecdote already conveyed as 'The Case of Alexander' in Dove's Second Despatch. In recycling the story (and effectively passing off an old anecdote as new), Dove again arguably demonstrates his limited involvement with the VDL exiles. The other journal entry that Dove sees fit to include dates from February 1840, and seems to be included in the Fourth Despatch to underline the apparent futility of the Christianising attempt. It is a particularly dramatic and illuminating entry, and demands to be reproduced at length. Dove writes,

> On going down this evening to the Native Square, for the purposes of instruction and prayer, I was assaulted in a furious style by the two Aborigines known by the names of Washington and Tippoo Saib.[139] The former came up to me with two waddies in his hand, and ordered me in a voice trembling with rage, to go back to my own house, as he would not allow the Blacks to wait on me. He stood at the door of the hut I was about to enter, and twice attempted to strike and push me away; but fear restrained him. Tippoo Saib spoke, also, in a similar strain, but used no menacing gestures ... Having prayed, and conversed with Alexander, Frederick and Edmund, who chose to tarry with me, I enquired into the cause of this uproar and excitement on the part of Washington, and was told that he was enraged on account of some bread which had been stolen from his hut ... Alexander muttered out something to the effect that I was not (as he was pleased to term it) 'a good one parson', because I did not supply them at will with sugar, and plums, and tobacco ... The waiting upon instruction is too plainly regarded by them as a task which ought to be rewarded from time to time by the issue of some extra indulgences.[140]

---

the Tasmanian Aborigines, 81-83.
139 Both Big River men.
140 From Dove's diary, included in his Fourth Despatch and reproduced in Miller, *Thomas Dove and the Tasmanian Aborigines*, 83-84.

CHAPTER 4

There are a number of important facets of Wybalenna life to be drawn from this anecdote, not the least of which was the minimal welcome Dove enjoyed to the homes, and lives, of the VDL exiles. We gain a glimpse into the sometimes fiery disputes on the settlement – often euphemised by the VDL people themselves as 'growling' – and the rapidity with which these could inspire armed conflict. Washington's 'fear' is almost certainly restraint: Dove is unaware – or pretends to be – of Washington's fame as a convicted killer. Most significantly, this passage also directly refers to the VDL people's expectation that the Government, as the Crown's agents, would provide them with payment for all of their work – this work clearly including going to church. This expectation, which stemmed from the agreed repayment for the colonising power's dispossession, and the honouring of what Richard Broome characterised as 'right behaviour' in the First Nations–coloniser contract,[141] would grow to be a much larger issue at Wybalenna in the years to come.

Tensions between all parties continued for the next two years at Wybalenna. Smith had negative relations with his officers and the Chaplain who, in turn, was often on unsatisfactory terms with those into whose hearts he was employed to ingratiate himself. There were constant allusions, accusations and counter-accusations of embezzlement and poor management, which inspired a series of official enquiries from 1839 onward. Robert Clark, the erstwhile catechist based in Hobart from May 1839, also keenly agitated through this disruptive period for a new model of management for Wybalenna. Although, amidst all this interest there was much talk about the management of the settlement from a range of administrators and

---

141 Richard Broome, 'There Were Vegetables Every Year Mr Green Was Here', *History Australia*, 3:2, 2006, 1-16.

colonial officials, we have very few clear glimpses of what day-to-day life might have been like for the VDL people at the centre of this settlement.

Some insight can perhaps be drawn from a Board of Enquiry which visited in May and June 1841, reporting to Sir John Franklin that VDL people had acquired 'few ideas of individual property', and were still living communally. It condemned the style of cottages built during Robinson's administration, which encouraged close proximity, and the practice of communal food preparation, and recommended:

> It surely would have been preferable that each man and wife should have had a separate cottage, with a small piece of land around it, all they produced from it which would have been their own.[142]

This idealisation of the yeoman farmer attempted to strip the VDL people of one of the key tenets which commonly characterises Indigenous land ownership and community function – collectiveness. A push towards individualism, and the ideas of private property, were probably inappropriate to the lifeways and goals of VDL people, just as the Reverend's distant, officious mode of instruction had been. However, the decision-makers in Hobart were far removed from Sir George Arthur's conviction that Christianity should precede civilisation. The civilising mission was now well entangled with the principles of capitalism. Led by a Governor who had spent less than one day with VDL people, but arrogantly claimed a great familiarity with them, cost saving was a priority: in June 1841, the Board of Enquiry decided to remove Smith, who was deemed inept. He

---

142 Board of Enquiry report dated 10 June 1841, cited in Plomley, *Weep in Silence*, 129.

CHAPTER 4

was replaced with a new superintendent, the surgeon Peter Fisher. Reverend Dove was also relieved of his posting. The battle for VDL souls had clearly been abandoned.

Plomley's assessment of this fractious period in Wybalenna's administrative history is brutal. He comments that from this point on, Wybalenna:

> … had now become little more than a home for the indigent: the Aborigines were to be cared for, but all attempts to give them a purpose in life, albeit a European life in which Christianity and labouring for one's subsistence formed the basis, were dropped. From this time any expenditure on the Aborigines was begrudged, it being held that the more quickly they died the better for the government purse.[143]

Plomley's bitter characterisation, steeped as it is in the view that any future for the VDL people must be a European one, is from some perspectives – white, European ones especially – undoubtedly accurate. However, there were still over sixty VDL men, women and children living on the island, mindful of the agreement made ten years previous that they would be protected and provided for so they could live in the manner of their choosing. In Plomley's assessment, and in all of the opinions rendered by supposed experts on the subject, including Franklin, Montagu, Smith, Dove, Clark and the various Boards of enquiry, one key factor was barely consulted or considered: the will of a free people.

---

143   Plomley, *Weep in Silence*, 130.

Chapter 5

EMPIRE, AGENCY AND A HUMBLE PETITION

In January 1842, the revolving door administration at Wybalenna since Robinson's departure took another turn. Peter Fisher, who had been at Wybalenna for less than six months, received word of his recall to England by the Admiralty.[1] The former catechist Robert Clark, who was maintaining a close interest in affairs at Wybalenna, would most certainly have applied if eligible. However, the position now called for the person filling the role of superintendent to serve as administrator, medical attendant *and* spiritual guide. This was in line with Sir John Franklin's more parsimonious approach towards the settlement.

It was now that one of the key European figures of the Wybalenna narrative, the Edinburgh-trained dentist, Doctor Henry Jeanneret, entered the record. Jeanneret's reputation for being a problematic individual was gained soon after his arrival in New South Wales in 1828. He had missed the deadline for grant bestowal, and set about battling authorities for a land grant to which he considered himself eligible. For twelve years he badgered the authorities, describing the

---

1 It appears Fisher would have been removed by Franklin if he had not resigned the position, due to contravening orders. Plomley briefly discusses Fisher's departure, and Franklin's displeasure with Fisher's administration, in *Weep in Silence*, 132-133.

process in his memoir, the very title of which serves as a window into his persecution complex.² Even before his appointment was confirmed, the Hobart press derided 'the singular nomination of Dr Jeanneret to the command of the kidnapped Aborigines' as 'absurd', as the position required a 'commanding exterior and physical energy'³ – implying he had neither. Jeanneret's appointment – which may well have been to quell his repeated agitations throughout the 1830s – raised concerns in a number of press and humanitarian quarters, but Sir John Franklin ignored them, having long since lost interest in Wybalenna. Almost certainly, he hoped Wybalenna would function quietly in the background, an embarrassing adjunct to the increase of the colony, and not demand any more of his attention. The series of events over the next few years would prove him monumentally wrong.

The Curious First Reign of Doctor Henry Jeanneret

It took eight weeks from the date of his appointment – and an impatient nudge from the Governor's office – for Henry Jeanneret to leave for Flinders Island. He arrived, with his wife Harriet and family, on 14 June 1842. Within a month, tensions had already escalated between Jeanneret and his staff: his orders to the military attachment to clean the VDL cottages met with refusal by Sergeant Ingram, and he also found it necessary to dismiss the coxswain Archer. This

---

2   Henry Jeanneret, *The Vindication of a Colonial Magistrate from the Aspersions of His Grace the Duke of Newcastle by Official Documents and Attestations, with a Remonstrance and Exposure of a Colonial Conspiracy, whereby Her Majesty the Queen has been Imposed upon in a Petition Against Henry Jeanneret, M.D., Late Superintendent of the Aborigines of Van Diemen's Land*, London, Hope and Co, 1854.

3   The *Courier*, Hobart, 1 April 1842, 2. The claim that Jeanneret's was the single nomination is contradicted by Jeanneret in his *Vindication*, where he states that he was chosen from a field of sixteen candidates.

carried on Wybalenna's administrative tradition of infighting between the Europeans. As Plomley commented, 'Flinders Island certainly brought out the worst in those who were unhappily confined there, both masters and servants'.[4]

Four weeks into his tenure as superintendent, Henry Jeanneret noted three very important arrivals. He wrote to George Boyes, the Colonial Secretary, that the community had just been bolstered by the arrival, via the schooner *Adelaide* from Port Phillip, of:

> ... three females, Aborigines of V. D. Land, named in the margin ('Truganini alias Lalla Rookh, Fanny, Matilda'). An old man named 'Wooradedy' died on the passage and was buried, I am informed, at Green Island.[5]

Thus, the three women, who had been at the centre of the terrible events six months previously at Port Phillip, were returned to Wybalenna as notes in a margin; and Doctor Wooreddy, who had witnessed the arrival of the first European ships, and gone on to play such a vital role in the VDL exile, was consigned to bureaucratic history.

At the same time as these three women arrived at Wybalenna, there were departures. Four children were sent to live with Robert Clark in Hobart.[6] The following month, events at Wybalenna grew even more vexed for the superintendent. In August, Private Reynolds, one quarter of the remaining military attachment, suffered a break to his leg. Jeanneret was a dentist, not a medical officer: Reynolds

---

4 Plomley, *Weep in Silence*, 136.
5 Henry Jeanneret to G W. Boyes, 16 July 1842, AOT CSO8/1/157, 63.
6 Both Governor Franklin and Superintendent Jeanneret were pushing for the children to be admitted to the Orphan School; however, their parents apparently insisted they be placed instead with Clark. Jeanneret to Boyes, 16 July 1842, AOT CSO 8/1/157/ 59-60.

CHAPTER 5

was permanently disabled. While the long-term effects would not have been obvious for some time, Jeanneret's problems with the military – already pronounced, after his early tensions with Sergeant Ingram – continued to simmer.

Jeanneret's relations with the VDL people also appear to have been very problematic at this early stage. We only have Jeanneret's very sketchy reports to go by, but it appears that some kind of strife was caused by the three women who had just returned from Port Phillip, Trugernanner, Matilda and Fanny. All three women had recently been widowed, but it must be noted that Trugernanner and Matilda had not been what might be called 'constant' in their marriages for a considerable time. Robinson's Port Phillip diaries make regular, vexed references to Trugernanner's absconding from Melbourne, often to be with European men.[7] It was almost certainly her behaviour which led to the Protector to effectively throw his hands in the air and decide to send the whole group back to Wybalenna. Moreover, Fanny had recently lost her husband, Tunnerminnerwait (Napoleon), to the brutality of a public execution in Melbourne. The sister of famed warrior Eumarrah,[8] Robinson's earliest records of Fanny describe a warlike woman who, just rescued from sealers, 'frequently said … she would teach the black fellows to kill plenty of white men'.[9]

These women must have led a rebellion of some kind, but we can only glimpse its aftermath. On 30 August, Henry Jeanneret complained to the Colonial Secretary about the disobedience of the

---

7 Trugernanner and Charlotte absconded numerous times, including on 7 August 1839 and 1 May, 7 June and 2 July 1840. Matilda at other times had been Trugernanner's companion. From Robinson's Port Phillip Journals, in Clark, *Journals of George Augustus Robinson, Volume 3*.
8 Michael Roe, 'Eumarrah (c.1798–1832)', *Australian Dictionary of Biography*, Supplementary Volume, Melbourne, Melbourne University Press, 2005, 117-118.
9 Fanny quote from McFarlane, 'Pevay: A Casualty of War', 289.

military party. It seems they – and other Europeans, probably convicts and sealers – had flatly refused orders to support him, and 'put down the shamefully immoral conduct of some of the Aborigines, particularly those lately imported from Port Phillip'.[10]

Two weeks later, this event escaped mention in Jeanneret's first official report as superintendent. His sprawling, detailed report to the Colonial Secretary – written in a distinctive, careful hand – supplies a very detailed glimpse into life at Wybalenna in this period. Importantly, he provides a full census, noting that three of the men – Alfred, Alexander and Tippo – 'claim the designation of King, and exercise a degree of authority over the others'.[11] This is an important change of seniority since Robinson's day, when the three kings were Alfred, George (Ben Lomond) and Alpha (Wooreddy, Bruny Island). King George had died in 1841, leaving the reduced Ben Lomond nation without a leader, and with the passing of Doctor Wooreddy, the only confirmed Bruny Island person on the settlement now was Trugernanner (known as Lalla Rookh in this period). From this list, we can see that the Big River–Oyster Bay alliance now claimed full leadership of the settlement, formed by a triumvirate of Alfred, who had replaced the famed King William at his death; Alexander, who had been exercising moral authority since 1838 when he led prayer sessions; and Tippo, an Oyster Bay man.

The report was structured in a patriarchal, hierarchical fashion. Once the leadership group was noted, Jeanneret's census of September 1842 went on to list the names of the fifteen married couples,[12]

---

10 The original report from Jeanneret unseen. Information on this event taken from Plomley, *Weep in Silence*, 139.
11 Henry Jeanneret to G W. Boyes, 15 September 1842, AOT CSO8/1/157 183.
12 Alfred and Emma; Alexander and Caroline; Tippo & Flora; Achilles & Agnes; Eugene & Sarah; Frederick & Anne; Neptune & Amelia; Noemy & Catherine;

CHAPTER 5

'if the connection they form can be so designated'. This hints at the ever-present problem for European and VDL men alike – inconstancy. The community at this time also comprised of six single men,[13] nine single women,[14] and seven children.[15] His report is a rich source of information regarding life in the community, and echoes the concerns of earlier administrators. He notes that the community on the whole 'agree better amongst themselves than might be anticipated', given the difference in language groups which had plagued the community from its outset:

> … considering they are of various tribes, so completely differing in dialect, as to be in some cases incapable of conversing, except in the barbarous English now the general medium of communication; which is replete with native words, and is pronounced with little regard to the distinction of consonants.[16]

At the time of writing this report, Jeanneret had only been at Wybalenna for three months, and some of his observations reflect only a superficial knowledge of the culture of the people he was now employed to superintend. Echoing the laments of previous superintendents, the writers of the *Flinders Island Chronicle*, and the men who sermonised at the prayer meetings, Jeanneret wrote, 'I find it

---

Andrew & Sophia; Washington & Juliet; Peter Pindar & Louisa; Augustus & Bessy; Bonaparte & Daphne; Henry & Lucy; Leonidas & Patty. Henry Jeanneret to G W. Boyes, 15 September 1842, AOT CSO8/1/157 183.

13 Alphonso, Edmund, Hannibal, Jem, Richard/'Cranky Dick' and Ajax. Henry Jeanneret to G W. Boyes, 15 September 1842, AOT CSO8/1/157 183.

14 Tinginoop, Harriet, Clara, Wild Mary, Big Mary, Fanny, Matilda, Rose and Trugernanner. (A tenth women, listed by Jeanneret as Fabracane, cannot be identified against earlier census lists published by Plomley in *Weep in Silence*.) Henry Jeanneret to G W. Boyes, 15 September 1842, AOT CSO8/1/157 183.

15 Fanny and Adam (children of Sarah), Martha (daughter of Catherine and Noemy); Hannah and Nanny (daughters of Big Mary); Jessy (daughter Jem), and Moriarty (son of Neptune and Amelia). Henry Jeanneret to G W. Boyes, 15 September 1842, AOT CSO8/1/157 183.

16 Henry Jeanneret to G W. Boyes, 15 September 1842, AOT CSO8/1/157 185.

exceedingly difficult to persuade them to keep their huts in a tidy state'.[17] Another enduring problem for administrators – matrimonial looseness – is also raised in Jeanneret's discussion of the VDL acceptance of Christian ideals. While, he observes, VDL people assented 'unreservedly' to Christianity and were equipped to 'readily converse on the subject' – setting them apart, in his estimation, to the New South Wales peoples – they did not seem 'prepared to admit its applicability, particularly as it respects the intercourse of the sexes'.[18] Jeanneret is able to record some very clear work done by the VDL people, such as Noemy tending the cattle and greater community effort in sheep care, and when boats arrive. Yet he displays a decided lack of knowledge of VDL social organisation when he states that polygamy was common[19] in pre-European VDL society, confusing polygamy with serial monogamy.

Jeanneret's report is ultimately patronising in the manner of its day, holding that VDL people 'resemble spoiled children, sometimes fretful and angry with little cause but easily reconciled'.[20] His recording of VDL cultural practices also displays his lack of familiarity:

> … the Aborigines continue their National dances, upon these occasions stripping themselves naked, the men at least, for I believe the women rarely if ever do so. I have ineffectually remonstrated against this, as well as the dirty custom they have of besmearing themselves with red ochre and grease.[21]

His comment about the women 'rarely if ever' performing rituals unclad undoubtedly speaks to the women's more secretive performance

---

17   Ibid., 190.
18   Ibid., 185.
19   Ibid., 186.
20   Ibid.
21   Ibid., 187-188.

of cultural practice, for in the next line he goes on to discuss how the VDL people frequently absented themselves from the settlement – a complaint as old as the settlement itself. The single women were especially the targets of his concern for refusing to be controlled. Those with children were seen to be negligent, sometimes going away for days on end, and:

> … in consequence of numerous complaints against them from the married ones, I insisted upon the single women remaining, neverthele∫s they managed to elude my vigilance and remained three weeks away.[22]

There were other observations, and references to previous administrators: Dr Fisher had allotted the VDL people a garden, but they would not exert themselves to tend it; and muskets had been given to them by Smith, but were now 'mostly disabled'.

Overall, Jeanneret seemed to be under the impression that he was supervising prisoners. Any ideas about VDL independence, or entitlement, seemed erroneous to him. He bemoaned how items retrieved from the wreck of the *Edinburgh Castle* 'proved a great evil to them, the spirits, wine and other now unattainable luxuries having rendered them less contented with their ample but more wholesome and homely fare', adding that he would like to stop their 'luxuries' of tobacco ration altogether and replace it with sugar. This was a long way from the relative generosity of Sir George Arthur's approach. His recommendation on stopping the tobacco ration caused Governor Franklin to make a note in the report's margin on the inadvisability of this course – not because it denied rights, but on account of the ill feeling it might introduce, them having been given tobacco freely for so long.[23]

---

22   Ibid., 188.
23   Ibid., 189.

Significantly, Jeanneret very briefly discusses education. He reports:

> A few of each sex can read and write a little and occasionally expreſs a desire to improve themselves. They all agree in wishing the children to have the benefit of education and, like all rude and uncultured races, they are highly amused and delighted with explanations of physical phenomena.[24]

This is an important observation, as it dispels one of the enduring myths about Wybalenna: that the VDL exiles had no interest in learning, or the ability to improve. Fuelling this assumption that the adults on Flinders Island could not or would not learn, Plomley stated that literacy was the domain of a select few of the younger, activist members of the community.[25] However, this younger, literate group were not present when Jeanneret made this report. Those living at Wybalenna during this period were – aside from the Sealing Women – generally what might be termed the least Europeanised of the exiles. Jeanneret's offhand observation, while demeaning, is a direct challenge to the long-running characterisation of literacy at Wybalenna as only being accomplished by a few select young people.

Jeanneret's 1842 observation goes a long way to argue for the authenticity of the writings which would come in several years: writings which he, himself, would charge to be inauthentic, leading to the general assumption followed by commentators and historians ever since. Put simply, the older Wybalenna community – even without its young, worldly literati – could already put pen to paper.

The desire for literacy was enduring. While historians have correctly noted that the civilising mission was focused on the use of

---

24 Ibid., 190.
25 Plomley insisted that, at the very most, only four or five VDL exiles in total were able to read and write 'with any fluency': *Weep in Silence*, 990.

CHAPTER 5

English to the exclusion of Indigenous languages as a form of cultural annihilation, the record demonstrates an aspiration for learning which extended over the entire history of the Wybalenna exile. Just as Henry Nickolls noted in 1835 that the men evinced a desire for literacy, so they could write to the Governor to return them to the VDL mainland, there was, among the older VDL population, a core who knew literacy to be crucial to their goals of repatriation.

The Second Return of Walter Arthur – October 1842

On 28 July 1842, a scene of tearful farewell took place on the beach at Williamstown, on the periphery of Port Phillip. Walter George Arthur, his wife Mary ann and their friend David Bruny were about to leave Melbourne to return south. The family who were bidding them farewell – the Robinsons, including the Chief Protector, his wife Maria and daughter Eliza, and probably one or more of his sons – were genuinely aggrieved to see this trio leave. The usually stoic Robinson noted in his diary:

> I parted with these people with reluctance, they cried and so did my family. I could wish they had remained but it is all for the best so I hope. I wrote for them to go to Launceston but sent them to Flinders, in consorting with as Flinders Island inhabitants are dull without them ...[26]

It was a far cry from two months earlier, when he had despatched another party of VDL exiles with relief. For Robinson and his family, the Arthurs had been an important part of their lives for seven years.

Mary ann and Eliza had almost grown up together, as had Walter and several of Robinson's sons, who were the same age. They had

---

26 Robinson's journal 23 July 1842, in Clark, *Journals of George Augustus Robinson, Volume 3*, 80.

worked together at the Robinsons' new farm in Port Phillip of recent times, and Walter had also travelled overland to South Australia with the Protector's son William Robinson, undoubtedly forming close bonds away from parental eyes. Mary ann was also distressed to be leaving the company of Charlotte, the former Tyereelore from New Holland who she had come to know at Wybalenna and who had travelled to the mainland with them. Mary ann carried a certificate written by the Chief Protector, addressed to 'The Superintendent, FI', testifying to her and her husband's good behaviour. It also specified 'They have both been baptised and were married according to the forms of the Presbyterian Church at Flinders Island by the Chaplain'. Curiously, the document also appears to leave the choice of their final destination up to them: it advises, 'I beg to state that they have expreſsed a wish to return to Launceston and I feel persuaded Sir John will not object to this arrangement when the circumstances of their Case is brought before him'.[27] Mary ann – already having a strong awareness of the power of the written word – would file this away for future use.

In an awful irony, the heartfelt farewell on the beach was to no avail, as the conveyance for the trio – the steamer to take them to the *Adelaide* – did not arrive to collect them. Instead, Mary ann and the two men spent a cold winter night, waiting on the beach, then made their way back to Melbourne the next day. Robinson was furious at what they had been through: he ensured that their next attempt at leaving, a few days later, did not end in such discomfort. Finally, on 30 August, the three sailed from Port Phillip on the *Adelaide*.

---

27 George Augustus Robinson to The Commandant, Flinders Island, 23 July 1842, CSO 11/26/378, SLV AJCP 280/195 Reel 544, 334.

CHAPTER 5

Their departure was noted at the highest level. In a report written ten days later, Charles La Trobe advised the Colonial Secretary in Sydney that the three – 'Walter George Arthur & wife Mary Ann, David Brunie son to Wooredde' – had left Port Phillip on 30 August. Referring to Robinson disparagingly, La Trobe added, 'there are now only two of their number originally brought over by him still in the Port Phillip district, and that it is his purpose to procure a passage for these, as soon as they come in from the country'.[28] These two he is referring to are Peter Brune and, most likely, Thomas Thompson – neither of whom would make the trip.

The *Adelaide* took the Arthurs and David Bruny straight to Hobart, arriving there on 9 September. The Hobart *Courier* would note their arrival in the shipping news, naming the ship, and its cargo – 'sheep and three Aborigines of Van Diemen's Land'.[29] We have no details of their first movements in Hobart, but it was highly likely that they were met by, or immediately visited, Robert Clark. They also met up with a fourth friend who they had first known in Melbourne.

John Allen was in his early twenties, like the Arthurs and David Bruny. He already had quite a long presence in the historical record, under a number of names.[30] His family were known to Robinson from as early as July 1830, when his parents Moneneboyerminer and Karnebutcher 'surrendered themselves' and were confined to jail in Campbell Town. From here, the family appears to have been separated: John's father disappears from the record, and his mother Karnebutcher was 'acquired' by Alexander McKay and taken to

---

28 C. J. La Trobe to Colonial Secretary, 10 September 1842, SLV MS 8454 Box 650/17.
29 The *Courier* (Hobart), 16 September 1842, 2.
30 Lennimeena/Lurnerminner/Paddy/Jacky/Batman's Jack/VDL Jack/Jack Allen/John Allen.

the North West, later joining Robinson's Friendly Mission.[31] The boy – then aged around eight – was 'placed' with John Batman.[32] Karnebutcher tried on multiple occasions to have her son returned to her, and Robinson agitated repeatedly on her behalf, first to Batman, and then to the Colonial Secretary, writing that the anxious mother 'has frequently importuned and solicited me in the strongest terms to have her son restored'.[33] This request was approved by an order from Sir George Arthur in January 1834, but Batman flatly refused to relinquish him.[34] This was the final straw for Karnebutcher: dejected, she abandoned the Friendly Mission party two weeks later on 20 January 1834, taking one of Robinson's key intermediaries, Pagerly, with her. Robinson wrote that 'The absconding of these women had caused an unpleasant sensation'.[35] She was eventually recaptured, and sent to Flinders Island, where it appears she died, never achieving her longstanding goal of being reunited with her son.[36]

John Allen's Port Phillip days are likewise reasonably well recorded. In July 1835, aged perhaps eleven or twelve, John sailed on the *Rebecca* to Port Phillip.[37] He arrived at Indented Head in early August, and in October is listed in Batman's journal as making the journey on foot to the Yarra settlement, to replace a broken hoe.[38] Allen is quiet in the record until October 1838, when he – or possibly

---

31 *Friendly Mission*, 448, 462, 518, 571, 615, 658, 759, 776, 800, 818.
32 A. H. Campbell, *John Batman and the Aborigines*, Malmsbury Vic., Kibble Books, 1987, 59.
33 *Friendly Mission*, 945-946.
34 Ibid., 866-868.
35 Ibid., 869-871.
36 There is a reference to Karnebutcher being dissatisfied with life at Flinders Island July 1834 (2 July 1834, *Friendly Mission*, 928), but it appears she had passed away before Robinson took up residence there in 1835.
37 See Cornwall Chronicle; *Friendly Mission*, 508.
38 Campbell, *John Batman and the Aborigines*, 128

CHAPTER 5

the other Batman's Jack, an Eora man who had been with Batman since his Sydney days – was charged with being drunk and disorderly, but no penalty was recorded.[39] Following Batman's death in June 1839, Allen connected with Robinson, now the Chief Protector in Port Phillip.[40] Allen's services were sought by Captain George Smyth of the Mounted Police, whose repeated recruitment attempts were rejected in June and July 1839.[41] Allen's refusal to work for Smyth may have been due to remuneration, which was to be in the form of a uniform and board, but no wages: he would also have been well aware of the police Captain's role in a recent massacre on the Campaspe River.[42] Finally, in July 1839, he signed a contract with David Hill and Walter Coates, at £26 per annum, the agreement witnessed and signed by Walter Arthur, Thomas 'Brunel', Robinson and W. Lansdown.[43] The following year, Allen was unjustly blamed for the death of a horse; although he was later acquitted, he had already fled to Hobart.[44] He appears to have remained in Hobart until August 1842, when he renewed his acquaintance with the Arthurs and David Bruny.

The four young VDL people would have formed an impressive group. All were comparatively literate and worldly, and possessed of a

---

39 Melbourne Court Register, 24 October 1838, reprinted in Michael Cannon (ed.), *Historical Records of Victoria, Foundation Series, Volume 2A, The Aborigines of Port Phillip 1835–1839*, Victorian Government Printing Office, Melbourne, 1982, 205.
40 Clark, *Journals of George Augustus Robinson, Vol. 1*, 53.
41 Robinson's journals, 26 June, 6 July, 24 July 1839, in Clark, *Journals, Vol. 1*, 63.
42 Robinson's journals mention Smyth's role in and report of the Campaspe massacre: Clark, *Journals, Vol. 1*, 56.
43 Reprinted in Michael Cannon (ed.), *Historical Records of Victoria, Foundation Series, Volume 2B, Aborigines and Protectors, 1835–1839*, Victorian Government Printing Office, Melbourne, 1982, 744.
44 Campbell, *John Batman and the Aborigines*, 231; Cannon, *Historical Records of Victoria, Volume 2B*, 737.

European polish. This was especially noticed when they were invited to visit Government House. As the *Hobart Courier* reported:

> We understand that on the afternoon of yesterday, the four Aborigines lately arrived on their way from Port Phillip to Flinders Island, attended by Mr Robert Clarke, their former Catechist, had the honour of waiting upon Lady Franklin, to whom they were introduced by Dr. Officer. Her Ladyship conversed with them for upwards of an hour, when she was joined by His Excellency the Lieutenant-Governor: both Sir John and Lady Franklin appeared much pleased with the natives, particularly with Walter George Arthur, the chief of the Ben-lomond tribe, and his lubra (wife) Mrs Arthur.[45]

The young VDL group also made the most of their humanitarian contacts. Aside from cultivating the Franklins, they befriended Dr Robert Officer, then a Hobart health inspector: he would go on to become Sir Robert Officer, noted politician. The Quaker George Washington Walker, who had first visited the VDL exiles in 1832 with his travelling partner James Backhouse, had discussions with the Arthurs and Bruny. The nature of this discussion is revealed in Walker's letter to Harriett Jeanneret, wife of the incumbent Wybalenna superintendent, of 16 September. After assuring her that she and her husband had not been forgotten in their 'exclusion from general society', Walker told her about the Arthurs and Bruny, who were currently on board the *Adelaide*. Warning her that the ship was soon bound to sail for Flinders Island, Walker wrote:

> They have for some time been resident in Port Phillip; & I find that they have been informed from what sources, I know not, impreſsions unfavourable as regards the present system of treatment of the Natives on Flinders. It may be wholly without

---

45   The *Courier*, Hobart, 14 October 1842, 2.

CHAPTER 5

cause. But if their minds have been any way prejudiced, it is better that you, & that the Doctor, should be aware of it ...[46]

Walker intimates that they had received accounts that the present mode of administration and treatment was austere, especially relating to the allowance of food, and that 'A feeling of aversion towards residing again on Flinders has been induced'. Walker either does not know the source of these reports or – more likely – he is diplomatically avoiding naming the messengers. We can only speculate.

Plomley habitually cited Robert Clark as the source of all VDL discontent. One of the key flaws of his monumental suite of works on VDL First Nations people was that, during the Wybalenna period, his clear dislike for Clark prejudiced all other analysis of VDL activity. Clark, however, had not set foot on Flinders Island for two years. How, then, might the reports of VDL dissatisfaction at Wybalenna have found their way to the ears of the Arthurs, Bruney and Allen, and through them to Walker?

There were several Wybalenna returnees in Hobart at the same time as the Arthurs and Bruney. They might well have crossed paths with erstwhile superintendent Peter Fisher, who had just come from Flinders six weeks earlier. Most certainly, they would have conversed with the VDL children who were staying with Clark. Officer, who was responsible for overseeing the Orphan Schools, would also have been apprised of events at Wybalenna. News of Jeanneret's failed attempt to use the military to subdue 'shamefully immoral conduct' may well have travelled. There was also the often-ignored network of sailors, sealers and VDL people based on the mainland, and the members of the general public who had, before Jeanneret was even

---

46   George Washington Walker to Harriet Jeanneret, 16 September 1842, AOT C1166 109-111.

confirmed, ridiculed his appointment. By September, there had been complaints about his administration from the military. There are any number of possible sources where the Arthurs, Bruny and Allen could have heard about the problems already surrounding Jeanneret's administration.

Tellingly, at no stage does Walker say that he does not believe the rumours. His diplomatic avoidance of siding with the Jeannerets speaks volumes. Instead, he tells Mrs Jeanneret:

> I need hardly remind the Doctor of the absolute necefsity that exists, in all dealings with the Aborigines, of winning their confidence & goodwill by kindnefs. Not as blind, indiscriminate acquiescence in all that they may ask, or desire, but such a course of behaviour as true Christian people.[47]

Despite their reservations, the Arthurs, David Bruny and John Allen were eventually sent to Flinders Island. The letter from Walker must have had an impact on Henry Jeanneret, because his report to the Colonial Secretary was very cautious, if not totally correct in its details:

> the Aboriginal persons Walter, Mary Ann, Jack and Stephen Brune arrived on this settlement on the Isabella and I hope they will be an advantageous [accefsion] to our party as they appear more completely afsimilated to the habits of Europeans than the others ... No effort will be spared to make them comfortable and induce them by orderly conduct to an example to the others.[48]

Jeanneret also made note that Harriet (or 'Hatty'), the mother of Thomas Thompson, was anxious to have him returned to her. He had

---

47   Ibid.
48   Henry Jeanneret to Colonial Secretary, 24 October 1842, AOT CSO8/1/157, 66.

CHAPTER 5

travelled to Port Phillip with Robinson's party and apparently absconded. Sadly for Harriet – although perhaps not for young Thomas – he was not to return to Wybalenna.

The community was bolstered in December 1842 by the arrival of the Lanny family, of Circular Head. They had been hiding from Europeans for some years in the North West, in the areas occupied by the Van Diemen's Land Company's pastoral lease. Comprised of a mother, father and five sons, a sixth child, known as Victoria Lanny, had been captured the previous January and had been living at Wybalenna since February. Tragically, the mother Nabrunga and the youngest son died soon after arrival. These deaths were noted, naturally, in the settlement reports. More significantly, they were also written about by Walter Arthur, in an extraordinary letter to Robert Clark written in March 1843.

This is Walter Arthur's first known letter written independently of European interference. It is also the moment when he announces himself – at the opening of the letter – as 'Mr Walter G Arthur, Chieftain of the Benlomond Tribe of Now Van D.L'. Here, he is assuming the position held by his father, King George, who had died on 1 June 1840, while Arthur was in Port Phillip. Interestingly, he does not claim the title of 'King', even though he would have been expected to. His letter to Clark begins:

> You will understand that I am not very well pleased with the Doctor processings at Flinders island
>
> Sir, You will understand I never received one thing from the Doctor which you yourself heard of in the Governour house Told to me in the Governour house and I will esteem it as particular Favour if you would have the Goodneſs as to insert this in your papers

and you do this for the sake of the poor Natives at Flinders Island Peajacket you will have the goodneſs to let the Colony at Large know how the poor Natives at Flinders Island are treated.[49]

There are a number of remarkable points raised by Walter Arthur's letter. Firstly, he specifies that promises given to him, in the Governor's house – presumably during his visit of September 1842 – had not been fulfilled. The 'things' never received from the doctor remain a mystery, but the intent of his request for Clark to 'insert this in your papers' is clear: Arthur wanted to ensure his objections to Jeanneret were lodged in the official record. He has a clear understanding, at this stage, of the importance of evidence. He also invites Clark to spread the word far and wide – to 'the Colony at Large' – of their mistreatment. But there was more to come. As well as making general complaints about Jeanneret's performance, he also sent Clark a record of deaths at Wybalenna:

> There are Four Natives
> the first is Rose
> the second is poor Henery hold Henery poor hold man die a very hard death.
> And there is poor little boy and his Mother the two that Latly came down from Swilleurhead.[50]

He was here referring to Big River woman Rose[51] who had been described in the 1837 school examinations as 'a shrewd intelligent woman and quite domesticated', and Henry, a man in his forties who

---

49 Walter George Arthur to Robert Clark, 17 March 1843, QVMAG Plomley Collection CHS53 2/10-2/13.
50 Ibid.
51 Myhermenanyehaner/Whytythecapperner/Gooseberry/Rose. Born around 1800, Big River nation (?): *Weep in Silence*, 867.

CHAPTER 5

had been noted in 1838 as 'Perfect in the alphabet' – clearly, one of the many older men who was on the way to literacy.[52] Both had died in December, since the arrival of Walter Arthur and the Port Phillip party. The other two deaths mentioned were those members of the Lanny family, Nahbrunga and her son, who had arrived from Circular Head. After passing on this information to Clark, Arthur again signed his name, Walter George Arthur, Chieftain of the Benlomond Tribe, Flinders Island Van D.L.

Henry Jeanneret's report of these four deaths was to come two weeks later, on 31 March, when he submitted his next report to the Colonial Secretary. He softened the bad news, however, by writing about new arrivals first:

> Subsequently to my last report the number of Aborigines has been augmented by the arrival of four from Port Phillip, viz, Walter George Arthur and his wife Mary Anne; John Allen; and Davy; of a family of seven from the main viz, John Lanna, Nabrunga (his wife) and their five sons Barney, Peter, Charley, William and Frank: and of two females Waberty and her daughter Beſsy Miti, who were left at the Settlement by a Sealer, with whom Waberty has cohabited for twelve years.[53]

Waberty – or Wapperty as she became better known – became an important addition to the community of exiles. One of the daughters of famed Coastal Plains chief Mannalargenna, she would remain with the exiles for the next two decades. After recording her arrival, and some information on the sealing men from whom she was received, Jeanneret went on:

---

52 Rose and Henry's school examinations, from Robinson Letterbook, QVMAG CY548.
53 Henry Jeanneret, Report to Colonial Secretary, 31 March 1843, AOT CSO8/1/157 230-238.

> Soon after the arrival of the people from the Main, the woman Nabrunga, an invalid at the time, was seized with Inflammation of the Lungs, and also her youngest boy; both refused, until too late, to submit to the active treatment requisite, and ultimately became victims to the disease.
>
> Two other fatal cases have occurred, those died from Fever, and Henry, a very old man, with Hydrothorax.

Jeanneret went on to blame the predominance of pulmonary disease on the high level of heat maintained, in the early evening, in the exiles' cottages. His solution was to alter the layout of the cottages, to enable more people to inhabit them, and thus dissuade any one individual, or couples, from sleeping too close to the fires. Jeanneret then returned to the subject of the Lanny family, and curiously – after previously stating that Nahbrunga and her son had refused any attempts at medical attention – drew attention to the family's obedience, saying, 'The poor creatures from Circular Head are very docile, cheerful and orderly, shewing no disposition to resort to the bush, always willing to make themselves useful, and amusing themselves with killing small birds with their short sticks'.[54] Here he was clearly infantalising them, perhaps to draw a firm distinction between them and the more querulous of his charge.

> Most of those from Port Phillip have proved more intractable. The women Truganini and Matilda abscond perpetually ... Allen and Davy, who have been brought up here, are without any material superiority over the rest, excepting that they speak our language more intelligibly, more indolent than any, and shew leſs desire to improve their circumstances.[55]

---

54 Ibid., 231.
55 Ibid., 231-232.

CHAPTER 5

Jeanneret wrote to the Colonial Secretary in very guarded language about how the 'disputes and jealousies noticed in my former report have vanished', but how 'reformation, in this instance, was not effected without coercion'. He does not clearly spell out what means of coercion he used, only:

> ... having repeatedly explained to all my determination not to allow the peaceably disposed to be annoyed by the riotous proceedings of the rest, this man in one of his domestic brawls committed a violent assault upon another; was in consequence subjected to a short confinement, and has ever been a pattern of propriety.[56]

This almost certainly relates to the case of a fight between Frederick and Eugene. As will later be discussed, Jeanneret reportedly took two loaded pistols to the square, threatening, according to witnesses, to shoot Frederick dead.[57] This was coercion indeed.

Jeanneret's report of 31 March makes no further mention of the problems on the settlement which had induced Walter Arthur to write such a dramatic plea for help to Clark. He makes general reports on the improvements which he attempts to take credit for – such as all now apparently attending church and school with regularity – and makes the observation that 'Many expreſs a desire for further education; but those who have enjoyed the greatest advantage in this respect, are the least useful, in fact, these boys, as they are called, are the laziest of all'. It is unclear to whom he is referring, though he does make clear that Walter, Mary ann, Washington and Bessy (presumably, Bessy Clark) assist in the Sunday School.

---

56 Ibid., 232.
57 Testimonies from David Bruney, Walter Arthur, King Alexander, Washington, Neptune and Frederick, October 13–14 1846, contained in the Friend Inquiry papers, AOT CSO11/1/27, C658.

The women – as always – remain the subject of scrutiny and anxiety for Wybalenna administrators. Jeanneret complained – as many had done before him – that the women refused to do any work, except when paid in sugar, tobacco or vinegar (used to clean shells for necklaces). It would seem, however, that it was for men that they would not work, for Jeanneret makes clear that the women:

> ... now make their own dreſses, and wash, cook and procure wood for themselves. They shew less disposition to obtain any education than the men, some are much addicted to fabricating mischievous and scandalous reports.[58]

Gammoning, it would seem, was still a popular pastime. Marriages – in the Wybalenna sense, occurring when couples expressed the public desire to cohabit – were still given the official sanction of the superintendent, but, in the absence of a chaplain, remained a very loose and impermanent affair. Jeanneret's report notes two recent ones – of David Bruny and Clara, and John Allen and Wild Mary. We know, from later records, that in three years' time David Bruny's wife was Matilda, so it seems that the VDL trend of serial monogamy was to continue. The only official marriage, presided over by an ordained minister, remained that of Walter and Mary ann Arthur.

The men, by Jeanneret's report, exhibit more of the habits of industry than the women. He notes that 'Several of the men are industrious, particularly Tippoo, Nomy, Hannibal and Dick'. There is, however, hints of problems to come when he states that,

> The men from Port Phillip have circulated exaggerated accounts of the value of their services, and have done mischief, as well as, by refusing themselves to render any aſsistance.[59]

---

58   Henry Jeanneret, Report to Colonial Secretary, 31 March 1843, AOT CSO8/1/157 233-234.
59   Ibid., 234.

CHAPTER 5

This was to become an important issue. Walter Arthur, David Bruny and John Allen had all been employed while at Port Phillip, at what were then the standard rates for any man with their training, white or black. They knew the value of their work, and also would have gained important insight into the burgeoning work ethic on the Australian frontier. Richard Broome notes how Indigenous workers accommodated the culture of the knockabout bush worker, which in turn resonated with their own traditional culture. The seemingly 'ill-disciplined' and 'likely to abscond' Australian Legend depicted by Russel Ward was a sound fit for workers who were compelled to down tools 'for ceremonies, to see kinfolk, or to travel their country'.[60] In short, Arthur, Bruney and Allen probably had far greater knowledge of the realities of Australian working life than Henry Jeanneret did. Their claims to have received a wage of £26 per annum, for example, which was Allen's remuneration in Melbourne, might have seemed an exaggeration to Jeanneret; however, he was still of the opinion that they were on the same social rung as convicts, deserving of no wage at all, but perhaps a little tobacco or sugar. His ideological approach to the people he was charged with superintending was at variance with both the precepts on which the settlement was first founded – that they were free people, not bound to work at all against their will – and with the true value placed on their labour in the open market. This attitude was to bring him into open conflict with the VDL exiles in the near future.

Another source of conflict was the VDL people's love of dogs. As has been well observed, dogs were embraced, when they arrived with Europeans, both for hunting and, more importantly, for companionship. This was somewhat at odds with European ideas of dogs as work

---

60   Broome, 'Aboriginal Workers on the South Eastern Frontier', 218-219.

animals: as Broome notes, 'Aboriginal attitudes to dogs … were seen by colonists as spoiling, and even as unnatural and abhorrent'.⁶¹ The VDL exiles gave their dogs English names, such as Prinny, Tinker, Thrumpty, Mountain and Groggy. Trugernanner's dog was Panty; Emma's was Lion.⁶² There had been dogs on the settlement for the length of its existence, but by Jeanneret's time their numbers had swelled to, according to his reports and those of Peter Fisher before him, over sixty. Jeanneret decided to cull the numbers drastically, keeping only a half dozen, which would be seen as the Government's property. He reported how the VDL exiles refused his offers to buy the dogs from them, and retreated to the bush to hide them. What he does not make clear in his report was his method of culling the numbers. It is known that he shot a number, and took many others to small islands, where they were left to starve to death. This was a heartbreaking brutality in the eyes of VDL people, and one which they would remember with bitterness for years to come.

Another issue which had caused consternation at the settlement – which Jeanneret mentions in his report – was his attempt, intimated in his previous report, to cut the allowance of tobacco. He wrote:

> For a time the <u>discontinuance of Tobacco and Sugar</u> [his underlining] as reward for industry caused amongst them an almost entire ceſsation from the labour they afford to the establishment.⁶³

This may very well be a minimisation of what we might term industrial action, or a strike. Jeanneret goes on to explain that during Peter Fisher's time, the flock of sheep, which were the property of the

---

61 Broome, *Aboriginal Victorians*, 22.
62 List made by Robert Clark, probably in the mid-1840s: *Weep in Silence*, 195.
63 Henry Jeanneret, Report to Colonial Secretary, 31 March 1843, AOT CSO8/1/157 234.

CHAPTER 5

VDL exiles, were sold by the then-superintendent, with the proceeds going to the Commissariat Officer at Launceston – effectively, into the colony's consolidated revenue. Thus, the previous source of funds for the exiles' luxuries, such as tobacco, was lost. It is almost certain that this sale of the sheep would have been brought to Jeanneret's attention by Walter Arthur who, from all we know of him, kept a close account of his father's and general VDL property. The reduction of their tobacco ration, Jeanneret again hinted, 'excited discontent, which I have mollified by promising to represent the matter'. He then recommended 'reappropriation of their flock to the supply of these extras, the proceeds being distributed as rewards for industry, and applied to their personal profit and advancement'.[64]

Crucially, Jeanneret also recommended adopting a scheme of paying wages for work performed. In a mode similar to that which would be adopted by Protection Boards across the Australian colonies, these wages would be held in trust, and issued piecemeal, and only for approved purposes. VDL people were not trusted with their own money. This is at some variance with the system of payment during Robinson's period as Commandant, when a Flinders Island currency was inaugurated, and the VDL exiles were given actual currency (albeit the Flinders Island coinage) to spend or save as they wished. Again, we see a strong sense of paternalism in Jeanneret's recommendations. Despite the clear advancement of people like the Arthurs, Bruny and Allen, he seems fearful of their sense of independence engulfing the whole community.

After Jeanneret's detailed and very insightful report of 31 March – and Walter Arthur's letter of two weeks previous, detailing his

---

64   Ibid., 236-237.

concerns about the administrator – three months pass with little information to shed light on events at the settlement. However, June 1843 saw an explosion of tensions.

On 6 June, Jeanneret wrote to the Colonial Secretary complaining about Walter Arthur's activities, alleging he had been 'assiduous in endeavouring to excite disaffection'.[65] At this time, the military detachment – led by Sergeant Ingram, with whom Jeanneret had previously clashed, and including Private Reynolds who had been permanently disabled by Jeanneret's poor medical care – were replaced. Sergeant Moore, accompanied by two privates from the 96th Regiment, arrived. Less than three weeks later, Sergeant Moore wrote to Hobart complaining about Jeanneret's treatment of him, and one week later Jeanneret returned the compliment, writing to the Colonial Secretary to complain about Moore. However, another writer – perhaps even more significant in the minds of the colonial authorities in Hobart, who were always concerned with what the humanitarian lobby back in England might think – was also voicing his displeasure at Jeanneret's management.

Walter Arthur wrote to George Augustus Robinson on 5 July 1843. Purposely making this a personal letter, not official, he addressed it to Mr Robinson, River Tarneat, Yearra Yearra. Opening it with an affectionate 'My Dear Old Master', he begins by acknowledging the arrival of the sheep belonging to the VDL exiles, which had just arrived from Port Phillip via the *Flying Fish*. Heartfelt enquiries are made regarding the health of Robinson's wife and family, and Arthur adds:

---

65   Jeanneret's report unseen, cited in Plomley, *Weep in Silence*, 142.

CHAPTER 5

> Myself and my wife and all my Countrymen are very well indeed and Mary Ann is often speaking about poor old Charlotte she is always talking about her.[66]

This affords a glimpse of the personal relationships which were made, and torn asunder, by the separation of Charlotte, a New Holland woman rescued from sealers with her child Johnny Franklin, from the Arthurs. She and Mary ann Arthur had lived and worked together for some years in the Robinson household, and obviously formed a deep bond, which is illustrated again later in the same letter by a repetition of the same concern – 'Mary Ann is doing very well and she hopes that old Charlotte is doing well'. This letter, though, is about more than keeping in contact with old acquaintances. Arthur requests:

> And you will try to send young Tommy Tompson and Peter Brune by any ship which may set sail for Hobart town and they will be sent down to Flinders Island.[67]

Here, Arthur was using his new position as leader of the community to voice the concerns of others. Harriet, as we had seen in an earlier letter from Henry Jeanneret, was anxious to have her son Thomas returned to her. David Bruny, now back at Wybalenna, was also concerned about his younger brother Peter, who had absconded from Robinson's care around the time of their return to Wybalenna. This would not be the last enquiry after the return of Peter Bruny, and clearly shows that – despite the apparent bad reputation of the island, the community was keen to consolidate itself there. Other family matters were raised in Walter Arthur's letter to Robinson: he

---

66 Walter Arthur to George Augustus Robinson, 5 July 1843, QVMAG CHS53 2/10-2/13, 1.
67 Ibid., 2.

also informed the erstwhile Commandant that he had seen his son, George Robinson, when he was last in Hobart town – presumably, the previous September when the group were en route to Wybalenna.

Then, possibly the true purpose of this letter is revealed when Arthur adds, 'This Doctor is a very bad man, he shoot all the natives dogs from them'.[68] The shooting of the dogs, as discussed earlier, was most certainly a very traumatic event for the VDL exiles, who placed a very high value on them, both for hunting and companionship. This was an issue which would be revisited, again and again, in the VDL complaints against Henry Jeanneret.

There is one other significant report in Walter Arthur's letter to Robinson, which gives valuable insight into life at Wybalenna. He tells Robinson:

> I am plough in a pice of land for my self and I always Gets Letters from Hobart Town every time the ships come to Flinders Island.[69]

This points to several key issues. Firstly, Arthur is clearly engaged in farming. Henry Jeanneret's earlier report had framed Arthur as somewhat lazy and disinterested in agriculture, but from this remark – and the many which would come in later letters – it is clear that the habits of agriculture, first established during Robinson's time at the establishment, were continuing. Further, the remark about getting letters from Hobart opens a number of possibilities. On one level, this acknowledges that VDL people – Walter Arthur especially – took a great interest and key role in the transference of goods which arrived at the settlement. His specific mention of letters is especially interesting, as it confirms that Arthur was in contact with persons

---

68   Ibid., 3-4.
69   Ibid., 4.

CHAPTER 5

outside Wybalenna – perhaps other than those of which we already have evidence.[70]

This letter seems to have been hurriedly written, as it is not in the careful copperplate of Arthur's official communications. However, he still finished it with a reminder of his youthful *Chronicle* sign-offs: a beautiful and elaborate 'Walter', followed by a repetition of his full name and title – 'Walter George Arthur, Chieftain of the Benlomond'. Most likely, this was so it could be carried in the *Flying Fish* to Hobart, then back north, to Robinson in Port Phillip. Many letters from Flinders Island were hurriedly scrawled to be conveyed in a waiting craft. Arthur would certainly have been hoping that, aside from his requests to have Thomas Thompson and Peter Bruney returned, Robinson would have used his influence to help get Doctor Jeanneret removed. However, what those at Wybalenna did not know – Jeanneret included – was that the doctor's days were already numbered.

It seems that the decision had been taken in Hobart some time previously that the appointment of Jeanneret had been a mistake. This might have been due to the doubts about his performance from the outset. It is not improbable, though, that Walter Arthur's very powerful letter to Clark, which would most certainly have been liberally tabled around Hobart, would have played a part. The terrible case of Private Reynolds, most certainly, was a deciding factor. In August 1843 – as Jeanneret and Moore were at loggerheads – the position of superintendent was quietly offered to former Van Diemen's Land medical inspector, Joseph Milligan. A trained doctor, naturalist and amateur ethnographer, Milligan was eminently more suited to the

---

70   Robert Clark, George Washington Walker, George Augustus Robinson.

position. Yet the colonial bureaucracy now had to find a way to dispense with the services of Henry Jeanneret.

In November 1843, Sir John Franklin's vice regal term was at an end. On leaving Van Diemen's Land, he made a point of visiting Wybalenna. Accompanied, as usual, by an illustrious party which included Bishop Nixon, Franklin writes:

> We then proceeded to Flinders Island, the dwelling-place of the sole remnant of the Aborigines of Van Diemen's Land, now scarcely exceeding fifty souls including some half-castes. A few of the younger members of this interesting black family were baptised by the Bishop, who promised himself another pastoral visit to them.[71]

Jeanneret took great heart from this visit, and from a perfunctory note written by Lady Franklin to his wife which Jeanneret interpreted as an official stamp of approval for his administration.[72] It appears he also took the opportunity to harangue the retired Governor about his issues with the military and new Governor. However, this was to be in vain, for when he wrote to Governor Eardley-Wilmot claiming to have Franklin's support, it was already too late. The decision had been well and truly made.

Henry Jeanneret's tenure as superintendent at Wybalenna was finally terminated in late November 1843, after the Colonial Surgeon found him incompetent in his treatment of Private Reynolds's leg. However, it is unclear as to when he actually received this advice. He was encountering problems with his administration as late as December 1843, when he pressed charges against Sergeant Moore. He advised the Colonial Secretary:

---

[71] Sir John Franklin, *Some Passages in the History of Van Diemen's Land*, [1845], Hobart, Platypus facsimile edition 1967, 97.

[72] Jeanneret, *Vindication of a Colonial Magistrate*, 7.

CHAPTER 5

> That on 4th December 1842, when called upon and directed both verbally and in writing to aid in apprehending the Aboriginal man 'Little Davey' charged with assault, he did conspire with Walter George Arthur and John Allen to liberate and rescue the said 'Little Davey' and did rescue him accordingly …[73]

This is a damning indictment of Jeanneret's administration. For the military detachment and the VDL exiles to band together to thwart Jeanneret's instructions is nothing short of mutiny. It also provides us with an example of the military presence at Wybalenna performing the exact role for which it was installed – protecting the VDL exiles. Jeanneret, a superintendent who had clearly lost control, further reported:

> Walter George Arthur, John Allen & others – joined in conspiracy to excite discontent and disaffection and did accordingly create diverse riots, assaults and affrays.[74]

Significantly, this is the only time – apart from in January 1832, under the leadership of Sergeant Wight – that such serious breaches of public order were recorded at Wybalenna. If the colonial administration in Hobart had not already resolved to dispense with Jeanneret's services, this incident would certainly have made the decision for them.

Meanwhile in Hobart, the machinations of change were already well underway. With Milligan already secured as Jeanneret's much needed replacement, Clark's steady efforts – ably supported by Walker – were rewarded, and he was offered his old position as catechist. Ten years after his first arrival on Flinders Island, Robert Clark was now

---

73 Henry Jeanneret to Colonial Secretary, 14 December 1843, AOT CSO 8/1/157, 335.
74 Ibid., 326

heading back to be with the people to whom he had grown so close. However, Henry Jeanneret – already having proved himself querulous regarding a land deal to which he felt himself served an injustice – would not take his dismissal by the Colonial Surgeon lying down. In the months to come, he would take his case for unfair dismissal from the far-flung colony to the home of the empire, London.

For now, though, an approach more sympathetic to the needs of the VDL exiles at Wybalenna was again in the ascendancy. More broadly across the empire, a full six years after the Select Committee into the Aborigines made their report, humanitarian policies relating to the treatment of First Nations peoples were still under discussion, at least in the colonial centres, if not on the frontiers. Across the Tasman, as tensions over land built, the *Southern Cross* carried a powerful editorial opinion:

> There is not one shadow of difference in principle between the crude adventurers who followed in the wake of Columbus on America, and those who followed Cook in the Pacific. The same hollow pretence to religion and humanity is made by both, and the same accursed scheme is pursued by both in their treatment of the aborigines: and will not the same fatal results ensue in both cases?[75]

On 4 February 1844, Milligan, Clark and their families arrived at Wybalenna on the *Isabella*. For a time, at least, the settlement would enjoy its smoothest, most accommodating and culturally rich days. The children separated from their families during Jeanneret's reign would be returned, and the young, worldly activists would, finally, find Europeans who treated them, generally, with respect.

---

75   Editorial, 'Progress of Civilization among the Natives', *The Southern Cross*, 28 October 1843, 2.

CHAPTER 5

There is little coverage of life at Wybalenna at this time, but some insight can be gained from the observations of J. B. Broadfoot, a passenger on the *Isabella* which was wrecked off Chappel Island in June 1844. In the memoir of his brief visit to Wybalenna, he owned that the community seemed comfortable, contented and healthy-looking, 'yet there seemed to be an air of melancholy depression hanging around everything I saw'.[76] Broadfoot goes on to lament the need for the VDL exiles to be thus confined to the island, and echoes the common lament that they would soon, surely, be extinct.

In July 1844, a personal tragedy struck the new superintendent. Joseph Milligan's wife of only three years died shortly after giving birth to their first child. For Milligan, this personal tragedy caused a re-evaluation of his life, and early in 1845 he resolved to return to Hobart with his infant son. Around this time, in February–March 1845, the artist John Skinner Prout visited Wybalenna and completed a set of evocative water colour landscapes and portraits of a number of the exiles.[77] In the absence of photography, these are some of the best records we have of life at Wybalenna.

The VDL exiles were at a crossroads. Faced with the prospect of having yet another administrator appointed over them, they began to consider alternatives. They were aided in this by Joseph Milligan, who seems to have been perhaps their most empowering administrator. Moves were afoot to try to shift the character of Wybalenna from

---

76   J. B. Broadfoot, 'An Unexpected Visit to Flinders Island in Bass's Strait', *Chambers Edinburgh Journal*, Vol. 4, 187-90 (original not seen, quoted from Plomley, *Weep in Silence*, 145).

77   These are now mostly in the British Museum, accompanied by short biographical notes from Robert Clark. Interestingly, Prout's daughter Matilda would remain in Van Diemen's Land after her family returned to England, and marry John Dandridge: the two would have a long relationship with VDL people at Oyster Cove and in Hobart.

a penal-style site of exile, to a self-supporting farming establishment. As Clark told George Washington Walker in early December 1845, if the Governor approved this plan, it would be 'the only piece of good service that has been performed for them since the departure of Sir George Arthur, that is to make Flinders Island a Self Supporting Establishment'.[78] The tenuous pathways of colonial power would soon find themselves revised, reorganised and reinvented. It is time they were reimagined.

Networks of Intelligence and Meshworks of Power

> It takes tremendous intellectual effort to even imagine what differentiation without hierarchy could be.[79]

As acknowledged at the outset, the vast majority of histories of Wybalenna have looked at the texts written by VDL people, and their actions, through a lens clouded by Eurocentrism and hierarchical thinking. The forms and functions of power at Wybalenna have been cast as ideas, legislation and directives emanating from London, sailing to Sydney, then south to Hobart, and from there, north to the Bass Strait islands, to be enacted by the Commandant at Wybalenna. From that point, authority – derived largely from written edicts – has been seen to be exercised over the VDL exiles. Such a view of the process is hardly surprising, as most of the histories which have been told are European histories, garnered from those many memorandums, instructions and determinations

---

78 Robert Clark to George Washington Walker, 3 December 1845, UTAS Library Quaker Collection S&RMC.

79 Elizabeth Brumfiel, 'Heterarchy and the Analysis of Complex Societies: Comments', in Ehrenreich, Crumley and Levy (eds.), *Heterarchy and the Analysis of Complex Societies*, Archaeological Papers of the American Anthropological Association, No. 6, Arlington, 1995, 125.

CHAPTER 5

which – apparently – constituted the written record. As earlier discussed, even sympathetic histories frame European control as absolute and the exiles as disempowered.

Power is seen as a metaphorical lightning bolt. It reigns downwards, running one-way, through colonial channels and the Commandant to the VDL exiles, ending only at the pens in the hands of VDL scribes. The words on paper have usually been seen as a mere earthing of this current, rendering it visible, through the archive. However, this view needs to be challenged. Lightning, in fact, often rises from the ground to meet the charge from above. It is an interaction of forces, not one acting on another.

There were multiple spheres of authority at Flinders Island, and the function of power took tangled, horizontal routes. For example, as shown in the *Flinders Island Chronicle*, Robinson as Commandant might have controlled the issue of flour and meat rations to the VDL people, but he could not curtail their movements and their gathering of bush foods, any more than he could control his often bickering staff and insubordinate convict servants. The Big River men, in Robinson's day, may have held influence over a large portion of the population, but not the people from the Ben Lomond nation. And no-one – at *any* stage – really had ultimate power over the remarkable ex-Tyereelore Sealing Women.

In the mid-1840s, there was a revolutionary change at Wybalenna. The beginnings of this could be seen with the return, from Port Phillip, of Walter Arthur and his circle of younger, more worldly friends. They were literate, had worked for wages, and knew the value that their labours commanded. They had observed the political machinations intrinsic to colonial administration, and they had a sound knowledge of the humanitarian ideals of the anti-slavery movement, thanks to their proximity to missionaries who harboured these ideals. Importantly, they also read newspapers, and kept abreast of events elsewhere in the empire. They were – as much as possible, given their confinement to an island – reasonably well informed and well-connected in terms of colonial networks. The level of sophistication gained by Walter Arthur and his circle, and the effect this would have had on a community which already had a staunch self-view of its own status as free people, has too often been overlooked by scholars who project their own values onto the cultures they encounter.

In Van Diemen's Land, Europeans looked for kings and a hierarchical structure. Scholars followed suit, reflecting what archaeologist Carol Crumley calls 'unconscious adoption of hierarchy-as-order'.[80] This made the colonisers and generations of commentators blind to the reality of a more horizontal, heterarchical group of societies in Van Diemen's Land, and a community in exile where a myriad of influences, often contradictory, overlap and resist. Henry Reynolds and Ian MacFarlane have noted the mosaic nature of nationhood in Van Diemen's Land, which was a 'patchwork of mini-states'.[81] Philosopher Mary Graham has also characterised Indigenous societies as based on multipolar organisation.[82]

The networks of order evident at Wybalenna differ demonstrably from a simple Commandant–military–exiles formula. They more closely resemble what Manuel de Landa terms 'meshworks'.[83] Although

---

[80] Carole Crumley, 'A Dialectical Critique of Heterarchy', in Patterson and Gailey (eds.), *Power Relations and State Formation*, Washington, American Anthropological Association, 1987, 157.

[81] McFarlane, *Beyond Awakening*, 3.

[82] Mary Graham, 'Some Thoughts about the Philosophical Underpinnings of Aboriginal Worldviews', *Australian Humanities Review*, 45, 2008, 181-194.

[83] Manuel de Landa, *One Thousand Years of Non-linear History*, New York, Swerve, 2000, 257-274.

it may have appeared there was a central power at Wybalenna, this is patently not the case. No Commandant could keep the exiles from going bush and maintaining culture if they so wished, and certainly no man could control the Sealing Women.

The renegade women serve as a strong example of the level of complexity and self-organisation occurring at Wybalenna. A disparate group of women from various nations formed their own society, which continually resisted centralised power. Traditionally, these women have been depicted as the most passive of all VDL people, but, as the records show, this was certainly not the case. Their identity was developed and maintained in Wybalenna's heterarchical social system. Interactions were often more lateral than hierarchical. The Sealing Women were not simply enacted upon in a static, one-way flow of power; they demonstrate what Beekman and Baden term 'the mutual interaction of many agents and variables' occurring at the settlement.[84]

The workings of power and order at Wybalenna were variable, heterarchical and complex: this can be evidenced in the forming and re-forming of national groupings, languages, alliances, and, finally, a pan-VDL identity. It is the only way to fully understand the events which were about to sweep the settlement.

Archaeology of a Stratagem

It is unclear exactly when the Wybalenna community first heard the shocking news that, after much hounding and eventually petitioning London, Henry Jeanneret was to be reinstated. This reinstatement was approved by the Secretary of State in London on 11 August

---

84   C. S. Beekman and W. W. Baden, 'Continuing the Revolution: Nonlinear Political and Economic Models for Archaeology', in Beekman and Baden (eds.), *Nonlinear Models for Archaeology and Anthropology: Continuing the Revolution*, Ashgate, Aldershot and Burlington, 2005, 3.

1845, and notification would feasibly have taken three months to reach Hobart. Some writers – Plomley and Ryan included – presume that both Joseph Milligan and the VDL community were aware of Jeanneret's reinstatement by December 1845, but there is no evidence of this. In fact, the documents we have point to the contrary.

When Robert Clark wrote a long and detailed letter to George Washington Walker on 3 December 1845 – effectively, a Return of the Settlement – marked 'Private and Important for the Aborigines',[85] there was no mention of Jeanneret's reinstatement. Clark's report includes financial accounts, and a plan – clearly hatched between the key Europeans, Milligan and Clark, and the VDL exiles themselves – to turn Wybalenna into a self-sufficient farm. Fully aware of Milligan's plan to return to England with his young son, Clark puts his own name forward as prospective superintendent, but begs Walker not to make it public until the time is right. Clearly, Wybalenna and its supporters still believed the superintendent position was up for discussion. This certainly would not have been the tone of Clark's letter if he had already known Jeanneret had been reinstated. Jeanneret himself records that the news of Lord Derby's order for his reinstatement, or being given a position of 'equal amolument', reached him in December 1845.[86]

It appears that even in late December 1845 the news had not yet reached Wybalenna, or at least been passed on to the VDL exiles. On 30 December, Walter Arthur wrote to George Washington Walker, pleading for his assistance. This was not to intervene, to help prevent Jeanneret's return – presumably, what he would have done had he

---

85   Robert Clark to George Washington Walker, 3 December 1845, UTAS Library Quaker Collection S&RMC.
86   Jeanneret, *Vindication of a Colonial Magistrate*, 8.

CHAPTER 5

known the news. Instead, this letter gives the impression of the superintendence of the community still being undecided. He requests Walker's advice on how to convince the colonial authorities to allow the community more autonomy, advising:

> ... myself and the remainder of my country people are desirous of doing all we can to support ourselves upon Flinders without our being any more expence to the Government as we will use our best endeavours to grow wheat and potatoes and gather mutton-Birds and their Eggs, &c. &c.
>
> Mr Clark will do us all the good he can, and assist us, but if the Governor would send down some person to see Flinders after Doctor Milligan leaves it, and before another comes in his place it might save the Governor a great deal of money.[87]

Arthur has clearly been informed, by Milligan, of the cost-cutting measures requested by the Colonial Secretary in his latest communications, and shrewdly cites this as an attractive prospect for the administration. This is a clear attempt to attain self-sufficiency, and echoes a report written by Milligan in early December, which recommended the appointment of a 'fit and proper person' to help the community refocus on farming activity. After complaining that the community would certainly read the 'Bible' more, if they had enough copies, Arthur advises Walker:

> ... we are doing very well except for the bad whitemen, the prisoners and soldiers are no good Sir. We cannot write to the Governor or else we would tell him how we would work and assist in feeding ourselves.[88]

---

87   Walter Arthur to George Washington Walker, 30 December 1845. Original letter located in the Calder Papers, Mitchell Library MS A612; typewritten copy entitled 'Letter written by a Tasmanian Aboriginal, the Station, Flinders Island, to Mr. G W. Walker, Hobart town', in QVMAG Plomley Collection CHS53 2/10-2/13.
88   Ibid.

This is both a typical, but quite extraordinary passage. Harassment from convicts, and occasionally the military, had been a recurring problem since the earliest days of the settlement. However, this is the first time this segment of the European community has been directly criticised by Arthur. We might wonder if this is included as part of his attempt for an autonomous, self-sufficient and demilitarised Wybalenna. Even more puzzling is the comment, 'We cannot write to the Governor'. It is unclear if this might be in relation to a direction from Milligan, or a response to some comment or directive filtered down from Sir John Franklin's replacement, Sir John Eardley-Wilmot, or his colonial secretary. This claim is echoed again later in the letter when, after testifying to his and Mary ann's dedication to Christianity and the Bible, and the kindness of Mr and Mrs Clark, he tells Walker:

> … the Blacks would all petition the governor to get land and to earn for themselves but they are afraid and when them will not work for other people they are called Idle and Lazy. Although We are paid but very little but indeed Sir we are not so. For we work very hard I cant write any more but thank you for your kindness to us poor Black people of Van Diemens Land.[89]

Arthur's guarded writing has led some writers such as Plomley to believe he had foreknowledge of Jeanneret's return. But, if this had been the case, a more explicit message is likely to have been sent to Walker. We might speculate that this message was encoded, and that Walker's reply – if one existed, for we have no trace of it – encouraged a more direct approach.

There is no hint of foreknowledge of Jeanneret's return in Milligan's or Clark's letters of that period. In fact, when Milligan wrote to

---

89 Ibid.

CHAPTER 5

Walker on 5 January 1846, having just returned from the mainland, he made no mention at all of the appointment.[90] It was on that same date – 5 January 1846 – that Governor Sir John Eardley-Wilmot officially advised the Colonial Secretary, James Bicheno, of Jeanneret's reinstatement.[91] Bicheno's letter to Milligan, advising him of the name of the new superintendent, is dated 6 January 1846.[92] It is likely that this mail did not reach Flinders Island for upwards of a week, or even longer. It is certain, then, that the news of Jeanneret's return would have reached Wybalenna by mid-January.

We do not know what events transpired in the weeks directly following the news of the imminent return of Henry Jeanneret. It is highly probable that Walker played a much larger role in ensuing events than has previously been estimated. On 2 February 1846, the shipping news reports a G. W. Walker Esq. sailing from Launceston on the *Union*, and yet he was back in Hobart by late February. Did Walker pay a clandestine visit to Wybalenna in this time? It can be no coincidence that he was busily advising Robert Clark during this period. Whatever Walker's involvement, the VDL community's next step was strategic. They decided to bypass the Governor, who they clearly did not feel comfortable or welcomed in writing to, and target the party they felt could be of most assistance: the very head of the empire to whom they had lost their land.

---

90 Joseph Milligan to George Washington Walker, 5 January 1846, UTAS Library Quaker Collection S&RMC, W7/50.
91 Eardley-Wilmot to Bicheno, 5 January 1846. CSO 11/10/242, 229. Unseen, cited from Plomley, *Weep in Silence*, 166.
92 Bicheno to Milligan, 6 January 1846. CSO 11/10/242, 246. Cited from Plomley, *Weep in Silence*, 166.

Chapter 6

DEFEATING WYBALENNA

On 12 February 1846, Governor Eardley-Wilmot wrote to Henry Jeanneret and told him to ready himself for his new position. A vessel was being prepared at Launceston, and would convey him to Wybalenna within a week.[1] It is highly likely that, as this intelligence was being delivered to Jeanneret, it was also on its way across the water to Flinders Island. Certainly, it had arrived at Wybalenna by 17 February 1846. Despite the Governor's letter, Jeanneret did not act promptly. However, the VDL exiles did. The news of the imminent return of Jeanneret inspired a rapid chain of events which was to reverberate in the highest offices of the empire, and have lasting ramifications for all the parties concerned. It is indisputably the first major act of First Nations political activism in Australian colonial history. And fortunately, for the historical observer, it was all conducted with careful documentation.

The Humble Petition of the Free Aborigines

The response to Jeanneret's reinstatement began, most fittingly, in the words and hands of the VDL community themselves. Walter Arthur penned a letter to Joseph Milligan, who had not yet left the island,

---

1 Eardley-Wilmot to Jeanneret, 12 February 1846, in Jeanneret, *Vindication of a Colonial Magistrate*, 8.

CHAPTER 6

which was signed by eight VDL men.² Their letter very clearly set out their intentions and how they aimed to achieve them – it is almost as if they knew the affair would be scrutinised, and they were ensuring transparency. They stated:

> We the free aborigine people of Van Diemens land do hereby request of you to order the Catechist Mr Clark to draw up for us a petition to the Queen Majesty of England for us. That she would not let Doctor Jeanneret come to Flinders Island again to be our Superintendent.
>
> We will tell Mr Clark what he will write for us in the petition as we are not able any of us and request you order Mr Clark to do it and each of us as can write a little will write our names to it for all the people wish it to be sent to the governor to send it to England to her Majesty the Queen who we all love.³

The paper trail was made abundantly clear. Milligan wrote to Clark, who complied with the instructions, penning the petition conveying the words and intent – as much as possible – of the VDL people. When the petition was complete, it was read back to the men, and those who could read it themselves did so. As we shall later see, they all had their own motivations for being involved, and all claimed it to be their own work. A common assertion would be, 'I wrote to the Queen', or 'I told the Queen'. Although it was physically penned by Clark, it certainly reflected the views, fears and aspirations of those whose names were appended to it.

Clark then sent the petition, with a covering letter, to Milligan. Milligan again read it back to the VDL contributors, to ensure they agreed with its contents, then he wrote a detailed, explanatory

---

2 Walter George Arthur, King Alexander, David Bruney, John Allen, Washington, Frederick, King Tippoo, Augustus.
3 Walter Arthur et al. to Joseph Milligan, 17 February 1846. CSO 11/26/378, AJCP Microfilm 280/195, Reel 544, SLV, 310-311.

covering letter to the Colonial Secretary. In this letter, he recounts the process of its creation, including that it was written by Clark at the request of the VDL people themselves. He also includes that the finished product was brought to him by a number of the VDL community, male and female. The excitement is almost palpable. We can be certain that the key activists Walter and Mary ann Arthur were among this number in Milligan's parlour, delivering the beautifully executed document, as most certainly were David Bruney, John Allen, Washington and King Alexander. This important document begins – after its address to Queen Victoria – with the following identification:

> The Humble Petition of the Free Aborigines Inhabitants of Van Diemens Land who live upon Flinders Island in Baſses Straits &- &-
>
> Most Humbly Sheweth
>
> That we your Majestys Petitioners are your Free Children, that we were not taken Prisoners but freely gave up our Country to Colonel Arthur then the Governor after defending ourselves.[4]

This multiple reiteration of their status as a free people is a continuation of the identity claimed since the very beginning of the exile. It reminds the Crown of the agreement with Sir George Arthur, and is reinforced thus:

> Your Petitioners humbly state to you Majesty that Mr Robinson made for us and with Colonel Arthur an agreement which we have not lost from our Minds since and we have made our part of it good.

---

4   Walter Arthur et al. to Queen Victoria, 17 February 1846. CSO 11/26/378, AJCP Microfilm 280/195, Reel 544, SLV.

CHAPTER 6

The petition went on to testify that 'when we left our own place we were Plenty of People, we are now but a little one'. This phrasing – almost a direct quote of Doctor Wooreddy's sermon to a prayer meeting some eight years earlier – leaves little doubt that the document is, in fact, drawn from the community's own words. 'Plenty' and 'a little one', as we will see, are common terms of measurement in the lingua franca. The Queen is also informed that, during the long period of confinement at Flinders Island, they had been a quiet and free people under many superintendents, and not imprisoned. The early part of the petition, then, is about reaffirming their acquiescence to the deal struck with Sir George Arthur, and their good behaviour.

Then, they turn to Henry Jeanneret, and the whole tone of the petition changes. A litany of abuses is detailed, and as we read through them, we can almost imagine a group of angry people, standing around Clark as he writes the petition, recalling one injury after another. For the purposes of analysis, it is useful to list the charges against Jeanneret raised by the VDL community, in the order they were conveyed:

1. He carried pistols, and often threatened to shoot VDL people.
2. He kept pigs in the VDL village.
3. His pigs entered VDL houses and ate bread and stole food.
4. His pigs entered VDL gardens and destroyed potato and cabbage crops.
5. He left VDL houses in a state of disrepair.
6. He left VDL houses uncleaned, and covered with vermin.
7. He did not issue sufficient clothing.
8. He did not tend to the sick until they were desperately ill.
9. Eleven people died during his administration.
10. He put VDL people into jail 'because we would not be his slaves'.

11. He withheld rations.
12. He issued bad rations of tea and tobacco.
13. He shot the VDL peoples' dogs before their eyes.
14. He sent the VDL peoples' dogs to the islands.
15. When told the dogs would starve, he said they might eat each other.
16. He forced VDL people to take up arms, alongside convicts.
17. They were to fight against the military.
18. This taking up arms was against the VDL community's will.
19. He did not teach the VDL people to read or write.
20. He did not teach the VDL people to sing to God.
21. The only instruction was delivered by his convict servant.
22. This same convict often took them to jail on Jeanneret's orders.

This explosive set of charges was then supported by the statement, 'The Lord Bishop seen us in this bad way and we told His Lordship plenty how Doctor Jeanneret used us'. This is referring to the visit of Bishop Nixon in 1843, when he visited Wybalenna briefly as part of Sir John Franklin's departing tour. In citing Bishop Nixon, they are calling on a very high moral authority indeed to support their claim. The basis of their claims would also be confirmed, in quite astonishing detail, in the journal of Wybalenna's erstwhile surgeon, James Allen, who was now living on Preservation Island.[5]

The petition is signed – in Clark's hand – by eight men, who all, according to both Clark and Milligan, were fully conversant in its contents. Interestingly, it is a different eight men to those named in the letter written by Walter Arthur, earlier that day, requesting

---

5   Allen's journal, which is in the Flinders Island Historical Society collection, strongly criticised Jeanneret's management as despotism, and mentions pigs destroying the garden, unfit meat supplies, and limited tea rations. Quoted in Edgecombe, *Flinders Island and Eastern Bass Strait*, 16.

CHAPTER 6

the clerical assistance. In this document, Frederick is replaced by Neptune. Though, as we will later see, Frederick definitely had cause to fear the return of Jeanneret.

The petition was dispatched to Hobart, where it appears to have caused a sensation at the Colonial Secretary's Office. Its covering letter is written on, from a number of directions, right to the very corners of the page. It was not sent on to London straight away, because a series of events in the intervening time period worked to cast doubt on its authenticity; namely, the return to Flinders Island of Jeanneret.

Jeanneret and his family did not arrive back at Wybalenna for another four weeks, and he had been fully apprised about the fact that a petition had been written about him. Milligan, who had remained in charge awaiting the chance to hand over control of the settlement, did not make the return a welcome one. Jeanneret demanded a copy of the petition from him, but Milligan protested not to have one. Clark, likewise, declined any knowledge of the contents of the petition, or location of a copy. Eventually, Jeanneret was forced to write to Hobart to obtain a copy. This drama is fully documented in a series of quarrelsome letters between Jeanneret, Milligan and Clark.[6] The casual reader, upon seeing them, would be forgiven for thinking that the parties were on separate islands, or even colonies, such is the distance in communication, when in fact they were actually only a few dozen metres from each other. The documents give a strong sense of the tense and fractious nature of the first weeks of Jeanneret's return. What we do not have, unfortunately, is a record of these events from the VDL perspective. It is clear, though, that Jeanneret was going to

---

6   Jeanneret to Milligan, 334; Jeanneret to Clark, 339; Jeanneret to Governor, 337, all dated 17 March 1846; Milligan to Jeanneret 338, Clark to Jeanneret, 340-341, 28 March 1846; Jeanneret to Governor, 344-345, 2 April 1846, CSO 11/26/378, AJCP Microfilm 280/195, Reel 544, SLV.

embark on a program of retribution against both the VDL activists and Clark. He only awaited Milligan's exit.

Clark and Walker remained in constant contact throughout, disproving assumptions that, after the departure of Robinson to Port Phillip, 'missionaries more or less abandoned the Tasmanians'.[7] It was far from the case. The catechist was dealing with a tragedy of his own – his youngest child died at Wybalenna – and this is a focus of his letters, as well as the ongoing events at Wybalenna. On 17 March 1846, he thanked Walker for sending 'Bibles' and newspapers, and told him:

> I hope please the Lord in about 3 weeks hence to forward you the plan which has originated with the people themselves, to render their independence for support from the Government, it is their aim in the first instance not mine – I have only to fill up some of the blank spaces which they have requested to – and submit to you for correction & improvements & to be handed to the Governor.[8]

It is clear that the VDL plan for self-sufficiency was continuing, despite Jeanneret's return. This is further detailed in a long letter from Clark to Walker, which describes in great detail the 'divide and conquer' methodology of Jeanneret. Upon his return, according to Clark, he had made use of '3 or 4 Natives who were favourites … have told him many untruths' about Milligan. It seems that another group loyal to Milligan were set on an opposing course, 'and a constant system of espionage between those 6 or 8 is carried on'. Clark had been told by others that, as soon as Milligan departed, 'we are to have a serious quarrel between both these parties and their adherents,

---

7   Davies, *The Last of the Tasmanians*, 197.
8   Robert Clark to George Washington Walker, 17 March 1846, Quaker Collection, UTAS Library S&RMC.

CHAPTER 6

which will not terminate without bloodshed'.⁹ Amidst these tensions, though, Clark also shares some very revealing information about the VDL exiles' level of literacy, and political awareness:

> Several of my people are able to read the news papers and Walter has read to them some of the Aboriginal periodicals that you gave me before I left ... the Aborigines are quite alive to the warfare going on in New Zealand and anxious to hear about their sable compatriots whenever I get a paper.[10]

This significant mention from Clark of the Land Wars in New Zealand – and the VDL awareness of them – gives a valuable insight into the level of transnational awareness, and solidarity, experienced and felt by the exiles.[11] We have known from the earliest editions of the *Flinders Island Chronicle* that the VDL people were aware of the colonial project as it existed in other countries and islands: they made mention of black men in other locations being taught the Bible by white men. Here, however, we have proof that they were actively following patriotic wars in other lands. They would have known very well that New Zealand was only a few days sailing away, and had certainly had experience with Maori sealers and mariners. Their familiarity with events in New Zealand, at this time, sheds new light on the activism at Wybalenna.

There is one more important issue that Robert Clark relayed to Walker in this letter: that is, the tendency for Europeans on the island to fraudulently claim the profits from work done by the VDL

---

9   Robert Clark to George Washington Walker, 3 April 1846, Quaker Collection, UTAS Library S&RMC, W7/34, 2.
10 Ibid.
11 Kristyn Harman gives an insight into this period, and the celebrity status which, several months later, would surround the arrival in Hobart, as transportees, of Maori war veterans. See Kristyn Harman, *Aboriginal Convicts: Australian, Khoisan and Maori Exiles*, Sydney, University of New South Wales Press, 2012, 207-236.

exiles. In one example, the proceeds of soda ash produced by Walter Arthur's barilla burning seem to have been appropriated.[12] Clark tells Walker, 'they anxiously enquire of me about their sheep and their wool and ask me will the Government keep them slaving as it has their Country'.[13] Financial security and freedom from slavery is obviously a very high priority for the VDL people. In a short, adjunct letter written the following day, Clark specifically requests, 'Will you be so good as to Forward me by the "Fortitude" now about sailing from Hobart, <u>Aborigines Magazines as many and as late dates as you can spare</u>' (his underlining).[14] Again, we are afforded a glimpse of the VDL thirst for knowledge and news of current events, especially affecting other First Nations people.

The same day as Clark made this request, Walter Arthur wrote Milligan a heartfelt letter. It was a fond farewell, and leaves no doubt of the esteem in which the Arthurs held Milligan. It also gives a strong sense of the stressful nature of the activists' current dilemma, and the state of fear they were already labouring under. Arthur told Milligan:

> Sir my wife and me are very sorry you are going to leave us and so I know are all my country men are but they are frightened a big one for to talk much about you Sir for fear of Doctor Jeanneret for he has growled them plenty for writing to the Governor about him and when you go away Sir they say he will growl them more we shall not forget you Sir we hope you will not forget us.[15]

---

12 There is no detailed information on this, but it is likely related to the production of soda ash (sodium bicarbonate) by the burning of salt-rich vegetation, perhaps seaweed.
13 Robert Clark to George Washington Walker, 3 April 1846, UTAS Library Quaker Collection, S&RMC, W7/34, 13.
14 Ibid.
15 W. G. Arthur et al. to Milligan, 4 April 1846, CSO 11/26/378, AJCP 280/195, Reel 544, SLV, 317.

CHAPTER 6

The letter also asked him to post the enclosed letter when he reached Launceston – 'it is from us Black fellows ourselves to the Governor'. Milligan dutifully complied, carrying the letter off Flinders Island with him. It is not known if he posted it in Launceston, or took it with him to Hobart, but it most certainly reached the desk of the Colonial Secretary. Its powerful words were destined to have a profound impact. The four leading Wybalenna activists wrote:

> We Black Fellows of Van Diemens Land want to know if their Father the Governor got a letter from us and a petition to the Queen of England. We write now to ask our Father the Governor to do something for us to send some good men down to Flinders Island Till we talk to them and tell them what we wrote in our letter was true … we Black fellows want to ask our Father the Governor if he will let us write to him when we want to Talk to him about ourselves.
>
> We remain his loving children,
>
> Walter G. Arthur, David Bruny, Washington, Mary Ann Arthur.[16]

The letter was personally signed by all four of the writers – an act which, in itself, leant credibility to the petition sent six weeks earlier. It also, crucially, was co-signed by Mary ann Arthur. She had clearly been one of the main instigators of the petition, and would be at the forefront of later activism at Wybalenna. This short letter undoubtedly shocked the Colonial Secretary, and the Governor, into action. The petition could no longer be dismissed as purely a fabrication of Milligan and Clark. On 14 April – a mere ten days after Walter Arthur had given the letter to Joseph Milligan to post – the following reply was dispatched to Flinders Island:

---

16   W. G. Arthur et al. to the Governor, 3 April 1846, CSO 11/26/378, AJCP 280/195, Reel 544, SLV, 313.

> The Colonial Secretary is directed to inform the Black Natives living at Flinders Island…that petition has been received and will be sent as desired as soon as possible … the Governor … will be glad to listen to anything they may wish to say about themselves.[17]

We cannot be sure when this letter, and invitation, was conveyed to Flinders Island, for there appears to be a silence in the archive for the best part of May. However, it is clear that by late May, the substance of this letter had been conveyed to Jeanneret, for he embarked on a campaign to discredit the petition writers. Clark hints at this in a letter to Walker hurriedly written on 27 May. First, he mentions the exiles' own recently-instituted Flinders Aboriginal Bible Society, which sought to be recognised by the Foreign Bible Society in London. He also passes on a request from Mary ann and Walter Arthur, for Walker to enquire after money left to her at the death of her father, a sealer. Again, we get an insight into the financial shrewdness of the Arthurs. Then, Clark discusses the tension on the island:

> The Aborigines and the Doctr are not friendly and the breach is widening … he intends bringing an action for libel against Walter George Arthur on account of the statements made by the natives in a petition to the Queen.[18]

The situation was becoming more stressful for the VDL exiles by the day. Jeanneret – as well as attempting to create divisions in the community – was now threatening its acknowledged leader with libel. His next step, as we shall see, was an attempt to pour discredit

---

17 Memorandum from James Bicheno, 14 April 1846, CSO 11/26/378, AJCP 280/195, Reel 544, SLV, 316.

18 Robert Clark to George Washington Walker, 27 May 1846, UTAS Library Quaker Collection, S&RMC, W7/36, 3-4.

CHAPTER 6

onto the charges contained in the petition to the Queen. It was this step, however, which would push the VDL people one step too far.

'We want a Protector': Epistolary Agency on Flinders Island

On 24 May 1846, Jeanneret instructed the coxswain, Sinclair Davie, to interview the individuals who had signed the petition to Queen Victoria – and others – respecting the veracity of the documents. Davie interviewed Walter George Arthur, John Allen, David Bruney, King Tippoo, King Alexander, Neptune, Washington, Frederick, Augustus, Eugene, Noemy, Edmund, and King Alphonso, and their testimonies were written up over several days. On the face of it, they appeared to contradict some of the claims made in the petition. Yet they were obviously questioned very briefly, and selectively.

Walter Arthur's testimony, for example, is extraordinarily brief: 'Walter George Arthur states that the whole of the Petition is true but cannot give any answers to the Petition or the Clothing being stopt that his tobacco was stopt for shooting a dog'.[19] Most of the other men's statements are similar, to the effect that Jeanneret never threatened to shoot him, gaol him, stop his rations, or refuse medical aid. However, there is some clear variance. King Alphonso made clear that while Jeanneret never threatened to shoot him, he did 'Growl at him with a Pistol in his hand'.[20] Frederick, likewise, said that Jeanneret had nor directly threatened to shoot him, but 'he heard something and ran away'.[21] Several mentioned their rations

---

19 Walter George Arthur, statement to Sinclair Davie, 28 May 1846, CSO 11/26/378, AJCP 280/195, Reel 544 373.

20 King Alphonso, statement to Sinclair Davie, 28 May 1846, CSO 11/26/378, AJCP 280/195, Reel 544, SLV, 374.

21 Frederick, statement to Sinclair Davie, 28 May 1846, CSO 11/26/378, AJCP 280/195, Reel 544, 374.

being stopped for various reasons, including 'fighting over a Lubara' (John Allen), 'allowing Davy and Matilda to be in his home all Night' (Frederick), and 'absconding off the Island and going among Sealers' (King Alphonso). Several said they could not write, but Mr Clark pencilled their names on the petition and they wrote over it (John Allen, King Tippoo, King Alexander and Neptune). David Bruney and Washington asserted that they wrote their own name, by their own hand. Interestingly, this question was not put to Walter Arthur.

There is a selectivity about the questions asked of these men, and a questionable brevity in their responses. Quite clearly, Jeanneret ensured that Davie asked leading questions of specific individuals, and the result – the collection of statements later sent to the Colonial Secretary – certainly gives the impression of doubt being cast over the veracity of the claims in the petition. However, Walter Arthur was later to give a very different impression of the nature of the Davie examinations: he assured the Governor, 'we all said over and over again what we wrote was true and we told the Coxswain that he knew himself that we told true'.[22]

The following day, Jeanneret and his son spread a rumour about the settlement that the petition had been rescinded, and the signatories had admitted lying. As Walter Arthur later explained, 'when we heard them talk this way we thought all of us that could write our names would send a little letter to our good Governor and tell him that we all told true and that we were not liars'.[23]

Clearly, the VDL activists were deeply concerned about how they were being represented. They drew up a memorandum themselves,

---

22 Walter George Arthur to the Governor, 15 July 1846, AOT CSO 11/1/27 C658.
23 Ibid.

CHAPTER 6

regarding their interview by Davie, and it was sworn to by eight signatories.[24] It testified:

> We the undersigned state that Mr Davy the Coxswain sent for us ... and when aſsembled in his house he asked us was it all true what we blackfellows wrote in the petition to her Majesty the Queen of England and was every thing true and we stated all over again and said it was all true which he wrote down and said he would give to Doctor Jeanneret and now we say again that the petition is all true.[25]

What happened next with this memorandum shows a high level of strategic thinking. It was not shown to Jeanneret, or sent to Hobart: instead, multiple copies were made by Walter Arthur and David Bruney, and these were carefully stored, along with other evidence, such as personal references from Robinson and Milligan. Some of these documents had been carried for years, awaiting the time when they might be useful, or necessary. As it turned out, that was very soon.

By the second week of June 1846, the situation between the VDL people and Jeanneret had deteriorated even further. Tensions had built up immeasurably since their receipt of the letter from the Governor. The VDL community knew that Jeanneret was working hard to misrepresent them to Hobart. Then – with one seemingly minor event – the floodgates were opened, and the tide of rebellion – through the medium of letters – was unleashed.

---

24 Davey Bruney, Walter G. Arthur, King Alexander, King Alphonso, Mr Washington, Noemy, Mary ann Arthur, John Allen. Multiple copies exist, some written by Walter Arthur, some by David Bruny.
25 Memorandum, Davey Bruney et al., CSO 11/26/378, AJCP 280/195, Reel 544, SLV: also have photograph of Walter G. Arthur's handwritten copy original in Friend Inquiry papers, AOT, CSO11/1/27, C658.

It began with Washington. As we already know, he was known as one of the convicted killers in the notorious Parker-Thomas case. It is also clear, from his fiery interactions with Reverend Dove, that Washington was a proud young man, with little tolerance for disrespect or intimidation.[26] As one of the signatories to the petition – all of whom were feeling the superintendent's wrath – he had also signed the letter to the Governor in April, which had elicited the response which so enraged Jeanneret. Tellingly, Washington was the only VDL man to have signed himself as 'Mr'.[27] On Friday 12 June, he was already working on his letter to the Governor. He began:

> Sir, My Father the governor will know by this little one letter that your black servant would like a big one to see him you if you please … Doctor Jeanneret he is a very bad man to me and to my country people …[28]

Washington was not able to finish his letter. The following day, he was jailed by Jeanneret. Writing from the island cells, he finished his letter, in the third person, 'Washington has told Walter his brother to write for him has he could write better than him and talk to most english'. It is highly significant that he calls Walter Arthur his brother: coming from the two traditional enemies, the Big River and Ben Lomond nations, this uniting in activism, in the face of oppressive behaviour from the current figurehead of their colonial disempowerment, is a crucial moment in Wybalenna history.

---

26 Diary of Thomas Dove, 5 February 1840, reprinted in Miller, *Thomas Dove and the Tasmanian Aborigines*, 83.

27 On the memorandum swearing to the authenticity of petition, 29 May 1846, CSO 11/26/378, AJCP 280/195, Reel 544, SLV 336.

28 Washington, 12 June 1846, CSO 11/26/378, AJCP 280/195, Reel 544, SLV, 327-328.

CHAPTER 6

Walter Arthur duly produced a letter on behalf of Washington, detailing the events of his incarceration and supplying documentary evidence. This jailing of Washington was, in itself, a damning indictment on life at Wybalenna under Jeanneret. Arthur's letter is an important window into the desperately poor state that relations had sunk to. It is also a very gripping narrative.

Rations were dealt out in an autocratic manner by Jeanneret's young son Charles, at twelve years old, an infant in the eyes of the VDL men. Walter Arthur relates how on Saturday 13 June, a dispute about tea rations between Washington and the younger Jeanneret ended with both parties threatening to put the other in jail. Arthur is in no doubt that the degrading manner in which Charles Jeanneret spoke to Washington was designed to incite him: as Arthur informed the Governor, 'Doctor Jeanneret will not let us alone but tells much to lies about us and trys to make us to much angry'.[29] A short time later, Washington was summoned by Jeanneret and tried for attempting to strike Charles Jeanneret (described later by Governor Denison as a 'whelp' who, like his father, deserved a whipping).[30] Jeanneret, as presiding judge, refused to hear the testimony of witnesses – including Clark – who would swear that Washington had not attempted to strike Charles.

Walter Arthur's letter details the shabby trial, how an impossible bail of £50 was set, and relays Washington's request for the Governor to pay bail for him. Enclosing a copy of the summons to trial – another example of the VDL activists' use of documentary evidence – Arthur also adds that:

---

29 Walter Arthur on behalf of Washington, 16 June 1846, CSO 11/26/378, AJCP 280/195, Reel 544, SLV, 332.
30 Notation by Denison, 20 November 1847, CSO 24/8/101, 2, cited in Plomley, *Weep in Silence*, 163.

> Washington hopes his Good Father the Governor will tell the big Judges to ask why he was put into Jail by Doctor Jeanneret for no thing at all but asking for his Rations and that the Judges will have him as well treatment as any white free man and not treated like a slave.[31]

Arthur wrote to the Governor on Washington's behalf on Monday 15 June. The following day, he added a postscript with news of Washington's release. The release itself is not unexpected, as the charges were spurious, but how it was achieved – and some details released in the telling of the story – are significant.

> Washingtons Father Alphonso a big Chief asked Doctor Jeanneret when he would let his son come out of Jail and the Doctor said he would keep him for three nights but Alphonso said well if you do we will all write to the Governor and tell him about you putting his Son in to Jail for nothing. Then Doctor Jeanneret was frightened and sent very soon and let him out.[32]

This sudden focus on King Alphonso – a 'big Chief' – is quite extraordinary. Until this point, in Wybalenna history, Alphonso had not put himself forward in any significant way. Here, however, he steps up to take responsibility for Washington's welfare. We get the sense of a patient senior man pushed too far. This passage also, quite remarkably, reveals that Alphonso is in fact Washington's father. It is unclear whether this is in a biological or kinship sense, but this is a biographical detail nowhere else documented.[33] The final fascinating insight gained by this narrative of Washington's arrest, incarceration and release was Jeanneret's demonstrated fear of being reported in

---

31   Walter Arthur on behalf of Washington, 16 June 1846, CSO 11/26/378, AJCP 280/195, Reel 544, 332.
32   Ibid.
33   This fact was not noted by Plomley, or any other writers: most likely, because these letters remain mostly unexamined.

CHAPTER 6

letters to the Governor: Arthur's narrative explains that Jeanneret 'told Washington he would forgive him ... the black people must write nothing about him to the Governor and said if it did he would not send their Letters for them'.[34]

This scene, depicted by Arthur, marks a monumental shift in political activism at Flinders Island. It illustrates the precision with which King Alphonso used the threat, and the uselessness of Jeanneret's own response. The threat of the letter is incredibly potent, and wielded confidently by King Alphonso. And as he predicted, the missive which depicted this scene, penned by Walter Arthur on behalf of his 'brother' Washington, found its target by reaching the local colonial representative in Hobart. The authors, as well as their foe, demonstrably knew the power of a well-directed written communication.

Letters were the engine of the colonial project. Requests and instructions were transmitted through a complex hierarchical structure. Any missive – be it a request for stores, or an allegation of abuse – might travel from an administrative outpost, such as Flinders Island, to the regional centre of Launceston, to Hobart, to Sydney, and finally to London. At many of these stages, copies were made and original material sent on. Official reports and more personalised letters from one colonial official to another enabled the function of empire. Obviously, King Alphonso knew the capability of the letter when he threatened Jeanneret with its use, and then, two days later, followed through on that threat.

Interestingly, King Alphonso did not mention the jailing of his son in his letter to the Governor. Instead, in a persuasive communication co-penned by King Alexander, King Alphonso complained that the

---

34   Walter Arthur on behalf of Washington, 16 June 1846. CSO 11/26/378, AJCP 280/195, Reel 544, SLV, 332.

superintendent was withholding clothing from the community unless they worked in his garden.[35] Noting that they did not want to be naked 'like long time ago in the bush, we wild man that time', they were reminding the Governor of their dispossession from their own Country, and the Crown's promise to care for their needs. Adding 'we all naked very soon', they were perhaps implying that Government neglect might result in a regression to the bush and – ominously – a return to guerilla warfare. The precarious state of Alphonso's health is also noted, with relation to the denial of clothing:

> Alphonso say he a sick man
> plenty to much cold come
> what that he do for to keep him warm
> he no able to work a big one.

King Alexander – the main narrator – also raises the issue of the petition, and the intimidation suffered since its writing. He hints at how Henry Jeanneret flaunted his previous victory over the Hobart administration, in having his dismissal overturned, boasting that local authorities had little power over him. Alexander tells the Governor:

> Doctor Jeneret fright me King Alexander a big one for me write my name to petition to the Queen what the fore to swear to black fellows to say they write lies we tell him all the petition is true but he say he no care for you Governor Queen take care of him and hang white and black man together.[36]

The two Kings are obviously very cautious, after the enquiry by Sinclair Davie, to be seen to be the authors of their own letter. They have most certainly signed their own names, both at the beginning

---

35 King Alphonso and King Alexander, 19 June 1846, CSO 11/26/378, AJCP 280/195, Reel 544, SLV, 329-330.

36 King Alphonso and King Alexander, 19 June 1846, CSO 11/26/378, AJCP 280/195, Reel 544, SLV, 329-330.

CHAPTER 6

of the letter, and at the closing, where they finish, 'Me write myself King Alexander, Me write myself King Alphonso'. This, in itself, is a small statement of both rebellion and pride.

Another very significant letter written on this day – despite the threats from Jeanneret, and promises he would not send them – was from Mary ann Arthur. Often a central figure in events at Flinders Island, this is the first time she fully steps into the documentary record, in her own hand. A formidable young woman by all accounts, she showed, according to James Bonwick who knew her well, 'not only vigour of intellect, but a strength and independence of will'.[37] She was known for being well read: John West noted 'looking lately at a picture of Don Quixote, she pointed him out as the man who fought with windmills',[38] and another visitor who knew her in later years noted that whilst some women asked for tobacco, 'Marianne asked for books'.[39]

On 16 June, as her husband was completing his letter to the Governor on behalf of Washington, Mary ann Arthur was also hard at work. Her elegant, moving letter to Governor Eardley-Wilmot is remarkable in a number of ways. First, it is the only letter by an Indigenous woman from Wybalenna in this series.[40] She speaks of the intimidation suffered by herself and her husband, including threats of being hung for their role in the petition to Queen Victoria, and includes character references from G. A. Robinson and Joseph

---

37 Bonwick, *The Last of the Tasmanians*, 282.
38 West, *The History of Tasmania*, Vol. II, 78.
39 Colonial Times quoted in *Examiner*, 10 December 1853, from S. Davis and S. Petrov (eds.), *Varieties of Vice-Regal Life (Van Diemens Land Section), by Sir William and Lady Denison*, Hobart, The Tasmanian Historical Research Association, 2004, 77.
40 In fact, she may be the only Indigenous woman letter writer from Tasmania in this period.

'ME WRITE MYSELF'

Milligan. Mary ann's use of supporting documentation illustrates her understanding of the importance of the written word as evidence.

> Doctor Jenneret does not like us for we do not like to be his slaves nor wish our poor country people to be treated badly or made slaves of.[41]

Mary ann was the first to directly raise the spectre of slavery, but it went on to be a common theme across the letters of June 1846. The VDL people were well aware of the Abolitionist movement, and would have known the potential impact of their accusations on the colonial government. They were at pains to situate themselves as free people, distinct from convicts. In addition, they knowingly asserted their rights to freedom from threat, the peaceful existence that they had been promised by Governor Arthur and successive administrations. And, in the case of the men, they asserted their rights to trousers.

The arrival of the supply ship *Fortitude* at Wybalenna would have been eagerly awaited. Any comings and goings would break the tedium and sense of isolation of island life. But more importantly, the VDL people were eagerly awaiting the cargo that the Fortitude contained. June on Flinders Island was bitterly cold, and the people were in need of clothing.

On 15 June, at different times of the day, or perhaps together, the leading men of the Wybalenna community – including David Bruney, John Allen, King Alphonso and King Alexander – had asked Jeanneret for the clothing which had been sent for them from Hobart. Jeanneret flatly refused: the Governor, he told them, had written that now the Aborigines had to work for their clothes. This

---

41 Mary ann Arthur, 16 June 1846, CSO 11/26/378, AJCP 280/195, Reel 544, 318-319.

CHAPTER 6

would have caused consternation enough, but Jeanneret's further clarification – that they must work in *his* garden – was a complete outrage. Four angry men set about planning and writing their letters.

John Allen was a relative newcomer to Wybalenna, but had clearly formed very strong bonds with the Arthurs and David Bruney. As we know, he had been taken as a child and raised by John Batman. He had accompanied Batman to Port Phillip in 1835, and spent much of his formative years among Eora men who Batman had brought to VDL from New South Wales. In many ways, he was probably the most worldly of all the exiles at Wybalenna. Like the Arthurs and David Bruney, he was in his early twenties by 1846, and possessed similar self-assurance in his communication.

Allen's letter regarding clothing rations is by far the most detailed. He mentions the passage of the *Fortitude*, the date of the confrontation with Jeanneret, and draws the Governor into the injustice experienced. Allen twice depicts Jeanneret as refusing the clothes that the Governor intended for him, and repeatedly and explicitly asks the Governor if he actually *did* tell Jeanneret they must work – specifically, in Jeanneret's garden – for their clothes. In framing his letter in this way, he is inviting the Governor to share the outrage. He closes his letter pledging the loyalty of his wife – an act repeated by all other male writers except for Walter Arthur, whose wife spoke for herself – and expresses trust in the justness of the Governor:

> … we know he will take care of us black fellows and not let white man do plenty bad to us and put us into jail.[42]

The following day, David Bruney composed his own letter to the Governor, on behalf of himself and his wife Matilda. Their alliance

---

42   John Allen, 16 June 1846, CSO 11/26/378, AJCP 280/195, Reel 544, 325-326.

had been forged shortly after Bruney returned to Flinders Island in 1842. Matilda (Maytepumminner) herself was a significant woman, being a central protagonist in the tragedy that unfolded at Port Phillip which culminated in the execution of Tunnerminnerwait and Maulboyheener. Like the Arthurs, Bruney planned a life of economic self-sufficiency. He was a literate, proud, and determined young man, and his letter to the Governor written on 17 June 1846 is executed in a fine copperplate hand second only to Walter Arthur's among the VDL people.

Bruney addresses familiar themes of intimidation and neglect, and, like the others, testifies to his hardworking character. He also raises three other issues which were vitally important to the VDL people at Wybalenna: family, dogs and tobacco. He relays Jeanneret's threat to shoot a dog given to him by Joseph Milligan, and complains that for his work in the boat he is only paid poor-quality tobacco. Most movingly, he asks the Governor:

> … would you write to Port Phillip to Mr La Trobe about a Brother of mine that is there I want to hear from him … he is now my one Brother that is alive his name is Peter Bruney Brother to Davey Bruney that was in Port Phillip with Mr Robinson Chief Protector.[43]

It is unclear whether Bruney ever received a response to his inquiry, but the news would not have been good. His brother Peter had died in December 1843.[44]

The letters of Kings Alphonso and Alexander, John Allen and David Bruney, all written in the aftermath of the dispute over clothing

---

43 Davey Bruney, 17 June 1846, CSO 11/26/378, AJCP 280/195, Reel 544, 323-324.
44 Peter Bruney died of dysentery, and was buried on Robinson's property. Robinson's journal, 8 December 1843, in Clark, *The Journals of George Augustus Robinson, Volume 3*, 219.

CHAPTER 6

from the *Fortitude*, provide a powerful united front against Jeanneret's abuses of power. Combined with Mary ann Arthur's humble plea to be saved from slavery, they formed a forceful moral argument. And with the addition of the final letter writer, they were irresistible.

Walter Arthur's letter of June 17 is a masterpiece of moral persuasion. It is a letter not from one man, but on behalf of the whole community. In a beautiful hand, he states the same plea, nine times in various permutations: 'we want a Protector'. Always capitalised, in using the word 'Protector' Arthur was drawing on his intimacy with Robinson, and knowledge of the office of the Protector of Aborigines. It was a reasonable request designed to shame the colonial government into action:

> ... we want very badly a Protector for the way in which we are treated it is shameful for any Person of any feeling to hear at Flinders island ...
> we want a Protector to take care of us from our father Governor until such time the Queen's Pleasure is known.[45]

The tone of the letter is modest but expectant. By referring twice to the fact that the Queen's pleasure was not yet known, Arthur is reiterating an expectation of a fair hearing of the February petition to Queen Victoria. As Reynolds has noted with regard to Arthur's other interactions with authority, he wanted justice, not pity.[46] In fact, in Walter's valediction of 'I remain Sir your humble Aboriginal black friend', he situates himself as both servant and equal. Although he makes clear that he and his community are in dire need of help, Arthur clearly writes from a position of moral authority.

---

45 Walter G Arthur, 17 June 1846, CSO 11/2 6/378, AJCP 280/195, Reel 544, 320-323.
46 Reynolds, *Fate of a Free People*, 26.

It is not known exactly where these letters were written, but the archaeological assembly from the VDL exiles' cottages includes remnants of ink bottles, suggesting at least some writing took place there.[47] It is clear, from the trace of Mary ann Arthur's hand in at least the letters by John Allen, Washington and the two Kings, that this young woman was at the forefront of the writing campaign, and logically follows that these letters were probably composed in the Arthurs' house. Her role has been largely overlooked by historians, with the notable exception of Henry Reynolds.[48] This follows a tendency noted by Jessica Horton of First Nations women's epistolary activism being framed as being on behalf of themselves or their family – women's issues, related to struggle – rather than as political action.[49]

These letters constitute a revolutionary, yet under-examined data set, considering their pivotal place in the history of pan-Australian Indigenous activism. Studies of resistance to colonial rule have often focused on armed responses led by charismatic individuals, such as Eumarrah, Mannalargenna or Walyer. The Wybalenna letters of June 1846, and the petition which preceded them, instead show the genesis of a communal, political response to the problems of colonisation.

At the heart of the letters, and the petition which preceded them, is the expectation of the Crown to fulfill its moral responsibilities. This would later manifest across Australia in a number of different settings and campaigns, in what Richard Broome called the claim on 'Right behavior': that is, the application of 'customary understandings about good conduct' in the client–patron relationship which

---

47 Birmingham, *Wybalenna*, 120.
48 Reynolds's *Fate of a Free People* places Mary ann Arthur's influence as almost equal to that of her more famous husband.
49 See Jessica Horton's discussion in 'Rewriting Political History: Letters from Aboriginal People in Victoria, 1886–1919', *History Australia*, 9:2, August 2012, 169.

developed between First Nations people and colonial agents.⁵⁰ This was to manifest in Port Phillip, when Woiwurrung elder Billibellary – who may have met Walter Arthur during his time there – undertook a number of steps to accommodate the colonisers, and also called for land to be handed back to his people for farming. This was a call for 'right behavior', and also an example, as Broome suggests, of what Johnathon Lear called Radical Hope – envisioning a future, in a traditional way.⁵¹

Letters and petitions became a major vehicle for Indigenous political activism across the Australian mainland. Texts in this tradition include letters to the press by William Barak and the petition to Queen Victoria from Coranderrk of the 1880s.⁵² Twentieth-century manifestations include William Cooper's petition to King George, and the Lake Tyers, Lake Condah, Yirrkala, Gurindji and Larrakia people's petitions.⁵³ Again, right behavior, and the fulfilment of obligations is paramount; as Maria Nugent notes, this is proven by the regularity of the statement 'Queen gave us the land'.⁵⁴ Heather Goodall also observes of the New South Wales frontier that these

---

50 Broome, 'There Were Vegetables Every Year Mr Green Was Here', 1-16.
51 Broome, *Aboriginal Australians*, 80.
52 For example, William Barak, letter to the *Argus*, 29 August 1882, reprinted in Heiss and Minter, *Macquarie PEN Anthology*, 15; Barak et al., *Petition of Coranderrk Station Aborigines to The Chief Secretary*, 21 September 1886.
53 For example, William Cooper's petition to King George IV, 1938, reprinted in Heiss and Minter, *Macquarie PEN Anthology*, 28-29; discussion of Lake Tyers petition of 1913 in Victoria Haskins, '"Give to us the People we would Love to be amongst us": The Aboriginal Campaign against Caroline Bulmer's Eviction from Lake Tyers Aboriginal Station, 1913–14', *Provenance*, Journal of Public Record Office Victoria, 7, 2008; discussion of Lake Condah material in Van Toorn, 'Hegemony or Hidden Transcripts? Aboriginal Writing from Lake Condah 1876–1907', *Journal of Australian Studies*, 29:86, 2005, 13-27; also Yirrkala Bark Petition, 1963, located at Parliament House, Canberra; Gurindji petition to Lord Casey, Governor General, 1967; Larrakia petition to the Queen, 1972, Office of Aboriginal Affairs A2354, 1973/86.
54 Maria Nugent, '"The Queen gave us the Land": Queen Victoria and Historical Remembrance', *History Australia*, 9:2, August 2012, 182-200.

beliefs about the Crown giving land, while sometimes dismissed as evidence of gullibility, 'underestimate the factual knowledge held by Aboriginal people in the period, and the symbolic power of their account'.[55]

It is not possible, from the evidence, to draw a direct link between the Wybalenna petition and letters and the activism of William Barak and others. However, it is reasonable to assume that news of the Wybalenna community's activism – and, as we shall see, subsequent success – would have spread through humanitarian and missionary circles to First Nations people on mission settlements. Henry Reynolds positioned Walter Arthur as linking the 'primary resistance' of the frontier and the political movements of the twentieth century.[56] In a similar vein, the epistolary activism of the VDL people at Wybalenna can be seen as instituting the rich tradition of protest letters and petitions to authorities that chart the rise of the civil rights and land rights movements.

These letters from Flinders Island straddle the genres of political, protest and petitioning letters, but refuse to be located firmly. While they ostensibly contain pleas for assistance, similar to the letters of Lucy and Percy Pepper,[57] or political agitation, such as the letters of Ernest and Maggie Mobourne,[58] the VDL texts and their writers are temporally positioned under a more humane regime (British

---

55 Heather Goodall, *Invasion to Embassy: Land in Aboriginal Politics in New South Wales, 1770–1972*, St Leonards, Allen & Unwin and Black Books, 1996, 102.

56 Henry Reynolds, 'Walter George Arthur: Pioneer Aboriginal Activist', *Island*, Issue 49, Summer 1991, 36.

57 Simon Flagg and Sebastian Gurciullo (eds.), *Footprints: The Journey of Lucy and Percy Pepper*, Canberra, National Archives of Australia, North Melbourne, Public Record Office Victoria, 2008.

58 Contained in Chapter 9 of Jan Critchett, *Untold Stories: Memories and Lives of Victorian Kooris*, Carlton, Melbourne University Press, 1998.

CHAPTER 6

Colonial, not Protection Board) and write from a unique position of inferred entitlement as free people in exile, not as second-class subjects to be managed. Their claims on the British Crown, to live up to the responsibilities guaranteed by Sir George Arthur, were a very potent moral assertion in their time.

The *Fortitude* carried the letters by the VDL complainants to Hobarttown in late June, along with a rambling defence by Henry Jeanneret against the charges leveled against him in the petition to Queen Victoria.[59] Framing the younger men as setting the others 'an example of roguery, dissoluteness and violence', Jeanneret also seeks to cast aspersions on the character of Mary ann Arthur. In what can be seen as an overtly gendered attack, he insinuates that Mary ann 'enjoyed the entrée' to Joseph Milligan's quarters 'at all hours of the day and night', and he also remarks on the fact that she was 'addressed conjointly' with her husband (i.e. at all) by the Governor in the invitation to communicate. Jeanneret's tone is impudent: he is inferring inappropriate behavior on the Governor's part.

The letters were received at the Colonial Secretary's office in Hobart on 1 July 1846. And as the bundle of explosive letters was crossing secretarial and vice-regal desks, back at Wybalenna the greatest drama was already underway. It centred around an unlikely source, and a very simple error in European hearing.

Noemy Merewick was seen as a compliant, even timid man, hailing from the mid West Coast of VDL. As we have seen, he was clearly the most committed Christian convert on Flinders Island, known for his characteristic harangues and exhortations to his fellow Countrymen to follow his lead. Notably, he was the only VDL exile

---

59   Henry Jeanneret, 5 June 1846, CSO 11/26/378, AJCP 280/195, Reel 544, 348-369.

of any nation lauded in the *Flinders Island Chronicle* – on multiple occasions – for his dedication to Christianity. For this reason, he is one of the most remarkable, and visible, of the VDL exiles in the Wybalenna record. While there are no images in existence of Noemy, and very little biographical data, he looms large in the Wybalenna story, a figure ever-present in both Indigenous and European accounts of religious education on the island. Noemy was regularly singled out by George Augustus Robinson and Robert Clark as an effective, emotive speaker.

Noemy was also one of the few supporters of Jeanneret among the VDL exiles. He would later testify at an Inquiry that he liked Jeanneret, and was happy for him to return to Wybalenna – 'Doctor a good one'.[60] However, he also unwittingly helped to 'bring down' the unpopular doctor, due to a simple misunderstanding – not his own – regarding the complex Flinders Island lingua franca.

The memorandum testifying to the veracity of the petition to Queen Victoria, which had been so carefully recorded and stored back in May 1846, was now to come into play. As the exiles prepared their letters to the Governor for transport on the *Fortitude*, Walter Arthur must have decided to play his hand. He went to Jeanneret's house with one of the copies of the memorandum, and formally asked the superintendent to read it and then forward it to the Governor. Then, by Arthur's account, he left Jeanneret's house.

This was a provocative act. Arthur would have been aware that Jeanneret was placing great stock on the statements taken by Sinclair Davie.[61] These were worded so to discredit the claims in the petition to

---

60 Noemy, Testimony to the Friend inquiry, October 1846, AOT CSO 11/1/27 C658, 178.
61 Sinclair Davie's relationship with the VDL exiles appears to be long and complex. He went on to run the Oyster Cove settlement for five years after the death of

CHAPTER 6

Queen Victoria, and appear as refutation of the claims. The memorandum was a direct challenge to these statements taken by Davie, and we can only imagine Jeanneret's dismay to read it. Even more shocking, perhaps, was the audacity with which Walter Arthur presented it to him. The signatories, we will remember, swore that when Davie questioned them, 'he asked us was it all true what we blackfellows wrote … and we stated all over again and said it was all true'.[62] Jeanneret would have been seething.

Walter Arthur's house was probably located approximately a hundred metres from the superintendent's quarters – less than a few minutes walk. Arthur had not reached his home that day, after presenting Jeanneret with the memorandum, when he was rapidly recalled to the superintendent's house. Walter Arthur tells the story:

> … he called me into his Parlour and said what does this paper mean and who drew it up to which I told him it was me who wrote it out Doctor Jeanneret then said how dare you offer to bring such a thing to me and then Doctor Jeanneret threw the paper at me and with great anger kicked it away and told me that if I wanted to send this letter to his Excellency we blackfellows must send it ourselves for he Doctor Jeanneret would not send any such paper for us he got into a great Paſsion and told me to be off out of his house and not to let him see me again …[63]

This was far from the end of Walter Arthur's trials that day. Jeanneret was determined to discredit the young man who had been an adversary since before they had even met (we will recall Arthur

---

Robert Clark, and one of his sons, named Walter George, married one of Fanny Cochrane's children.

62   Memorandum, Davey Bruney et al., CSO 11/26/378, AJCP 280/195, Reel 544, SLV: also Walter G. Arthur's handwritten copy original in Friend Inquiry papers, AOT, CSO11/1/27, C658.

63   Walter George Arthur to the Governor, 15 July 1846, AOT CSO 11/1/27 C658.

expressed concern about reports of Jeanneret's administration before ever meeting him). And Jeanneret clearly thought he had an ally in his campaign to discredit Walter Arthur, in the compliant West Coast man Noemy.

In the wholesale questioning around the community regarding the petition and other documents, Noemy had been heard to say that Walter *lanny* him to sign a letter. Knowing this was a common word for beat or strike, Jeanneret must have thought he finally had his proof, that Walter Arthur had threatened the other men to sign the petition. Enraged by the memorandum – which actually bore Noemy's signature – and determined to gain control over the rebellious menace of Walter Arthur once and for all, Jeanneret made his stand.

Jeanneret recalled Walter Arthur to his parlour. Also in attendance were Noemy, Walter's wife Mary ann, a group of other VDL Countrypeople, Jeanneret's family, their nurse, Robert Clark and Sinclair Davie the coxswain. This was clearly a major showdown, and Jeanneret wanted an audience. He was sure he had the upper hand. Walter Arthur recounts what happened next:

> He told Mr Clark to write down Nommy depositions then Doctor Jeanneret called this Black man Nommy and asked him did Walter threaten to Lanny (him the aborigine word for beat strike) if he would not sign this Memorandum … but all I heard Nommy say when they asked Nommy this question was that Walter Laarne me on his way of describing the word learn to teach me … Nommy said very plain to Doctor Jeanneret that I like to write my name myself and said it in his own Language Ludiwi na Potheac tuanaperrea memenea (his way of stating) white man do not understand me …[64]

---

64   Ibid., 109.

CHAPTER 6

Noemy, the peaceable man suddenly cast into the centre of this drama, apparently did his best to placate Jeanneret. But there was no avoiding letting the superintendent know that he had made a simple error of language. As Noemy later explained:

> I told Dr Jeanneret that Walter said he would learn me to write my name to the paper ... It was only to learn me to write. I did not mean that Walter said he would beat me if I did not sign a paper but that he would teach me to write my name.[65]

Incensed and humiliated by his confusion of *lanny* and *laarne*, Jeanneret, according to Arthur, 'flew up in a great rage before us all with Nommy and call him a great liar and desired him to go out of his house'.[66] Jeanneret then refused to hear any other VDL witnesses, or take Robert Clark's expert advice on the clear linguistic difference between *laarne* and *lanny*. He consulted the coxswain and the nurse, who testified to having heard Noemy say Walter *lanny* him, and sentenced his nemesis, Walter Arthur, to indefinite incarceration.

Walter Arthur's imprisonment lasted seventeen days, and was a clear turning point in the fight for power at Wybalenna. Jeanneret's blatant abuse of power was obvious from this point on, and as soon as the colonial authorities in Hobart became aware of it, it gave them the ammunition needed to launch a full investigation. Upon his release from the settlement's jail, Walter Arthur penned a long and detailed letter to the Governor, dated 15 July 1846, describing the series of events in great detail. His release was only obtained when Mary ann – who had boldly and repeatedly confronted Jeanneret over

---

[65] Noemy, Testimony to the Friend Inquiry, October 1846, AOT CSO 11/1/27 C658 163.
[66] Walter George Arthur to the Governor, 15 July 1846, AOT CSO 11/1/27 C658, 110.

the situation – claimed that Arthur's health was suffering. And indeed, being incarcerated, with no fresh air, sun or exercise in the middle of a Bass Strait winter, was certainly damaging. In describing his release, Arthur tells the Governor that Jeanneret:

> … wants now to say he only treated me as he would his children But please your Excellency I feel I am a Man and a Free Man too and cannot be satisfied of being shut up in a dungeon for 17 days …[67]

Walter Arthur's statement 'I am a Man and a Free Man too' is an assertion. By appropriating and answering the Abolitionist propaganda of 'Am I not a Man?' in the affirmative, Arthur is jogging the memory of colonial functionaries. If receiving the bundle of provocative letters and papers written in June was not enough to force his hand, Governor Eardley-Wilmot was left with no choice once he had received Walter Arthur's letter describing his incarceration, and an equally damning cover letter. Henry Jeanneret's trouble-plagued eight month reign demanded review. In September 1846, the Colonial Secretary wrote to Lt Matthew Curling Friend, the George Town Harbour Master, ordering him to convene an enquiry into the problems at Wybalenna. James Bicheno told Friend:

> … it would appear that Dr Jeanneret had thought it necessary to imprison a black Walter G. Arthur, for 17 days, and that man is complaining of this confinement and of binding him over in a penalty, charges Dr J with general maltreatment of the natives, and with issuing rations of bad meat.[68]

It was the beginning of the end for both Henry Jeanneret, and Wybalenna.

---

67   Ibid., 114-115.
68   James Bicheno to Matthew Friend, 14 September 1846, AOT CSO11/1/27 C658, 3-4.

CHAPTER 6

The Friend Inquiry

> I do not like Dr Jeanneret because he is an ugly fellow.[69]

Matthew Friend was given a complex, unenviable assignment. On the one hand, he was to hear evidence from the VDL exiles regarding their claims against Jeanneret in the petition to Queen Victoria. He was also instructed to investigate the circumstances of Walter Arthur's imprisonment, and gauge the true feelings of the VDL exiles regarding Jeanneret's administration. In addition, he was to investigate a series of charges raised by Jeanneret against Robert Clark, alleging brutal treatment of the children in his care. The most sensational of these claims involved the hanging of a child, by the neck, from the roof of the school house. Friend was advised by the Colonial Secretary that the Governor 'deemed it expedient to institute an enquiry upon the spot, not only into the complaints themselves, but into the general management of the Establishment'.[70]

Walter Arthur, having managed to secure the Inquiry, sought to ensure that it was conducted, as much as possible, on his own terms. On October 6 he wrote to Matthew Friend, who had presumably just arrived at Wybalenna, with what is effectively a pre-emptive strike:

> Sir, I lay this before you that I have heard that my fellow Country-men said that I made them Sign the petition to the Queen, that it has always been said by Doctor Jeanneret that I force them to Sign the petition of which I was put into Jail for, and laybelled me a wicked man and my wife we were both very bad people.[71]

---

69 Frederick, Testimony to the Friend Inquiry, October 1846, AOT CSO 11/1/27 C658, 185-186.
70 James Bicheno to Matthew Friend, 14 September 1846, AOT CSO11/1/27 C658, 3-4.
71 Walter George Arthur to Matthew Curling Friend, 6 October 1846, AOT CSO 11/1/27 C658, 120.

Assuring Friend that he could prove these accusations to be false, Arthur sought permission from Friend for Robert Clark to directly ask these parties if they were ever forced to sign documents without their consent. This, presumably, was to ensure a balance, as Jeanneret would certainly be putting forth that opinion. Arthur is ensuring that he is at least beginning the Inquiry on an equal footing to Jeanneret. To further cement this position, he requested:

> Will you be please Sir to allow me to Call up my own wittneſses either black people or white people and to allow Mr Clark to be my interpreter. Will you pleas to allow me now to have any one present but those I think right to have when the wittneſses are examined.[72]

This request may well stem from lessons learnt during the trial, in Port Phillip, of Tunnerminnerwait and Maulboyheener who, due to their Aboriginality, were unable to testify. They were thus positioned as being unable to understand the law, but paradoxically – and fatally – responsible for its consequences. This note from Arthur to Friend shows a clear comprehension of judicial processes, and works as an assurance of his civilisation. Tellingly, he signed this letter 'Your Aboriginal and black friend, Walter G. Arthur'. He is positioning himself as a respectable citizen, and equal to a free white man, before the Inquiry had even commenced.[73]

The hearings recorded by Matthew Friend in October 1846 offer us some of the most compelling insights yet into life at Wybalenna. If the school examinations afforded glimpses into individuals who

---

72 Ibid.
73 There is no conclusive proof from Friend's report that Arthur's request was granted, and that VDL exiles were interviewed without Jeanneret being present; however, it is implied by their often candid testimonies, which might have been more guarded in his presence.

CHAPTER 6

are nowhere else in the record given a voice, with the Friend Inquiry these people are given a virtual stage and megaphone. This especially relates to the children, who were ignored in the earlier examinations, and certainly throughout the record. Much of this is thanks to the sensitive reportage of Matthew Friend, who advised the Colonial Secretary, in his subsequent report:

> … In eliciting the answers from the black man, I endevoured to get at the spirit of their replies, which was not effected without some difficulty, but I have no doubt that I at length accomplished according to their true intent and meaning …[74]

Case 1: Contested Authorship

> I told the Queen that we had given up our Country and came to this Island and we expected in return to have what we wanted.[75]

The key area of inquiry which Matthew Friend was charged to investigate was the authenticity of the petition to Queen Victoria, and the letters which were written in its wake. This was paramount to the Governor, who needed to be able to advise the Colonial Office in London of the veracity of the claims against Jeanneret. If Jeanneret was going to be ousted a second time – which seemed to be the goal of everyone, except the superintendent himself – the evidence had to be correct, so there was no chance of him regaining his position yet again on appeal.

The method of the petition's creation – being actually penned by Robert Clark – leant itself to claims that it was not truly representative

---

74 Matthew Curling Friend to James Bicheno, 31 October 1846, AOT CSO11/1/27 C658, 37.
75 David Bruney, Testimony to the Friend Inquiry, October 1846, AOT CSO 11/1/27 C658, 168-172.

of the attitudes of the VDL exiles. This cloud over the petition and the letters – initiated by Jeanneret – has been an enduring one, and has spawned two distinct discourses. It is useful to briefly touch on these, before we examine precisely what the VDL exiles themselves had to say.

The first of the discourses around the petition and letters is that of contested authorship. It was introduced by Jeanneret at the time of writing, and consolidated by James Bonwick in his very influential 1870 work *The Last of the Tasmanians*. A fervent admirer of Jeanneret, Bonwick wrote, 'A petition against him was got up by somebody, and signed by eight of the Natives …The poor men afterwards repudiated their own act, and attributed it to bad counsel'.[76] This is a very selective reading of the facts. Bonwick takes into account the statements made to Sinclair Davie in May 1846, but does not give any credit to the rebuttal memorandum, letters to the Governor, or even the testimonies to the Friend Inquiry which, as we shall soon see, tell a very different story. This curious omission by Bonwick of the findings of Friend's Inquiry is perhaps explicable in light of Bonwick's admiration of Jeanneret: it also set the tone for Clive Turnbull who, in 1948, and taking largely from Bonwick's work, likewise dismissed the petition as worthless. Turnbull frames the June 1846 letters as 'curious documents … chiefly remarkable for their faked simplicities of style, references to "our father the Governor" and whatnot', and asserts that the political machinations surrounding Jeanneret's troubled appointment were high matters that 'passed the natives by'.[77] Turnbull's work, fed by Bonwick, was to have a similar influence on a host of other writers.

---

76 Bonwick, *The Last of the Tasmanians*, 267.
77 Turnbull, *Black War*, 224.

CHAPTER 6

N. J. B. Plomley, certainly the most informed and thorough of all historians of the Flinders Island period, addresses the petition and June letters relatively briefly in his *Weep in Silence* chapter which examines the problematic administration of Jeanneret. Like Turnbull and Bonwick, Plomley was dismissive of the role of the petition and the June 1846 letter writers. He characterised the key Indigenous writers – presumably, Walter Arthur and David Bruney – as 'the counterpart of that modern youth who sees the world as having no future for him and therefore wants to destroy it'. Thus, they are some 1840s version, presumably, of the anarchist-nihilist punks Plomley observed in the 1980s. Plomley also states that the letters 'appear to have been composed by the same person, and that not an Aboriginal'.[78] This is rather astounding, considering the variation in handwriting and language use, and suggests that perhaps he had not sighted the original letters. Hence, Plomley's assessment that the June letters were concocted by the agitator Walter Arthur and interfering catechist Robert Clark (who Plomley vehemently disliked, and called 'a mealy mouthed crawling creature'[79]) must be viewed with some degree of caution.

The petition's claim that the agreement with the Crown was 'not lost from our Minds' is disputed strongly by Keith Windschuttle, and indirectly by Brian Plomley. Claiming that only one or two younger members of the community were behind the petition, Windschuttle asserts that they could not possibly be aware of transactions between their elders and Robinson, as the agent of the Crown.[80] However, this ignores several key points. Firstly, a number of senior men who

---

78 Plomley, *Weep in Silence*, 152-153.
79 Ibid., 678.
80 Windschuttle, *Fabrication*, 233-234.

had been part of the original negotiations with Robinson fifteen years earlier testified to the veracity of this claim – it was still fresh in their minds. Secondly, one of the younger petitioners, David Bruney, far from being unaware of these previous events, was physically present on at least one of the conciliatory missions with his father, the chief negotiator Doctor Wooreddy, and so was also a direct witness. Thirdly, and perhaps most importantly, other younger members of the group had clearly internalised their elders' view of being a free people. Knowledge of the deal made with Governor Arthur and the King was in fact the great creation story of Wybalenna, and this negotiation – tied up with their status as a free people – is present from the earliest record of the settlement, to the very last.[81]

A second stream of scholarship around the petition and subsequent letters highlights the agency shown by the Wybalenna exiles. Lyndall Ryan quotes briefly from the letters of Walter and Mary ann Arthur, David Bruney, John Allen and Washington.[82] Henry Reynolds has done much to raise the profile of both the Petition and the activism of Walter Arthur and his circle: Reynolds draws on the Petition and links it to what he sees as a negotiated treaty for the Tasmanian mainland. Noting that politics is 'assumed to be a European prerogative,'[83] Reynolds asserts that at Flinders Island the reverse was the case. He also laments that historians have long overlooked Walter Arthur's activism, and notes that 'Jeanneret's was a significant political scalp'.[84]

---

81   Windschuttle's denigration of the petition to Queen Victoria is therefore not only spurious, but an exemplar of the perniciousness which characterises a century and a half of problematic historiography based on poor scholarship.

82   The language is heavily corrected, and Ryan erroneously cites Denison as Governor in this period. Lyndall Ryan, *Tasmanian Aborigines*, 249-250.

83   Reynolds, *Fate of a Free People*, 11.

84   Ibid., 13.

CHAPTER 6

Sally Dammery, in her biography of Walter Arthur, argued that the petition was less about land rights (as Reynolds claimed) but specifically to prevent Jeanneret's return.[85] While acknowledging Walter Arthur's letters to the Governor convinced colonial authorities that the Petition had indeed been written by the VDL exiles, Dammery concentrates chiefly on Arthur's communications and activism, barely mentioning the other letter writers.[86]

Penny Van Toorn has worked extensively on the literature which emerged from Wybalenna and other locations of Indigenous exile and control. Of the Petition, which she sees as a tactical document which 'played British colonial authorities at their own game'[87] and a 'communally generated story about the community's experience'[88] she notes that the deferential terminology was 'designed to reassure …that the petition was not a proclamation of rebellion'.[89]

Van Toorn raises an important point. The letter writers of June 1846 display seemingly gratuitous deference, especially the senior men Washington, Alphonso and Alexander, but this can be understood as a strategic assurance, in the style of the petitioning genre. They were first and foremost, as Ravi De Costa notes, positioning themselves as imperial subjects.[90] They were also persuading the current Governor that they understood civilised protocols, at the same time demanding the rights agreed to by a previous regime. Theirs was a very strategic approach, and it paid rich dividends: their careful

---

85   Dammery, *Walter George Arthur: A Free Tasmanian?*, 29.
86   Ibid., 29-34.
87   Van Toorn, *Writing Never Arrives Naked*, 122.
88   Van Toorn, 'Indigenous Australian Life Writing', 7.
89   Van Toorn, *Writing Never Arrives Naked*, 122.
90   Ravi de Costa, 'Identity, Authority, and the Moral Worlds of Indigenous Petitions', *Comparative Studies in Society and History*, 48:3, July 2006, 675.

language and strong but respectful persuasions eventually managed to make Hobart take notice, and launch an inquiry. And Matthew Friend was the man charged with ascertaining whether the petition really was the work of the men whose names were appended.

The claims of the VDL community as to their authorship of the petition and subsequent letters were both complex and, as we might assume, knowing what we do of life at Wybalenna, idiosyncratic. No two responses to Matthew Friend's questioning were the same. The influence of Robert Clark and Walter Arthur are very strong – in many cases, those who participated in the petition said they were told to, or advised to, by either Clark or Arthur. Yet virtually all still claim direct ownership.

> Alexander:
> I remember writing a Petition to the Queen. Mr Clark told me to write it. Nobody else. I remember that it said I did not want Dr Jeanneret to come down.[91]
>
> John Allen:
> I recollect writing a letter to the Queen. Dr Milligan and Mr Clark advised me to write that letter, the purpose of it was not to let Dr Jeanneret come again. I signed my name it was pencilled for me. Mr Clark pencilled it. [92]
>
> David Bruney:
> I recollect writing a letter to the Queen some time ago, it was about Dr Jeanneret, about stopping our tobacco, no one told me to do so, I can write. I signed it myself. I can read. I read it myself first and afterwards had it read to me.[93]

---

91 King Alexander, Testimony to the Friend Inquiry, October 1846, AOT CSO 11/1/27 C658, 179-180.
92 John Allen, Testimony to the Friend Inquiry, October 1846, AOT CSO 11/1/27 C658, 175-177.
93 David Bruney, Testimony to the Friend Inquiry, October 1846, AOT CSO 11/1/27 C658, 168-172.

CHAPTER 6

Neptune:
I remember writing a Petition to the Queen. Mr Clark told me to write the Petition. Mary Ann tell me to go to Mr Clarks house to write the Petition. It was not to let Dr Jeanneret come down to Flinders Island, because people no like him.[94]

Walter George Arthur:
I recollect signing a Petition to the Queen about six months ago. I wrote not to let Dr Jeanneret come again. I did not wish him to come again for the sake of my own Countrymen ... I remember the Petition. I did not read it myself. Dr Milligan read it to me. My Countrymen were present when Dr Milligan read it.[95]

Washington:
I recollect writing a Petition to the Queen. I wrote to the Queen to ask her for some money. I wrote to tell her that I work in the garden every day and to prevent the Doctor from scolding every day, because the Doctor want to make the black fellow work ... Walter told me to write to the Queen. Dr Milligan told and no one else. Mr Clark tell me a little ... I did not write my name to the Petition, it was leaded first. I can read writing a little. I read some of the Petition first & Walter read it afterwards. Walter pencil my signature & I wrote over it.[96]

It is important to note here that these men, although some not having physically written the petition, claim full ownership and authorship as though they had put ink to paper themselves. Throughout history, it was a common practice for letters to be written, for a sender, by a scribe. The business was conducted at post offices, and at court houses. John Hirst documented convict petition-writing as a 'minor

---

94   Neptune, Testimony to the Friend Inquiry, October 1846, AOT CSO 11/1/27 C658, 173-174.
95   Walter George Arthur, Testimony to the Friend Inquiry, October 1846, AOT CSO 11/1/27 C658, 140-146.
96   Washington, Testimony to the Friend Inquiry, October 1846, AOT CSO 11/1/27 C658, 182-184.

industry', and how a well-positioned clerk, or literate convict, could make a substantial income.[97] These communications, even though written by paid professional scribes or clerks, were still interpreted as messages from the named sender. Indirect authorship was also common among First Nations people in colonial settings. Vukile Khumalo noted a similar tradition in Kwazulu-Natal, with 'indirect authorship' a common practice in letter-writing from the mission setting at Ekukhanyeni.[98] Claims which discredit the petition to Queen Victoria conveniently ignore this well-established tradition, or especially as it relates to First Nations people.

There were also testimonies concerning other documents surrounding the petition, and here the issues are more complex. King Tippoo, for example, admits no knowledge of what was in the petition which bears his name; he told Friend:

> I remember a short time ago I wrote a Petition to the Queen. I was ill at the time. I did not sign it myself. Walter signed it for me, no one else but Walter told me to sign the Petition. I do not know what was in the paper.[99]

Interestingly, Tippoo claims to have written the petition, while at the same time disavowing any role in it. We might speculate that Tippoo was, at this stage, following along with the majority of his Big River Countrypeople, who were vehemently opposed to Jeanneret.

---

97 John Hirst, *Convict Society and Its Enemies*, Sydney, George Allen & Unwin, 1983, 128-129.
98 Vukile Khumalo, 'Ekukhanyeni Letter-writers: A Historical Inquiry into Epistolary Network(s) and Political Imagination in Kwazulu-Natal, South Africa', in Karin Barber (ed.), *Africa's Hidden Histories: Everyday Literacy and Making the Self*, Indiana University Press, Bloomington, 2006, 122.
99 Tippo Saib, Testimony to the Friend Inquiry, October 1846, AOT CSO 11/1/27 C658, 181.

CHAPTER 6

However, Tippoo's opinion of Jeanneret was, by October 1846, quite favourable: he told Friend, 'Doctor good one'.[100]

Noemy's role in the May memorandum is even more complex. Being a supporter of Jeanneret, he did not sign the petition of February 1846, and knew nothing about it. Besides, as he told Friend, 'I like Dr Jeanneret to come down – black fellows not like him to come down, but I liked him to come down'.[101] Yet his signing of the memorandum, swearing to the truth of the petition, warranted examination by Friend, for this was the justification for the jailing of Walter Arthur for seventeen days. The scene which led to the jailing – with its linguistic confusion between *lanny* and *laarne* – was explained by Noemy to Friend:

> I told Dr Jeanneret that Walter said he would learn me to write my name to the paper – I did not know what was in the paper – It was only to learn me to write. I did not mean that Walter said he would beat me if I did not sign a paper but that he would teach me to write my name.[102]

Noemy's name being affixed to the memorandum certainly goes some way to explaining some of Jeanneret's rage when he read it, and his actions in calling Noemy in for interrogation about the statement 'Walter laarne me'. Matthew Friend called Sinclair Davie to give evidence, and he testified regarding the contested memorandum. He explained, 'Dr Jeanneret asked him [Noemy] what induced him to sign the paper & he said blackfellow frightened him too much and that Walter "Lanny" him as I understood it, meaning to beat. There

---

100 Ibid., 181.
101 Noemy, Testimony to the Friend Inquiry, October 1846, AOT CSO 11/1/27 C658, 178.
102 Ibid., 144.

were several together some inside & some outside the door, making a great noise'.¹⁰³ Noemy also testified:

> When I said I signed I was frightened & therefore signed my name I meant that I was afraid of the Blackfellows but did not mean one in particular. I was also frightened too much that Mr Clark would growl me.¹⁰⁴

A clearer picture seems to emerge here, of a man, loyal to the returned superintendent Jeanneret, being bullied and probably tricked. Walter Arthur, it would appear, used less than honest means to get Noemy's signature on the memorandum. It also seems blatantly clear that Noemy was, to some degree, intimidated, probably by the new alliance of Big River and Ben Lomond men. As we learnt from Robert Clark's letter to George Washington Walker of 3 April 1846, the community had been divided between a small group of Jeanneret's favourites, and those violently opposed to him. Noemy's position, as a supporter of Jeanneret, put him at odds with the majority who were against him, especially the powerful Big River men. He was also clearly uncomfortable with Robert Clark. When questioned about his signature appearing on a letter dated 6 August, he told Friend, 'the signature "Nommy Merewick" is my writing, it was pencilled for me by Mr Clark. I did not wish to write it. Mr Clark growled me. I wished my child [Martha] to be taken away from Mr Clark but Catherine her mother did not wish it'.¹⁰⁵

As we will see, Noemy probably had very good cause to want his daughter to be removed from the Clarks, even though he was

---

103 Sinclair Davie, Testimony to the Friend Inquiry, October 1846, AOT CSO 11/1/27 C658, 144-145.
104 Noemy, Testimony to the Friend Inquiry, October 1846, AOT CSO 11/1/27 C658, 145.
105 Ibid., !63-164.

overruled by his wife. For, in the case of at least a small group of the children under their care, the stories emerging from the children's dormitory at the Clark's house were horrific.

Case 2: Child Brutality – The Hanging of Hannah McSweeney

A second key issue that Matthew Friend was charged with investigating was the sensational counter-charges laid against the catechist Robert Clark and his wife Catherine by Henry Jeanneret.[106] The most disturbing of these was that of the hanging of Hannah McSweeney. According to Jeanneret's report, this event had taken place around two years earlier. Hannah McSweeney's brief testimony – her only 'voice' in the archive – deserves to be relayed in full:

> I am about 7 years old. I have been at School under Mr & Mrs Clark. I recollect a long time ago, I was hanged up by the neck. Mrs Clark hanged me, she did it by herself. No one helped her. Mr Clark was not there. Mary Ann, Walter, Mathinna, Nancy, Fanny, Martha, Miss Fanny Clark were there. I was hanged up to a beam in the Hall. I was hanged up quite high to the top of the beam. I did not cry very much when they hanged me up. I did not cry very much when they took me down again. I did cry but not very much. I could see all about me when I was hanging up. My neck was all swelled up when I was taken down. I told my Mother about it.[107]

Questioned directly afterwards, Clark's wife denied that such an event ever took place, stating that the statement was wholly false. Yet other children asserted – with minor variations – that it was the

---

106 Contained in Jeanneret's lengthy report to the Colonial Secretary in June 1846 defending himself against the charges in the petition, CSO 11/26/378, AJCP 280/195, Reel 544, SLV; and also in his *Vindication of a Colonial Magistrate*, 10-13.
107 Hannah McSweeney, Testimony to the Friend Inquiry, October 1846, AOT CSO11/1/27, C658, 126.

truth. The next child examined in relation to the charge was Fanny Cochrane. The half-sister of Mary ann Arthur, she was already well known among the community for her rebellious behaviour, and – as we will see – was most certainly the recipient of brutal corporal punishment from the Clarks. With regard to Hannah McSweeney's story, Fanny was in no doubt:

> I remember Hannah being hanged up by the neck, it was in Dr Milligans time, it was Mrs Clark who hanged her, I saw her hang her. Mrs Clark put the rope around her neck. She hanged her in the hall ... As soon as Hannah was hanged I went out with Walter to saw wood, and did not wait to see her taken down ... When I left her hanging up I thought she would die.[108]

Fanny Cochrane testified that she was outside cutting wood with Walter Arthur during most of the hanging, and that when she returned to the school room, Hannah 'was doing nothing particular, she was standing in the room she was not crying. I did not notice whether she had any mark around her neck'.[109] The only variance from Hannah's story is that Fanny specifically states that Mathinna was not there at the time of the hanging; instead, she was looking after the baby. Again, Mrs Clark declined responding to this testimony, claiming it was a story of Fanny's own invention. Walter Arthur was questioned about Fanny's testimony, given that he was a central actor in it. He denied being present when a child was hanged, and said, 'I never saw a child hanged up by the neck ... I remember often cutting wood with Fanny. I was in the habit of talking to her when we were cutting up wood together. I do not think Fanny would have seen Hannah hanged up by the neck without mentioning it to

---

108 Fanny Cochrane, Testimony to the Friend Inquiry, October 1846, AOT CSO11/1/27, C658, 130.
109 Ibid.

CHAPTER 6

me, if it were as she states'.[110] Mary ann Arthur, likewise, disavowed any knowledge of the hanging.[111]

Yet the children held a firm line: the hanging had in fact occurred. Their evidence, on the whole, was very similar. The next child questioned over the hanging was Martha, the daughter of Noemy and his wife Catherine, who told Friend:

> I am about twelve or thirteen years old. I recollect Hannah being hanged up by the neck, Mrs Clark put the rope around her neck and hanged her up … it was for looking at Fanny Cochrane. She was not speaking to her – Hannah cried when she was hanged. She did not cry when she was taken down. She did not cry when she was hanging up. I thought she would die. She did not speak when she was taken down.[112]

Nanny, Hannah McSweeney's sister, also gave evidence to witnessing the hanging. She told Friend:

> I am between eight and nine years old. I recollect Hannah being hanged up by the neck. Mrs Clark hanged her, it was in the Hall … She was hanged because she stealed Mrs Clark's eggs. She did not hang her up long … When Hannah was taken down, she did nothing, but stopped outside in the yard.[113]

The final person questioned regarding the hanging of Hannah McSweeney was the girl's mother, listed in the Inquiry papers as Mary Henrietta, but better known to us as 'Big Mary' or Tylerwinner. Big Mary had been one of the key instigators of the escape conspiracy

---

110 Walter Arthur, Testimony to the Friend Inquiry, October 1846, AOT CSO11/1/27, C658, 128.
111 Mary ann Arthur, Testimony to the Friend Inquiry, October 1846, AOT CSO11/1/27, C658, 128.
112 Martha, Testimony to the Friend Inquiry, October 1846, AOT CSO11/1/27, C658, 132.
113 Nanny, Testimony to the Friend Inquiry, October 1846, AOT CSO11/1/27, C658, 135.

during the reign of Sergeant Wight back in 1832, and she had also been castigated by Henry Jeanneret – and the married women – for loose behaviour in 1842. She testified to Matthew Friend:

> I am the mother of Hannah. I was told by her a long time ago that she had been hanged up by the neck. She said Mrs Clark has hanged her & flogged her too much. I did not believe it. I could see her every week, both my daughters were there … The Children tell me this a long time ago.[114]

These testimonies from the children are deeply troubling. It is highly likely that the story about Hannah McSweeney – then aged no more than five years old – being hung by the neck for ten minutes is an exaggeration. In all likelihood, the children were threatened with hanging for misbehaviour – the tragic fate of Tunnerminnerwait and Maulboyheener in Port Phillip could, feasibly, have been good fodder for adults warning children about what happens to naughty children. The suggestion that Mrs Clark probably did not hang Hannah McSweeney by the neck, however, is in no way meant to imply that there was no brutality visited on the children under the Clarks' care, for it is very obvious that at least some of the children were treated harshly.

Mathinna – who would become immortalised by writers long after her untimely death – was certainly one of the children who received harsh treatment from the Clarks. Her testimony to Friend is worth relaying in full, as it is the only place in the documentary record where this often-written-about child speaks in her own voice:

> I do not know how old I am. I lived with Lady Franklin for some time. I have been under the care of Mr & Mrs Clark, when I was flogged I was placed across a table and my hands

---

114 Mary Henrietta, Testimony to the Friend Inquiry, October 1846, AOT CSO11/1/27, C658, 134.

and feet were tied. I was flogged every day. I did not do my work and if I did my work, it was needle work. I made my clothes, I have no father or Mother. I think I was flogged when I ought not to be flogged. I told Dr Jeanneret that I was treated badly. Dr Jeanneret took me away and placed me at Mr Lee's. Hannah and Nanny were also flogged. I do not know if they had been naughty. I was once flogged when the blood ran down my head, the stick struck my head when I was running away. Mrs Clark struck me. She intended to hit me in the head. I had not done all the needle work that she bid me, I never complained about being flogged.[115]

Catherine Clark, when questioned, reported that she had been told by Joseph Milligan that Mathinna 'is a great liar and I was not to depend on any thing she said. She used to tell lies very frequently'. Giving the impression that this propensity for fabrication had abated somewhat, Mrs Clark did not deny the final charge, where blood had run down Mathinna's head: this was accidental, as she had aimed to hit the girl in the back, and she had run away, the stick accidentally hitting a scab on her head. Mrs Clark added, 'I consider she was the least chastised of any in the school'.[116]

The catechist's wife was not the only dispenser of discipline. The testimony of Adam, the half-brother of Mary ann Arthur, again gives the impression of beatings taking place at the school:

I am about Seven or Eight years old, I told Dr Jeanneret that Mr Clark had beaten me, the mark on my face had been made by a stick. Mr Clark struck me … I was also flogged for the talk. I had opened the gate and let the Cow out.[117]

---

115 Mathinna, Testimony to the Friend Inquiry, October 1846, AOT CSO11/1/27, C658, 93.
116 Catherine Clark, Testimony to the Friend Inquiry, October 1846, AOT CSO11/1/27, C658, 94.
117 Adam, Testimony to the Friend Inquiry, October 1846, AOT CSO11/1/27, C658, 75.

Perhaps one of the most bizarre and disturbing stories, aside from the alleged hanging of Hannah McSweeney, is that of 'Fanny Cochrane's box'. It appears that Fanny Cochrane – who was clearly the least controllable of the children – was for a time put into a small box to sleep as punishment. This is testified to by Adam, who claimed 'Mr Clark put me into Fanny Cochrane's box. A nail hurt me which was in the box'.[118] Hannah McSweeney also claimed that her hanging occurred 'at the time Fanny used to sleep in the box'.[119] Mary ann Arthur also acknowledged the use of the box, when discussing Adam's injury from the nail.[120]

Clearly, the Clarks were at times brutal towards the children. Even setting aside the perhaps more outlandish hanging, which could well be an exaggeration if not fabrication, errant behaviour resulted in whippings and other forms of physical punishment which, to the modern sensibility, seem heavy handed and barbaric. Yet it is important to remember that violence was a part of everyday life. It is one of the key characteristics of colonialism, and of children's lives in wider society. Beatings and corporal punishment were common in homes, educational institutions such as they existed at that time, and in the workplaces, where apprentices were beaten by their masters.

VDL people had experienced violence in myriad forms. From the invasion of their land; to the blatant frontier violence where they were hunted, hounded and shot by settlers; to the officially sanctioned violence of their removal from Country and exile to Flinders Island.

---

118 Adam, Testimony to the Friend Inquiry, October 1846, AOT CSO11/1/27, C658, 75.

119 Hannah McSweeney, Testimony to the Friend Inquiry, October 1846, AOT CSO11/1/27, C658, 126.

120 Mary ann Arthur, Testimony to the Friend Inquiry, October 1846, AOT CSO11/1/27, C658, 75.

CHAPTER 6

Once there, violence was again a key feature of everyday life. It came up time and time again in the sermons spoken by the men. As well as frontier violence, flagellation – that graphic, state-sanctioned violence often seen as one of the legitimate tactics for maintaining control – was common on the mainland penal settlement, and also at Wybalenna. For a time, the settlement had its own flagellator – incidentally, a black man – to discipline rowdy convicts for offences as seemingly minor as speaking disrespectfully to a master.[121]

Among the VDL community there was, it must be acknowledged, a seemingly steady stream of small, violent episodes. There were tensions, often breaking out into violence, between nations during at least the first decade of the exile. Domestic violence – euphemised in the record as a husband 'ill-using' his wife – definitely occurred.[122] In all probability, it was not quite as widespread as chroniclers of the day purported: they had a vested interest in demonising Indigenous men, and depicting the women as needing rescue. And, from what we know of the spirited VDL women at Wybalenna, they were often capable of rescuing themselves. However, it seems there was – as in any society – a proportion of the population enacting violence, and this extended to the female population, as there are also incidents of women perpetrating violence on other women.[123] These were times,

---

121 John Pierre, aka 'Black Pierre the Flagellator', was the Grenadian convict usually stationed on Clark or Chalky Island tending sheep during 1836–38, who was called upon to discipline transgressive convicts.

122 There are records of Walter Arthur 'ill-using' Mary ann, and David Bruney beating Matilda.

123 The spoken sermons of the men make a number of references to women fighting and tearing their frocks. At the subsequent settlement at Oyster Cove, the visiting Doctor William Smith was called on at least two occasions to attend to Emma, who had been badly beaten, and part of his prescription was to isolate her from the other women, especially Mary ann Arthur. 19 April and 1 August 1862, Oyster Cove Visitor's Book, AOT CSO 89/1/1.

it must be reiterated, when violence *was* a major part of the colonial language.

It was not extraordinary, then, for the Clarks to beat the children under their care. Whippings were, in this period – and in fact right up until the 1970s – a legitimate part of the disciplinary repertoire of educating children. The reported hanging of Hannah McSweeney, however, was deemed as excessive, and when investigated, according to Matthew Friend, 'the evidence was given in a manner which caused me to doubt whether the whole was not a fiction'.[124] Friend was also persuaded by the testimony of Walter and Mary ann Arthur, the two independent witnesses, who he called 'the two most intelligent persons amongst the Aborigines'. For all their obvious loyalty to the Clarks, it is doubtful that the Arthurs would have tolerated such extreme behaviour as the hanging of a child by the neck for ten minutes; and even more improbable that such a punishment would not result in death. Yet we might read from this case that the *threat* of being hung – having special salience after the execution of Tunnerminnerwait and Maulboyheener – was undoubtedly used on the children, and that the Clarks most certainly used corporal punishment on at least some of the children.

What is also glaringly obvious from this report, and others filtering down through official journals over the years, is that a group of the children – especially Fanny Cochrane, Mathinna and Hannah McSweeney – were openly rebellious. They showed many of the same examples of everyday resistance written about by James C. Scott, and common at Wybalenna (and, in fact, with school children across racial, class and temporal divides). At times, this escalated into open

---

124 Matthew Curling Friend to James Bicheno, 31 October 1846, AOT CSO11/1/27, C658.

CHAPTER 6

acts of rebellion, such as Fanny Cochrane's deliberate burning down of the school house, and many smaller documented acts of sabotage and disobedience. More often, this resistance took the form of causing a myriad of minor disruptions – telling lies, spreading stories, gossiping and, in this case, in all likelihood extrapolating on one incident of brutality towards Hannah. As we will see, this conscious manipulation of the truth – or gammoning – was actually one of the key forms of resistance enacted at Wybalenna.

Case 3: The Charges Against Henry Jeanneret – Rumour and Reality

Matthew Friend's job was to look into the both the veracity of the charges, and whether it was, in fact, representative of the wishes of those whose names appear on it. In both cases, multiple levels of meaning and complexity were revealed, leaving few very clear answers. Truth represents something of a postmodern dilemma: it definitely existed, but it was ethereal, collective, positional, and in a constant state of flux. To get a closer idea of the veracity of the issues raised in the petition, and the Wybalenna version of truth they represented, we might look closely at a sample selection of the issues raised in the petition to Queen Victoria.

The first claim of many against Henry Jeanneret in the petition is that he had carried loaded guns and threatened to shoot the VDL exiles. The petition specifically stated, 'He used to carry Pistols in his Pockets and threatened very often to shoot us and make us run away in a fright.'[125] This was a very serious charge, as coercion was never intended to be a facet of daily life at Wybalenna. Eight months after

---

125 Walter Arthur et al. to Queen Victoria, 17 February 1846. CSO 11/26/378; AJCP 280/195, Reel 544, SLV.

writing this in the petition, the men of Wybalenna told Matthew Friend:

> David Bruney:
> I remember mentioning in the letter that Dr Jeanneret carried pistols and threatened to shoot us. He never said so to me, nor did I hear him say so, I only heard some of the chaps say so.
>
> Walter Arthur:
> I heard say that he threatened to shoot Frederick. I was not on the Island at the time. Frederick himself as well as several others told me so.
>
> King Alexander:
> I saw Dr Jeanneret with pistols. He did not say he would shoot me, he ask where is Frederick, he only look out for Frederick. Frederick run away.
>
> Washington:
> I saw the Doctor with big pistols in the Square. The Doctor never said he would shoot me. Doctor make frighten Frederick because two men were fighting.
>
> Neptune:
> Dr Jeanneret never threatened to shoot me. I heard him tell Frederick he would shoot him, it was because two fellows fell fighting.
>
> Frederick:
> I do not like him to shoot me. He never did shoot me.[126]

The truth behind the pistol-packing doctor story seems to be that, three years earlier, Frederick and Eugene were fighting in the square. Eugene's wife Sarah ran to Jeanneret, who was then in the earliest stage of his first tenure, in fear for her husband's life. Jeanneret took

---

126 Testimonies from Davey Bruny, Walter Arthur, King Alexander, Washington, Neptune and Frederick, October 13–14 1846, contained in the Friend Inquiry papers, AOT CSO11/1/27, C658.

CHAPTER 6

his two pistols, and it seems that Sarah ran ahead, telling Frederick that the doctor was coming to shoot him. Frederick ran away, in justified fear. This is most likely the event Jeanneret described in his report of March 1843.[127]

In the petition, it was remembered differently: strategically, this event was recounted more dramatically and more threateningly to the whole community, to make an impact for the Crown. These six different responses to the question of the doctor carrying loaded pistols illustrate the complexity of meaning at Wybalenna. On one level, these statements in part contradict some of the details in the petition to the Queen. Jeanneret obviously did not carry pistols 'very often' (as there would have been more stories), or regularly threaten to shoot them. Yet, this is not an outright untruth. The doctor was seen carrying pistols, and at least one man, Frederick, was obviously threatened with being shot. For the VDL exiles, this was enough to make a case.

For the purposes of their political campaign, a one-time threatening of one man became a 'very often' threatening of 'us'. The exiles at Flinders Island stretched, or in contemporary parlance finessed, the truth, to make the desired impression of a beleaguered people. Three years after the fact, and in a colonial climate steeped in rumour and gossip, Sarah's screams of warning to the men became a very useful tool in the political struggle to self-represent as a community under siege. This could be seen as the kind of act of everyday resistance that James C. Scott refers to as 'the only weapons of the relatively powerless groups' – including dissimulation.[128]

---

127 Henry Jeanneret, Report to Colonial Secretary, 31 March 1843, AOT CSO8/1/157, 232.
128 Scott, *Weapons of the Weak*, xiv.

Several of the other charges against Jeanneret display a similar constitution to the pistol-packing story: part rumour, but with a basis solidly in fact, of a sort. Incidents experienced by one or two individuals were recounted, manipulated and extrapolated to involve the whole community. Yet the stories were always paradoxically true. None were *complete* fabrications. Another good example is the claim that Jeanneret put people into jail, or threatened to, because they would not be his slaves. This was a claim directly raised by Mary ann Arthur in her letter of 16 June. Four months later she told Friend:

> The Doctor did not tell me that he would put me into jail or that he would hang me for signing the Petition to the Queen, I never heard him say so, but my Countrymen told me so, Washington told me so and the Women told me so.[129]

Again and again, charges made in the petition, or in the letters of June 1846, boiled down to information given by others. In almost every case, Jeanneret's excesses were witnessed, heard of or experienced by one person, then broadcast to the community, who took the issue on as their own, often magnifying the incident or injury in the process. The issues were consciously and deliberately framed to show Jeanneret in the worst light possible, to give weight to their claims for him to be prevented from returning, or later, for an inquiry so he could be removed. Each one of their claims was based on the moral claims they had against the Crown, for reneging on the deal made between the VDL people and Sir George Arthur. And each one of the claims was, to some degree, based in fact.

Rumours – or unofficial, manipulated facts – played a very important role in the claims raised in the petition and letters, and this was

---

129 Mary ann Arthur, Testimony to the Friend Inquiry, October 1846, AOT CSO11/1/27, C658, 165.

CHAPTER 6

acknowledged by all parties. In fact, we know that rumour, gossip and gammoning were a key part of everyday life on the isolated community of Wybalenna for its whole existence. Certain elements in the community, especially the Sealing Women, and apparently the children, took constant delight in playing jokes or gammoning. It was a tool of humour and also subversion. Sermons delivered by VDL men Nommy, Neptune, King Alexander and Leonidas all encouraged the community – specifically the women – not to tell lies.[130] Likewise, G. A. Robinson's Flinders Island journals contain numerous instances of confusion and even serious turmoil caused by rumours, innocent and intentional.

'True' news, or intelligence, was at a premium in such an isolated location. At Flinders, like other colonial contexts described by Ann Laura Stoler, 'Incomplete knowledge was the rule and not the exception'.[131] Sometimes it was many weeks or even months between official mail deliveries: the news of King William of England's death, as we recall, did not reach Flinders Island until his successor Queen Victoria had been on the throne for six months. The *Flinders Island Chronicle* often reflected the keen interest in news from other centres, as Thomas Brune wrote:

> The brig Tamar arrived this morning at green Island I cannot tell perhaps we might hear about it by and by when the ship boat comes to the Settlement we will hear news from Hobartown.[132]

The Island was isolated from the colonial news centres of London, Sydney and sometimes due to wild and inclement seas even Hobart,

---

130 Sermons recorded by Robert Clark, February–April 1838, Robinson Letterbook QVMAG CY548.
131 Stoler, *Along the Archive Grain*, 231.
132 Thomas Brune, *Flinders Island Chronicle*, 17 November 1837, ML A7073, Vol. 52, part 4, 61.

but was often visited by sealers, Straitsmen and their wives, and other maritime arrivals. The line between news and rumours was often blurred. Sometimes, they were one and the same. In 1837, for example, Robinson repeatedly heard rumours which were circulating Launceston that the entire Flinders Island community was about to be moved to the New Holland mainland.[133] Rumours continually filtered to Wybalenna from Launceston, Hobart and beyond, and were shared between VDL exiles and Europeans alike. This Wybalenna experience was not unique: a number of writers have discussed the prevalence and influence of rumour on many colonial frontiers.[134] Kirsten McKenzie noted in particular the role of gossip in Antipodean settler colonies 'as an agent that bound the community together by means of talk, defined insiders and outsiders, and policed its members while reinforcing moral values'.[135]

There is a wide scholarship on the role of rumour, to which the Wybalenna experience can be related. Once interpreted mainly as aberrations, or signs of a sick society according to Allport and Postman's influential work,[136] rumours or 'unofficial news', according to Jean-Noel Kapferer, 'challenge official reality by proposing other

---

133 Robinson's journal, 27 November 1838: *Weep in Silence*, 751.
134 Stoler, 'In Cold Blood', 151-188; Tom Arne Midtrød, 'Strange and Disturbing Events: Rumor and Diplomacy in the Colonial Hudson Valley', *Ethnohistory* 58:1, Winter 2011, 91-112; Raymond D. Fogelson, 'The Ethnohistory of Events and Nonevents', *Ethnohistory* 36:2, Spring 1989, 133-147; Raymond Firth, 'Rumor in a Primitive Society', *Journal of Abnormal and Social Psychology*, 53:1, July 1956, 122-132.
135 Kirsten McKenzie, *Scandal in the Colonies*, Carlton, Melbourne University Press, 2004, 10.
136 G. Allport and L. Postman, 'Analysis of Rumor', *Public Opinion Quarterly* 10, 1946 and *The Psychology of Rumor*, New York, Henry Holt & Co, 1947, cited in Jean-Noel Kapferer, [1987], *Rumors: Uses, Interpretations and Images*, first English translation 1990, Transaction Publishers, New Jersey, 1990, 2-4.

CHAPTER 6

realities'.¹³⁷ The strength and prevalence of rumours is an important social signifier. The anthropologist Raymond Firth pondered the 'functional significance, if any, of rumor in relation to the structure and organization of the society where it occurs',¹³⁸ and, in the case of Wybalenna and the petition and letters, rumour definitely points to a largely cohesive community, with clear aspirations, using rumour as a tool. Tom Arne-Midtrød, who studied the spread of rumours on the colonial Hudson Valley, asserts that rumours can be interpreted as 'a sign of the continued strength and vitality of the indigenous political and social landscape in this area'.¹³⁹ In fact, Midtrød postulates that rumours represent: 'the tip of a vast iceberg of social and political interaction hidden from contemporary European colonists and modern researchers alike'.¹⁴⁰

Thus, the gun-toting doctor episode, where the whole community took on the threat against one man, both reflects the prevailing anxieties which fed the perceived communal threat, and constitutes a new truth or reality, which was included in the petition to the Queen and defended at the inquiry. The threat against one man, relayed by rumour, became a broader reality. Or, as Ann Laura Stoler puts it more simply, discussing rumour on the Dutch–Sumatran colonial frontier, 'Facts were constituted out of rumour as often as the other way around'.¹⁴¹ In colonial India, as is well known, the Sepoy rebellion of 1857 was allegedly initiated, in part, by rumour.¹⁴²

---

137 Kapferer, *Rumors*, 263.
138 Firth, 'Rumor in a Primitive Society', 122.
139 Midtrød, 'Strange and Disturbing Events', 94.
140 Ibid., 98.
141 Stoler, *Along the Archive Grain*, 231.
142 Porter, *Religion versus Empire*, 69.

Five years later, John West would sum up some of the complexities facing Matthew Friend's enquiry, and the range of stories circulating, both from VDL exiles and Europeans alike. He wrote:

> The stories which float in the colony, respecting the little empire of Wybalenna, are grotesque and humorous. No modern author will venture to look into the abyss of despatches, which develop its policy. To arrive at the truth would require an amount of labour, perhaps not beyond its intrinsic worth, but involving large discussions and questions not without peril.[143]

Matthew Friend was, in fact, charged with examining those questions. It seemed he was a man well equipped for the task, and his report of 31 October 1846 deftly negotiated the myriad agendas, stories, truths and rumours which muddied the Wybalenna story during Henry Jeanneret's contested second reign. While he found no direct evidence for most of the claims against Jeanneret, and reported that most of his administration was achieved as well as possible under the difficult and under-funded circumstances, one of the chief complaints against Jeanneret – that of Walter Arthur's imprisonment – was discussed in no uncertain terms:

> Walter George Arthur is an intelligent man, quite capable of writing the letters bearing his name and signature – How far the statements made in the petition to the Queen may be borne out I would leave to the better judgment of His Excellency but I must observe that I cannot perceive any reasonable ground for the incarceration of this man for seventeen days.[144]

It is worth visiting for a moment the analysis of N. J. B. Plomley in this matter, for his reading of the Friend Inquiry, and by extension

---

143 West, *The History of Tasmania, Vol. II*, 68-69.
144 M. C. Friend to J. E. Bicheno, 31 October 1846, AOT CSO 11/1/27 C658, 38.

CHAPTER 6

the agency of the VDL exiles in it, is symptomatic of the traditional, Eurocentric approach to the Wybalenna period. Plomley's estimate was ultimately very similar to that of James Bonwick, in that he felt Jeanneret was a humanitarian man, effectively wronged by the system. Of the claims in the petition, Plomley states, 'Most of the statements seen to have been made by the natives against Jeanneret were either not made at all or made by one and in particular circumstances'.[145] He also holds that in the minutes of evidence there were 'many statements in favour of Jeanneret – and none supporting Clark which can held to be unbiased'. This includes, presumably, the many VDL testimonies which clearly did not support Jeanneret. This claim of bias against Jeanneret is reminiscent of sociologist Howard Becker's seminal *Whose Side Are We On?* which points out that claims of bias are only ever lodged against the subordinate group.[146] In Plomley's estimation, opinions supporting Jeanneret are legitimate, and those against him biased. Further, Plomley wrote: 'There is no doubt that Jeanneret's methods were the cause of antagonism, but this did not mean that his principles were wrong'.[147] As usual, Plomley laid the blame for the affair – and indeed, the failure of the Flinders Island Settlement – on that 'despicable rogue' Robert Clark. This assessment, naturally, gives no credit whatsoever to VDL activism or agency, besides Walter Arthur. *Weep in Silence* is essentially a European history, about Europeans running a European settlement, with a few inconsequential VDL faces thrown in.

In fact, it can be argued that Friend paid a good deal of mind to the VDL people who he spoke to at Wybalenna through the month

---

145 Plomley, *Weep in Silence*, 155.
146 Becker, 'Whose Side Are We On?' 239-247.
147 Plomley, *Weep in Silence*, 156.

of October 1846, and the case against Jeanneret was effectively sealed with his comment that the jailing of Walter Arthur was unwarranted. It will be remembered that Walter Arthur had met, and impressed, Governors, whereas Jeanneret was already seen as somewhat unhinged. Friend's finding on this point marked the beginning of the end for both the second-time superintendent, and Wybalenna itself.

When Friend left Wybalenna on 28 October, Jeanneret travelled with him, apparently to state his case to Interim Governor La Trobe, in person.[148] However, La Trobe ordered Jeanneret straight back to Flinders Island – an order that Jeanneret, emboldened over his previous win over the VDL Government, chose to ignore. On the basis of this meeting, La Trobe also remarked, on a letter from Jeanneret, that the man was 'not quite sane'.[149] A meeting in Hobart with the Colonial Secretary also went badly. Undeterred, Jeanneret – who had also dismissed Robert Clark, against La Trobe's orders – stayed on the mainland for another month, and when he finally returned to Wybalenna, in December, the problems intensified. Friend was again drawn into the problems at Wybalenna, receiving letters of complaint from Robert Clark about his unfair dismissal. It seems, though, that one particular letter, sent to Friend, was the straw that broke the camel's back – and in this case, the camel was C. J. La Trobe's patience.

In December 1846 – two months after the Inquiry – Friend received a letter from Washington. It was a reminder that, even though the process had been enacted and now they had to await the Crown's pleasure, for the VDL people at Wybalenna life under a vindictive

---

148 Eardley-Wilmot had retired suddenly, then died; La Trobe was filling in until the replacement, William Denison, arrived.

149 Multiple correspondence, 5 November 1846, AOT CSO 11/1/27 C658, summarised by Plomley, *Weep In Silence*, 156.

CHAPTER 6

superintendent continued. Washington told Friend, 'I want to tell you plenty that Doctor Jennert no good man to me he take him away my garden me no like that'.[150]

A litany of complaints ensued, very similar to the letters of June 1846. Washington touched on Jeanneret's 'divide and conquer' tactics, mentioning twice how Tippo and 'another one black fellow' had been given items from the store to make them like the superintendent, but not the general population. And again, Jeanneret appears to have warned them against reporting his actions to those off the island:

> ... he growl me to much he say I a bad man to tell you to much I am frighted he put me in jail he say if I be a good man no tell any thing to you any more that he a bad man.[151]

Washington details Jeanneret's attempts to bribe him into silence, promising that if he 'put away' Mr Clark 'and no more talk to him he will like me and give me fine thing out of the store', like Tippo. However, Washington wants to be seen as a man telling the truth:

> ... me like to tell true and me tell you all true and me know you a fine white man me want you to ask Governor not to let Doctor Jent do as he like with my things and take away my Garden and make me a prisoner black people like you well would like to see you and talk plenty more they frightened to tell you.[152]

Washington closes this letter to Friend 'I love you sir and am your black friend, Washington'. It is a moving, intimate, and ultimately strategic letter to a new influential contact, and it illustrates that

---

150 Washington to Matthew Friend, 26 December 1846, AOT CSO 11/1/27 C658 294-297.
151 Washington to Matthew Friend, 26 December 1846, AOT CSO 11/1/27 C658 294-297.
152 Ibid.

despite the Inquiry being concluded, the VDL activists at Wybalenna were still, constantly, looking for ways to make their case. And Matthew Friend complied, forwarding Washington's letter – and his own concerns that 'the aborigines feel all the consequences' of the problems between Jeanneret and Clark – to the Colonial Secretary. When La Trobe saw the correspondence – including Washington's letter – he ordered that Clark be reinstated, and left a directive, recommending to his successor that Jeanneret was unfit for the office, and should be replaced as soon as possible. Washington's letter to Friend was, for La Trobe, the final straw.

Repatriation to Country

In February 1847, Walter Arthur wrote to George Augustus Robinson. It had been five years since the two had any physical contact, though it appears they exchanged letters regularly. Robinson certainly would have been keeping abreast of the problematic reign of Henry Jeanneret. Contrary to the views of most writers, Robinson did maintain an interest in the affairs of at least some of his VDL friends, to the extent of having letters smuggled in to them. Walter Arthur made this clear in the opening of his letter. After addressing himself to 'Mr Dear Friends Mr & Mrs Robinson & family' – a far cry from the previous letter to him, which was addressed to 'My Dear Old Master' – he writes:

> I received your letter in the very channel in which you expected, by the sealers as you have stated in your letter to me and now I feel it my duty both on the part of myself, wife and country people to accomplish your express and worthy wishes.[153]

---

153 Walter G. Arthur to G. A. Robinson, 1 February 1847, QVMAG Plomley Collection, CHS 53 2/10–2/13.

CHAPTER 6

Robinson's 'express and worthy wishes' remain unknown, but the fact that this letter arrived by unofficial channels – through the sealers – indicates that some kind of subterfuge was afoot. The significance of the Chief Protector of Aborigines in Port Phillip lowering himself to have his mail passed on through the sealers, who had been the bane of his administration, cannot be understated. This indicates that the VDL exiles were not the only ones who did not trust the mail service which was presided over by the superintendent. While any instructions or advice Robinson might have given to Walter Arthur are lost to us, it is possible that these might have related to the ongoing campaign to achieve some kind of self-sufficiency for the community. Arthur's next question to Robinson directly speaks to this goal:

> Sir I want to know how I am to get my sheep appertained to my father. I do not think for one moment myself that any body has a better right to them than myself. I am told the sheep are turned into the Government they are always sheared and the wool is sent away I do not know what is become of the wool, I should be very glad for you to ascertain for me where the wool goes too.[154]

This continuing interest in his father's sheep, and the profits from their wool, is the latest step in an enduring battle by Walter Arthur for control of, or compensation for, lost income. The shrewdness which was noted in him as a young boy was still manifest in the man. Arthur then turns his attention to the treatment of the VDL community:

> The natives are having been treated shamefully just like savages brought lately from the bush, poor people they are never

---

154 Ibid.

learnt any thing at all, the Superintendent and people (white people) I mean use the natives as they please and they do not dare speak one word in their own defence and why, because Doctor Jeanneret carrys his pistols in his pockets and puts the blacks in jail.[155]

Arthur is reiterating the claims made in the petition and to the Friend Inquiry. Despite the bravery of the people in speaking up to Matthew Friend when he visited to hear their testimonies, they were based on the island – most of the time – with a superintendent they feared. And they had good reason to fear that the Inquiry, however judicious, might easily be overruled in London, just as Jeanneret's initial dismissal had been reversed. Arthur pointedly requested Robinson to forward any future mail for him to Matthew Friend at the Georgetown Port Office. He went on to assure him of his own and Mary ann's good health, and begged Robinson not to forget him. After signing off as 'Walter G. A. Chieftain of the Benn Lomond Tribe', there is a powerful postscript: 'Mr Clark is the only friend of myself and the blacks. W.G.A'.[156]

In March, Robert Clark had still not been officially reinstated by Jeanneret, despite clear instructions from Hobart. Clark took leave of Wybalenna and, from Hobart, sent a barrage of reports and complaints about events at Wybalenna to the Colonial Secretary. Among these were accusations that Jeanneret was abusing his power and conspiring with sealers to marry off young girls, such as Fanny Cochrane and Victoria Lanny, against their will.[157] Jeanneret, likewise, sent his annual report in March 1847 which, among other things, criticised

---

155 Ibid.
156 Ibid.
157 Clark to Colonial Secretary, 30 March 1847, AOT CSO 11/1/27, C978, 444-46, Fanny, 458.

CHAPTER 6

Clark's legacy. The new Governor, William Denison, then took matters into his own hands. On 5 May, after reviewing the whole affair, as well as the competing reports from Jeanneret and Clark, and the settlement's books, Denison dismissed Jeanneret and reinstated Joseph Milligan as superintendent of the Wybalenna settlement. This was to be a temporary placement, as the community was to be repatriated to the VDL mainland. In late May, probably before this advice had reached Wybalenna, Walter Arthur wrote again to the Colonial Secretary, complaining about the abuses of power of Jeanneret and his son Charles, who had now been appointed a special constable.[158] However, the die had already been cast.

In July, an epidemic of catarrh (inflammation of the mucous membrane) swept through the settlement, rendering much of the population, VDL and European, seriously ill. Tragically, four of the already depleted VDL population died within a week. This included a young woman whose family had been the last group brought to Wybalenna from Circular Head five years previously, Victoria Lanny.[159] Achilles, thrice mentioned in the *Flinders Island Chronicle* as a hard worker, yet said in the school examinations to neglect his studies, also passed away in this epidemic, as did a woman who once had lived with the infamous bushranger Musquito, Big River woman Lucy.[160] The fourth to perish was King Alphonso, senior Big River man, father of Washington, and one of the bold letter writers of 1846. Tragically, despite his important hand in the campaign against Jeanneret when

---

158 Walter George Arthur to James Bicheno, 22 May 1847 (unseen). Cited by Dammery, *Walter George Arthur*, 33.
159 Deborahkanni/Tabracane/Victoria Lanna/Lanny. Born around 1822, North West nation. Her family was captured in December 1842. Sister of William Lanny.
160 Nertaweeartheer/Treenkoteyaner/Trooneguediana/Lucy. Born around 1798, Big River nation: *Weep in Silence*, 862.

he threatened the superintendent with writing to the Governor, Alphonso was never to set foot on VDL soil again.[161]

18 October 1847 was a momentous date. After years of agitation by the VDL exiles, and months of planning by the colonial authorities, the VDL exiles boarded the *Sisters*. The journey took them south of Hobart, to Oyster Cove, where a former probation station had been prepared to house them. The VDL group which finally made the return to the mainland consisted of ten men, twenty-three women and ten children. Joseph Milligan was their official caretaker, and Robert Clark was their catechist. Wybalenna was history, and they were exiles – on an island, at least – no more.

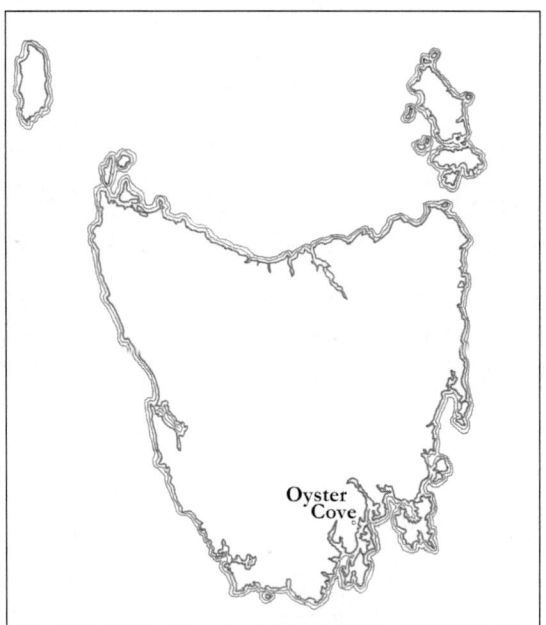

Oyster Cover station location. © L. Stevens 2017

---

161   Two others – Agnes, the ex-Tyereelore who had once travelled to Mauritius, died on 13 October of influenza; and a man, possibly a member of the Lanny family from Circular Head, died in October just before the removal, but there is scarce information on this. See *Weep in Silence*, 944.

CHAPTER 6

Conclusion

> Some dark secrets run so deep that they slip from view. The hole left in our collective conscience is gradually plugged with shallow distractions and awkward half-truths. Questions, if uttered, pass unheard. An uneasy and enduring silence prevails. So it has been in Tasmania since the end of our war.
>
> Greg Lehman.[162]

The return of the Wybalenna community to the Tasmanian mainland is often seen as the final chapter in their story. The traditional narrative holds that, after returning to the former penal station at Oyster Cove, the listlessness of Wybalenna turned into full depression. There are reports of alcoholism, prostitution, destitution and neglect. These reports, however, match the generalisations previously made about the Wybalenna exile, in that their perspective is contaminated by the doomed race narrative. The chroniclers saw what they wanted to see.

In fact, the community who returned to Oyster Cove adopted a varied range of responses to their newfound freedom. There were frequent extended returns to Country to hunt and maintain culture, punctuated by reliance on staples provided at the settlement.[163] Most of the men sought work, often at sea in the whaling industry.[164] Some, such as Walter Arthur, farmed and ran small businesses.[165] Others

---

162 Greg Lehman, 'Tasmanian Gothic: The Art of Australia's Forgotten War', *Griffith Review*, 39, Autumn 2013, 201.
163 The Oyster Cove Visitors Book, and reports by John Strange Dandridge and others, report continual comings and goings over two decades.
164 Walter Arthur, David Bruny, John Allen, Adam, Tippo Saib, Washington and William Lanny and others all spent some time at sea. See Russell, *Roving Mariners*.
165 Arthur farmed near Oyster Cove, ran the ferry and mail services, kept track of the lives and burials of his Countrypeople, and continued petitioning the Government for his rights as a free man – including applying for a convict servant – until his death in a boating accident in May 1861.

merged with the Hobart community through employment and marriage.[166] Some entered Hobart society and there is little trace; others followed the gold rush across Bass Strait in the 1850s.[167] Some sailed the oceans and never returned.[168] Some became legends.[169] Some simply disappear from the record.[170] The Oyster Cove story is yet to be fully told, but certainly holds the potential to challenge traditional representations, just as the Wybalenna narrative has been revolutionised by this study.

Wybalenna, as we have seen, was a vibrant, noisy, and often rebellious community. The exiles did not see themselves as prisoners, but as free people. Their lives were difficult and at times traumatic, but they were also full. For most of the period of exile, they ensured that the Europeans worked for them. People hunted, swam, sang, played marbles and sports. They steadfastly maintained traditional language and culture, at the same time incorporating aspects of European living and spirituality as it suited. There were multiple spheres of power and authority, and when their European managers overstepped their

---

166 Fanny Cochrane married and had eleven children, blending European and traditional worlds. Wax cylinder recordings of her songs have been vital to revitalisation of Palawa-kini (the new Tasmanian language). After Walter Arthur's death, Mary ann remarried.

167 Brother and sister Thomas and Mary Anne Thompson were last heard of in 1852, when in communication with Walter Arthur. Thomas was in the gold diggings in Victoria; Mary Anne had been in service in Hobart, but moved to Sydney. Their mother Harriet the ex-Tyereelore was then in Hobart.

168 Adolphus, who lived for a short while with Sir John and Lady Franklin, was last known to have sailed for England.

169 Trugernanner as 'The last Tasmanian'; Mathinna a tragic heroine. Both are fallacies.

170 A number of people left Oyster Cove, and on current information disappeared from the record. This includes the ex-Tyereelore and Port Phillip-era widows Fanny and Matilda, 1832 rebellion plotter Big Mary, King Alexander, warrior-turned-activist Washington and his wife Juliet, renowned preacher Noemy, Amelia, Daphne, Port Davey woman Tingernoop or the man who actually had been threatened by Jeanneret with loaded pistols, Frederick. At least three boys are also unaccounted for. See *Weep in Silence*, 945.

CHAPTER 6

authority, they resisted. Sometimes the resistance was subtle; at other times, it was overtly political.

The *Chronicle*, sermons, letters and petitions penned by the First Nations people of Van Diemen's Land during their seventeen year exile at Wybalenna offer a compelling counter-narrative to the traditional, erroneous representation of a depressed, dispossessed people's final days. This study has merely been an overview; this rich resource of First Nations texts, which has never been fully examined before on its own merits, has many more stories to impart. It all depends on how we read, and how we listen; whose values we prioritise, and whose voices we credit.

BIBLIOGRAPHY

Abbreviations:

AOT – Archives of Tasmania, Hobart
ML – Mitchell Library, State Library of New South Wales
SLV – State Library of Victoria
QVMAG – Queen Victoria Museum and Art Gallery, Launceston
   (location of the Plomley Collection)
UTAS S&RMC – Quaker Archive, University of Tasmania Library Special and Rare Manuscripts Collection

Texts Written by VDL Authors

Flinders Island Chronicles:
Papers of George Augustus Robinson, Mitchell Library, ML A7073, Vol. 52, Part 4.
Other copies located in George Augustus Robinson Letterbook 1838–39, Mitchell Library, ML A7045 (Vol. 24), State Library of New South Wales.
Plomley Collection, QVMAG, plus additional copies and drafts in colonial and personal archives.
Sir George Arthur papers regarding Aborigines, 1825–1837 A2188. Mitchell Library, Arthur papers Vol. 28.
Letters:
Colonial Secretary's Office CSO 11/26/378, AJCP Microfilm 280/195, Reel 544, SLV.
Archives of Tasmania, Colonial Secretary's Office CSO 11/1/27, Correspondence Civil Branch C658.
Plomley Collection, QVMAG.

Other Primary Sources

Flinders Island School Examinations (May 1837 and February 1838) and Sermons recorded in 1838:
Mitchell Library, Robinson's Letterbook, ML A7044 Vol. 23.
QVMAG, Plomley Collection, Robinson's Letterbook, Microfilm Reel CY548.
Early Flinders Island Administrative records (1832–34), QVMAG Plomley Collection CHS53.
Flinders Island Settlement Office Journal, QVMAG Plomley Collection CHS53.
Sir George Arthur papers regarding Aborigines, 1825–37 A2188. Mitchell Library, Arthur papers Vol. 28.
C. J. La Trobe papers, SLV MS 8454 Box 650/17.

BIBLIOGRAPHY

Reports from Flinders Island to Colonial Secretary 1842–44, AOT CSO8/1/157.
Friend Enquiry papers, Archives of Tasmania, Colonial Secretary's Office CSO 11/1/27, Correspondence Civil Branch C658.
Walker, G. W. letters, Quaker Archive, UTAS Library S&RMC.
Backhouse, J. and Walker, G. W., Reports of Visits to Penal Settlements at Port Arthur and Norfolk Island and Aboriginal Settlements at Flinders Island, 1833–35, Royal Commonwealth Society relating to Australia Letters, AJCP M1693, SLV.
Report from the Committee on the Aborigines Question with Minutes of Evidence (NSW), Ordered by the Council to be printed 12th October 1838, Votes and Proceedings of the Legislative Council Sydney, J. Spilsbury (microfilm, LTU).

19th Century Texts and Facsimilie Editions

Backhouse, J., *A Narrative of a Visit to the Australian Colonies*, [1843], New York, Johnson Reprint Corporation, 1967.
Bischoff, J., *Sketch of the History of Van Diemens Land*, [1832], Australiana Facsimilie Editions No. 102, Adelaide, Libraries Board of South Australia, 1967.
Bonwick, J., *The Last of the Tasmanians*, [1870], Facsimilie Edition No. 87, Adelaide, Libraries Board of South Australia, 1969.
Bonwick, J., *Daily Life and Origins of the Tasmanians*, [1870], First Reprinting, New York and London, Johnson Reprint Corporation, 1967.
Bonwick, J., *The Lost Tasmanian Race*, [1884], New York, Johnson Reprint Corporation, 1970.
Calder, J., *Some Account of the Wars, Extirpation, Habits etc. of the Native Tribes of Tasmania*, [1875], Hobart, Fullers Bookshop, 1972.
Franklin, J., *Some Passages in the History of Van Diemen's Land*, [1845], Hobart, Platypus Facsimile Edition, 1967.
Jeanneret, H., *The Vindication of a Colonial Magistrate from the Aspersions of His Grace the Duke of Newcastle by Official Documents and Attestations, with a Remonstrance and Exposure of a Colonial Conspiracy, Whereby Her Majesty the Queen Has Been Imposed Upon in a Petition Against Henry Jeanneret, M.D., Late Superintendent of the Aborigines of Van Diemen's Land*, London, Hope and Co, 1854.
Walker, J. B., 'Notes on the Aborigines of Tasmania, Extracted from the Manuscript Journals of George Washington Walker', from *Early Tasmania, Papers Read before the Royal Society of Tasmania during the years 1888 to 1889*, Tasmania, H. H. Pimblett, Government Printer, 1950.
West, J., *History of Tasmania Vol. II* [1852], Australian Facsimilie Editions No. 35, Adelaide, Libraries Board of Australia, 1966.
Minutes of Evidence before Select Committee on Aborigines (British Settlements), Imperial Blue Book, 1836, nr VII, 538, Facsimilie reprint, Cape Town, C. Struik Pty Ltd, 1966.
Report of the Parliamentary Select Committee on Aboriginal Tribes (British settlements). Reprinted, with Comments by the 'Aborigines Protection Society', London, Ball, Chambers, Row, Hatchard & Son, 1837.

Republished 19th Century Journals and Historical Material

Backhouse and Walker: Oats, W. M. (ed.), *Backhouse and Walker: A Quaker View of the Australian Colonies 1832–1838*, Hobart, Blubber Head Press, 1981.

Darwin, C., *Voyage of the Beagle: Charles Darwin's Journal of Researches*, [1839], Abridged, London, Penguin, 1989.

Dredge, J., 'The Hanging of Two Aboriginals, 1842', *La Trobe Library Journal*, no. 7, April 1971, 77-78.

Jorgenson: Plomley, N. J. B. (ed.), *Jorgen Jorgenson and the Aborigines of Van Diemen's Land: being a reconstruction of his 'lost' book on their customs and habits and on his role in the Roving Parties and the Black Line*, Hobart, Blubber Head Press, 1991.

Knopwood: Nicholls, M. (ed.), *The Diary of the Reverend Robert Knopwood, 1803–1838*, Launceston, Tasmanian Historical Research Association, 1977.

Robinson (1835–39): Plomley, N. J. B. (ed.) *Weep in Silence: A History of the Flinders Island Settlement, with the Flinders Island Journal of George Augustus Robinson*, Hobart, Blubber Head Press, 1987.

Robinson (1829–39): Plomley, N. J. B., *Friendly Mission: The Tasmanian Journals and Papers of George Augustus Robinson, 1829–1834*, Second edition, Launceston, Queen Victoria Museum and Art Gallery and Quintus Publishing, 2008.

Robinson (1939–45): Clark, I. D. (ed.), *The Journals of George Augustus Robinson, Chief Protector, Port Phillip Aboriginal Protectorate, Vol. 1*, January 1839–September 1840; *Vol. 2*, October 1840–August 1841; *Vol. 3*, September 1841–December 1843; *Vol. 4*, Jan 1844–Oct 1845. Melbourne, Heritage Matters, 1998.

Newspapers

Hobart Town Courier
The Cornwall Chronicle
The Southern Cross (NZ)
Launceston Examiner
Port Phillip Herald

Secondary Sources

Aitken, W., 'Community Voices', in A. Johnston and M. Rolls (eds.), *Reading Robinson: Companion Essays to Friendly Mission*, Hobart, Quintus Publishing, 2008, 95-96.

Alexander, A., *The Ambitions of Jane Franklin*, Crows Nest, Allen & Unwin, 2013.

Alderton, L. M., 'A Historical Overview of Tasmanian Aboriginal Women who Co-habited with Sealers and Whalers in the First Four Decades of the 19th Century', Honours Thesis, University of Ballarat, 2012.

Allen, J., *Peer Review of the Draft Final Archaeological Report on the Test Excavations*

BIBLIOGRAPHY

of the Jordan River Levee Site, Southern Tasmania, Robert Paton Archaeological Studies, August 2010.

Anderson, K., *Race and the Crisis of Humanism*, Routledge, London and New York, 2007.

Anderson, I. P. S., 'A People Who Have No History?', in A. Johnston and M. Rolls (eds.), *Reading Robinson: Companion Essays to Friendly Mission*, Hobart, Quintus Publishing, 2008, 59-76.

Auty, K. and Russell, L., *Hunt Them, Hang Them: 'The Tasmanians' in Port Phillip 1841–42*, Melbourne, Justice Press, 2016.

Ballantyne, T., 'Christianity, Colonialism and Cross-Cultural Communication', in J. Stenhouse (ed.), *Christianity, Modernity and Culture: New Perspectives on New Zealand History*, Adelaide, ATF Press, 2005, 23-56.

Ballantyne, T. and Burton, A., *Bodies in Contact: Rethinking Colonial Encounters in World History*, Durham and London, Duke University Press, 2006.

Battiste, M., 'Micmac Literacy and Cognitive Assimilation', paper presented to Mokakit Indian Education Research Association, London, Ontario, July 26 1984.

Becker, H., 'Whose Side Are We On?' *Social Problems*, 14 (Winter 1967), 239-247.

Beekman, C. S. and Baden, W. W., *Nonlinear Models for Archaeology and Anthropology: Continuing the Revolution*, Ashgate, Aldershot and Burlington, 2005.

Begg C. and Begg, N., *The World of John Boultbee, Including an Account of Sealing in Australia and New Zealand*, Christchurch, Whitcoulls, 1979.

Berndt, R. M. and Berndt, C. H., *The World of the First Australians*, fourth edition (revised), Adelaide, Rigby, 1985.

Bird Rose, D., 'Ned Kelly Died for Our Sins', *Oceania* 65:2, 1994, 175-186.

Birmingham, J., *Wybalenna: The Archaeology of Cultural Accommodation in Nineteenth Century Tasmania*, Australian Society for Historical Archaeology, 1992.

Boyce, J., *God's Own Country? The Anglican Church and Tasmanian Aborigines*, Hobart, Social Action and Research Centre, Anglicare Tasmania, 2001.

Boyce, J., *Van Diemen's Land*, Black Inc., Melbourne, 2008.

Brantlinger, P., *Dark Vanishings: Discourse on the Extinction of Primitive Races*, Ithaca and London, Cornell University Press, 2003.

Brantlinger, P., 'King Billy's Bones: Colonial Knowledge Production in Nineteenth-Century Tasmania', in A. Johnston and M. Rolls (eds.), *Reading Robinson: Companion Essays to Friendly Mission*, Hobart, Quintus Publishing, 2008, 45-57.

Breen, S., *Contested Places: Tasmania's Northern Districts from Ancient Times to 1900*, Hobart, Centre for Tasmanian Historical Studies, 2001.

Broome, R., 'Aboriginal Workers on the South Eastern Frontier', *Australian Historical Studies*, 103, October 1994, 202-220.

Broome, 'The Statistics of Frontier Conflict', in B. Attwood and S. G. Foster (eds.), *Frontier Conflict: The Australian Experience*, Canberra, National Museum of Australia, 2003, 88-98.

Broome, R., 'Entangled Histories: The Politics and Ethics of Writing Indigenous Histories', *Melbourne Historical Journal*, 33, 2005, 6-10.

Broome, R., *Aboriginal Victorians: A History since 1800*, Sydney, Allen & Unwin, 2005.

Broome, R., 'There Were Vegetables Every Year Mr Green Was Here', *History Australia*, 3:2, 2006, 1-16.

Broome, R., *Aboriginal Australians: A History since 1788*, fourth edition, Crows Nest, Allen & Unwin, 2010.
Brumfiel, E. M., 'Heterarchy and the Analysis of Complex Societies: Comments', in R. M. Ehrenreich, C. L. Crumley and J. E. Levy (eds.), *Heterarchy and the Analysis of Complex Societies*, Archaeological papers of the American Anthropological Association, No. 6, Arlington, 1995, 125-131.
Burrows, E., 'Resisting Oppression: The Use of Aboriginal Writing to Influence Public Opinion and Public Policy in Van Diemen's Land from 1836 to 1847', *Media History*, June 2014. Published online, DOI: 10.1080/13688804.2014.925684.
Cahir, F., *Black Gold: Aboriginal People on the Golfields of Victoria, 1850–1870*, Aboriginal History Monograph 25, Canberra, ANU E-Press, 2012.
Calder, G., *Levee, Line and Martial Law: A History of the Dispossession of the Mairremmener People of Van Diemens Land 1803–1832*, Launceston, Fuller's Bookshop, 2010.
Cameron, P., *Grease and Ochre: The Blending of Two Cultures at the Colonial Frontier*, Launceston, Fuller's Bookshop, 2011.
Campbell, A. H., *John Batman and the Aborigines*, Malmsbury, Vic., Kibble Books, 1987.
Cannon, M., (ed.), *Historical Records of Victoria, Foundation Series, Volume 2A, The Aborigines of Port Phillip 1835–1839*, Victorian Government Printing Office, Melbourne, 1982.
Cannon, M., (ed.), *Historical Records of Victoria, Foundation Series, Volume 2B, Aborigines and Protectors, 1835–1839*, Victorian Government Printing Office, Melbourne, 1982.
Chakrabarty, D., 'Postcoloniality and the Artifice of History: Who Speaks for "Indian" Pasts?', *Representations* 37, Winter 1992, 1-25.
Clark, I. D., *Scars in the Landscape: A Register of Massacre Sites in Western Victoria, 1803–1859*, Canberra, Aboriginal Studies Press, 1995.
Clark, J. 'Devils and Horses: Religious and Creative Life in Tasmanian Aboriginal Society', in M. Roe (ed.), *The Flow of Culture: Tasmanian Studies*, Occasional Paper No. 4, Canberra, Australian Academy of the Humanities, 1987, 50-72.
Clements, N., *The Black War: Fear, Sex and Resistance in Tasmania*, Brisbane, University of Queensland Press, 2014.
Clendinnen, I., 'Reading Mr Robinson', in M. Fraser (ed.), *Seams of Light: Best Antipodean Essays: A Selection*, Sydney, Allen & Unwin, 1998, 58-78.
Collingridge, G., *Discovery of Australia*, [1895 Hayes Brothers Sydney], Facsimilie Edition, Silverwater, Golden Press, 1989.
Cotter, R., *A cloud of Hapless Foreboding: Assistant Protector William Thomas and the Port Phillip Aborigines 1839–1840*, Sorrento, Nepean Historical Society, 2005.
Cox, R., *Steps to the Scaffold: The Untold Story of Tasmania's Black Bushrangers*, Pawleena, Tas, Cornhill Publishing, 2004.
Cree, N., *Oyster Cove, Last Home of the Tasmanian Aboriginal*, Toorak, Cree, 1979.
Critchett, J., *A Distant Field of Murder: Western District frontiers, 1834–1848*, Carlton, Melbourne University Press, 1992.

BIBLIOGRAPHY

Critchett, J., *Untold Stories: Memories and Lives of Victorian Kooris*, Carlton, Melbourne University Press, 1998.

Crowley, T., 'Tasmanian Aboriginal Language: Old and New Identities', in M. Walsh and C. Yallop (eds.), *Language and Culture in Aboriginal Australia*, Canberra, Aboriginal Studies Press, 1993, 51-71.

Crumley, C., 'A Dialectical Critique of Heterarchy', in T. C. Patterson and C. W. Gailey (eds.), *Power Relations and State Formation*, Washington, American Anthropological Association, 1987, 155-159.

Cushman, E., 'The Cherokee Writing Syllabary: A Writing System in its Own Right', *Written Communication*, 28:3, 2011, 255-281.

Dammery, S., *Walter George Arthur: A Free Tasmanian?*, Monash Publications in History, 35, 2001.

Davies, D., *The Last of the Tasmanians*, Sydney, Shakespeare Head Press, 1973.

Davies, R. H., 'On the Aborigines of Van Diemen's Land', *Tasmanian Journal of Natural Science, Agriculture, Statistics & c*, Vol. II, 1846, 409-420.

Davis, J. B., 'The Life and Work of Sequoyah', *Chronicles of Oklahoma*, 8:2, June 1930, 149-180.

Davis, S. and Petrov, S. (eds.), *Varieties of Vice-Regal Life (Van Diemens Land Section)*, by Sir William and Lady Denison, Hobart, Tasmanian Historical Research Association, 2004.

De Costa, R., 'Identity, Authority, and the Moral Worlds of Indigenous Petitions', *Comparative Studies in Society and History*, 48:3, July 2006, 669-698.

De Landa, M., *One Thousand Years of Non-linear History*, first paperback edition, Brooklyn NY, Swerve, 2009.

Debelle, B., 'Aboriginal Customary Law and the Common Law', in E. Johnston, M. Hinton and D. Rigney (eds.), *Indigenous Australians and the Law*, Sydney, Cavendish, 1997, 81-100.

Dening, G., *Islands and Beaches: Discourses on a Silent Land, Marquesas 1774–1880*, Honolulu, University Press of Hawaii, 1980.

Denoon, D., with Firth, S., Linnakin, J., Meleisea, M. and Nero, K., *The Cambridge History of the Pacific Islanders*, Cambridge, Cambridge University Press, 2004.

Dickison, O. and Newbigging, W., *A Concise History of Canada's First Nations*, second edition, Ontario, Oxford University Press, 2010.

Edgecombe, J., *Flinders Island and Eastern Bass Strait*, Thornleigh, Edgekirk, 1986.

Edmunds, P., 'Travelling "Under Concern": Quakers James Backhouse and George Washington Walker Tour the Antipodean Colonies, 1832–41', *The Journal of Imperial and Commonwealth History* 40:5, December 2012, 769–788.

Elder, B., *Blood on the Wattle: Massacres and Maltreatment of Aboriginal Australians since 1788*, third edition, Sydney, New Holland Publishers, 2003.

Evans, J., Grimshaw, P., Philips, D. and Swain, S., *Equal Subjects, Unequal Rights: Indigenous Peoples in British Settler Colonies, 1830–1910*, Manchester and New York, Manchester University Press, 2003.

Fels, M. H., *Good Men and True: The Aboriginal Police of the Port Phillip District*, Melbourne, Melbourne University Press, 1988.

Fels, M. H., Clark, D. and White, R., 'Mistaken Identity, Not Aboriginal Resistance', *Quadrant*, Vol. 58, No. 10, Oct 2014, 74-83.

Firth, R., 'Rumor in a Primitive Society', *Journal of Abnormal and Social Psychology*, 53:1, July 1956, 122-132.
Flagg, S. and Gurciullo, S. (eds.), *Footprints: The journey of Lucy and Percy Pepper*, Canberra, National Archives of Australia, North Melbourne, Public Record Office Victoria, 2008.
Flood, J., *Archaeology of the Dreamtime: The Story of Prehistoric Australia and its People*, revised edition, Marleston, J.B. Publishing, 2004.
Fogelson, R. D., 'The Ethnohistory of Events and Nonevents', *Ethnohistory* 36:2, Spring 1989, 133-147.
Folds, R., *Crossed Purposes: The Pintupi and Australia's Indigenous Policy*, Sydney, University of New South Wales Press, 2001.
Gilligan, I., *Another Tasmanian Paradox: Clothing and Thermal Adaptations in Aboriginal Australia*, Oxford, Archaeopress, 2007.
Goodall, H., *Invasion to Embassy: Land in Aboriginal Politics in New South Wales, 1770–1972*, St Leonards, Allen & Unwin and Black Books, 1996.
Graham, M., 'Some Thoughts about the Philosophical Underpinnings of Aboriginal Worldviews', *Australian Humanities Review*, 45, 2008, 181-194.
Gunson, N. (ed.), *Australian Reminiscences and Papers of L. E. Threlkeld, Missionary to the Aborigines,* Australian Aboriginal Studies No. 40, Ethnohistory Series No. 2, 1974.
Hancock, W. K., *Australia*, [1930, London], Brisbane, Jacaranda, 1964.
Harkins, J., 'Linguistic and Cultural Differences in Concepts of Shame', in Parker, D., Dalziell, R. and Wright, I. (eds.), *Shame and the Modern Self*, Melbourne, Australian Scholarly Publishing, 1996, 84-96.
Harman, K., *Aboriginal Convicts: Australian, Khoisan and Maori Exiles*, Sydney, University of New South Wales Press, 2012.
Haskins, V., '"Give to us the people we would love to be amongst us": The Aboriginal Campaign against Caroline Bulmer's Eviction from Lake Tyers Aboriginal Station, 1913–14', *Provenance, Journal of Public Record Office Victoria*, 7, 2008, 53-63.
Hau'ofa, E., 'Our Sea of Islands', *The Contemporary Pacific*, 6:1, Spring 1994, 147-161.
Heiss, A. and Minter, P. (eds.) *Macquarie PEN Anthology of Aboriginal Literature*, Crows Nest, Allen & Unwin, 2008.
Hirst, J., *Convict Society and Its Enemies*, Sydney, George Allen & Unwin, 1983.
Hiscock, P., *Archaeology of Ancient Australia*, London and New York, Routledge, 2008.
Horton, J., 'Rewriting Political History: Letters from Aboriginal People in Victoria, 1886–1919', *History Australia*, 9:2, August 2012, 157-181.
Hughes, R., *The Fatal Shore*, London, Collins Harvill, 1987.
Jallard, P., *Australian Ways of Death: A Social and Cultural History, 1840–1918*, Melbourne, Oxford University Press, 2002.
Johnson, M. and McFarlane, I., *Van Diemen's Land: An Aboriginal History*, New South Publishing, Sydney, 2015.
Johnston, A., 'The "little empire of Wybalenna": Becoming Colonial in Australia', *Journal of Australian Studies*, 28:81, 2004, 17-31.
Jones, R., 'The Tasmanian Paradox', in R. V. S. Wright (ed.), *Stone Tools as Cultural*

BIBLIOGRAPHY

Markers: Change, Evolution and Complexity, Canberra, Australian Institute of Aboriginal Studies, 1977, 189-204.

Jones, R., Ranson, D., Allen, J. and Kiernan, K., 'The Australian National University–Tasmanian National Parks and Wildlife Service Archaeological Expedition to the Franklin River, 1982: A Summary of Results', *Australian Archaeology*, No. 16, June 1983, 57-70.

Kapferer, J. N., *Rumors: Uses, Interpretations and Images*, [1987], first English translation, Transaction Publishers, New Jersey, 1990.

Kenny, R., *The Lamb Enters the Dreaming: Nathanael Pepper and the Ruptured World*, Carlton North, Scribe, 2007.

Khumalo, V., 'Ekukhanyeni Letter-writers: A Historical Inquiry into Epistolary Network(s) and Political Imagination in Kwazulu-Natal, South Africa', in K. Barber (ed.), *Africa's Hidden Histories: Everyday Literacy and Making the Self*, Indiana University Press, Bloomington, 2006, p. 113-132.

Lawrence, S., 'Excavations at Kelly & Lucas' Adventure Bay Whaling Station', *Newsletter, Australasian Society for Historical Archaeology*, 28:1, 1998, 5-6.

Lawrence, S., *Whalers and Free Men: Life on Tasmania's Colonial Whaling Stations*, North Melbourne, Australian Scholarly Publishing, 2006.

Lear, J., *Radical Hope: Ethics in the Face of Cultural Devastation*, Cambridge, Harvard University Press 2008.

Lehman, G., 'Telling us True', in R. Manne (ed.), *Whitewash: On Keith Windschuttle's Fabrication of Aboriginal History*, Black Inc. Agenda, Melbourne, 2003, 174-185.

Lehman, G., 'Reconciling Ruin: The transformation of Tasmanian Aboriginal culture', *Historic Environment*, 17:1, 2003, 1-8.

Lehman, G., 'Tasmanian Gothic: The Art of Australia's Forgotten War', *Griffith Review*, 39, Autumn 2013, 193-204.

Lemkin, R., 'Tasmania', *Patterns of Prejudice*, 39:2, 2005, 170-196.

Lester, A., 'George Augustus Robinson and Imperial Networks', in A. Johnston and M. Rolls (eds.), *Reading Robinson: Companion Essays to Friendly Mission*, Hobart, Quintus Publishing, 2008, 27-43.

McFarlane, I., 'Pevay: A Casualty of War', *Tasmanian Historical Research Association Papers and Proceedings*, 4: 84, 280-305.

McFarlane, I., *Beyond Awakening: The Aboriginal Tribes of North West Tasmania – A History*, Launceston, Tas, Fuller's Bookshop, 2008.

McGrath, A., *Contested Ground: Australian Aborigines Under the British Crown*, St. Leonards, Allen & Unwin, 1995.

McGregor, R., *Imagined Destinies: Aboriginal Australians and the Doomed Race Theory 1880–1939*, Melbourne University Press, Carlton, 1997.

McKenzie, K., *Scandal in the Colonies*, Carlton, Melbourne University Press, 2004.

Memmi, A., *The Colonizer and the Colonized*, London, Earthscan, 2003.

Merry, K., 'Dancing with Devils: The Aboriginal Women and the Sealers of Bass Strait and Kangaroo Island in the Early Nineteenth Century', in G. Bastin, K. Douglas, M. McCrea and M. X. Savvas (eds.), *Journeying and Journalling: Creative and Critical Meditations on Travel Writing*, Kent Town, Wakefield Press, 2010, 112-120.

Miller, R. S., *Thomas Dove and the Tasmanian Aborigines*, Melbourne, Spectrum Publications, 1985.

Midtrød, T. A., 'Strange and Disturbing Events: Rumor and Diplomacy in the Colonial Hudson Valley', *Ethnohistory*, 58:1, Winter 2011, 91-112.

Mollison. W. and Everitt, C., *The Tasmanian Aborigines and Their Descendants: Chronology, Genealogies and Social Data*, Hobart, University of Tasmania, 1978.

Morgan, A. T., 'Aboriginal Education in the Furneaux Islands (1788–1986): A Study of Aboriginal Racial Policy, Curriculum and Teacher/Community Relations', Thesis, Centre for Education, University of Tasmania, 1986.

Morgan, S., *Land Settlement in Early Tasmania: Creating an Antipodean England*, first paperback edition, Cambridge, Cambridge University Press, 2003.

Mudrooroo (as Colin Johnson), *Doctor Wooreddy's Prescription for Enduring the Ending of the World*, Melbourne, Hyland House, 1983.

Mudrooroo Narogin, *Doin Wildcat*, Melbourne, Hyland House, 1988.

Mulvaney, J. and Kamminga, J., *Prehistory of Australia*, St Leonards, Allen & Unwin, 1999.

Nugent, M., '"The Queen gave us the Land": Queen Victoria and Historical Remembrance', *History Australia*, 9:2, August 2012, 182-200.

Perdue, T., 'Rising from the Ashes: The Cherokee Phoenix as an Ethnohistorical Source', *Ethnohistory*, 24:3, Summer 1977, 207-218.

Plomley, N. J. B., 'Robinson's Adventures in Bass Strait', in *Bass Strait: Australia's Last Frontier*, Sydney, Australian Broadcasting Commission, 1969.

Plomley, N. J. B., *A Word-List of the Tasmanian Aboriginal Languages*, Launceston, N. J. B. Plomley in association with the Government of Tasmania, 1976.

Plomley, N. J. B., *Weep in Silence: A History of the Flinders Island Settlement, with the Flinders Island Journal of George Augustus Robinson*, Hobart, Blubber Head Press, 1987.

Plomley, N. J. B., *The Tasmanian Tribes & Cicatrices as Tribal Indicators among the Tasmanian Aborigines*, Occasional Paper No. 5, Launceston, Queen Victoria Museum and Art Gallery, 1992.

Plomley, N. J. B. (as Brian Plomley), *The Tasmanian Aborigines*, Launceston, Plomley Foundation, 1993.

Plomley, N. J. B., *Friendly Mission: The Tasmanian Journals and Papers of George Augustus Robinson, 1829–1834*, second edition, Launceston, Queen Victoria Museum and Art Gallery and Quintus Publishing, 2008.

Porter, A., *Religion versus Empire? British Protestant Missionaries and Overseas Expansion, 1700–1914*, Manchester and New York, Manchester University Press, 2004.

Prickett, N., 'Trans-Tasman Stories: Australian Aborigines in New Zealand Sealing and Shore Whaling', *Terra Australis*, 29, 351-366.

Pybus, C., *Community of Thieves*, Melbourne, William Heinemann Australia, 1991.

Pybus, C., 'A Self-Made Man', in A. Johnston and M. Rolls (eds.), *Reading Robinson: Companion Essays to Friendly Mission*, Hobart, Quintus Publishing, 2008, 97-109.

Rae-Ellis, V., *Trucanini: Queen or Traitor?*, Hobart, OBM Publishing, 1976.

Rae-Ellis, V., *Black Robinson, Protector of Aborigines*, first paperback edition, Carlton, Melbourne University Press, 1988.

BIBLIOGRAPHY

Ratcliff, P. R., *The Story of Wybalenna*, Launceston, The Glendessary Press, 1975.
Reynolds, H. 'Aborigines and European Social Hierarchy', *Aboriginal History*, 7, 1983, 124-133.
Reynolds, H., 'Walter George Arthur: Pioneer Aboriginal Activist', *Island*, 49, Summer 1991, 36-39.
Reynolds, H., *This Whispering in Our Hearts*, St Leonards, Allen & Unwin, 1998.
Reynolds, H., *Why Weren't We Told? A Personal Search For the Truth About Our History*, Camberwell, Penguin Australia, 1999.
Reynolds, H., 'The Written Record', in B. Attwood and S. G. Foster (eds), *Frontier Conflict, The Australian Experience*, Canberra, National Museum of Australia, 2003, 79-87.
Reynolds, H., 'Genocide in Tasmania?', in A. D. Moses (ed.), *Genocide and Settler Society: Frontier Violence and Stolen Indigenous Children in Australian History*, New York and Oxford, Berghahn Books, 2004, 127-148.
Reynolds, H., *Fate of a Free People*, revised edition, Camberwell, Penguin, 2005.
Reynolds, H., 'George Augustus Robinson in Van Diemen's Land: Race, Status and Religion', in A. Johnston and M. Rolls (eds.), *Reading Robinson: Companion Essays to Friendly Mission*, Hobart, Quintus Publishing, 2008, 161-170.
Reynolds, H., 'Revisiting Risdon Cove', presentation at Tasmanian Historical Research Association Conference, University of Tasmania, 4 September 2010.
Reynolds, H., *A History of Tasmania*, Cambridge and Melbourne, Cambridge University Press, 2012.
Reynolds, H., *Forgotten War*, Sydney, Newsouth, University of New South Wales Press, 2013.
Roberts, J., *Jack of Cape Grim: A Victorian Adventure*, Melbourne, Greenhouse Publishers, 1986.
Robson, L., *A History of Tasmania*, Vol. 1, Melbourne, Oxford University Press, 1983.
Robson, L. and Roe, M., *A Short History of Tasmania*, second edition, 1997, Oxford and New York, Oxford University Press, 1997.
Roe, M., 'Eumarrah (c. 1798–1832)', *Australian Dictionary of Biography*, Supplementary Volume, Melbourne, Melbourne University Press, 2005, 117–18.
Rose, M., *For the record: 160 years of Aboriginal Print Journalism*, Sydney, Allen & Unwin, 1996.
Rowley, C. D., *The Destruction of Aboriginal Society*, Harmondsworth, UK, Penguin, 1978.
Russell, L., *Roving Mariners: Australian Aboriginal Whalers and Sealers in the Southern Oceans, 1790–1870*, Albany, State University of New York Press, 2012.
Russell, P., 'Girl in a Red Dress: Inventions of Mathinna', *Australian Historical Studies,* 43:3, 2012, 341-362.
Russo, K., *Practices of Proximity: The Appropriation of English in Australian Indigenous Literature*, Newcastle, Cambridge Scholars Publishing, 2010.
Ryan, L., *Tasmanian Aborigines*: A *History since 1803*, Crows Nest, Allen & Unwin, 2012.
Sagona, A., *Bruising the Red Earth: Ochre Mining and Ritual in Aboriginal Tasmania*, Carlton, Melbourne University Press, 1994.

Scott, J. C., *Weapons of the Weak: Everyday Forms of Peasant Resistance*, New Haven, Yale University Press, 1985.
Seddon, G., *Landprints: Reflections on Place and Landscape*, Melbourne, Cambridge University Press, 1997.
Shaw, A. G. L., *Sir George Arthur, Bart: Superintendent of British Honduras, Lieutenant-Governor of Van Diemen's Land and of Upper Canada, Governor of the Bombay Presidency*, Carlton, Melbourne University Press, 1980.
Silva, N. K., *Aloha Betrayed: Native Hawaiian Resistance to American Colonialism*, Duke University Press, Durham and London, 2004.
Stevens, L., 'The Phenomenal Coolness of Tunnerminnerwait', *Victorian Historical Journal*, 8:1, June 2010, 18-40.
Stockings, C. 'Introduction', in C. Stockings (ed.), *Zombie Myth of Australian Military History*, UNSW Press, Sydney, 2010, 1-9.
Stoler, A. L., '"In Cold Blood": Hierarchies of Credibility and the Politics of Colonial Narratives', *Representations*, 37, Winter 2002, 151-189.
Stoler, A. L., *Along the Archive Grain: Epistemic Anxieties and Colonial Common Sense*, Princeton University Press, Princeton and Oxford, 2009.
Taylor, J., *Cultural Evolution in Palawa (Tasmanian Aboriginal) Societies 40,000 BCE to 1803 AD*, PhD Thesis, University of Tasmania, Incomplete.
Taylor, R., *Unearthed: The Aboriginal Tasmanians of Kangaroo Island*, Kent Town, Wakefield Press, 2008.
Taylor, R., 'Reliable Mr Robinson and the Controversial Dr Jones', in A. Johnston and M. Rolls (eds.), *Reading Robinson: Companion Essays to Friendly Mission*, Hobart, Quintus, 2008, 111-126.
Thompson, E. P., 'The Moral Economy of the English Crowd in the Eighteenth Century', *Past & Present*, 50, Feb 1971, 76-136.
Thompson, E. P., 'The Politics of Theory', in R. Samuel (ed.), *Peoples History and Socialist Theory*, London, Routledge and Kegan Paul, 1981, 396-408.
Travers, R., *The Tasmanians: The Story of a Doomed Race*, Melbourne, Cassell Australia, 1968.
Turnbull, C., *Black War: The Extermination of the Tasmanian Aborigines*, [1948], Melbourne, Cheshire-Lansdowne, 1965.
Van Toorn, P., 'Indigenous Australian Life Writing: Tactics and Transformations', in B. Attwood and F. Magowan (eds.), *Telling Stories: Indigenous History and Memory in Australia and New Zealand*, Sydney, Allen & Unwin, 2001, 1-20.
Van Toorn, P., 'Hegemony or Hidden Transcripts? Aboriginal Writings from Lake Condah 1876–1907', *Journal of Australian Studies*, 29:86, 2005, 13-27.
Van Toorn, P., *Writing Never Arrives Naked: Early Aboriginal Cultures of Writing in Australia*, Canberra, Aboriginal Studies Press, 2006.
Watson, I., 'Naked Peoples: Rules and Regulations', *Law/Text/Culture*, 4, No. 1, 1998, 1-17.
Windschuttle, K., *Fabrication of Aboriginal History, Volume One: Van Diemen's Land, 1803–1847*, Sydney, Macleay Press, reprinted with corrections, 2003.

INDEX

Aboriginal people– see Ben Lomond, Big River, Bruny Island, Coastal Plains, Western, South West, North Midlands, VDL

Achilles   86–7, 117, 124, 126, 169n.32, 222n.12, 327

Adam   223n.15, 309–10, 329n.164

Adaptation
   to colonisation   xiii, 15, 204
   to post-glacial climate   5, 117

Adolphus   84, 87, 132, 137–8, 197, 330n.168

Adventure Bay whaling station   16, 19, 219n.127

Afterlife
   Heaven   xxxix, 104, 111, 120, 155, 157, 165, 170, 174, 177, 179–80, 184, 186–89
   Hell   156–7, 165, 176–7, 179, 181
   Ponedim   200

Agnes   32n.11, 222n.12, 328n.161

Aitken, Wendy   xviii, xxxiv

Ajax   120, 131, 137, 160, 203n. 111, 223n. 13

Alexander – see King Alexander

Allen, James   52, 97, 109, 117–8, 264

Allen, John
   activism and letter writing   20n.53, 261–62, 271–73, 280–82, 284, 298
   early years with Batman   229–231
   testimony to the Friend Inquiry   300–301
   whaling   329
   at Wybalenna   233–34, 237–238, 240–41, 243, 249

Alpha – see Doctor Wooreddy

Alphonso – see King Alphonso

Amelia   222n.12, 223n.15, 330n.170

Andrew   223n.12

Anti-semitism   166

Arthur, Mary ann
   early years at Wybalenna   80, 175, 178
   early years with Walter Arthur   138–9, 141, 168, 174–6, 178, 193, 240
   fighting for rights   262, 270, 284, 287, 290–91, 301, 305–07, 309–11, 330
   letter writing   xli$n$.84, 269, 273n.24, 279–80, 283–84, 298
   mentioned in husband's letters   245, 258, 326
   move to Port Phillip   199n.97, 204, 211
   return to Wybalenna   227–229, 232, 234, 237
   role as teacher   80, 168, 239
   testimony to the Friend Inquiry   310, 312, 316
   use of supporting documents   228, 280

Arthur, George (Sir)
   advising the Select Committee   57–58
   architect of exile   17–21, 26, 30, 34, 41, 43, 46–47, 51–53, 225
   as Governor   xvi, xxiii, xxxvi, 12, 67–68, 78, 152, 162, 216, 230, 252, 262–63, 287, 316
   plans for removal of community   133, 196
   setting up Protectorate   206

Arthur, Walter George
   assumes title of Chief of the Ben Lomond   xiv, 235
   battles with Jeanneret   244–46, 249, 270–73, 288–93, 302, 325–27
   business acumen   128, 243, 257, 268, 270, 325, 329
   claims status as free man   xxiii–iv, xxviii, xxix–xxx, 254, 292
   early years at Wybalenna   31, 41, 62, 64, 77, 80–81, 83–84, 87, 89, 95, 98
   early years with Mary ann Arthur   138–39, 174–76, 178, 196

Flinders Island Chronicle xxxiv–xxxvii, 98, 105–10, 113–16, 120–22, 124–31, 136–38
  letters to colonial officials 269–70, 272–77, 283–84, 289–94, 304, 327
  letters to friends 22, 211*n*.131, 235–37, 244–47, 256–58, 268–69, 324–45, 330*n*.167
  move to Port Phillip 199, 204, 211
  petition to Queen Victoria 20, 260–265, 300–01, 313–14
  relationship with Robinson 139, 142–45, 151
  relationship with Washington 120–21, 274
  return to Wybalenna 227–9, 231–234, 237, 239–41
  sermons xxxviii, 80, 152–57, 164, 171, 174, 176
  status as political activist xli, 283–7, 298–99, 312
  testimony to the Friend Inquiry 306–307, 312, 314, 320, 322
Arwenia – see Mathinna
Augustus 20*n*.53, 77, 85*n*.28, 98, 105, 223*n*.12, 261*n*.2, 271
Awabakal language 45
Backhouse, James xvi, xxiv*n*.48, xliii, 5*n*.12, 47–50, 58, 72, 84, 117–18, 232
'Bad White Men' 15, 23, 132, 170, 183–84 179, 183, 188
Badgers Corner 108, 110
Ballantyne, Tony 46*n*.49, 94, 190
Bannister, Saxe 59
Barak, William 285–86
Bass Strait Islands viii, xix, xx*n*.33, xxii, 14*n*.36, 24, 27–28, 32, 51, 128, 150, 182, 252
Batman, John 14*n*.34, 31, 230–31, 281
Batman's Jack – see Allen, John
Battiste, Marie 56
Becker, Howard xxviii, 321
Benjamin 154
Ben Lomond nation
  individual members xiv*n*.10, 31, 34, 35, 41, 60, 80, 83, 86–87, 143, 173, 175, 190, 199, 222, 232
  tensions with Big River nation 7, 11, 38, 56, 58, 62, 78, 120, 274, 304
  at Wybalenna 47, 53, 77–78, 92–93, 205, 253
Ben – see Augustus
Bet, Big – see Queen Elizabeth
Bet, Cranky – see Daphne
Bible
  calls to read in Flinders Island Chronicle 132, 142, 267
  calls to read in Sermons 151, 153, 173, 177–79, 185–87
  popularity of Genesis stories 86, 88, 165, 167–68, 174
  source of solace 212, 257–58, 266, 270
  tool of assimilation 83, 107
  translation 45–46
Bicheno, James 259, 270*n*.17, 292–93
Big River nation
  resisting invasion 10–13, 30–31, 33, 38
  in Country 6–7
  individual members ix, xiv*n*.10, xl, xlii, 31, 34, 82, 85, 87, 95, 103, 110, 119–120, 131, 135, 137, 144, 155, 165, 173, 175, 179, 183–92, 196, 199, 201–02, 214, 236, 302, 327
  tensions with the Ben Lomond 7, 11, 30, 56, 58, 62, 78, 120, 274, 304
  at Wybalenna xxxviii, xl, 38, 47, 53, 77–78, 116, 119, 127, 205, 222, 253
Billibellary 285
Billy, Big – see King Alfred
Birmingham, Judy 129*n*.143, 284*n*.47
Birth control 157
Bischoff, James xvii*n*.18, 14, 21*n*.54, 56
Black Line – see Line Operation, The
Black Pierre the Flagellator – see Pierre, John
Black Tom 24–25
Black War – see War, the
Boatswain – see Jane
Bock, Thomas 167, 197, 199*n*.99, 203*n*.111

INDEX

Bonaparte 223*n*.12
Bonenerveve – see Noemy
Bonwick, James xix, xxvii*n*. 54, xxxi*n*.59, xli, 51*n*.64, 117, 279, 296–97, 321
Booker, Mary ann – see Arthur, Mary ann
Boonwurrung 69, 205
Bowle – see Maria, Old
Boyce, James xxxi*n*.61, 1*n*.2, 10*n*.25, 30*n*.4, 31*n*.10, 196*n*.89
British Empire xvii, xxvi–vii, 57, 66, 75, 150, 190, 299
Broadfoot, J. B. 251
Broome, Richard xii–xiv, xiii, xxxii, 12*n*.29, 15*n*.37, 53, 146, 207*n*.118, 215, 241–42, 284–85
Broomterlandenner – see Smith, Bet
Broughton, William 58, 196
Brune, Thomas
    death 211–212
    Flinders Island Chronicle xiii, xxxv–vii, 18–19, 64–66, 92*n*.50, 97–106, 109–10, 113–116, 118–19, 122–26, 129–135, 137–42, 145–147
    move to Port Phillip 199*n*.96, 204
    sermons xxxvii–viii, 80, 151–54, 156–157, 160, 164, 171, 174, 177–78, 181, 192
    youth 63–64, 73*n*.4, 81, 88–89, 166, 193, 196
Bruny Island xiv*n*. 10, 8–9, 16–18, 20, 43, 63, 88*n*. 44, 45, 97, 163, 184, 210*n*. 127, 222
Bruney, David xiv*n*.10, 9*n*.19
    move to Port Phillip 199*n*.97, 204
    petition and letter writing 20*n*.53, 261–62, 269, 271–73, 280–82, 295n.75, 297–298
    return to Wybalenna 211, 227, 229, 231, 234, 237–41, 241, 249
    testimony to the Friend Inquiry 300, 311*n*.122, 314, 329*n*. 164
    youth 25*n*.66, 42, 61, 88, 118, 132, 142
Bruney, Peter 9*n*.19, 42, 88, 160, 199*n*.97, 229, 245, 247, 282

Bucham, David 59
Building of cottages 78, 94, 97, 99, 109, 115, 118, 122–23, 127, 129, 131–32, 158, 190
Bullrer – see Louisa
Bung's Jacky – see Phillip
Burials 99, 112, 119, 131, 193, 329*n*.165
Burton, Antoinette 94, 190
Calamarowenye – see King Tippo
Calder, Graeme xxiii*n*.45, 1*n*.1, 7, 10*n*.24, 117*n*.112
Calder, James xxxi*n*.59, 257*n*.87
Calerwarrermeer – see King Tippo
Cameron, Patsy 1*n*.1, 5*n*.12, 6*n*.13, 7, 10, 28, 32, 34*n*.17, 35*n*.23, 37*n*.27, 92–93, 101*n*.64, 112*n*.102, 182, 200*n*.101
Catherine 79*n*.15, 222*n*.12, 223*n*.15, 304, 307
Chakrabarty, Dipesh xxvi
Chalky Island 38, 128, 176, 178, 193, 311*n*.121
Charlotte 121*n*.125, 134, 199*n*.97, 204, 221*n*.7, 228, 245
Cherokee syllabary xiii, 56*n*.80
Christianisation xxxv, 79, 81, 84, 94, 103, 127, 152, 170–71, 187, 189, 202
Christopher 173
Clara 85, 95, 110*n*.95, 187, 223*n*.14, 240
Clark, Bessy 87, 172, 223*n*.12, 239
Clark, Charles xxxiv, 121–122, 197*n*. 93
Clark, Edward – see Teddy
Clark, Ian D. xlii, 197, 207
Clark, Catherine 93, 125, 168, 258, 305–09
Clark, Robert
    accusations of brutality 305–06, 308–310, 312
    based in Hobart 195–96, 212, 215, 217–18, 220–21, 229, 232–37, 239, 247
    catechist xxxvii–viii, xlii, 50–51, 105, 109, 131, 135–36, 141, 154, 157–59, 162–64, 174
    disliked by Plomley 50, 233, 297, 321

dismissed by Jeanneret 322–24, 326–28
educator 55–56, 66, 89–90, 118, 121–22, 125, 169
petition and aftermath 261–72, 275, 288–95, 297, 300–01, 304
return to Wybalenna 249–252, 256–60
translator 96, 111, 171–72, 177, 181–82, 184–92, 317n.130
Clark, Teddy xxxiv, 121, 130–31, 138, 197n.93
Coastal Plains nation
in Country 7, 10, 28
individuals 35, 37, 92, 108n.86, 111–112, 119, 155n. 10, 190, 200n.101, 203n.111, 237
Cochrane, Fanny xix$n$. 30, 80n.16, 223n.15, 289n.61, 305–307, 310, 312–13, 326, 330n.166
Cochrane, Mary ann – see Arthur, Mary ann
Cochrane-Smith, Fanny – see Cochrane, Fanny
Collingridge, George 3n.5
Colonial Times 63, 279
Constantine 108, 154
Continuity of culture x, xx, 93, 104, 127, 156, 172, 183, 255, 329–30
Convicts xvii, xxiv, xxvi, 12, 14, 17, 30–31, 53 54, 72, 72, 97, 101, 120, 198, 222, 241, 258, 264, 280, 311
Cooper, William 285
Corinpardune – see Benjamin
Cornwall Chronicle 161n.22, 230n.37
Corrobery – see Helen
Count Alexander – see King Alexander
Count Alpha – see Doctor Wooreddy
Cranky Bet – see Daphne
Cranky Dick – see Richard
Cranky Poll – see Jemima
Credibility of VDL texts xxiii–xxx, xli, 226, 269, 295–05
Cree, Nicholas 77
Crook – see Sabina
Crowley, Terry xx, 51, 171, 187n.64
Crumley, Carole 254

Curr, Edward 14n.24
Currency 77, 243
Dammery, Sally xxiii–iv, xxviii–ix, 299, 327n.158
Daphne 85, 186, 223n.12, 330n.170
Darling, Sir Ralph 41, 45
Darling, William 41–45, 47, 49–50, 52, 62
Darwin, Charles xvi
Davie, Sinclair 271–73, 278, 288–91, 296, 303, 304n.103
David – see Leonidas
Davies, John B xxii, 76, 82, 266n.7
Davies, R. H. 5n.12, 51
Death – see mortality
Deborah 136, 173
Deborahkanni – see Lanny, Victoria
Dening, Greg xxv, xxxii
Denison, William 275, 279, 322n.148, 327
Denoon, Donald xxxiii
Dick, Cranky – see Richard
Dickinson, Loftus 91, 128, 185
Diplomacy 20, 21, 52, 61, 81, 136, 144, 203, 205
Dispossession – see Removal
Doctor Wooreddy
at Port Phillip 204, 209, 211
at Wybalenna xxxvi, 44, 61, 77, 88, 103–04, 142–43, 145–6, 148–49, 159–60, 222
before Europeans 9, 16
death 211, 220
diplomat 17–21, 42, 48, 52, 69, 81n.20, 204-05, 298
sermons 184–85, 189–90, 263
Doctor Wooreddy's Prescription for Enduring the Ending of the World 9n.21, 15, 17, 148–149
Dogs 33, 48, 95, 98, 114, 128, 145, 241–42, 246, 264, 282
Doomed race doctrine xv, xviii, xxi, xxiii, xxv, xxxi$n$.61
Dove, Dora 163, 169, 191
Dove, Thomas 158–59, 162–63, 165–69, 172, 180, 185–86, 191–92, 198, 201–04, 213–15, 217, 274

– 346 –

INDEX

Dowwrunggi – see Leonidas
Drayduric/Dray – see Sophia
Dredge, James 206*n*.116, 209–10
Dremipunner – see Bonaparte
Drieblem – see Hannibal
Drierlergenerminner – see Queen Elizabeth
Drinene – see Neptune
Dromedeene – see Daphne
Drowlepuner – see Achilles
Droyerloinny – see Bruny, Peter
Druemerterpunner – see King Alexander
Druleerpar – see King George
Drummerlooner – see Louisa
Drunteherniter – see Clark, Charles
Duterreau, Benjamin 48
Eardley–Wilmot, John xl*n*.79, xlii, 248, 258–60, 279, 292, 322*n*.148
Eastbynown – see Queen Andromache
Edmunds, Penelope xvi
Edmund 156, 214, 223*n*.13, 271
Edward 126, 144, 200
Education
    Flinders Island school 45, 64, 73, 79–92, 98, 105, 111, 123, 125, 128, 138, 159–60, 163, 169–73, 186, 239, 305, 309, 312–13
    literacy 55–56, 62–64, 74, 81–83, 106, 115, 168, 213, 226–227, 237, 267
    Orphan School xxxv, 41, 53–54, 62–63, 195*n*.78, 121*n*.128, 197*n*.93, 220*n*.6, 233
    school examinations xxxvii–ix, 73, 81–92, 99–100, 138*n*.171, 157*n*.17, 164–70, 173*n*.42, 180, 188, 191, 194, 200*n*.100, 236–37, 294–95, 327
    traditional literacies 56
    VDL desire to learn 45, 55–56, 105, 173, 181, 190, 226–27, 264, 290–91, 303, 325–26
    VDL Teachers xxxix, 78*n*. 13, 80, 81, 88–89, 138, 221, 239
Ekukhanyeni letter writers 302
Elder, Bruce xxii

Ellen – see Helen
Emma 95, 155, 222*n*.12, 242, 311*n*.123
English, use of – see Languages
Epidemics 198–199, 327
Errors in recording of names xi–ii
Errors in hearing 287, 291
Eugene 80*n*.16, 175*n*.46, 222 *n*.12, 239, 271, 314
Eugenics xv, xviii, xxi
Eurocentrism ix, xii, xxv–vii, xxix, 252, 321
Europeans dismissed from Wybalenna 47, 49, 213, 250, 278, 322, 327
European exploration 3, 8–10
Evangelism 17, 45, 57, 59, 61, 83, 111, 152, 158, 163, 179
Eveline 194
Ewunermanarer – see Washington
Extinction myth ix, xvii–xx, xxi, xxiii–xxv, xxi, xli*n*. 83, 21, 22, 59
Fabications – see Gammon
Fanny (Planobeena) 81*n*.20, 199*n*.97, 203–04, 210, 220–21, 223*n*.14, 330*n*.170
Fanny Cochrane – see Cochrane, Fanny
Fels, Marie 209–210
Fenton, James 31*n*.10, 67
Firth, Raymond 318–19
Fisher, Peter 217–218
Flinders Aboriginal Bible society 270
Flinders Island
    general/environment 9, 26–29
    lagoons settlement 30–43
    Wybalenna settlement 43–205, 212–331
Flinders Island Chronicle
    analyses ix, xxvii–viii, xxxv–vii, 147–52
    first appearance 64–70, 74–75, 211
    observations from 18, 19, 54*n*.73, 92–93, 97–151, 158, 173, 177, 182–83, 189, 223, 247, 253, 267, 288, 317, 327, 331
    peak production 97–151
    written parallel with Sermons 152–54
Flood, Josephine 27–28

Flora 34, 40, 85–86, 95, 106, 122, 155, 180, 222*n*.12
Fosbrooke, Edward 213
Francis 191, 193
Franklin, Johnny xxxiv, 121, 160, 199*n*.97, 204, 211, 245
Franklin, Jane 79, 138, 158–62, 173*n*.43, 197–98, 232, 248, 308, 330*n*.168
Franklin, John (Sir) 78–79, 81*n*.19, 91*n*.47, 94–96, 112, 133, 138, 152, 158–62, 194, 197, 208, 216–220, 225, 232, 248, 258, 264
Frederick 29, 85*n*.28, 108, 156, 214, 222*n*.12, 239, 261n.2, 265, 271, 272, 293, 314–315, 330*n*.170
Free People – see Status as Free People
Friday – see Arthur, Walter George
Friend, Matthew Curling 292–324
Friend Inquiry, the
    commissioning 273*n*.25, 289*n*.62, 292–293
    findings 312, 320–22
    testimonies 29*n*.4–6, 239*n*.57, 288, 291, 293–96, 300–16, 326
Friendly Mission xxii, 18–21, 24, 52, 61, 69, 78, 82, 83, 112n. 102, 143n. 184, 144, 147, 151, 167, 188, 190, 203–205, 209–10, 230
Frontier violence – see Violence
Furneaux group – see Bass Strait Islands
Gamble, Robert 34–35, 37, 39
Games 122, 129–30
Gammon 72, 94, 149, 176, 178, 184, 240, 269, 275, 278, 309, 313, 317
Gilligan, Ian 5*n*.12, 117
Gipps, George 207, 211*n*.130
Gnashing of teeth 151, 157
Goodall, Heather 285–86
Gooseberry – see Rose
Gossip 93, 149, 313–18
Graham, Mary 254
Great Island – see Flinders Island
Green Island 35, 43, 61, 66, 74, 124–25, 128, 134, 193, 211, 220, 317
Gun Carriage Island 21, 24–25
Hannibal 78*n*.12, 194, 223*n*.13, 240

Harriet 34*n*.20, 88*n*.43, 180, 188, 193, 223*n*.14, 234–35, 245, 330*n*.167
Hau'ofa, Epeli 7–8
Hawai'i xxvii, 46
Heaven – see Afterlife
Hector 111–12, 118–19
Helen 87, 191–92
Hell – see Afterlife
Henry 110, 213, 223*n*. 12, 236–38
Heterarchy 253–55
Hierarchy of credibility xvi–xx
Hierarchy of nations at Wybalenna 78, 175
Historiography ix–xliii, xxx–xxxiii
Hobart Town Courier 37–38, 41*n*.38, 42, 44*n*.44, 48, 54–55, 60, 62–63, 67
Hurlanerhener – see Queen Elizabeth
Ice Age 5–6, 117
Ingram, Sergeant 219, 221, 244
Isaac 119, 144, 155, 199*n*.97, 204, 211
Isolation 6–8, 28, 75, 163, 193, 280, 311*n*.123, 317
Jack of Cape Grim – see Tunnerminnerwait
Jackanoothara – see Sarah
Jacky, Big – see Constantine
Jane 180, 200
Jeanneret, Charles 275, 290, 327
Jeanneret, Harriet 232, 248, 290
Jeanneret, Henry
    battles with Walter Arthur 128, 235–36, 244, 249, 268–293
    first appointment 218–226, 233–250
    inquiry into administration 293–322
    petition against 260–265
    second appointment 54, 147, 255–256, 258–60, 265–268, 324
Jemima 87, 135–37, 155*n*.11
Jemmy – see Isaac
Jemmy, Big – see King Alphonso
Jemmy, Big Mary's – see Francis
Jenny – see Semeramis
Jessy 223*n*.15
Joanna – see Rose
Jock – see Fanny

INDEX

Johnson, Colin – see Mudrooroo
Johnson, Murray xxvii*n*.55, 148
Jones, Rhys 5, 7
Jorgensen, Jorgen 32
Juliet 180, 223*n*.12, 330*n*.170
Kallerromter – see King Tippo
Kalloongoo – see Charlotte
Kapferer, John Noel 318–319
Karnebutcher 229–230
Kartitteyer – see Hector
Keetewa – see Amelia
Kenny, Robert 46, 207*n*.119
Killercrankie Point 112, 117
King Albert 31*n*.10, 103, 144, 185
King Alexander
   letter writing ix, xiv, xl–ii, 273, 277–80, 282, 299
   at Oyster Cove 330*n*.170
   petition 20*n*.53, 261*n*.2, 262, 271–72
   Sermons 179, 180, 183, 186, 189, 317
   testimony to the Friend Inquiry 239*n*.57, 300, 314
   at Wybalenna 77, 85, 110, 167, 201–02, 213–14, 222
King Alfred 159, 175, 222
King Alphonso
   letter writing ix, xiv, xl–ii, 276–80, 282, 299
   petition 271–73
   at Wybalenna 155, 223*n*.13, 327–28
King George 31, 41, 62, 77, 83–85, 92, 112, 128, 156, 175, 190*n*.72, 193, 222, 235
King Tippo 20*n*.53, 77, 86*n*.34, 117, 167, 214, 222, 240, 261, 271–72, 302–03, 323, 329n.164
King William 34, 78*n*.12, 82, 91–92, 135*n*.162, 201, 222
Kit, Little 37*n*.27, 200
Kit, Old 108, 112, 118–119
Kittewer – see Amelia
Kitty – see Kit, Old
Knopwood, Robert 68, 110, 145
Kolebunner – see Robinson, George

Koonerpunner – see Robinson, George
Lacklay – see Isaac
Lagoons, the 30–32, 40–41, 43, 108, 128, 274
Lake Condah 285
Lake Macquarie 45, 51
Lake Tyers 285
Lalla Rookh – see Trugernanner
Languages
   english, use of xxvii, 33, 46, 51, 66, 86–88, 107, 160, 172, 187, 189*n*.69, 223, 227, 242, 274
   lingua franca 45, 51–52, 85, 96, 107, 171–72, 178, 181, 183–184, 186, 187n.64, 223, 263, 288
   pidgin 33, 51, 85, 187
Lanne, William 327*n*.159, 329*n*.164; see also Lanny family
Lanny, Victoria 235, 326, 327
Lanny, William – see Lanne, William
Lanny family 235, 237, 238
Larcurkenner – see Isaac
Larhertounge – see Queen Andromache
Larmoderick – see Deborah
Larratong – see Queen Andromache
La Trobe, Charles 196, 207–08, 211–12, 229, 282, 322, 324
Launceston Advertiser 49
Lear, Jonathan 17, 72, 285
Leati – see Leonidas
Leenererkleener – see Jane
Leepunner – see Edward
Lehman, Greg xix, xxiii*n*.45, xxxvii*n*.73, 148, 329
Lemkin, Raphael xxi–ii
Leonidas
   sermons 173, 184, 189, 317
   at Wybalenna 137, 164–66, 213, 223*n*.12
Lerpullermenner – see Henry
Lewis, Gidley 134, 139, 186
Line Operation, the 13, 23, 191, 205
Little Billy – see Edward
Little Davey – see Bruny, David
Little Jacky – see Bonaparte
Little Kangaroo Island 38
Little Kit – see Sabina

Little Mary – see Mary, Little
Little Sally – see Paulina
Little Tuery – see Emma
Lockjaw Poll – see Susan
Long Billy – see King Alexander
Looerryminer – see Jane
Louisa   37, 40, 86, 106, 136, 223*n*.12
Lucy   110, 223 *n*.12, 327
Lygdudge – see Trugernanner
Maccamee – see Washington
Maclachlan, Archibald   24–25, 40
Macquarie, Lachlan   54
Mairremmener   xxxviii, 10, 38, see also Oyster Bay nation
Makeadru – see Constantine
Maleteherbargener – see Ajax
Mangbopeer – see Deborah
Maniyercoyertutcher – see Susan
Mannalargenna   xxvi, 24, 48, 111*n*.96, 119, 237, 284
Mannapackername – see King Alphonso
Mansell, Edward   40
Marbles   78*n*.12, 129, 146, 153, 330
Maria, Old   196
Marnetti – see Pindar, Peter
Martha   223*n*.15, 304, 305, 307
Martin, Walter Juba – see Arthur, Walter George
Marwerreek – see Noemy
Mary, Big
    testimony to the Friend Inquiry 307, 308
    at Wybalenna   35, 191*n*.75, 78, 223*n*.13, 330*n*.170
Mary, Wild   34–35, 184–85, 223*n*.14, 240
Mary Henrietta – see Mary, Big
Mason, Thomas   34–35, 37–39
Mathabelianna – see Matilda
Mathinna
    testimony to the Friend Inquiry 308–09
    with the Franklins   197–98
    at Wybalenna   305–06, 312
Matilda
    at Port Phillip   199n. 97, 204, 210

    at Wybalenna   69–70, 155–56, 220–21, 223, 238, 240, 272, 281–82, 311, 330*n*.170
Maulboyheenner (Robert)
    diplomat   81
    at Port Phillip   204, 210, 282, 294, 308, 312
    sermons   186, 190
    at Wybalenna   112, 118, 199
Maytepueminner – see Matilda
McKay, Alexander   229
McFarlane, Ian   xxvii*n*.55, 37*n*.27, 148, 204, 221*n*.9, 254*n*.81
McSweeney, Hannah
    testimony to the Friend Inquiry 305, 310
    at Wybalenna   223*n*.15, 305–13
McSweeney, Nanny
    testimony to the Friend Inquiry   307
    at Wybalenna   223*n*.15, 305, 309
Meelathinna – see Agnes
Meenabaekamenna – see King Alphonso
Meenerkerpackerminer – see King Alphonso
Meerterlatteenner – see Rebecca
Meethecaratheeanna – see Emma
Memmi, Albert   xv–vi
Menerletenner – see Agnes
Merappe – see Neptune
Merewick – see Noemy
Metatalyrerparrelcher – see Christopher
Meterlatteyar – see Rebecca
Metterluerurparrityer – see Christopher
Midtrød, Tom Arne   318*n*. 134, 319
Mierpunner – see Washington
Milligan, Joseph   247, 249–51, 256–66, 268–69, 273, 280, 282, 287, 300–01, 306, 309, 327–328
Milton   98–99
Mittimer – see Mathinna
Moarna – see Mohanna
Mobourne, Ernest and Maggie   286
Mohanna   110–111
Mokerminer – see Constantine
Montagu, John   24, 49, 55, 133, 217
Moomereriner – see King Alexander
Moontehener – see Pindar, Peter

INDEX

Moouner – see Mohanna
Morerenoun – see Catherine
Morerenung – see Catherine
Moriarty   223
Mortality
   death camp characterisation of Wybalenna   xxi–xxii
   deaths at Wybalenna   72–73, 91, 97–99, 109–13, 117–20, 130–31, 135–138, 142, 147, 154, 157, 173, 178, 185, 188, 193–94, 197, 199–201, 210–11, 222, 235–37, 308, 312, 229–30
   infanticide   35–36
   introduced disease   13
   recording of deaths   44, 72n.2, 83, 85, 99
Mother Brown   36, 156
Moyhenny – see Mohanner
Moyhenung – see Mohanner
Mudrooroo   9n.21, 15, 17, 65–66, 148–49
Munro, James   37, 86
Musquito   87n.40, 327
Mutton-birds   124, 125, 139, 257
Myapanna – see Washington
Myhermenanyehaner – see Rose
Myungge – see Bruny, David
Nahbrunga   237–38
Nakedness   116, 190, 224, 278
Naming
   naming to shame   98, 105, 116, 122, 155
   use of European names   xi–xv, 76
   VDL names for dogs   343
Napoleon – see Tunnerminnerwait
Narlarrernilare – Paulina
Narthebynoune – see Queen Andromache
National boundaries   xliv
Native Court   77, 121, 157
Neerhepeererminer – see Hector
Neernnerpatterlargener – see King Alphonso
Neptune
   petition   20n.53, 265, 271–72
   sermons   170, 172–4, 179, 181, 183–84, 187, 317
   testimony to the Friend Inquiry   29, 239, 301, 314
   at Wybalenna   77, 114, 164, 166–67, 222n.12, 223n.15
Nertaweerartheer – see Lucy
New Holland   49, 55, 100, 121n.125, 123, 134, 199n.97, 204, 228, 245, 318
New Maria – see Matilda
New Zealand   14n.36, 22, 46, 47, 57, 74, 267
Nicermenic – see Eugene
Nickamanick – see Eugene
Nickerermargerer – see Mary, Little
Nickerumpowerer – see Mary, Little
Nickolls, Henry   52–58, 60, 74
Nixon, Francis   248, 264
Noble Savage   xv, xviii
Noemy
   petition   271, 273, 287–91, 303
   sermons   79, 96, 102–03, 107, 120, 160, 172–74, 177–18, 181, 187–88, 213n.137, 317
   testimony to the Friend Inquiry   29, 288, 291, 303–304
   at Wybalenna   79n.15, 90n.15, 85n.28, 127, 166, 222n.12, 223n.15, 224, 307, 330
Nolahallker – see Sabina
Noluollarrick – see Sabina
Nomerrucer   109–10
Nomime – see Noemy
Nommy – see Noemy
North Midlands Nation   10n.24, 11, 14, 200n.100
Nowlywollyger – see Kit, Little
Nuenonne   8, 9, 16, 19, 43, 63, 69; see also Bruny Island
Nugent, Maria   285
Numbloote – see Semeramis
Nunneatheganner – see Helen
Nurnepattenner – see Jemima
Obscene dance   36, 156
Ochre   5, 5n.12, 13, 79, 93, 103–04, 107, 121, 126, 156, 172, 189–90, 213, 224
Old Kit – see Kit, Old

Old Maria – see Maria, Old
Old Tom – see King George
Oyster Bay Nation
    alliance with Big River nation 7, 10n.24
    individual members 34n.16, 70n.109, 82n.21, 85n.31, 91, 111n.97, 117, 167, 186, 196n. 86, 200–01
    resisting invasion 11–13, 38
    at Wybalenna 47, 78, 205, 222
Oyster Cove Station 182, 251n.77, 288n.61, 311n.123, 328–30
Pagerly 19, 25n.66, 230
Pallawah xiv; see also Van Diemen's Land or VDL
Palle – see Hannibal
Pallooruc – see Frederick
Pangernowideic – see Clark, Bessy
Panghum – see Flora
Pannabuke – see Robinson, William
Parker-Thomas murders 31n.10, 87n.39, 103n.71, 117n. 112, 120, 137n. 168, 144n. 188, 165, 274
Parlin – see Hannibal
Parpemelenyer – see Francis
Parramatta Native Institution 54
Parumgmunermooner – see Achilles
Paulina 196
Pea Jacket Point 43, 61, 236
Peevay – see Tunnerminnerwait
Pelloneneminner– see Flora
Pendemurrernuic/Pendewurrewic – see Benjamin
Pendowtewer – see Rodney
Penermoke – see Hannibal
Pennemeroe – see Milton
Pennemoonooper – see Clark, Charles
Pepper, Lucy and Percy 286
Pepper, Nathanael 46
Peterlarrack – see Noemy
Petition to Queen Victoria
    charges in 263–264
    communal authorship 299–303
    creation of 269–265
    discourse on 295–300
Phillip 86

Phlebotomy 108, 136
Pignaburg – see Clark, Bessy
Pincommininer – see Mary, Wild
Pindar, Peter 167, 223n.12
Planobeena – see Fanny
Pleenperrenner – see Mother Brown
Plerpleroparner – see King Alfred
Plomley, N. J. B. (Brian)
    view of Europeans xlii–iii, 49–50, 217, 220, 233, 297, 321
    view of VDL people ix, xxi, 23–24, 39–40, 46, 51, 82, 171, 217
    view of VDL texts xxv–xxvi, xxvii, xli, 148–49, 226, 258, 276n.33, 297, 320–21
    work on Robinson's journals xiin.6, xxxi, xlii, 62n.95, 72n.2
Plorenernoopenner – see Fanny
Plorermininer/Plownneme – see Flora
Political activism xxiv, xli, 15–16, 55–56, 80, 121, 253–56, 255–67, 272–87, 295–304, 315–16, 319, 321–24, 331
Poll, Blind – see Agnes
Poll, Cranky – see Jemima
Pompy – see Richard
Pondanarip/Ponedimerneep 130
Porter, Andrew 60, 319n.142
Port Phillip
    Port Phillip Protectorate 205–208
    proposed relocation 75–76, 122–23, 133–34, 194–197
    VDL people at 70n.109, 167, 199, 204, 208–212, 227–232
Power, pathways of 252–253
Preservation Island 37, 264
Prince Adolphus – see Adolphus
Probelattener – see Isaac
Proletarianisation 42, 53, 101, 209
Protection
    by God 101, 166
    humanitarian initiatives 57–60
    protector (office) 67–69, 195–97, 199, 205–211, 221, 227, 231, 283, 325
    from violence 16, 20–21, 24–25, 30, 34, 41, 55, 101, 163, 193, 198, 217, 249, 283
    of women 92, 94

INDEX

Prout, John Skinner   110*n*.93, 251
Pulmonary disease   13, 112, 173, 194, 238
Purlurrepennener – see Emma
Purngerpar – see King Alfred
Putumpatecher – see King William
Pyreparnner – see King William
Queen Andromache   138
Queen Elizabeth   135*n*.162
Racism   xv–xxiii
Radical Hope   17, 72, 285
Rawee – see Clark, Charles
Rebecca   92, 155–156, 180, 199*n*.97
Redhica – see Sophia
Removal
   of body parts for collectors   99, 173, 193
   of children to Orphan School   42, 54, 197, 220, 250
   exile to Flinders Island   15–26, 30, 66, 310
   planned move to Port Phillip   xxxvi*n*. 72, 55, 76n. 5, 122–23, 133–34, 196, 204
Repatriation after exile   227, 324, 328–330
Reynolds, Henry   xiv, xli, 6, 10*n*.25, 19–20, 76, 101, 115, 254, 283–84, 286, 298–299
Reynolds, Private   220, 244, 247–48
Richard   81n. 20, 143–45, 223n. 13
Right behaviour   284–285
Rinehebigger – see Neptune
Risdon Cove   10, 16
Robert – see Maulboyheener
Robinson, Charles   167, 198
Robinson, Eliza   193
Robinson, George   199–200
Robinson, George Augustus
   administrator of Wybalenna   52–64, 68–196
   deterioration of relationships   139–147
   Friendly Mission   xvi, xxiii, 9, 13, 17–26, 38, 29–32, 39–41
   influence on Flinders Island Chronicle   xxxv, 64–68

maintains contact with Walter Arthur   244–247, 324–326
   move to Port Phillip   196–228
Robinson, George Jr   212, 246
Robinson, Maria   80*n*.17
Robinson, William   84, 109, 157
Robinson, William (son of GA)   228
Robson, Lloyd   xxii
Rodney   136*n*.165, 194
Rolepa – see King George
Romeo   86
Roonthadauna – see Richard
Rose   87, 223*n*.14, 236–37
Rose, Michael   xxxvii*n*.73, 128*n*.138, 133*n*.156, 138, 140, 148
Rowlepanna – see Achilles
Rumanaloo – see Louisa
Rumour   93, 234, 272, 315–319
Russell, Lynette   22*n*.58, 101*n*.64, 210n.126, 329*n*.164
Ryan, Lyndall   xiv, xix*n*.26, xli*n*.84, 16*n*.39, 76–77, 93, 148, 256, 298
Sabina – see Kit, Little
Sagona, Antonio   5*n*.12, 104
Sally Lagoon   143
Sally – see Rebecca
Sarah   80, 175, 222*n*. 12, 223*n*.15, 314–15
Scott, James C   94, 140, 144, 176, 312, 315
Sealers   10, 26, 31–40, 51, 69, 75, 92, 100–01, 198, 203, 212, 221–22, 233, 245, 267, 272, 318, 324–26
Sealing Women   32–34, 92, 94–96, 108–09, 122, 127, 134, 143, 200, 226, 253, 255, 317
Select Committee Report 1837   xvii, 21, 57–61, 150, 250
Self-sufficiency, aspirations for   xlii, 246, 251–252, 256–58, 266, 282, 285, 325
Semeramis   199, 204
Sermons
   general discussion   ix, xxv, xxvii–iii, xxxix
   spoken   170–174, 177–191, 210, 311, 317

– 353 –

written 152–57, 164, 171, 174, 176, 181, 192, 211
Shame xix, 116, 222, 233, 283
Sheep owned by VDL people 78, 101, 125, 128, 193, 204, 242–44, 268, 325
Shipwrecks 225, 251
Silva, Noenoe xxvii
singing 78n.13, 80, 87, 103, 125–28, 130, 160–61, 187
Slavery 33, 57, 92–93, 253, 268, 280, 327
Smallboy – see Maulboyheener
Smith, Bet 34
Smith, John 30, 33, 35–35, 80n.16, 200
Smith, Malcolm Laing 212–13, 215–17, 225
Smythe, George 231
Sophia 189, 223n.12
South East nation xixn.26; see also Bruny Island
South West nation 7, 98, 127, 130, 144
Status as Free People ix, xxiv, xlii, 54, 72, 217, 241, 254, 262–63, 280, 287, 298, 330
Stoler, Ann Laura xxvii–viii, 317–19
Story, George 117
Straitsmen 10, 22, 24, 33, 35–36, 40, 80n.16, 88, 92, 101n.64, 318
Strange, John 34–35, 37–39
Strugnell, John 100–01
Sunday Corroboree 103–104, 185
Susan 196
Swan Island 13n.32, 23, 25, 30
Tabracane – see Lanny, Victoria
Tamoer, Boesack 57
Taneeberrick – see Clara
Tarenootairer – see Sarah
Tarentuthick – see Andrew
Tarramaneve 109
Taylor, John 4–6, 10
Taylor, Rebe xviin.22, xix
Teddeheburer – see Clara
Teengerreenneener – see Richard
Teldredmoorer – see Maria, Old
Tensions between Ben Lomond and Big River Nations 11, 38, 62, 78, 120, 274

Thermanope – see Augustus
Thielewanna – See Mary, Big
Thomas, William 174, 208n.116
Thompson, E. P. xxx, 73
Thompson, Thomas 22n.59, 88, 122, 166, 204, 211, 229, 234, 245, 247, 330n.167
Thomson's Sall – see Rebecca
Thoonock – see Edmund
Threlkeld, Lancelot 45–46, 51, 91, 196–197
Tibb – see Sarah
Tilaway – See Mary, Big
Timemenidic – see Adolphus
Timme – see Adolphus
Timmy – see Maulboyheener
Tingeroop – see Tinginoop
Tinginoop 223n.14, 31n.10
Tippoo Saib – see King Tippo
Titterrarpar – see Ajax
Toanac – see Edmund
Toinneburer – see Tarramaneve
Tolelerdurrick – see Andrew
Tommy – see Adolphus
Tommy – see Frederick
Tonee – see Edmund
Tongelongeter – see King William
Towterrer – see Romeo
Travers, Robert 82, 170
Treenkoteyaner – see Lucy
Tremebonner – see Bonaparte
Trerpummeleher – see Edmund
Trooneguediana – see Lucy
Trowlebunner – see Achilles
Trowunna – see Van Diemen's Land, or VDL
Truganini – see Trugernanner
Trugernanner
    face of extinction myth xix, xxvi, 330
    as Friendly Mission diplomat 17–19, 25n.66, 48, 81, 204
    at Port Phillip 204, 210, 221n.7
    at Wybalenna 77, 82, 109, 136, 137, 143, 221–223, 242
Tuberculosis 154, 173, 191, 194, 196

INDEX

Tunemerniddic – see Adolphus
Tunnerminnerwait
    as Friendly Mission diplomat 25, 81
    at Port Phillip 210, 221, 282, 294, 308, 312
    sermons 186, 188
    at Wybalenna 117, 118, 128, 167, 194n.82, 203n.111, 204–05
Turnbull, Clive xxi, xxxi$n$.60, xli$n$.80, 296
Twopence – see Helen
Tyereelore 10, 22, 24, 32, 34–37, 69, 108, 112, 136, 155n.10, 175, 182, 193, 200, 203, 228, 253, 330n.167, 170; see also Sealing Women
Tylerwinner – see Mary, Big
Tylo – see Sabina
Van Diemen's Land
    choice of name for this study xiv–xiv
    deep History 2–8
    european name 8
Van Toorn, Penny xxxvii–viii, xli, 65, 81–82, 107, 133n.156, 148, 285n.53, 299
Victorian gold rush 22, 330
Violence
    against women 31–33, 35–36 92–93, 311–12
    of colonisation xvii, xxxiii, 14, 31, 57–60, 310–311
    corporal punishment 305–12
    frontier xvii, xxxi, 10, 16, 179, 183, 206–07
    'Line' Operation 13, 23, 191, 205
    resistance xxxiii, 12–14, 35, 39
Wages – see Payment for work
Walker, George Washington
    early contacts xvi–ii, xliii, 47–50, 68–69, 72, 84, 117–118
    supporting VDL activists 232–34, 249, 252, 256–59, 266–68, 270, 304
Walsh, Matthew 109, 111–12, 118, 130, 136, 139, 154n.8, 195–96, 212, 213
Walyer 25, 175n.46, 284

Wapperty 237
Warkernenner – see Old Kit
Warrameenaloo – see Juliet
War, The (AKA Black War)
    armed resistance xxii, 10–21, 25, 30–31, 33–40, 42, 55, 64–65, 82n.21, 165, 185, 191, 221, 267, 278, 329
    political response xiii, xxiv, xli, 15–16, 48, 56, 69, 75, 253, 260, 267, 277, 284–86, 298, 315, 319, 331
Warwe – see King Albert
Washington
    letter writing 274–277, 279, 284, 298–99, 322–324
    life after repatriation 330n.170
    petition to Queen Victoria 20n.53, 261–262, 269–72
    relationship with Walter Arthur 120
    testimony to the Friend Inquiry 239n. 57, 301, 314, 316
    warrior 31, 127n.168, 215
    at Wybalenna 119, 127, 128, 167, 214–15, 223n.12, 239, 327
Watty/Wat – see Harriet
Wawme – see King Albert
Weltepellemeener – see Francis
Western nation
    individuals mentioned 79, 84, 109–10, 121, 136, 138, 150, 154, 167, 175n.46, 178, 187, 194, 200, 205, 230, 235, 287, 290, 327n.159
    at Wybalenna xxxviii, 47, 56, 77
Whaling industry xiii, 14, 16, 19, 22, 150, 210, 329
Wight, Alexander 25–26, 30–34, 38–41, 48, 54, 71, 85, 93, 185, 249, 308
Wilkinson, Thomas 45–50, 58, 158
Willis, John Walpole 210
Windeyer, Richard xvi
Windschuttle, Keith xxixn.62, xli, 297–298
Women
    refusal to do housework 115, 127, 181–83, 224

– 355 –

refusal to marry 94–96, 155–56
see also Tyereelore, Sealing Women
Wongeneep – see Eveline
Wongerneep – see Eveline
Wonghowrum – see Catherine
Wonginner – see Old Kit
Wooraddy/Wooradeddy/Woureddy –
see Doctor Wooreddy
Worekenna – see Old Kit
Work
    'bad' work 155, 178
    Bass Strait Islands 10, 36, 182
    in colonial society 14*n*.36, 31, 150, 329–30
    mentioned in the *Chronicle* 67, 92, 97–98, 100–02, 106–07, 114, 118, 121, 139, 141, 147, 153
    payment/wages xlii, 71, 78, 97, 147, 215, 231, 243, 253
    at Port Phillip 209, 211, 227–228, 231, 253
    at Wybalenna xxxiv, 53–54, 71, 78, 80, 89, 97, 114, 149, 158, 169, 181–82, 187, 215, 224, 240–241, 243, 245, 257–58, 267–268, 278–282, 301
Wotycowwidyer – see Harriet
Wot – see Harriet
Wowee – see King Albert
Wybalenna, meaning of name 53-44

CPSIA information can be obtained
at www.ICGtesting.com
Printed in the USA
JSRC041238120920
7746JS00006B/214